CONSTRAINED BY JESUS' LOVE

THEOLOGISCHE ACADEMIE UITGAANDE VAN DE
JOHANNES CALVIJN STICHTING TE KAMPEN

CONSTRAINED BY JESUS' LOVE

AN INQUIRY INTO THE MOTIVES OF THE MISSIONARY AWAKENING IN GREAT BRITAIN IN THE PERIOD BETWEEN 1698 AND 1815

Proefschrift

TER VERKRIJGING VAN DE GRAAD VAN DOCTOR
IN DE GODGELEERDHEID, OP GEZAG VAN DE RECTOR
DR G. M. DEN HARTOGH IN HET OPENBAAR TE
VERDEDIGEN OP DINSDAG 29 MEI 1956 DES NA-
MIDDAGS TE HALF DRIE IN DE AULA DER THEO-
LOGISCHE HOGESCHOOL, OUDESTRAAT 6,
TE KAMPEN

DOOR

JOHANNES VAN DEN BERG

GEBOREN TE ROTTERDAM

J. H. KOK N.V. KAMPEN 1956

IN MEMORY OF MY MOTHER
TO MY WIFE

STELLINGEN

I

De betrekkelijk geringe belangstelling der Reformatoren voor de zending onder niet-christelijke volkeren dient gedeeltelijk verklaard te worden uit de ongunst der tijden, voor een ander deel echter uit een zekere terughouding die haar oorzaak vond in de critische houding der Reformatoren ten aanzien van de anthropocentrische bepaaldheid der Rooms-Katholieke missie.

II

E. Schick gaat te ver, wanneer hij meent dat slechts van echte, Bijbels-gefundeerde zendingsarbeid gesproken kan worden na het losmaken van de verbinding tussen kolonizatie en zending.
(Zie: E. Schick, *Vorboten und Bahnbrecher*, Basel 1943, S. 20).

III

Het karakter der Anglicaanse zendingsgenootschappen die omstreeks 1700 werden gevormd is bepaald door een samentreffen van pietistische en rationalistische invloeden.

IV

Het ontwaken der zendingsgedachte in Methodistische kring is in hoofdzaak tot soteriologische motieven te herleiden.

V

De brede vlucht, die de zendingsgedachte tegen het einde der 18de eeuw in de Angelsaksische wereld nam, is voor een groot deel te danken aan de directe en indirecte invloed van Jonathan Edwards.

VI

Het feit dat het eschatologisch motief een zeer sterke invloed kon verkrijgen op de ontwikkeling van het zendingswerk der London Missionary Society vindt mede zijn oorzaak in het samentreffen van theologische en politiek-sociale factoren.

VII

De zending onder Israël vindt hierin haar diepste grond, dat het Evangelie der verlossing gebracht dient te worden aan allen die leven buiten het licht van Jezus Christus — maar zij ontvangt een bijzonder accent door het feit dat de Joden „geliefden zijn om der vaderen wil" (Rom. 11 : 28).

VIII

In haar benadering van het probleem van de Islam bouwe de Elenctiek voort op de uitspraak van Kuyper, dat de zending onder de Mohammedanen dient aan te sluiten „zoo aan het anti-paganistisch streven van den Islam, als aan de ware bestanddeelen, die in zijne belijdenis van Mozes en den Christus nog zijn overgebleven".

(Zie: *Acta van het Zendingscongres gehouden te Amsterdam volgens opdracht der Voorloopige Synode van Nederduitsch Gereformeerde Kerken op den 28sten, 29sten en 30sten Januari 1890*, Amsterdam 1890, blz. 5: Stelling XVI van het Referaat van Dr. A. Kuyper)

IX

Terecht handhaaft L. G. Rignell voor Zacharia 6 : 1—8 de masoretische text.

(Zie: L. G. Rignell, *Die Nachtgesichte des Sacharja*, Lund 1950, S. 202)

X

In zijn schildering van het uitgaan van de profetische verkondiging van Gods gericht èn genade tot de heidenen legt het boek Jona getuigenis af van het feit dat het Oudtestamentisch heilsuniversalisme mede een centrifugaal aspect vertoont.

XI

De in de Brief aan de Philippenzen aanwezige gegevens pleiten voor de veronderstelling dat deze brief vanuit Epheze geschreven is.

XII

De suggestie van R. Schippers, dat Openbaring 20 verstaan dient te worden als profetie van een vrederijk dat telkens aanwezig is in de historie wanneer de geest der martelaren het regiment der wereld aangrijpt, wijst een weg ter oplossing van het probleem van de historische datering van het Millennium.

(Zie: R. Schippers, *Geestelijk Chiliasme*, Bezinning I 1946, blz. 41)

XIII

Terecht verklaart W. H. van de Pol: „De reformatorische leer van de wedergeboorte en de nieuwe mens betekent niet een herroeping van de leer van de „rechtvaardigmaking door het geloof alleen" noch ook een verzwakking maar veeleer juist een bevestiging en bekrachtiging daarvan. Daarom betekent het reformatorisch spreken van „wedergeboorte" en „de nieuwe mens" ook in geen geval een toenadering tot de katholieke leer".

(Zie: W. H. van de Pol, *Karakteristiek van het Reformatorisch Christendom*, Roermond en Maaseik 1952, blz. 380)

XIV

Ten onrechte verklaart E. Hirsch dat het Pietisme „die aufgeklärte Moralisierung des Heilsprozesses eingeleitet hat".

(Zie: E. Hirsch, *Geschichte der neuren evangelischen Theologie*, II, Gütersloh 1951, S. 160)

XV

De gedachte der z.g. „Bewährungsethik", door K. Fröhlich aldus weergegeven: „Aus dem Erwählungsbewusztsein entspringt das eigentümliche Motiv der *Bewährung* in der calvinischen Frömmigkeit", doet niet voldoende recht wedervaren aan het terecht door J. Bohatec geconstateerde feit dat uiteindelijk bij Calvijn alléén Christus de bron van onze heilszekerheid is en blijft.

(Zie: K. Fröhlich, *Gottesreich, Welt und Kirche bei Calvin*, München 1930, S. 35, en J. Bohatec, *Calvins Lehre von Staat und Kirche*, Breslau 1937, S. 710)

XVI

Tussen de ethiek en de liturgie van het Puritanisme bestaat een nauw verband.

XVII

De herleving van het Calvinisme in de Anglicaanse Kerk gedurende de tweede helft van de achttiende eeuw vond buiten de kring dezer Kerk haar oorsprong.

XVIII

De Afscheiding van 1834 dient mede verklaard te worden uit de invloed van het Réveil.

XIX

Het deelnemen van de ouderlingen aan de kerkvisitatie is een consequentie van het karakter van het ouderlingambt.

XX

De huidige structuur onzer maatschappij leidt slechts schijnbaar tot een beperking der diaconale taak.

XXI

Ten einde de dubbele functie der Wet ook in de Eredienst duidelijk te doen uitkomen, verdient het aanbeveling vóór de Schuldbelijdenis de samenvatting der Wet, na de Genadeverkondiging de Decaloog of een paraenetisch Schriftgedeelte te lezen.

XXII

Het z.g. formuliergebed dient in de Gereformeerde Eredienst een vaste plaats naast het z.g. vrije gebed te behouden, c. q. te hervinden.

XXIII

Het zou zowel de breedte als de diepgang der gymnasiale vorming ten goede komen, indien in het leerplan der hoogste klassen een plaats kon worden ingeruimd voor de lectuur van enkele Griekse en Latijnse patres.

PREFACE

Now that I have reached the end of my academic studies I want to express my deep gratitude to all who have been willing to give me their guidance and assistance on this road. First of all, I give thanks to the professors of the *Theologische Hogeschool* and the *Johannes Calvijn Academie* at Kampen: Dr. G. Brillenburg Wurth, Dr. K. Dijk, Dr. G. M. den Hartogh—who inspired me with a love of Church History which I have not been able to disavow in the present study—, Dr. J. L. Koole, Dr. J. J. Koopmans, Dr. A. D. R. Polman, Dr. J. Ridderbos and Dr. H. N. Ridderbos, while with piety I mention here the names of the deceased professors Dr. S. Greijdanus and Dr. K. Schilder. But in a special sense I am grateful to Professor Dr. J. H. Bavinck, my *promotor,* whose inspiring guidance in the field of missionary science has opened my eyes to the fascinating aspects of this sector of theology, and whose unfailing interest and stimulating assistance have made the work for the completion of my dissertation a source of continuous joy. I also wish to include within my thanks the professors of *New College,* Edinburgh, of whom I mention in particular Principal Hugh Watt D. D., Professor J. H. S. Burleigh D. D., and Professor N. W. Porteous D. D., while together with them I mention Professor A. M. Renwick D. D. of *Free Church College,* Edinburgh: they all have given me their help and assistance in a most friendly and cordial way.

A great debt of gratitude I owe to my friend and former fellow-student at *New College,* the Rev. J. Mc Michael Orr B. D. of Auchterarder, Scotland, who has rendered me invaluable service by correcting the language of my dissertation. I also thank Mr. R. Abels, drs. litt., of Zutphen, who was always ready with help and advice in linguistic problems.

I want to express my gratitude to the Libraries which have made it possible to me to make a thankful use of their services. Apart from the Library of the *Theologische Hogeschool* and the *Missionary Libraries* of Amsterdam, Baarn and Oegstgeest I mention here the *Koninklijke Bibliotheek* at the Hague, the *Universiteitsbibliotheek* at Utrecht and the Library of the *Vrije Universiteit* at Amsterdam. At the same time I thank the various British Libraries which have given me all the facilities I needed—with special gratitude I think here of the help, given to me by the staff of the Library of the *British Museum,* the Library of the *Church Missionary Society* and *New College Library*.

I am deeply grateful for the way in which my parents have enabled me to continue my theological studies even outside the bounds of our country and to complete them in the writing of this dissertation. That my father, who has supported with so much enthusiasm the cause of the adjudication of the *ius promovendi* to the *Theologische Hogeschool*, lives to see at least the partial fulfilment of one of his great wishes in a double sense, is not only for him a reason for special joy. But above all I am thankful that my parents have shown me the way to the source of all knowledge. In this context my thoughts go out to her who in her living and dying gave testimony to the value and the greatness of the love of Jesus. The blessing of her memory has accompanied me during the course of my theological studies and has guarded me in days of doubt and uncertainty.

The word of thanks to my wife for the part which she has taken in the completion of this work has a more than traditional meaning. It is not only her "technical" assistance which evokes my gratitude: the fact that during several years when practically all spare hours had to be passed in the study she has followed the writing of this work with active and stimulating interest, has made me understand the deep sense of the biblical title of honour: "an help meet for him".

I thank the "kirk-sessions" of my former congregation, Ottoland, and of my present congregation, Zutphen, for their understanding of the exigencies of my study; thanks to the facilities which they have granted to me, I have had the opportunity to begin and to complete the writing of this dissertation. A word of special thanks to my colleague, the Rev. G. S. Oegema of Zutphen, who in particular during the last year has been so kind to relieve me from some of my tasks.

But above all I thank Him who, though He did not allow me to take part in the missionary work in Indonesia, still gives so many opportunities for fruitful service in his Kingdom, that the last sentence of this foreword cannot be but this one: "what shall I render unto the Lord for all his benefices toward me?"

CONTENTS

CONTENTS

PROLOGUE

We live in a time of renewal and reorientation. Old foundations are shaken, old schemes are thrown away or are subjected to such a drastic revision that it is sometimes difficult to discern any continuity with the past. The deep incision of the second world war and its aftermath has confronted us with a new situation in almost every sector of life. In this time of crisis and fermentation the Church has to face new problems with regard to its missionary task. The home base has changed: the last rests of the *corpus christianum* have broken down, the mission-field has come alarmingly near to the doors of the older Churches. And there have also been fundamental changes in the old mission-fields: almost everywhere the way to reach those who are living without Christ runs through the „younger" Churches, who have joyfully accepted their responsibility to proclaim the gospel in their own country. [1]

This can mean that a time of crisis has approached for the work of missions. It certainly means that the Church sees itself faced with the task of regauging its missionary values in the light of the present and of the past. It has been remarked in an interim report to the meeting of the I.M.C. at Willingen in 1952, that not since the seventh century has the message of the Christian mission been so searchingly tested and tried, and that consequently it will not do to say the same old things in the same old way. [2] At the same time, however, we have to avoid the danger of a missionary thinking which is so much determined by the present situation that it loses the sense of continuity with the work of foregoing generations. Some degree of discontinuity is unavoidable: the Church can only live up to the high requirements of its missionary calling if it bravely accepts the challenge of the present day. But across the breach runs the bridge of an abiding continuity, which makes historical study an essential part of missiology.

All this holds true especially with regard to the inquiry into the missionary motive. The crisis of this day throws the Church back upon the old fundamental question: „Why foreign missions?" Ultimately, the answer to this question can neither be derived from the present situation nor from the circumstances of the past. The decisive answer can only be found in the revelation of God. Revelation however is no

---

[1] Cf. W. Freytag, *Vom Sinn der Weltmission*, E.M.M. XCIV (1950), SS. 67—68.
[2] N. Goodall (ed.), *Missions under the Cross*, London 1953, p. 238.

1

mere dictate from heaven, but finds its sequel in a dialogue between God and man, in which God thrusts upon man ever and anew his divine command, while man gives response in broken deeds of human obedience. And we cannot presume to find the answer for our present situation, if we have not tried to listen to the dialogue of former generations with Him whose call to missions goes out afresh in every new period in the history of the Church.

This makes it necessary to put the quest for the missionary motive against a historical background. Besides, in this way we are guarded against the danger of an abstract thinking which blinds the eye to the concrete and practical aspects of the problems that are under consideration. But from the fact, that the decisive answer must be found in God's revelation it follows that historical study is not sufficient. History has no norm in itself. In a time of crisis, the Church is not only compelled to a reconsideration, but also, as Dürr puts it, to a purification of the missionary motives. [3] The Church has to confront the human motives which have contributed to the growth of the missionary work with the one great motive of God. The motives which we find in the way of historical research stand in a certain relationship to the divine motive, [4] but this relationship is not a continuous one: it is nearly always broken by human errors and human misunderstandings. There is an open space, a dimension of non-empirical values behind the empirical motives. Here historical research finds its limit; here theology has to speak its penultimate critical word [5], which points to the ultimate one: the Word, spoken by God himself, the Word of crisis and forgiveness. So our study has a twofold aim: first to find the empirical motives, the spokes within the wheel of the missionary work, and then to consider how they are related to the axle of the wheel, the centre of the work, the motive, which is enshrined in the biblical call to missions.

In the meantime, the word „motives" asks for explanation. In the context of our present study it does not mean in the first place the psychological motive which finds itself at the background of the individual's decision to enter into the sphere of missionary work, [6] but primarily the impelling forces which stand behind the missionary awakening as a whole—though it is evident that there is an interaction between the communal motives and the first stirring of the missionary ideal in the individual: without the work of „awakened" individuals the missionary awakening at the end of the eighteenth century is

---

[3]   H. Dürr, *Die Reinigung der Missions-Motive*, E.M.M. XCV (1951), SS. 2—3.
[4]   J. H. Bavinck, *Inleiding in de Zendingswetenschap*, Kampen 1954, blz. 276.
[5]   K. Barth, *Die Theologie und die Mission in der Gegenwart*, Zwischen den Zeiten X (1932), passim.
[6]   Chiefly in this sense the word "motive" is used by Miss Rouse: R. Rouse, *The Missionary Motive*, I.R.M. XXV (1936), p. 251.

simply unthinkable, while on the other hand the individual's decision was determined by the attitude of the group to which he belonged. Apart from this, however, several other factors have influenced the revival of the missionary ideal. Political, cultural and sociological circumstances have played a part. Much depended on the ecclesiastical and theological situation. These factors have become *motives* as soon as they found a place either in the conscious or in the unconscious life of the Christian community, where they could act as forces which contributed to the awakening of the idea of missions and impelled to take the missionary work in hand. And behind them stands the hidden, mysterious work of the great mover, God's Spirit: the ultimate ground of the fact that the deepest cause of awakening and revival escapes all explanation. [7]

In this study, we have as object to consider the motives which have worked in one of the most important stages of missionary history: the eighteenth century in Great Britain. This brings with it a twofold limitation, of time and of place. The eighteenth century has been chosen. because it is the period in which the missionary ideal in Protestantism took form in a growing stream of missionary activities—from the formation of the S.P.C.K. in 1698 to the origin of the great missionary societies around 1800. It is our intention to follow the course of events till about 1815, when the formative period has finished and a time of broader expansion has begun—an expansion whose roots we find in the preceding century. Our second limitation finds its cause in the fact that the missionary awakening in England and Scotland has developed a character of its own, and, though not unrelated to the revival of missions in Germany, [8] is yet so deeply rooted in the soil of Britain's spiritual and cultural life that it asks for separate treatment.

An introductory chapter will give attention to the history of missionary thought in Protestantism before the eighteenth century, with special regard to the first British missionary endeavours. Then follows in the next chapters a historical exposé of the growth of the missionary ideal in Great Britain till the beginning of the nineteenth century combined with a systematical treatment of the missionary motives in that period. Ultimately, this leads to a critical confrontation of the separate motives with the one great motive of the Bible, centred in Jesus Christ, God's *apostolos*, in whom alone the work of missions finds its judgment and its justification.

---

[7] Cf. O. Riecker, *Das Evangelistische Wort*, Gütersloh 1935, S. 6. in every revival moment can be found next to the working of human laws the influence of the "pneumatische Impuls".

[8] E. Benz, *Pietist and Puritan Sources of early Protestant World Missions*. Church History XX (1951), p. 29.

Chapter I

EARLY PROTESTANT MISSIONARY THOUGHT AND ACTIVITY

In order to get an insight into the causes of the British missionary awakening it is necessary to go back to the Reformation and post-Reformation periods, in which at least some of the roots of the later development are to be found. In this introductory chapter we will first give attention to those Reformers whose world of thought has more or less influenced the later missionary development: Luther, Bucer and Calvin. After that we will consider the growth of the missionary idea in the period after the Reformation, with special regard to the Dutch missions in the seventeenth century — which unfolded in a situation, in some respects analogous to that of England — and, of course, to the first beginnings of missionary life in Great Britain itself.

1. THE REFORMERS

a. *Their attitude towards missions*

The history of Protestant missions begins with a much discussed, but as yet not fully solved riddle: that of the missionary vacuum during the period of the Reformation. The existence of this vacuum is evident with regard to practical missionary work. While there was a great outburst of Roman Catholic missionary activity, it is very difficult to find one real missionary venture at the Protestant side during the sixteenth century. This fact, however, is not the most embarrassing side of the riddle: it finds its easy explanation in the external circumstances of the time. The political situation made it almost impossible for Protestants to cross the seas and to go to the "antipodes", as Calvin calls them [1]), to those who lived outside every direct Christian influence: Spain and Portugal, the Roman Catholic sea-powers, dominated the entrance to the non-Christian world. From the world of Islam — near as it had approached since the attack of the Turkish realm on the heart of Europe — the Western countries were separated

---

[1] *C.R.* 73 (*O.C.* XLV), c. 656 (*Comm. in Matth. 24. 14*).

by an "iron curtain". [2] Moreover, the hands of the Reformers were tied by the struggle against Rome, a struggle in which the law of self-preservation and the necessity of consolidation absorbed almost all the dynamic energies of the young Protestant Churches [3] — just as in some Roman Catholic countries, e. g. France, the efforts to win back the ground which had got lost diverted the attention of Roman Catholic circles from the direct missionary task. [4] So it is not difficult to bring forward very valid excuses for the lack of missionary enterprise in the Protestant circles of that time. It is, however, generally felt that they do not solve the riddle! We could imagine an analogous situation in our own time, in which the impossibility of taking up the missionary work would be felt as painful. But the great problem for most of the missiologists who have occupied themselves with the beginnings of Protestant missions is this, that they cannot find even a *latent* missionary zeal: according to them, the vacuum lies below the surface, in the Reformers' *world of thought*.

In this connection one previous question has to be put: what do we expect from the Reformers, which standard do we apply to them? In recent times some Lutheran authors on this subject have remarked that it is unfair as well as scientifically inadmissible to summon the Reformers before the tribunal of a modern missionary concept, which has itself its historical limitations and its theological defects. [5] Too often indeed, missions have been identified with the "business of missions", with the organizational aspect of modern missionary life. On the other side however there is the not imaginary danger of an understatement of the part which man has to play in the fulfilment of God's plan, the danger that the factor of necessary human activity is not sufficiently accentuated. Mission is indeed the work of God, God-in-Christ is the great subject of all missionary work. [6] God is not dependent on man in the transmission of the kerygma. He is free in his acting. In this sense the missionary idea had quite definitely an important place in the thinking of the Reformers: they clearly saw the dynamic relation between Christ and the ends of the earth, as we

---

[2] W. Holsten, *Reformation und Mission*, Archiv für Reformationsgeschichte XIVL (1953), S. 13.

[3] O. Dibelius, *Die Epochen der Kirchengeschichte und die Mission*, V, E.M.Z. IV, 1943, S. 134.

[4] K. Scott Latourette, *A History of the Expansion of Christianity*, III, New York and London 1939, p. 27.

[5] W. Elert, *Morphologie des Luthertums*, I, München 1931, S. 336: the idea of missions is not identical with a "Betriebstheorie"; W. Holsten, *Reformation und Mission*, op. cit., SS. 2 ff.: modern missions are alien to the spirit of the Reformation when and in as far as they are a child of Catholicism as the mediator of the anthropocentric motives of humanism.

[6] J. H. Bavinck, *Inleiding in de Zendingswetenschap*, op. cit., p. 65; cf. also W. Holsten, *Das Kerygma und der Mensch*, München 1953, S. 70: "Subjekt der Mission ist das Kerygma", or "...Gott, der im Kerygma entscheidend handelt, ist das Subjekt", but never "Gott, abgesehen vom Kerygma".

shall see below. But the word "mission" is also related to the aspect of the human deed. The way of God's acting in this world is that of intermediation: it has pleased God to lay the task of the transmission of the faith in the hands of men; according to his plan of salvation, a bridge of human work and human activity has to be laid between Christ and the ends of the earth; men have to go out into the world and to teach the nations. [7] Of course, every time has its own forms and methods, and it would be unfair to measure the Reformers by the shape—relative as it is—which the work of mission had to take in a later time. But in biblical light it is fully legitimate to ask: did the Reformers have an open eye, not only for the universal character of the Gospel, but also for the Church's vocation to carry the message by the way of human activity to the ends of the earth? Our answer to this question is of dominant importance for our evaluation of the missionary work of a later period.

The works of the Reformers contain no doctrine of missions, not even fragments of such a doctrine—and this omission does not have the same background as it has in the New Testament, where the self-evidency of the missionary vocation is continuously supposed. [8] There a fullness—here a vacuum. The word "heathen" is often used by Luther, but mostly in the sense of "Christians from the gentiles", [9] though here and there he uses it in the sense of "non-Christians". [10] Luther knows that the preaching of the Gospel has not reached as yet the whole of the heathen world: repeatedly he declares that the Gospel is still on its way. [11] But this knowledge remains on the margin of his thinking and is counterbalanced by the thought that the most important part of the world has already heard the message, [12] that

---

[7] Cf. the book of Acts, in which this human factor takes a great place. From his theological point of view (Luther seen through Bultmannian spectacles, with an extreme accentuation of the "extra nos": the kerygma is "die Botschaft vom entscheidenden und zur Entscheidung rufenden Handeln Gottes in Christus"; as the starting-point of missiology we have to take "das reformatorische Verständnis vom Menschen... hominem fide iustificari", *Das Kerygma und der Mensch, op. cit.*, SS. 43—45), Holsten criticises the book of Acts, in which according to him the centre of gravity has been shifted from Easter to Pentecost (*op. cit.*, S. 124).

[8] J. R. Brutsch, *La pensée missionnaire dans le Protestantisme, de Luther à Zinzendorf* (thèse en manuscrit de l'université de Genève), Genève 1946, p. 11.

[9] G. Warneck, *Abrisz einer Geschichte der Protestantischen Missionen*, Berlin [10] 1913, S. 9.

[10] *W.A.* 31 [I], 231, 12 (*Der 117. Psalm ausgelegt*, 1530): "Heyden, das yn Ebreschem Goim lautet, heissen die Juden gemeiniglich alle volcker, die nicht Juden sind, gleich wir auch thun und heissen alle volcker Heyden, so nicht Christen sind..."

[11] *W.A.* 10 [I] a, 22. 1—8 (*Kirchenpostille*, 1522): "... der Apostel redet von der artt des Euangeliums"; *W. A.* 10 [III], 139, 17—21 (*Sermon am Auffahrttage über Mark. 16. 14*, 1522): "Auch seynd vil inseln erfunnden worden noch zu unseren zeiten, die da heiden seind und niemant hat in gepredigt..."

[12] *W. A.* 10 [I] a, *in loco citato*: "... und zu der Aposteln zeyt schon ynsz groste und beste teyl der welt kommen war".

in principle the name of Christ is known throughout the world and that in accordance with the nature of the realm of God the message will spread itself to the furthest corner of the earth. [13] The most pressing problem was for Luther the problem of Islam. There is a seeming dualism in Luther's attitude towards it, which is connected with his doctrine of the two swords. [14] On one side he calls upon the Christian princes to combat the Islamic power, on the other hand he vehemently rejects the ideology of the crusades: the Church has to fight against Islam with spiritual weapons [15]—and for this fight he sees as the only way the personal testimony of Christians who have fallen into the hands of the Turks. [16]

In the works of Bucer we find another accent. Though his presuppositions do not differ much from that of Luther, still it is as if he has a more disquieted conscience with regard to the situation of the heathen world. When Luther in his Kirchenpostille of 1522 remarks that the Gospel is "auf der ban und geschehen, doch nicht gar", Bucer, in his latin translation of 1525/1526, gives the following paraphrase: "quamquam interim haud parum multi sint, qui adhuc nihil de ea (gratia) audierint". [17] Bucer has a special interest in the conversion of the Jews [18], he also gives more attention than Luther does to the human element in the proclamation of the Gospel; [19] yet he does not come to a full appreciation of the missionary task of the Church. [20]

On Calvin the opinions are much divided. While from one side his ideas on the spreading of the Gospel are considered as poor in comparison with those of Luther and Bucer, [21] other authors on this subject see in Calvin's world of thought the source of the modern missionary enterprise. [22] In fact there is not much difference between the practical attitude of Calvin and that of the other Reformers. Calvin knows as well as Luther and Bucer that not all the nations have as yet heard the Gospel: he speaks of the antipodes and other far removed peoples

---

[13] Cf. P. Drews, *Die Anschauungen reformatorischen Theologen über die Heidenmission*, Zeitschrift für praktische Theologie XIX (1897), SS. 15, 23; cf. also W. Holsten, *Reformation und Mission, op cit.*, SS. 11—12.

[14] E. Kellerhals, *Der Islam*, Basel 1945, S. 314.

[15] *W. A.* 8, 708, 27—32 (*Bulla coenae domini*, 1522): "Wen ehr [= the Pope] aber Christus stadthalter were, so wurde er auf seyne fusse tretten, hyngehen und den Turcken des Euangeli predigen, daran setzen leyb und leben: das were eyn Christlich weysze, die Turcken zubestreytten..."

[16] *W.A.* 30 II, 195, 1—8 (*Heerpredigt wider den Türken*, 1529).

[17] *W.A.* 10 I a, 22, 11—14 (with fragments of Bucer's translation in the footnotes).

[18] W. Holsten, *Das Evangelium und die Völker*, Berlin 1939, SS 63—67.

[19] H. Frick, *Die Evangelische Mission, Ursprung, Geschichte, Ziel*, Bonn—Leipzig 1922, SS. 41—46.

[20] P. Drews, *art. cit.*, S. 217.

[21] *In loco citato*, S. 289.

[22] E.g. S. M. Zwemer, *Calvinism and the Missionary Enterprise*, Theology Today VII (1950), pp. 206—216.

whom even the least fame of Christ has not reached; [23] though the world of Islam did not come as much within his horizon as was the case with Luther, his correspondence with the Brazilian emigrants has certainly directed his attention towards the distress of the heathen world; [24] everywhere in his works, in particular in his commentaries on the prophets, we meet the thrill of expectation; the missionary zeal is present in a latent way in his prayer for the conversion of the heathen and in his desire to draw all men in this world to Christ [25] — but Calvin, too, does not come to the full recognition of the missionary obligation of the Church.

b.   The theological background of their attitude

In all this the most important question is: how can we *explain* the rather negative attitude of the Reformers? Have only accidental factors—as, *e.g.*, the political situation—played a part, or are there deeper causes, connected with the Reformers' theological views—and if so, is there perhaps an interaction between both sets of factors?

Gustav Warneck has sought [26] the causes of Luther's attitude in his *eschatology* and his *doctrine of election*. [27] With regard to Luther's eschatology it can be remarked, however, that on other points his expectation of a speedy Second Coming of Christ has not been a brake on his dynamic activity; and the history of missions shows more than one instance of a strong eschatological tension which became a powerfull stimulus in a missionary awakening, as we shall see hereafter. There is no sufficient proof that eschatology in itself is the cause of the missionary vacuum. However, in combination with the circumstances in which Luther lived, the nature of his eschatology—according to Prof. Torrance "mainly an eschatology of judgment, going back to early Latin fathers like Cyprian, with their emphasis on the decay and collapse of the world" [28]—may have strengthened Luther's pessimism with regard to the actual possibility of missionary work: he saw, in a certain period at least, the Church surrounded by devils on

---

[23]   *C.R. 73 (O.C. XLV), c. 656 (Comm. in Matth. 24. 14).*

[24]   Cf. the vivid picture of the "barbarians", given by the preacher P. Richer in his letter to Calvin of April 1557, *C.R.* 44 (O.C. XVI), c. 434 (ep. 2609). The latest study on the Brazilian expedition is that of G. Baez-Camargo, *The earliest Protestant Missionary Venture in Latin America*, Church History XXI (1952), p.p. 135—145.

[25]   See my: *Calvin's Missionary Message*, E.Q. XXII (1950), p. 181.

[26]   "dans un élan de sincérité", according to G. Goyau, *L'idée missionnaire dans le Protestantisme et dans le Catholicisme aux seizième et dix-septième siècles*, L'Eglise en marche, 1re série, Paris 1933, p. 93.

[27]   G. Warneck, *op. cit.*, S. 14.

[28]   T. F. Torrance, *The Eschatology of the Reformers*, in: W. Manson and others, *Eschatology*, Scottinsh Journal of Theology Occasional Papers No. 2, London and Edinburgh s.a., p. 40.

each and every side![29] Therefore he saw the possibility of missionary work limited to a kind of "spontaneous expansion".[30] A certain quietism in Luther's attitude may also have its cause in a reaction against Rome, in a fear for the anthropocentric element in the Roman Catholic missionary activity. God does the work![31] That Luther's doctrine of election has played a part here is improbable: Luther knows too well that grace is offered to all men! In his doctrine of the ecclesiastical office we perceive a double reaction: against Rome with its doctrine of the apostolic succession, Luther accentuated the unrepeatable character of the apostolate; against the sectarians with their too loose conception of the office, he laid stress upon its fixed and stable character.[32] By the static doctrine of *vocatio* every official activity was limited within the bounds of the parish.[33] Yet it would be wrong to assume a too direct connection between this concept and the "missionary vacuum"—Luther was too much of a living theologian to be the slave of his own ideas! Some authors, on the Protestant[34] as well as on the Roman Catholic side[35], see as one of the main causes the falling away of the ascetic motive. Here, however, is a terminological misunderstanding: the Reformers dropped asceticism as a meritorious work, but not as an attitude of willingness to make personal sacrifices in the service of God. And while the loss of the monastic orders evoked indeed in later time some problems with regard to the practical fulfilment of the missionary task, it could have no direct influence on the missionary idea itself.

It is difficult to reduce the different factors, which have arrested the growth of the missionary idea with Luther, to one denominator. One thing is evident: that there is a place in Luther's world of thought for the idea of mission, but that reaction against Rome as well as difficult outward circumstances coloured some of his theological concepts in such a way,[36] that they became the cause of an

---

[29] *W.A.* 30 II, 196, 1—4 (*Heerpredigt wider den Türken*, 1529): "Eitel teuffel auff beiden seiten und allenthalben. So stehet es leyder itzt ynn der welt ... ynn den letzten tagen...".

[30] Which was for him na "missionary principle", as appears from the often quoted "stone-passage" (the message spreads itself like circles of water around a stone), in which he leaves room for *preachers of the Gospel* — W.A. 10 III, 140, 6—10 (*Sermon am Auffahrttage über Mark. 16. 14*, 1522): „... und wird durch die prediger weiter getrieben...".

[31] W. Holsten lays a special emphasis upon this point (*passim* in his quoted works) — once again: with a one-sided accentuation of the "extra nos" with Luther.

[32] E. Schick, *Vorboten und Bahnbrecher*, Basel 1943, S. 16.

[33] H. Frick, *op. cit.*, SS. 15—16.

[34] P. Drews, *Mission und Askese*, Die Christliche Welt XI (1897), Sp. 538.

[35] M. Galm, *Das Erwachen des Missionsgedankens im Protestantismus der Niederlände*, St Ottilien 1915, S. 8.

[36] K. Scott Latourette, *op. cit.*, III, p. 25, sees in the attitude of the Reformers "perhaps an unconscious outgrowth" of the difficult position of early Protestantism.

attitude of reserve. This "epochè" has become a distinct denial with the Lutheran orthodox theologians of a later period; on the other hand, it has guarded Protestant missions against an uncritical imitation of the missions of the Roman Catholic church. Luther's attitude was not purely negative: it has also had the meaning of a "purification of the missionary motive". [37]

After this it is not necessary to say much about the other Reformers. In Bucer we have found a more open mind towards the idea of missions than Luther possessed. Holsten sees here the danger of the anthropocentric motive: according to him, Bucer has left the standpoint of the pure reformatory "extra nos"; the factor of human piety, together with a different valuation of the non-Christian religions, make him a forerunner of the pietist missions. [38] There lies a partial truth in this view of Bucer: his world of thought knew indeed a more active element, and his eschatology was less quietistic and more dynamic, leaving more room for the renewal of this world and for the realization of the will of God in history, than that of Luther [39] — though certainly the difference between the two Reformers is more a matter of emphasis than of principle. Bucer, too, did not come to a full recognition of the missionary task, but his theology gave an opening towards the side of human activity and dynamism in the realization of the missionary idea. As in later Pietism and Methodism, we find already with Bucer the motive of compassion with the state of the heathen and the desire to win their souls for Christ. [40] Bucer has had a twofold influence in Great Britain: directly through his stay in England and through his writings, in an indirect way through his influence of Calvin.

It is not difficult to point out some parallels between the attitude of Luther and that of Calvin towards the idea of missions. With Calvin we also find a certain "epochè", a fear for arbitrary action; for

---

A Roman Catholic author supposes that there also is a relation with pre-Reformation ideas: H. de Lubac, *Le Fondement théologique des Missions*, Paris 1946, p. 60: "L'état d'esprit des premiers réformateurs s'explique en partie par un état d'esprit antérieur à la Réforme".

[37] H. Dürr, *art. cit.*, SS. 5—6.

[38] W. Holsten, *Christentum und nichtchristliche Religion nach dem Auffassung Bucers*, in: *Das Evangelium und die Völker, op cit.*; idem, *Reformation und Mission, op cit.*, SS. 14—19.

[39] T. F. Torrance in: *Eschatology*, op cit., p. 54: „...the *regnum Christi* in Butzer's theology constitutes a third dimension, the *corpus Christi* which through the Word and Spirit is visibly and actually realised in the Church on earth...". What Holsten sees as humanistic influences with Bucer (the part which the *doctrina pietatis* plays in his works), Torrance sees as the result of a broader understanding of the teaching of Scripture: Word and Spirit are seen in their conjunction, Ephesians and Galatians are interpreted together.

[40] Cf. the quotation of Bucer's "Von der wahren Seelsorge", given by O. Michaelis in his: *Zur Frage des Missionsverständnisses der Reformatoren*, Z.M.R. XLI (1926), SS 340—342.

him, too, mission is primarily the work of God; [41] a seeming quietism is not strange to him: he waits and teaches to wait until God will open the door [42]—though in fact this is no passivity, but rather a realism behind which an expectant activism hides itself. This brings us on to the differences between Luther and Calvin. The principal difference is not this, that Luther's interest was mainly soteriological, while the theology of Calvin had a more theocentric character: both elements are present with both Reformers, [43] albeit that especially with Calvin the idea of the *gloria Dei* takes a prominent place. There is a real difference in circumstances. Calvin had not Luther's feeling of being closed in between walls: for him great parts of the world began to open themselves out, as his broad correspondence shows. In his works we find another tone: that of a strong dynamism. [44] In his eschatology he has more eye than Luther had for the renewal of this world [45] and for the participation of the Church in the mighty acts of Christ: „. . . throughout all his works, Calvin made it a point of prime importance to teach the combination of the *meditatio vitae futurae* with the unceasing activity of the Church on earth in the growth and extension of the Kingdom." [46] With him asceticism turns its face towards the Christian's task in the midst of this world. In his concept of the ecclesiastical office there is an initial break-through of some of his views with regard to the limitation of apostolate [47]: though he makes a sharp distinction between the temporary and the non-temporary offices, he still finds a way-out in the acknowledgement—perhaps inconsistent—of the fact that God in the time of the Reformation could raise apostles for special tasks. [48] And the soteriological element gives a certain fervour to some of Calvin's utterances: he is moved by compassion to save the poor souls of perishing people from hell [49] and driven by humanity to the help of those who are in distress. [50]

---

[41] W. F. Dankbaar, *Het Apostolaat bij Calvijn*, N.Th.T. IV (1949—1950), p. 184.

[42] *C.R. 78 (O.C.L.)*, c. 31 (*Commentarius in II Cor. 2. 12*): " . . . progressus faciunt servi Domini, quum datur facultas. Clauditur ostium, ubi nulla spes fructus ostenditur".

[43] Cf. G. C. Berkouwer, *Geloof en Rechtvaardiging*, Kampen 1949, pp. 55—56.

[44] Cf. T. F. Torrance, *Calvin's doctrine of man*, London 1949, p. 71: "*Imago Dei* is not a dead but a living image, not a mute expression of the divine glory, but a witness-bearing image . . .".

[45] T. F. Torrance in: *Eschatology, op. cit.*, p. 40.

[46] *Op. cit.*, p. 55.

[47] See W. F. Dankbaar, *art. cit.*, passim.

[48] *Inst. IV, 34:* "Quanquam non nego quin apostolos postea quoque, vel saltem eorum loco Euangelistas interdum excitarit Deus, ut nostro tempore factum est"; cf. J. R. Brutsch, *op. cit.*, p. 95: " . . . sa [— Calvin's] définition de l'apôtre est favorable à la pensée misionnaire".

[49] W. F. Dankbaar, *art. cit.*, p. 185.

[50] *C.R. 57 (O.C. XXIX*, c. 175) (*Sermons sur Deut. 24. 10—13*): "Notons bien donc que si nous ne sommes pitoyables, que nous n'ayons compassion de ceux qui

That in spite of this the idea of missions takes no greater place in Calvin's works is due to the coincidence of political and sociological factors with the theological factor of an "epochè" which was for the great part a result of his strong reaction against Roman Catholic missions. It must quite emphatically be stated that his doctrine of election is not the culprit: [51] Calvin himself is explicit enough in his Institutes. [52] Only a hyper-Calvinism in which Christ is not seen as the *speculum electionis* and in which a static doctrine of predestination gets a tyrannical power, is anti- or at least non-missionary.

We conclude: though various circumstances hindered the outgrowth of the missionary idea with the Reformers, we still find with them many positive elements, which became missionary motives as soon as the impeding factors fell away. They had a clear consciousness of the universality of the Gospel, they knew the soteriological tension of love and compassion, [53] and in particular with Calvin we find the theocentric ideal of the expansion of the Kingdom of God.

c. Humanism, Spiritualism and "Corpus Christianum"

Finally, we have to make three remarks:

1. In this inquiry we have left aside the ideas of Erasmus and Zwingli: Erasmus was no Reformer, Zwingli's thoughts have had neither direct nor indirect influence on the missionary idea in Great Britain. The latter statement can not be made of Erasmus. Thomas Bray, who played such an important part in the foundation of the S.P.G. and the S.P.C.K., had a great admiration for Erasmus' *Ecclesiastes,* of which he even produced a new edition. [54] Already because of this relation between Erasmus and the British missions it is necessary to deal for a moment with the grounds of Erasmus' missionary interest. The Christian humanist, who had tried to disengage the biblical ethics of love from their background of ascetic idealism and otherwordly piety and whose interests were more with the moral than with the soteriological, sacramental and ecclesiastical aspects of biblical theolo-

---

ont faute de notre aide, pour les secourir, et que nous n'usions d'humanité, que nous n'aurons nul accez à nostre Dieu...".

[51] As, *e.g.,* J. McLeod Campbell contends in his *Christian History in the Making,* London 1946, p. 29: Calvin's theology is "a theology which cuts the nerve of evangelistic impulse".

[52] *Inst* III, 23, 13 (in a quotation from St. Augustine): "Cursum igitur suum habeat praedicatio ... Neque tamen impediatur praedestinationis cognitio ..."; 14: "... quia nescimus quis ad praedestinatorum numerum pertineat, vel non pertineat, sic nos affici decere ut omnes velimus salvos fieri".

[53] Though Luther and Calvin made no speculations, they were anxious about the eternal destiny of those who lived outside the revelation of Jesus Christ (see P. Eppler, *Die Gedanken der Reformatoren über die Frömmigkeit und Seligkeit der Heiden,* E.M.M. LXII (1918), SS. 6—15, 43—52).

[54] W. K. Lowther Clarke, *Eigteenth Century Piety,* London 1944, p. 99.

gy, [55] gave in the evening of his life, in his work on the art of preaching, written between 1529 and 1535 (*Ecclesiastes sive concionator evangelicus*, Basel 1535), a moving testimony of his love for the missionary cause. [56] In this call to missions we hear, in a certain sense, more the voice of the catholic Christian than that of the humanist: Erasmus is impelled by a pure desire to see many souls freed from Satan's tyranny and won for the Redeemer. The moral element, however, dominates the soteriological interest: it is the *philosophia christiana*, the *christiana sapientia*, which has to be propagated, and missionary work is seen as a taming of wild peoples. [57] All this remains too much on the lines of human activity: sympathetic and noble as Erasmus' call may be, we miss in it the dimension of grace—it makes us better understand the "epochè" of the Reformers.

2.   Of late, some attention has been given to the missionary idea in sectarian circles during the Reformation period. K. Goldammer sees in the German mystic Paracelsus the first herald of the missionary idea in Protestantism; [58] he assumes the existence of hidden links with Herrnhut and perhaps also with Halle, while E. Beyreuther has traced some remarkable parallels between Paracelsus and J. von Welz, one of the seventeenth century propagandists for the missionary idea in Germany. [59] In Paracelsus we see a representative of the spiritualist type, which finds itself outside or at the margin of the institutional Church; it has a certain contempt for the static forms of ecclesiastical life; its eschatology is fervent, but often overlooks the category of historical development; its missionary zeal is strong, but remains in the individualistic sphere; it tries to dynamise the concept of the ecclesiastical office, sometimes by denying its special character. It is valuable as a corrective of a too static concept of the Church, but its individualism, its anti-institutionalism and its non-historical eschatology are not favourable for a quiet and steady realisation of the missionary idea. There are no direct lines traceable from the German sectarians to British missionary life, but often in the history of missions a certain spiritualism has helped to open the eye to the forgotten category of the dynamism, which lies in the indwelling force of the Spirit. [60]

---

[55]   As J. Lindeboom says it in his: *Het Bijbels Humanisme in Nederland*, Leiden 1913, pp. 114—121.

[56]   J. Schmidlin has given the Latin text of the passage in question (taken from the Lyon edition, *Opera* t. V, p. 813 ss.) with German translation in his article: *Erasmus von Rotterdam über die Heidenmission*, Z.M. IV (1914), SS. 1—12.

[57]   Erasmus in: J. Schmidlin, *art. cit.*, S. 6: "Novimus circurare bestias feras et horribiles vel ad voluptatem vel ad usum vulgarem, et non novimus mansuefacere homines, ut serviant Christo?"

[58]   K. Goldammer, *Aus den Anfängen evangelischen Missionsdenkens, Kirche, Amt und Mission bei Paracelsus*, E.M.Z. IV (1943), SS 44—70.

[59]   E. Beyreuther, *Die Bedeutung des 17. Jahrhunderts für das deutsche Missionsleben*, E.M.Z. VIII (1951), SS. 71—77.

[60]   Cf. the description of the "Pentecostal type" by L. Newbigin, *The Household of God*, London 1953, pp. 87—110.

3. In our description of the missionary elements in the Reformers' world of thought we have not taken into account the idea of the *corpus christianum*: it does not affect the missionary idea in its core and essence, but in its practical realization. J. R. Brutsch sees in the notion of the *corpus christianum* one of the main causes of the absense of the missionary idea in the thinking of the Reformers. [61] Perhaps this judgment is too much influenced by the modern conception of the separation between Church and State. The Reformers had another view of the function of the State. Luther's ideas on this point were conservative, influenced by medieval conceptions, [62] but with Calvin we find a clear doctrine of the relation between Church and State. Calvin recognizes the possibility of a Christian government, which stands as well as the Church under the dominion of God and which has as its task the promotion of God's Kingdom and his glory. [63] He has a clear conception of the distinction between Church and State—but he also sees that because they have the same goal, they have to cooperate in order to bring the government of Christ to the ends of the earth. [64] We find the echo of these ideas in the *Confessio Belgica* (Art. 36) and in the *Westminster Confession* (Chap. 23). Since the days of the Reformers the *corpus christianum*, the unity of political, social and religious life, has broken down; the State has radically changed through the disintegration of the various spheres of life, and our view of the task of the State has also undergone a profound change: there are not many Churches now, who still adhere to the literal interpretation of the above mentioned articles in their confessions. We have learned to see the limitations and the dangers of the old concept of the *corpus christianum*. In the sphere of that concept missions get a special accent: the theocratic motive is there stronger than the motives of love and compassion, and the danger is not imaginary that missions are used for illegal purposes (imperialism!). However: while the sociological structure of the age of the Reformers left few possibilities for missionary work other than some form of government-controlled missions, [65] this dit not mean—especially for Calvin— an abandonment of its task by the Church, but the fulfilment of it by means of an instrument which was seen as given by God to promote his Kingdom and to serve the Church as its "nursing father" (Isa. 49. 23). Therefore it is incorrect to let the beginning of biblically-

---

[61] J. R. Brutsch, *op. cit.*, p. 167.
[62] G. Schrenk, *Gottesreich und Bund im älteren Protestantismus, vornehmlich bei Joh. Coccejus*, Gütersloh 1923, S. 155.
[63] *Inst.*, Praefatio: "Nec jam regnum ille sed latrocinium exercet qui non in hoc regnat ut Dei gloriae serviat".
[64] K. Fröhlich, *Gottesreich, Welt und Kirche bei Calvin*, München 1930, S. 83: "Eine politische Machterweisung des Protestantismus bedeutet ihm Zuwachs zum Reiche Christi".
[65] W. Holsten, *Reformation und Mission*, *op cit.*, S. 4.

grounded missions coincide with the breaking of the *corpus christianum*[66]
—though it must be conceded that in practice the corpus-christianum-
idea has been a real hindrance to the full and free development of the
missionary ideal in the Church.

2. THE POST-REFORMATION PERIOD

a. *The development in Germany*

On Lutheran soil the post-Reformation period is a time of remarkable
sterility with regard to the cause of missions. It is as if after Luther
a process of stiffening had lamed the spiritual energies of theologians
and church-leaders. Real missionary ventures are out of the question—
the efforts of Gustav Wasa to bring the Lapps to the Christian faith
can still less be considered as genuine missionary endeavours than the
heroic ecumenical attempts of Peter Heyling and others to reawaken
the Eastern Churches. [67] It would be unfair not to mention the outward
circumstances which contributed to this frigidity toward the missionary
task. The stimulus from the outer world was missing almost absolutely: there was but little colonial activity, and the Islamic power, which
had arrested Luther's thought in such a great degree, had receded
and was no longer a direct challenge for the Christians of Western
Europe. In addition the closed and particularistic form which the
corpus christianum took in Germany after Augsburg ("cuius regio,
eius religio") kept in check the desire for spiritual expansion which
had so often been the concomitant of the idea of the responsible
Christian state. So there was nothing to break by outward force the
strong barrier, erected by the Lutheran orthodox theologians of that
time. The most notorious plank of that barrier is perhaps the verdict,
given by the theological faculty of Wittenberg in 1651, in which
several pro-mission arguments were rejected as "absurd". [68] Some
notions which were already present with Luther, but with him found
their counterbalance in several other factors, we meet again—now in
a congealed form—with many of his orthodox followers: the idea of
"vocatio"—after the apostles every "Pfarrherr" has his own parish,
which limits his work strictly within its boundaries—, [69] and that of
the fulfilment of the missionary task by the apostles in their preaching
of the Gospel to the ends of the earth (with a recurrent appeal on

---

[66] As E. Schick does, *op. cit.*, S. 20: "Von einer echten, biblisch begründeten
Missionsarbeit können wir erst sprechen von dem Augenblick an, da diese Ver-
bindung von Kolonisation und Mission gelöst wurde".
[67] G. Warneck, *Abrisz, op cit.*, SS. 23—24.
[68] Idem, *op cit.*, SS. 26—30.
[69] H. Frick. *op cit.*, S. 15: "... es lähmte auch — im Unterschied vom Calvinismus — nicht selten die Aktivität, besonders wo es die Initiative auf bisher
noch unbetretenen Bahnen galt".

Ps. 19. 5). This attitude originated in a strong reaction against Rome and a not less determined opposition against the ideas of Saravia, which led the orthodox theologians to cover with theological arguments the factual impossibility of missionary activities. [70] On the other hand we must concede to Holsten, the brave champion of Luther and Lutheran orthodoxy, that the emphatic "no" of these theologians was not directed against the missionary ideal itself, but against the foundation of it on the command of Matt. 28. 19. [71] From time to time we find with them more positive utterances. Even in the rather chilly atmosphere of seventeenth century Lutheran orthodoxy the missionary ideal could not die, though it had to sit in silence, wings clasped! The orthodox theologians had lost the broad view of the world-wide task of the Church, bound as they were by the elements of negative reaction in their own concepts; at the same time, however, they have preserved the doctrine of saving grace in such a way that in later time the soteriological motive could become a powerful force in the development of German missions.

Two names convey another association: that of Von Welz and that of Leibniz. Other names could be mentioned—but these two men are, each in his own way, the most important representatives of a growing missionary interest. Von Welz was a man of deep religious experience; he stood firmly on the base of the Lutheran confession, while at the same time an ecumenical interest was not strange to him. [72] It became his great passion to call his people to the work of missions. In 1664 he sent into the world his urgent appeal to found a society for the propagation of the evangelical religion, [73] which shows him as a precursor of the pietist revival. [74] As motives for his call to missions he gives: the will of God (he does not refer in first instance to Matth. 28. 19 [75], but among others to Rom. 10. 18, the text which by orthodox theologians was used as a proof that the missionary command already had been fulfilled!), the example of pious men, the ecclesiastical prayer (in the litany of the prayer of the Neurenberg liturgy) for the augmentation of the kingdom, and the establishment of the "congregatio de propaganda fide" on the Roman Catholic side. Two points are of special importance: with von Welz the motive of love plays an important rôle in combination with an ascetic trend [76]—and

---

[70]   H. W. Schomerus, *Missionswissenschaft*, Leipzig 1935, S. 159.
[71]   W. Holsten, *Die Bedeutung der altprotestantischen Dogmatik für die Mission*, in: *Das Evangelium und die Völker*, Berlin-Friedenau 1939, SS. 148 ff.
[72]   E. Schick, *Vorboten und Bahnbrecher*, Basel 1943, SS. 47—50.
[73]   Edited by W. Faber as: *Der Missionsweckruf des Baron Justinian von Welz in treuer Wiedergabe des Originaldruckes vom Jahre 1664*, Leipzig 1890.
[74]   H. Frick, *op. cit.*, S. 149, calls his work a "Weissagung auf den Pietismus".
[75]   This he did in a later writing, together with a proposal to reinstitute the apostolic office: E. Schick, *op cit.*, S. 60.
[76]   J. von Welz, *op cit.*, S. 3: "... weilen ein rechtes Christliches Einsidler-Leben nicht nur die Liebe gegen Gott/sondern auch gegen den nechsten erfordert".

to bring his ideas into execution he sees as the most suitable instrument the missionary society: also on this point he appears to be a forerunner of a later situation, in which the society within the Church is an accepted phenomenon.

Von Welz was a herald of the pietist awakening, Leibniz stands in history as one of the fathers of the "Aufklärung". The great philosopher was strongly influenced by the example of Roman Catholic missions. China had his main interest; with him the great emphasis lies on the cultural aspect of missionary work: "propagatio fidei christianae per scientias" [77]. This was attended by a very positive valuation of the elements of truth in other religions. [78] Leibniz was moved by his vision of the kingdom of God: a realm which leads up to moral and spiritual perfection, a realm in which the glory of God and the common good are integrated into a harmonious unity. [79] Because Leibniz did not believe in an eternal judgment and because he saw the situation of the civilized non-Christian peoples in the most favourable light, the soteriological motive—always so strong on Lutheran soil—with him made place for the motive of the cultural expansion of Christianity, in which the purely religious fervour was not wanting altogether, but was enfeebled in such a way, that his "bold and farsighted missionary plans were translated into the sphere of action only by the glowing faith of pietism". [80] In a certain sense Leibniz stands halfway on the line between Erasmus and Hocking. [81] It was Leibniz who struck the key-note of the general feeling of the eighteenth century. He had some influence on people such as Francke and Mel, who in their turn had relations with missionary leaders in England, [82] while there also runs a direct line from Leibniz to the missionary development in Great Britain: his *Novissima Sinica* were read with approval by many people in England, among them the Primate of the Church of England, and

---

[77] F. R. Merkel, *Des Philosophen G. W. Leibniz erste Berührungen mit der Mission*, Mededeelingen LXIV² (1929), p. 126; cf. p. 124: "Sein genialer Blick erkannte sofort die zivilisatorisch-kulturelle Bedeutung der Mission..."

[78] L. J. Frohnmeyer, *Freiherr von Leibniz und die Mission*. E.M.M. LXI (1917), S. 491.

[79] See: E. Hirsch, *Geschichte der neueren evangelischen Theologie*, II, Gütersloh 1949, S. 17.

[80] F. R. Merkel, *The missionary attitude of the philosopher G. W. von Leibniz*, I.R.M. IX (1920), p. 409.

[81] W. E. Hocking was the chairman of the "Laymen's Commission", which published the famous work *Rethinking Missions* (New York 1932). Hocking stood for a "sharing" between the world religions. See for his ideas: W. M. Horton, *Between Hocking and Kraemer*, in: *The Authority of the Faith*, "The Madras Series", I, London and New York 1939.

[82] A. H. Francke had a living interest in the work of the S.P.C.K.: E. Benz, *art. cit.*, SS. 28—55; and M. Galm, *op. cit.*, S. 79, mentions that Conrad Mel sent in 1711 his *Missionarius Evangelicus* to the president of the S.P.G.

in this way became a factor in the process which led to the foundation of the S.P.G. [83]

b. The missionary idea in Holland

In the meantime we find a more positive development of the missionary idea in Holland than in Germany during the seventeenth century. Behind this development we can see the influence of socio-political circumstances as well as of theological factors. Holland belonged to the rising sea-powers: Dutch merchants and explorers prepared the way for a rapid mercantile and colonial expansion in several parts of the world. The barrier, which kept Protestant Christianity enclosed within the limits of Western Europe, was broken; the heathen world came into sight. This fact coincided with an important theological development within Calvinism: the so-called "Second Reformation", which was nothing but a continuation of the reformatory work of Calvin with a special accent on pneumatology in both its aspects: the work of the Spirit in man's soul as well as on the broad front of life, the renewal of man's inner life and the renewal of the "face of the earth". [84] The Second Reformation shows at least in its first stage a remarkable blending of the soteriological and the theocratic elements in Calvinism; its weakness was an under-accentuation of the objective value of the *justificatio impii*, [85] which would bring the movement in a later stage into the narrow waters of a sterile mysticism. The men of the Second Reformation in Holland have formed a bridge between the British Puritans and the German Pietists. From the latter group they distinguish themselves by their theocratic interest. Here too lies the relation between the incipient colonial expansion and the missionary aspect of the Second Reformation: [86] the explorers and merchants had their spiritual background in a "corpus christianum" which, though on the point of breaking by inner weakness, still represented some of the theocratic tendencies of original Calvinism, while the theologians had almost all of them a living interest in the broadening of the horizon because they were moved by the vision of "an earth, filled with the knowledge of the Lord". At the same time the soteriological element in their thinking guarded them against a cold and formal "imperialism of the Christian spirit": they saw the earth and its fulness—they saw man in his need.

---

[83]   As Leibniz writes in his *Bedenken* of November 1701: see L. J. Frohnmeyer, *art. cit.*, S? 496.

[84]   Cf. A. A. van Ruler, *De Bevinding*, Kerk en Theologie I (1950), pp. 71—90.

[85]   J. van Genderen, *Herman Witsius*, 's Gravenhage 1953, p. 222.

[86]   According to A. A. van Ruler the point of contact between the inner experience and the apostolic outlook lay in the Puritan point of view: see *De Bevinding in de Prediking*, in *Schrift en Kerk, Een bundel opstellen ... aangeboden aan Prof. Dr Th. L. Haitjema*, Nijkerk 1953, pp. 177—178.

An attempt has been made to explain their missionary interest as due to the influence of Roman Catholic missions. [87] Now the men of the Second Reformation were indeed interested in and stimulated by the activities of the Roman Catholic Church. But the motives which prompted them to missionary work were not a "Fremdkörper" in their reformatory world of thought. If some aspects of these motives show a more or less striking parallel to what we find in Roman Catholicism, we must not forget that Roman Catholics and Calvinists have still much in common in their "catholic" heritage, while on the other hand some notions, which are formally analogous, are determined on either side by a different theological background, which gives them another function and sometimes even another meaning. It is this factor which Galm overlooks when he sees in the presence of the ascetic motive in some of the missionary writings of the Second Reformation the proof of an inner dependence on Roman Catholicism. With Heurnius and his Calvinistic contemporaries the ascetic idea has another background: asceticism is not seen as a means to attain salvation along the road of human efforts, which cooperate with the grace of God, but as a way in which the certitude of salvation is confirmed and in which the grateful response to God's redeeming acts can be realized. [88]

Well-known names are to be found on the list of the champions of the missionary cause in Holland: that of W. Teellinck (who was strongly influenced by English Puritanism; he made an urgent appeal to the East India Company in the foreword of his *Ecce Homo*); J. Heurnius (who gave as a "cri de coeur" his *De Legatione Evangelica ad Indos capessenda Admonitio* and afterwards played an important part in the ecclesiastical life of the East Indies); G. Voetius (the famous professor at Utrecht, who approached the cause of missions more from the theoretical side); J. Hoornbeek (who gave a missionary doctrine in the spirit of his teacher Voetius in his *De Conversione Indorum et Gentilium*) and J. van Lodensteyn (the pietistic poet-minister of Utrecht). As motives we find with them: compassion with the temporal [89] and eternal [90] fate of the heathen, thankfulness to God for his benefactions, [91] obedience to the command of

---

[87]   M. Galm, *op cit.*, passim.

[88]   See also A. Goslinga, *Die Anfänge des Missionslebens in Holland*, A.M.Z. IL (1922), SS. 79—80.

[89]   J. Heurnius, *De Legatione Evangelica ad Indos capessenda Admonitio*, Leiden 1618, p. 191: "Indi ... quorum miseriae et aerumnae inexplicabiles, jamdudum ad hoc opus misericordiae nos vocat".

[90]   W. Teellinck, *Ecce Homo ofte Oogen-Salve voor die noch sitten in blintheyt des Ghemoets*, Dordrecht 1646, p. **3: "... ontferme dijner/Heere der genade/ over soo veel duysent duysenden zielen/die daer noch al henen woelen sonder achter-dincken op den wegh des verderfs..."; cf. also J. Hoornbeek, *De Conversione Indorum et Gentilium Libri Duo*, Amsterdam 1669, p. 195: the heathen have to be brought "ab inferno ad coelum".

[91]   Among others with J. van Lodensteyn, *Beschouwinge van Zion*, Amsterdam 1729, pp. 19, 20.

Christt, [92] awareness of the universal character of the Gospel call. [93]

Apart from these general motives some special stimuli ask for our attention. Interesting is the place which the ascetic motive takes with a man as Heurnius. As we saw already, the word has been the cause of some misunderstandings. The matter itself, however, certainly occurs with him in this sense, that the Christian life is a "militia", and not always an easy one: [94] Heurnius points out again and again that he who wants to follow Christ "in regeneratione Ethnicorum" has to flee the manifold snares of this bad world, "nam Deus noster, Deus zelotes est". [95])

Now that Protestantism had become a settled power next to Roman Catholicism, the idea gained a foothold that a counterpart had to be given for the missionary activities on the other side. Hoornbeek used the term "aemulatio" [96]; he went so far as to propose the foundation of a *collegium de propaganda fide* in the spirit of the Roman Catholic "Propaganda", [97] but Voetius could not see the good of it as long as there was not a general correspondence among all the Reformed Churches. [98]

It is important to notice that the thought of the fulfilment of the missionary task and the missionary command in the time of the apostles (an idea, already present with Thomas of Aquino, and in a rather strong form advocated by Beza and some orthodox Lutheran theologians) almost completely disappeared in the time of the Second Reformation, though Voetius tried to maintain some formal elements of the old theory. [99] The new discoveries, which led to a realistic, world-wide outlook, made the serious maintenance of such a theory simply impossible!

One remarkable fact is that eschatological expectations played a not insignificant part in the development of the missionary idea. We find the thought that the conversion of the Gentiles precedes that of the Jews, which in its turn will be the sign of the renovation of all things. [100] In this way missions become a constituent factor in the

---

[92] With J. Heurnius, *op. cit.*, p. 11, still without explicit reference to Matth. 28. 19; apparently in a later period the controversy around Matt. 28. 19 has lost its actuality: J. Hoornbeek at least appeals more than once to the missionary command of that text — *op cit.*, pp. 193, 195, 199.

[93] H. A. van Andel, *De Zendingsleer van Gisbertus Voetius*, Kampen 1912, pp. 62—63; cf. J. Heurnius, *op. cit.*, p. 20: " ... Deus est is qui omnes ad se vocat, quis ille qui voluntate ejus resistet?"

[94] *Op cit.*, p. 89: " ... vita nostra est militia, per multas nos afflictiones intrare oportet in hoc regnum coelorum".

[95] See: *op. cit.*, Cap. VII, pp. 209—263.

[96] J. Hoornbeek, *op cit.*, p. 201.

[97] In 1622 the *Sacra Congregatio de Propaganda Fide* was instituted by the Pope; see K. Scott Latourette, *op. cit.*, III, pp. 33—35.

[98] G. Voetius, *Politica Ecclesiastica*, III, Amsterdam 1676, p. 352.

[99] H. A. van Andel, *op. cit.*, pp. 67—69.

[100] W. Teellinck speaks of an acceleration of the Second Coming by the con-

realization of God's total plan for the world: a relation becomes visible between the going out to the ends of the earth and the coming of the end of the times! Something of the same idea is present with a theologian who stood outside the circle of the Second Reformation in its strict sense: J. Coccejus. Though he did not expect the great break-through of missions before the last days, yet Christianity had to prepare the way for the events of that time by the *propagatio regni Christi*. [101] The realm of God has for him a complex character: the strongest accent he gives to the dominion of God in the hearts of men. Because of this, Schrenck sees in him a forerunner of the pietist revival with its emphasis on the "salvation of souls". [102]

The practical effect of the pleas for missions during the period of the Second Reformation was not proportionate to their fervour and depth. The reason for this is a twofold one. In the first place the system of the East India Company, which had taken the missionary work under its wings in its function of Christian government for the Eastern realm, [103] was not favourable to the missionary idea: the indigenous people were rather seen as objects of material profit than of spiritual testimony — and while the theocratic interest counterbalanced the lack of human affection in the initial stage of the Company, a later period saw a lack of spiritual vitality which proved to be disastrous for the missionary expansion of Dutch Christianity. In the second place the Church as a whole did not respond to the passionate appeals of some of its prominent men [104]—and during the period of general decay of Dutch religious life in the eighteenth century the missionary idea went almost completely to sleep in pietist as well as in rationalist circles. The results of this tragic interaction between political and religious factors could only be broken in the beginning of the nineteenth century by the coincidence of the downfall of the old governmental system in the East Indies with a reawakening of religious fervour as a result of the evangelical revival.

c. *British missions before 1700*

Now we turn to Great Britain. There too the awakening colonial interest was accompanied by a certain degree of zeal for the expansion of the Christian Church. This appears already in the naval enterprises

---

version of the gentiles and the Jews, *op. cit.*, p. **3; J. Heurnius sees the conversion of the Jews as a sequel to that of the gentiles, "novum in terram creans gaudium, et rerum omnium innovationem", *op. cit.*, p. 173.

[101] G. Schrenk, *op. cit.*, SS. 232, 273—275.

[102] G. Schrenk sees in his doctrine of the realm of God "eine Mischung von Calvinismus, Barockbiblizismus, Täufertum und Staatskirchentum", *op. cit.*, S. 293.

[103] C. W. Th. Baron van Boetzelaer van Asperen en Dubbeldam, *De Protestantsche Kerk in Nederlandsch Indië*, 's Gravenhage 1947, p. 126.

[104] As a favourable exception we mention the interest which some "Clas-

during the reign of Elisabeth. It was not a time of deep religious feelings, but there was an awareness of the unity of life, of the mutual integration of the religious and the political spheres, which made religious propaganda the self-evident sequel of political expansion. Here we meet again the idea of the "corpus christianum", though it was not, as in the Middle Ages, the Church, but the State that was in the ascendent: "the spheres of King and magistrates covered religion". [105] Further, the seafarers, who went out to open the world for English commerce, were staunch Protestants, desirous of crippling Rome's power and planting the banner of Protestant Christianity even on the most distant coast. [106] In these strivings they were backed by many of the clergy at home, especially by the Puritan preachers, whose party advocated an aggressive anti-Spanish policy. [107] This does not mean that the "soul of the heathen" lay outside the range of interest of English Protestantism. On the contrary: the idea of the conversion of pagan peoples played a not unimportant part in the westward expansion of England from the first voyage of Martin Frobisher in 1576 onwards. The pagans were pictured as thirsting after salvation, as looking forward to the eternal blessings of the Gospel as much as to the temporal blessings of the English culture—which were generally considered as two aspects of one matter! Patriotism, anti-Roman attitude, real concern for perishing souls—all these elements, blended together in a naive way, functioned as motives behind the awakening missionary interest. Remarkable arguments were brought to the fore: one author sees the prospect of new markets for English clothiers when the converted heathen would have been taught to dress in Christian apparel [108]! The idea of the "destined time", which we already met with Calvin, also played a part: so R. Hakluyt wrote that God "hath his tyme for all men", and he was firmly convinced that England's time for evangelical enterprise had come. [109] And behind all this stood the dream of a Christian empire which would extend itself to the ends of the world—though this dream had its limits: how much it was bound up with the *westward* expansion appears from the fact that no big hope was fostered with regard to the conversion of the Eastern peoples. [110] "The unity of Church and State made the extension of

---

ses' in the resort of the Synod of North-Holland took in the missionary cause: see [J. A. Grothe], *Archief voor de Geschiedenis der oude Hollandsche Zending*, I, Utrecht 1884, passim.

[105] G. M. Trevelyan, *English Social History*, London² 1946, p. 174.

[106] Idem, *op cit.*, pp. 194—195.

[107] See for this and for what follows: L. B. Wright, *Religion and Empire*, Chapel Hill 1943, passim.

[108] L. B. Wright, *op. cit.*, p. 26.

[109] Idem, *op. cit.*, p. 45.

[110] Idem, *op. cit.*, p. 57.

ecclesiastical control corrolary to the establishment of civil jurisdiction over newly occupied regions". [111]

The imperialistic missionary attitude was reflected in the charters of the trading and colonizing companies and of the colonies in America. Now the element of conversion, now the factor of civilization was dominant: " ... a work, which may ... in time bring the Infidels and Savages ... to human civility", but also " ... as their [i. e. the settlers'] good life and orderlie conversacon maye winn and incite the natives of country to the knowledge and obedience of the only true God and Savior of mankinde ...". [112] At any rate, the religious motive played a part in the foundation of the colonies across the Atlantic—strongest in the Puritan colonies, whose inhabitants had been driven by the double desire to escape from the infringements on freedom of religion in the mother-country and to build the Kingdom of God in theocratic fashion in the new land! [113] In this theocratic ideal the missionary interest found its place as well as its limitations. Already in Holland the "Pilgrim Fathers" were moved by "an inward zeal, and great hope of laying some foundation, or making way for the propagating and advancing the Gospel of the Kingdom of Christ to the remote ends of the earth ..." [114] This theocratic attitude could lead either to such a noble work as that of Eliot or to the cruel and bloody Indian wars. [115]

We are brought into quite a different climate by the scholarly expositions of H. Saravia. Though Saravia spent the first period of his theological career in the Netherlands we treat of him here, because he gave his thoughts on missions as an Anglican in a defence of the episcopal system of Church government. [116] His main work [117] seeks to prove the existence of a biblically-grounded relation between the existing episcopate and the historical apostolate. It is in this context that Saravia maintained the permanent validity of the missionary command (Matt. 28. 19): "Tantum concludo illius legationis et mandati

---

[111] O. W. Elsbree, *The Rise of the Missionary Spirit in America*, Williamsport 1928, p. 7.
[112] Idem, *op. cit.*, pp. 8 and 10; the first quotation is from the charter of the Virginia Company, the second one from that of the Massachussets Bay Company.
[113] G. M. Trevelyan, *op. cit.*, p. 40.
[114] E. Hoyt Byington, *The Puritan as a Colonist and a Reformer*, London 1899, p. 206 (in a quotation from W. Bradford's *History of Plymouth Plantations*, Mass. Hist. Socy Coll. 4, IV, p. 24).
[115] So W. Bradford describes a bloody victory over a group of Indians in 1637 as "a sweete sacrifice", L. B. Wright, *op. cit.*, p. 158 (in a quotation from W. Bradford, *op. cit.*, III, p. 357).
[116] Saravia was professor in Leiden from 1582 till 1587; in that year he went to England, where he became a Canon in Canterbury: B. Glasius, *Godgeleerd Nederland*, III, 's Hertogenbosch 1886, pp. 260—265.
[117] H. Saravia, *De Diversis Ministrorum Evangelii Gradibus, sicut a Domini fuerunt instituti*, etc., Frankfurt 1591; the London edition appeared one year earlier, the English translation in 1640.

vim et obligationem de praedicando Euangelio manere vim et obligationem in ecclesia" [118] Beza answered by denying the validity of Matth. 28. 19 for the Church of all times, though he recognized in principle the Church's missionary obligation. [119] The positive moment in Saravia's thought is, that he saw a relation between ecclesiology and missions: in this way he became the pioneer of a better understanding of the missionary command in its actual meaning. [120] The fact however that he saw the bishop as the successor of the apostle and that he made Matt. 28. 19 a proof-text in his defence of the "apostolic succession", helped to perpetuate the misunderstandings which existed with regard to the real meaning of the missionary command in Reformed and— more persistently still—in orthodox Lutheran circles. It is difficult to assess Saravia's influence on the missionary development. Drews [121] and Galm [122] suppose some influence on Heurnius, which cannot be proved however; Galm's opinion that Eliot was influenced by Saravia is improbable. Saravia's plea for missions was bound up with the defence of a system which in the time when Eliot took the work of missions in hand was contrary to his ecclesiastical convictions. [123] Eliot may in addition have read the work of the Puritan author Richard Sibbes, who showed himself in his *Light from Heaven* (London 1638) a strong advocate of missions among the Indians [124] And of course he also knew the "Public Prayer before Sermon" of the Synod of Westminster's *Directory for the Publick Worship of God*, in which the prayer for the conversion of the heathen had even been put in an eschatological context: "To pray for the propagation of the gospel and kingdom of Christ to all nations; for the conversion of the Jews, the fulness of the Gentiles, the fall of Antichrist and the hastening of the second coming of our Lord . . ." [125]

Puritan interest in the cause of missions culminated in the work of the "New England men". On Martha's Vineyard worked the Mayhews, while near Boston John Eliot began his splendid work in 1646, after a time of linguistic preparation. [126] Several motives cooperated in making Eliot a shining example of pure love for the cause of missions —but among them one of the most important certainly was his *"pitty for the dark souls of these natives"*, as Cotton Mather writes: "he

---

[118] Idem, *op cit.*, p. 66.
[119] Th. Beza, *Ad Tractationem de Ministrorum Evangelii Gradibus . . . Theodori Bezae Responsio*, 1593 s.l., pp. 106—107.
[120] Cf. J. R. Brutsch, *op. cit.*, p. 150: "Sa forte préoccupation ecclésiologique est ce qui nous semble devoir être retenue de la thèse de ce précurseur".
[121] P. Drews, *art. cit.*, p. 315.
[122] Cf. A. Galm, *op. cit.*, p. 37.
[123] Cf. A. Goslinga, *art. cit.*, p. 82.
[124] See A. Lang, *Puritanismus und Pietismus*, Neukirchen 1941, SS. 162—163.
[125] Cf. Answer 191 of the Larger Catechism of Westminster (on the Second Petition of the Lord's Prayer).
[126] K. Scott Latourette, *op. cit.*, pp. 218—220.

thought men to be *lost* if our *gospel* be hidden from them . . ." [127] In
Eliot the theocratic elements in Puritanism—he tried to give form
to the life of the converted Indians in Christian communities after the
Puritan pattern—combined itself with the soteriological interest which
was the main link between Puritanism and Pietism, [128] while the thought
of the gradual approaching of "the perfect day" through the work of
missions reminds us of the eschatological expectation which we find
in the above quoted "Public Prayer". [129] Eliot's work was most important—not so much because of its actual results (wars devastated the
flourishing work), as because of the influence which his activities
exercised in several countries. In America the cause of the Indian
missions was brought before the conscience of the Puritan colonists,
some of whom had been "inclined to think that the Indians were wild
beasts whom God called them to fear and fight". [130] According to
Professor J. Leusden of Utrecht, Eliot's example stimulated the Dutch
to further activity in the East Indies. [131] In England itself the knowledge of Eliot's work gave rise to a wave of missionary enthusiasm.
The Long Parliament gave, in 1648, in answer to a request made by
some Scottish and English ministers, a proclamation in support of the
cause of missions; a society was founded to give financial help; one year
later the society was incorporated by Parliament as the "President
and Society for the Propagation of the Gospel in New England", and
a collection was taken which brought in nearly £ 12.000. [132] This
splendid result will certainly have been due in the first instance to
the fact that a great deal of publicity had been given to Eliot's missionary activities; no doubt the feeling of spiritual relationship between
English Puritanism in the time of Cromwell and the Congregationalism
of Massachusetts has contributed to the success of the collection; [133]

---

[127]   C. Mather, *Magnalia Christi Americana*, III, Hartford 1820, p. 503; cf. a
quotation from Eliot in E. H. Byington, *op. cit.*, p. 218: "God first put into
my heart a compassion over their poor souls . . ."
[128]   Cf. R. Bronkema, *The Essence of Puritanism*, Goes 1929, pp. 98—100.
[129]   Cf. the title of a work of one of Eliot's friends, H. Whitefield: *Light
appearing more and more towards the perfect day* (London 1651); that Eliot did
not expect that great things would happen in a sudden way appears from what he
wrote to Baxter in 1669: "Pray for this day of small things" (see F. J. Powicke,
Some unpublished Correspondence of Rev. R. Baxter and Rev. John Eliot, Bulletin of the John Rylands Library XV (1931), p. 455.)
[130]   F. J. Powicke, *art. cit.*, p. 141.
[131]   Dr Leusden mentions this in his correspondence with Increase Mather, see
Cotton Mather, *op cit.*, p. 510. There is no reason to make such a great distinction
between the work of Eliot and the Dutch missions as H. Frick does, *op. cit.*, SS.
84—86: both types of work sprang essentially from the same root, though circumstances greatly differred.
[132]   See E. Schick, *op. cit.*, SS. 42—43, and K. Scott Latourette, *op. cit.*, p. 45.
[133]   Eliot was a Congregationalist with Presbyterian tendencies — see among
others D. H. Yoder, *Christian Unity in Nineteenth-Century America*, in: R. Rouse
and S. G. Neill, ed.), *A History of the Ecumenical Movement*, London 1954, p. 227.

but the fact that the tidings from across the Atlantic found such an enthusiastic response in Cromwell's England—rent though it was by civil war as well as by ecclesiastical divisions—has still a deeper cause. A great old dream was dreamed again in Cromwell's days: the dream of a theocratic realm, which would expand the glory of God wherever its influence reached. [134] Once again the theocratic ideal of Calvin seemed to revive in an integration of religion and politics which was intended to reflect the will of God for Church and nation. The tragic blunders which were made do not detract from the fact that those who from deep religious motives supported the new order were moved by nothing less than the idea of a mission for more than Britain alone. Only this general feeling can sufficiently explain the sudden wave of missionary interest; it also explains why Cromwell seems to have fostered the thought of a council for the Protestant religion in opposition to the *congregatio de propaganda fide* at Rome. Though we have no convincing proof of the presence of this idea in Cromwell's mind, the story which Bishop Burnet heard from Stoupe, who assisted the Protector in the management of his foreign affairs, sounds probable enough. [136] It is in accordance with the general aspect of Cromwell's "Protestant Interest", which had theocratic as well as secular-political roots. [137]

The Restoration was the natural consequence of the inner collapse of Cromwell's theocratic ideals. A religious ebb-tide seemed to draw with it what remained of the missionary ideals of the Commonwealth. But also in that time the flame of missions kept burning on—again partly fed by the oil of Eliot's unceasing activity and holy enthusiasm. One of Eliot's British correspondents was the famous Richard Baxter, who wrote in 1670 to his New England friend: "The industry of the Jesuits and friars and their successors in Congo, China and Japan

---

[134] With many followers of Cromwell this dream was blended with a strong eschatological expectation: a man such as J. Goodwin "filled all people with such expectations of a glorious thousand years speedily to begin, that it looked like a madness possessing them", G. Burnet, *History of his own Times*, I, Edinburgh 1753, p. 94.

[135] The theocratic dream connected missionary ideals with eschatological expectations: in 1654 the representatives of the General Baptist group, who drew up a "humble representation and vindication", declared: „And in as much as our Saviour Christ has given this as one sign, not long preceding his next coming, saying, This Gospell of the Kingdom shall be preached in all the world, for a Witness unto all Nations, and then shall the end come. Their hope therefore is, that in these latter daies, at least for a time, God will, by the hands of such Civill Powers as shall favour the Saints, open a door of greater liberty to the Saints, for the spreading of the Gospell in the Nations of the World, than usually has been enjoyed in times past", W. T. Whitley (ed.), *Minutes of the General Assembly of the General Baptist Churches in England*, I, London 1908, p. 4.

[136] G. Burnet, *op. cit.*, p. 109.

[137] Cf. J. N. Bowman, *The Protestant Interest in Cromwell's Foreign Relations*. Heidelberg 1900, p. 66, who gives however only small attention to the theocratic background of Cromwell's ideals.

shame us all, save you". [138] They were of the same spirit: both stood
in the line of the Calvinist tradition— though especially in Baxter's
later years there appears a tendency towards neo-Nomianism and
universalism [139]—; both had a strong desire for ecclesiastical unity, for
which they contended each in his own surroundings, though they never
lost their Puritan flavour; both were mission-minded to such a degree
that either of them can be called a pioneer of the modern missionary
movement. The unity of spirit between Baxter and Eliot appears in
a moving fashion from what is probably Baxter's last letter (to Dr
Increase Mather, Aug. 3, 1691): "I knew much from Mr Eliot's opinions by many letters which I had from him. There was no man on
earth whom I honoured above him. It is his evangelical [i. e. his missio-
nary] work that is the apostolic work I plead for. I am now dying,
I hope as he did" [140] Baxter gave his support to the "New England
Company", which had taken the place of the old society. [141] At the
same time he directed his attention towards the Eastern part of the
world-map. So the East Indian Company's Court Minutes Book mentions (Nov. 14, 1660) a letter from Baxter, in which he suggested
that some copies of the arabic translation of Grotius' "De Veritate
Religionis Christianae" might be spread by agents of the Company
"to the end Christianity may be established among those infidels..." [142]
This interest in the spread of the Gospel was born of a deep conviction:
in the "Reliquiae Baxterianae" Baxter writes: "No part of my prayers
are so deeply serious as that for the conversion of the infidel and
ungodly world... Except the case of the infidel world, nothing is
so sad and grievous to my thoughts as the case of the divided
Churches..." Though Baxter was moved by a desire for "the winning
of such miserable souls", he did not go so far as to deny salvation
to those who had not heard the Gospel: "Yet I am not so much
inclined to pass a peremptory sense of damnation upon all that
never heard of Christ, having more reason than I knew of before to

---

[138]   H. Martin, *Puritanism and Richard Baxter*, London 1954, p. 164.
[139]   Baxter had a deep respect for the Synod of Dordt and the Westminster
Assembly: see N. Sykes, *Ecumenical Movements in Great Britain in the seventeenth and eighteenth centuries*, in: *A History of the Ecumenical Movement, op cit.*,
p. 132. He came under the influence of Amyraldism (H. Bavinck, *Gereformeerde
Dogmatiek*, Kampen[4] 1929, p. 456), but sometimes a distinction is made between
Baxter himself and "Baxterianism" (a middle way between Calvinism and Armia-
nism): see G. F. Nuttall, *Richard Baxter and Philip Doddridge*, London 1951,
p. 3 and N. 5 on p. 22. Though Baxter's views on certain problems no doubt have
undergone some change during the course of his life, still the general tone of his
works has always remained much akin to that of the men of the "Second Reformation".
[140]   F. J. Powicke, *art. cit.*, p. 145.
[141]   The charter of the old society was renewed by Charles II in 1661 under the
title of "The Company for the Propagation of the Gospel in New England and
the Parts adjacent in America", K. Scott Latourette, *op. cit.*, III, p. 45.
[142]   F. Penny, *The Church in Madras*, London 1904, p. 36.

think that God's dealing with such is much unknown to us . . . [143]

During the Restoration period the flame of missionary interest not only burned within the circle of the Nonconformists: in the Established Church also some voices rose on behalf of the cause of missions. Robert Boyle, a layman of warm religious experience, in ecclesiastical respect an Anglican „low-churchman", in theology most akin to that type of broad-minded orthodoxy which in its comprehensiveness would become "fashionable" in the Church of England after the "Glorious Revolution", supported the missionary cause in various ways [144]. He was the first governor of the renewed "New England Company"; the propagation of the faith in India also had his lively interest: he bore the expense of the arabic translation of Grotius' "De Veritate Religionis Christianae" (recommended by Baxter to the East Indian Company), and stimulated the Company to give attention to the conversion of the natives. [145] His plea for missionary activity in the East evoked response from a few Anglican clergymen: Bishop Fell of Oxford and the later Dean of Norwich Dr Prideaux. [146] There are many points of contact between the missionary interest of Baxter and that of Boyle — but yet we feel that with Boyle we have passed into a new spiritual climate, of which we shall see in the next chapter that it has contributed to the formation of the S.P.C.K. and the S.P.G. Boyle stands in between the Calvinist and the Erasmian line — and he is typical in so far as in a later age the partial combination of these two lines would appear to be one of the main characteristics of British missions.

d. Survey of some motives

We conclude this chapter by stating that:

1. Theocratic motives played an important part in post-Reformation missionary interest — especially in the Dutch missionary enterprises and in the missions of the English Puritans.

2. The idea of the "corpus christianum" was a powerful factor

---

[143] J. M. Lloyd Thomas, *The Autobiography of Richard Baxter, being the Reliquiae Baxterianae, abridged from the Folio (1696)*, London 1925, pp. 117—118. From these quotations it appears that R. Allen in his *The Spontaneous Expansion of the Church*, London 1927, p. 68, gives too much accent to the "hell-fire-motive" behind Baxter's interest in foreign missions: this motive was stronger in his approach of the unconverted Christians, who "knew the way".

[144] Cf. R. Hooykaas, *Robert Boyle, Een Studie over Natuurwetenschap en Christendom*, Loosduinen s.a., pp. 15—16, 110—115.

[145] K. Scott Latourette, *op. cit.*, III, pp. 45, 277.

[146] F. Penny, *op. cit.*, pp. 96, 120—121. John Fell, who rose to the see of Oxford in 1676, was a patristic scholar of high-church tendency (see: N. Sykes, *D. E. Jablonski and the Church of England*, London 1950, p. 8); Humphrey Prideaux was an orientalist, who after the "Glorious Revolution" became an able, though sometimes difficult supporter of ecclesiastical reform (see among others E. Carpenter, *Thomas Tenison*, London 1948, pp. 113, 157).

in the blending of the theocratic motive with the concept of government-sponsored missions. [147]

3.   The cultural motive was interwoven through Eliot's theocratic experiments; [148] it also found a place, though in another context, with some of the promotors of missions during the Restoration period in England; in the same period it came to full development in Germany in the ideas of Leibniz—this in accordance with an interpretation of the Gospel in which the moral element got a greater place than in reformatory thinking: cultural elevation was not only seen as a result of, but also as a form of the conversion to God.

4.   Only gradually did the explicit command of Christ begin to play a part in the awakening of the missionary interest.

5.   The soteriological motive was not only strong on Lutheran soil, but also in the circle of the Calvinistic "Second Reformation"; pity and compassion were powerful incentives to take the work of missions in hand. This compassion was engendered as fully by the empirical knowledge of the state of the heathen as by the theological view of it. All their distress was reduced to the one great cause: their standing outside the light of God. Not always did this take, however, the form of a pronouncement on their eternal fate.

6.   Eschatological motives only played an incidental part.

7.   The idea of the glory of God was almost invariably present as the background of all other considerations—though most explicit in Calvinistic circles. [149]

---

[147]   Also Eliot's missionary work was backed by the state: in November 1646 the General Court of Massachussets took positive steps with regard to the missionary work among the Indians. E. H. Byington, *op. cit.*, p. 208.

[148]   Eliot felt it necessary "to carry oncivility with religion": W. Brown, *History of the Propagation of Christianity among the Heathen*, I, London³, 1854. p. 34, quoting from Shepard's *Clear Sunshine of the Gospel*.

[149]   In his *Der junge Wesley als Heidenmissionar und Missionstheologe*, Gütersloh 1955 — a work which appeared after the greatest part of the present study had been written — M. Schmidt calls attention to Richard Sibbes, who saw the missionary task from a theocentric point of view, and to John Eliot, who combined the eschatological and the theocratic motive: *op. cit.*, SS. 7—13.

Chapter II

BETWEEN PURITANISM AND METHODISM

Two swallows don't make a summer—the formation of two societies with at least in part a missionary character did not yet ring in the full summer of the great missionary awakening in England and Scotland. Still, it is a remarkable fact that after about forty years in which almost [1] all the missionary interest that had remained since the downfall of Cromwell's plans was to be found in dissenting circles—and even there the flame burned low!—, leading circles in the Church of England awoke to a broader vision and to a better understanding of the Church's transatlantic task. The years between the flowering-time of Puritanism and the beginnings of Methodism are often considered as a period of spiritual barrenness—but that same period witnessed the birth of a new interest in missions which took shape in the work of the S.P.C.K. and the S.P.G. and which can be considered as one of the waves that foreboded the flood of nineteenth century Protestant missions. In this chapter we shall try to see the motives of this awakening missionary interest against their political, cultural ecclesiastical and theological background.

1. THE CHARACTER OF THIS PERIOD

a. *The first signs of a new development*

During the period after the Restoration, the Church of England was closely related to the State. With the exception of a few years under the dominion of James II the *Ecclesia Anglicana* was the privileged Church, which in its turn by its stability and its loyalty was a guarantee of the existing order. Yet the complete integration of religious and political life, which had been one of the characteristics of the periods before the Restoration, belonged to the past. Below the surface a process of secularization had set in, which announced the breaking of the *corpus christianum* and the distintegration of the old religiously-sanctioned alliance between Church and State. Cromwellian

---

[1] Such Anglicans as supported the missionary cause had not the cooperation of the community to which they belonged.

England had seen the last great attempt to realize the theocratic ideal, though the tolerance of the Commonwealth already foreboded a new situation. The Restoration period was conservative, but the clock of historical development could not be put back; though some Tories looked wistfully back to Laudian times and some Independents still fostered their theocratic ideals, a new spirit gained ground, which stood for toleration in religious matters and for a separation of the political and the ecclesiastical sphere. [2] This new trend of thought was represented on the theological field by the "Cambridge Platonists", a group of theologians who can be considered as the vanguard of the Latitudinarian movement. They elevated morals above dogmas; they were broadminded in their view of the salvation of heathens and infidels; their influence was strong with a number of ecclesiastical leaders of the period after 1689, who had, however, more congeniality with the moralist element than with the mystical vein in their teaching. [3]

From a spiritual point of view, the Restoration period was one of low ebb, a fact reflected in the waning interest for the cause of missions: as we saw in the preceding chapter, only some isolated figures were really concerned about the fact that England on its transatlantic frontier was confronted with peoples that lived outside the light of the Christian revelation. The colonial imperialism of Cromwell's England was continued without the concomitant of a fervent religious ideal. The Pennsylvanian experiment was an exception which proves the rule—and New England Puritanism was no longer fed by the religious resources of the old country.

Yet it would be unfair to declare this period void of all religious depth. Without as well as within the Church of England, in High Church as well as in Low Church circles, there were ecclesiastical leaders of real piety—though most of them shared with their surroundings the lack of vision on the Church's world-wide task. One of the means through which the latent piety of this period would be converted into fertile activity, was the movement of the "Religious Societies". When the later Prussian court-chaplain and Moravian Bishop, Jablonski, came on his first visit to England, the existence of these Societies was for him a sign that the pious spirit of the "Brüdergemeinde", in which he had been reared, was also present in the Church of England. [4] The Religious Societies were the result of a happy combination of German Pietism and English Puritanism. [5] Their founder, Dr A. Horneck, was a German who in Heidelberg had been a pupil of Professor Spanheim, the publisher of Anna Maria van

---

[2] C. M. Trevelyan, *English Social History*, *op. cit.*, pp. 255—256.
[3] See: G. R. Cragg, *From Puritanism to the Age of Reason*, Cambridge 1950, pp. 33—95.
[4] N. Sykes, *Daniel Ernst Jablonski and the Church of England*, *op cit.*, p. 9.
[5] A. Lang sees in the Religious Societies a reawakening of the old Puritan "prophesyings": *op. cit.*, S. 308.

Schuurman's works. [6] In 1671 be became preacher at the Savoy-Chapel in London, where the warm sincerity of his sermons, in which he insisted on the necessity of holiness and new birth, made a deep impression. [7] Under the influence of Horneck and of other London ministers a number of young people began to meet regularly for religious purposes. In the original Societies (formed around 1678) the pietist element was dominant: the first aim was personal edification, though the practical needs were not forgotten. [8] The fact that they put themselves under ecclesiastical leadership guarded them against such mystic extravagancies as we find in the "Philadelphian Society" of Jane Leade-Ward. [9] Following a period of partial eclipse under James II, they revived again after 1689, this time with new possibilities for practical work: J. Woodward saw as one of their chief purposes "the making of our peace with God by effectual *Reformation*". [10] It is impossible to explain the new interest in missions and the new concern for the religious character of English public life during the reign of William and Mary without taking into account the silent work of these Societies, which were already in their own time considered as a parallel phenomenon to what had come into being in Halle. [11] Their influence began to wane in the second quarter of the eighteenth century: other societies had arisen which took over the greatest part of their practical activities—and British soil was not favourable to societies of too introverted a character. [12] But before the second half of the eighteenth century began, their place was taken by a new society-movement which was to have a still deeper influence on British life: Methodism.

b. The breaking of the corpus christianum

In more than one respect the year 1689 made a deep incision in the life of the British people. By the "Glorious Revolution" Britain not

---

[6] G. A. Wauer, *Die Anfänge der Brüderkirche in England*, Leipzig 1900. S. 41 n 2.

[7] J. S. Simon, *John Wesley and the Religious Societies*, London 1921, pp. 10—11.

[8] They worked among the poor and the prisoners, took care of students and orphans, and played an active part in the "anti-popery-movement": W. T. Whitley in *Hastings Encyclopaedia of Religion and Ethics*, VI, Edinburgh ond New York 1920, p. 326a.

[9] See: C. W. H. Hochhuth, *Jane Leade und die Philadelphische Gemeinde in England*, Zeitschrift für die historische Theologie XXXV (1865), SS. 171—290, and: N. Thune, *The Behmenists and the Philadelphians*, Uppsala, 1948.

[10] J. Woodward, *An Account of the Rise and Progress of the Religious Societies*, London[3], 1711, p. 88. Woodward was a chaplain in Poplar; in 1710 he asked the Directors of the East India Company to take in hand missionary work in India: F. Penny, *op. cit.*, p. 21.

[11] J. Woodward, *op cit.*, p. 9.

[12] G. A. Wauer, *op. cit.*, SS. 45—46.

only entered a new political sphere, but also a new spiritual climate, with new conceptions and new forms of thought. The idea of the *corpus christianum* began to give place to a new relationship between Church and State. The idea of an established Church was not discarded altogether, but it was brought into the sphere of practical convenience. [13] Some people still clung to the old world of thought, especially the "non-jurors" [14]—but "the Revolution of 1689 had crossed the Rubicon which divided such theological politics from the utilitarian policies of the eigteenth century". [15] Henceforward theocratic dreams would belong to the past, henceforward colonial and ecclesiastical expansion would be two separate things. The Church was losing at least part of the external support which it had possessed since the days of Constantine. At the same time, however, it was regaining the chance to approach the world in a new way: in purity and freedom. But it would take a long time still before the Church would come to realize the full implications of the new situation, a long time also before it would seize the opportunities, offered for free development and for the use of its prophetic function in its contact with the State. The eighteenth century witnessed the after-effects of the corpus christianum-idea in the fact of an unimaginative partnership between a secularizing State and a Church which readily accepted a semi-erastian position.

It is no wonder that in this period colonial expansion had lost all traces of its theocratic past. The expansion on the Western frontier of the empire served the consolidation of the American possessions, which were chiefly threatened by French aspirations, while the contact with the Eastern world had a mercantile character, combined during the second half of the eighteenth century with imperialist inclinations. [16] In the period of the "Aufklärung" the concepts of peace and justice, which were the constituent elements of the *pax Brittanica* in its ideal form, lost their religious associations, their relationship with the expansion of the Kingdom of God [17]—though in the first half of the nineteenth century colonial expansion would once again be associated with religious purposes! [18]

---

[13] In a later stage of the development we meet the idea of Bishop Warburton, that the largest religious body ought to be made the official Church, just because it is convenient for the state to deal with such a body: R. N. Stromberg, *Religious Liberalism in Eigtheenth Century England*, London 1954, p. 134.

[14] The Anglicans, who were not prepared to take the oath of allegiance to William and Mary; as a rule they were extremely "High-Church".

[15] N. Sykes, *Church and State in England in the Eighteenth Century*, Cambridge 1934, p. 114.

[16] The first Empire had a mercantile character: see Jhr. P. J. van Winter, *De Aanloop tot het Britse Imperialisme*, Groningen-Djakarta 1954, p. 5.

[17] K. Völker, *Die religiöse Wurzel des englischen Imperialismus*, Tübingen 1924, p. 26.

[18] Jhr. P. J. van Winter, *op. cit.*, pp. 6—10.

c. The Churches of the new period

The events of 1689 inaugurated a new situation not only in the
political, but also in the ecclesiastical sphere. Immediately after the
Revolution, the leadership in the Church of England passed into the
hands of a group of men who were in a greater or less degree representatives of the spirit of a new age. The new Archbishop of Canterbury, John Tillotson, was the main link between the Cambridge Platonists and the Latitudinarians. [19] His successor on the archiepiscopal
see, Thomas Tenison, was of the same spirit; he was a protagonist of
moderation and comprehension in ecclesiastical affairs. [20] The new
Bishop of Salisbury, Gilbert Burnet, was very outspoken in his Low-
Church proclivities and his theological moderatism; [21] he had a lively
correspondence with Leibniz. [22] These men were not distinguished by
an impressive depth and fervour, [23] they expected more from knowledge
and education than from the emotional side of religious life, their
world of thought was marked by a sometimes almost naive optimism.
But at the same time their out-look was not confined within the walls
of English ecclesiastical life, they had an eye for the possibilities which
the new spirit of the time offered to the Church in an expanding
realm. And finally, they were not afraid of new forms and new ways
in the defence of the cause of religion. Something of this spirit was
also present in groups outside the Low Church circle. So the non-
juring layman Robert Nelson, who afterwards returned to the Established Church, had as the basis for his ideas the thought that "religion is not a metaphysical idea but a life which pours itself out in
prayer and praise before God, and in justice and charity towards
man". [24] It may be that in High-Church circles the elements of praise
and prayer, in the Low-Church group the elements of justice and
charity received the heavier accent; in some cases High-Church leaders
stood rather aloof with regard to organisations in which churchmen
and dissenters worked together; [25] but as a whole they were broadminded enough to cooperate with and to give support to those organisations, which in the forms of a new age helped to guard and to

---

[19] A. Plummer, *The Church of England in the Eighteenth Century,* London
1910, pp. 83—84.
[20] E. Carpenter, *Thomas Tenison, Archbishop of Canterbury,* London 1948,
p. 95.
[21] E. Carpenter, *op. cit.,* p. 309.
[22] F. R. Merkel, *G. W. von Leibniz und die China-Mission,* Leipzig 1920,
SS. 191 ff.
[23] J. Stoughton misses in their writings "intensity of utterance and glow of
passion": *History of Religion in England,* V, London 1881, p. 249.
[24] E. Carpenter, *op. cit.,* pp. 268—270.
[25] So John Sharp, Archbishop of York, was opposed to the Societies for the
Reformation of Manners: A. Tindal Hart, *The Life and Times of John Sharp,
Archbishop of York,* London 1949, pp. 179—184.

build the old Church. Moreover, with their greater respect for the doctrinal tradition of their Church they formed a valuable corrective to some latitudinarian tendencies. But to the Anglican Church of this period can be applied in general what N. Sykes said of its leaders: "The religious tradition of eighteenth-century churchmanship was admittedly homespun and practical". [26]

The groups outside the Church of England also found themselves affected—to a greater or less extent—by the influence of the new age. The Quakers, who once formed a popular revival-movement, had now become a settled, quiet, well-to-do community, [27] whose moralist accent gave them much in common with the Latitudinarians. [28] The Presbyterians, once a strong body which stood in the direct line of the Calvinistic tradition, had rapidly come under Arian influences since the leaders of the "old dissent" had fallen away. In many Presbyterian congregations the atmosphere grew chilly and sterile: social uplift and spiritual decline here went hand in hand. With the Independents, however, the situation was different: the greater part of their ministers withstood Unitarian influences and remained loyal to the trinitarian creed as it was contained in the Confession of Westminster. [29] Something of Baxter's spirit lived on in figures like Isaac Watts and Philip Doddridge. [30] Leslie Stephen found in Watt's sermons something of the old unction of Puritanism and in Doddridge's work a certain reflection of the old Puritan zeal. [31] As Independents they helped to keep in the evangelical line the congregations whose spiritual leaders they were. The third greater dissenting group, that of the "General Baptists", came partly under Unitarian influences, while the uninfluential group of the "Particular Baptists" maintained the orthodox doctrine in a rigid way. [32]

The Church of Scotland, which had been brought back on the line of its Calvinistic tradition by the events of 1689, remained practically immune to Arian and Unitarian tendencies. Yet it was also, to a certain extent, influenced by the English latitudinarian movement: the early eighteenth century witnessed the rise of Moderatism—"a temper rather than a system" [33]— which derived its name from an expression,

---

[26] N. Sykes, *Church and State*, op. cit., p. 283.
[27] G. M. Trevelyan, *English Social History*, op. cit. pp. 267—268.
[28] J. Stoughton, *History of Religion in England*, IV, London² 1881, p. 346.
[29] See for the events of 1719, when the ways of many of the Presbyterians on the one side and most of the Independence on the other side parted on the point of the subscription to the confessional formulation of the Trinitarian creed: J. S. Simon, *The Revival of Religion in England in the Eighteenth Century*, London s.a., pp. 112—124.
[30] See: G. F. Nuttall, *Richard Baxter and Philip Doddridge*, op. cit., passim.
[31] L. Stephen, *History of English Thought in the Eighteenth Century*, II, London 1876, pp. 385—388.
[32] J. S. Simon, *in loco citato*.
[33] A. J. Campbell, *Two Centuries of the Church of Scotland*, Paisley 1930,

used by King William in his message to the General Assembly of
1690: ,,Moderation is what religion requires . . .''. As a rule they were
at least in formal agreement with the Confession of Westminster, but
they were not free from a certain moralism and rationalism—a modern
author sees in them "affinities with the humanism of the Renaissance". [34] As much as the English Latitudinarians they were men
of the middle way, men who missed the glow and intensity of a former
generation. Partly as a reaction against their legalism arose the group
of the so-called "Marrow-Men", who produced a new edition of the
Marrow of Modern Divinity (first edition: London 1645), an anti-
legalistic work. [35] The "Marrow-Men" possessed something of the
warmth of Pietism; their trend of thought was soteriological; though
believing in a limited atonement they laid a special stress on the universal offer of grace: "Go tell every man without exception that there
is good news for him: Christ is dead for him". [36] It has been remarked
that the "missionary passion which, a century later, began to possess
the Church, owed much to their unswerving tenacity". [37] To this group
belonged the leaders of the Secession of 1733 (among others the well-
known brothers Erskine). Within the Church of Scotland, this extended confrontation with the ideas of the "Marrow" helped to hold the
door open for the advancing influences of Methodism and Evangelicalism: "Historically, it was the Marrow Men who recaptured the
evangelical note . . .". [38] During almost the whole of the eighteenth
century, however, Moderatism was in the ascendant, bravely trying
to adapt the life of the Scottish Church to the exigencies of a new
age, but amidst all its activities failing to proclaim the essence of the
biblical message with the passionate fervour of the Pauline appeal:
"we pray you in Christ's stead, be ye reconciled to God!" [39]

d. *Some characteristics of the new spirit*

We have seen something of the political and ecclesiastical background of the period after the "Glorious Revolution". It has become

---

p. 35; see for the theology of that period also: J. Macleod, *Scottish Theology*,
Edinburgh 1943, pp. 103—138.
 [34] A. J. Campbell, *in loco citato*.
 [35] See for the Marrow Controversy: D. Beaton, *The "Marrow of Modern Divinity" and the Marrow Controversy*, Records of the Scottish Church History
Society I (1926), pp. 112—134, and: S. Mackie, *The Marrow Controversy Reviewed*, E. Q. XXII (1950), pp. 20—31.
 [36] D. Beaton, *art. cit.*, p. 128.
 [37] J. Macinnes, *The Evangelical Movement in the Highlands of Scotland*,
Aberdeen 1953, p. 180.
 [38] H. Watt, *The Influence of Martin Luther on Scottish Religion in the
Eighteenth Century*, Records of the Scottish Church History Society VI (1938),
p. 150.
 [39] II Corinthians 5. 20.

clear to us that the events around 1689 meant more than a rather fortuitous change of the scene in State and Church: they inaugurated the commencement of a new age, they opened the door for new ideas, they prepared the way for a new understanding of the problems of life. We observe the remarkable fact, that the new development of missionary activity, which is the subject of this chapter, took place just when the age of reason set in. So the question arises whether there is a relation between both phenomena, and, if so, what is the character of this relationship and which elements in the spirit of the period have helped to bring it about.

The two poles around which the life of the new period circled were those of *moralism* and *rationalism,* poles, which in turn were connected by the same view of the natural possibilities of the human heart. Moralism found its reflection in the *Societies for the Reformation of Manners,* offshoots of the Religious Societies: they sprang up all over the country, and fought a brave battle against the many moral deficiencies of their time. Churchmen and Dissenters worked here together in fair harmony, distributing tracts, trying to put a stop to swearing, drunkenness and immorality and invoking the help of the magistrates when persuasion failed. [40] Formally there is a strong resemblance between the ideals of these Societies and that of the earlier Puritans. But there is also an element of discontinuity: while the old Puritans lived and thought in the reformatory "dimension of grace", the new Societies had felt the influence not only of the Religious Society movement, but also of the prevailing legalism and moralism of the early eighteenth century. There is a fundamental difference between the spirit of the old Puritan authors and that of a man such as Archbishop Tillotson, who was convinced that an emphasis on morality was the great need of his time. [41] This was more than an additional accent, it was a shifting of the emphasis from grace to works. The sense of sin made room for a moral optimism, [42] parallel to that of Leibniz, who saw the Kingdom of God as a "vernünftig-sittliche Weltordnung", and grace as a means of bringing the moral evolution of life to perfection. [43] In this way the moralism of the period was closely connected with an optimistic view of man. That the Cambridge Platonists were broadminded with regard to the problem of the salvation of the heathen was not so much the result of a deep belief in the greatness of God's saving grace, as a consequence of the fact that they failed to see the

---

[40] See for a vivid description of the activities of these Societies: G. M. Trevelyan, *English Social History, op cit.* pp. 327—328.

[41] G. R. Cragg, *op. cit.,* pp. 78—79.

[42] R. N. Stromberg, *op. cit.,* p. 118: "Even Bishop Butler's system seemed to find no place for original sin nor any very pressing need for atonement".

[43] E. Hirsch, *Geschichte der neueren evangelischen Theologie,* II, Gütersloh 1951, SS. 34 ff.; according to Hirsch, this opinion of Leibniz "bestimmt seine frohe Entschlossenheit zum Wirken in der Welt", S. 47.

state of fallen man in the light of biblical revelation. The Latitudinarians never went so far as the Deists, who held that purely by the light of natural religion man could find his way to God—but the urgent passion to call those living outside Christ from the darkness of their own ways to the light of God's saving grace gave way to the feeling that it was good to add to the tenets of natural religion the values of God's revelation to Moses and Christ. [44] This general outlook could not but affect the view of the heathen world and, consequently, the character of missionary work.

At the same time the character of all ecclesiastical work was profoundly influenced by the *rationalism* of the period. It is almost tragic to see how the defenders of the Church's tradition accepted the challenge of the Deists to fight the battle on the field where Deism had gained its greatest victories: the belief in the capacity of human reason to climb up to the great mysteries of God. [45] This holds good especially for the period before 1730: after that time it is possible to discern a certain "retreat from reason". [46] But the beginning of the eighteenth century is characterized by a belief—sometimes a very naive belief— in the possibility of spreading the faith through the propagation of "Christian knowledge".

Related to the rationalist-moralist background of this period were the ideas of *benevolence* and *charity*. "In Faith and Hope the world will disagree, but all Mankind's concern is Charity", sang Alexander Pope. [47] A sympathetic example of this spirit is to be found in the Charity-School movement: a movement, which has done splendid work by founding schools for the children of the poor. It is impossible to disentangle the various motives which were at work behind the movement. The idea, for instance, that the minds of children, being *tabulae rasae*, could by education and instruction be brought to a better condition (the psychology of John Locke!) will have played its part. Also to be considered is the serious desire of the "puritans of the eighteenth century" to put their faith into practice through deeds of philanthropy and humanity. [48] Finally, the fact that so many "laymen" cooperated in the Charity-School movement as much as in the various societies of this period was a symptom of that "laicisation of religion" which N. Sykes sees as the keynote of the ecclesiastical development of the eighteenth century. [49]   •

We conclude by remarking that in more than one respect British

---

[44]   N. Sykes, *Church and State, op. cit.*, p. 346.
[45]   E. Hirsch, *op. cit.*, I, S. 351.
[46]   R. N. Stromberg, *op. cit.*, p. 96.
[47]   Quoted by N. Sykes, *in loco citato.*
[48]   M. G. Jones, *The Charity School Movement. A Study of Eighteenth Century Puritanism in Action*, Cambridge 1950, pp. 4—8.
[49]   N. Sykes, *Church and State, op cit.*, p. 379.

ecclesiastical life in this period moved along the "Erasmian line": God was seen as the benevolent Creator, man as intrinsically capable of moral betterment, the Kingdom of God as the crown of the steady progression of Christianity. We must, however, not forget that, though we miss here quite definitely the depth of the Reformers' theology, this period also had important points to its credit: it had the courage to use intellectual weapons in the service of God's Kingdom and it tried to listen to the command of Christ: ,,Thou shalt love thy neighbour as thyself". These notes, of course, were not new, nor were these elements the exclusive possession of the men of Latitude. But in order to avoid an unfair judgment we have to state that they at least made a serious effort to put religion into practice. And though Latitudinarianism and Moderatism often barred the way to a right understanding of the heart of the biblical message, yet there were other tendencies present which prevented an inner estrangement from the genuine Christian tradition. Pietist factors (think of the pietist influences in the Religious Societes), High-Church traditions in the Church of England (see only the religious life of John Wesley's mother), evangelical elements among the dissenting groups, the various types of Calvinism in Scotland—all these have counterbalanced the "spirit of the age" in such a way that in the background of the movements which are under our special consideration we find again and again the presence of the real Christian heritage.

There is a link between the spirit of the age and the missionary awakening—but it has a complex character. It is possible to discern a correlation between moralism and ecclesiastical activity, between rationalism and the propagation of Christian knowledge, between a broadening of the horizon and a renewed expansion of the Church, between the idea of charity and the awakening interest in the fate of Indians and negros. But the spirit of the new age could also lead to such a shallow optimism with regard to man's natural capabilities that the urgency of the missionary task was but weakly felt; it could infringe the purity of the missionary ideal in such a way that missions threatened to be transformed into articles of ecclesiastical or even cultural propaganda. A certain influence of "the age of reason" upon the reawakening of the missionary ideal cannot be denied—but that influence had a negative as well as a positive aspect: it has stimulated the churches on some points, while at the same time it imposed such limitations on missionary work as could only be broken through where a living confrontation with the heart of the biblical message opened

---

[50] According to Ch. W. Lowry, the High-Church tradition in Anglicanism has helped to check the inroads of liberal and latitudinarian tendencies: *The Spiritual Antecedents of Anglican Evangelicalism*, Historical Magazine of the Protestant Episcopal Church, XII (1943), p. 138.

men's eyes to the primary meaning of missions: to call the nations to
the cross of Christ.

2. THE REAWAKENING OF THE MISSIONARY IDEA
WITHIN THE ANGLICAN CHURCH

a. *The influences which played a part in the foundation of the S.P.C.K. and the S.P.G.*

On 8 March 1699 an event took place which would appear to be
of great significance for the awakening of the missionary spirit in the
Church of England. Five friends met on that day in Lincoln's Inn,
London, and constituted themselves into the "Society for the Propagation of Christian Knowledge". [51] Four of them were "laymen",
belonging to the Church of England; [52] the initiative, however, had
been taken by Thomas Bray, vicar of Sheldon and commissary of the
Bishop of London for the ecclesiastical affairs of Maryland. As Bray
has played a dominant part in the foundation of the S.P.C.K. and the
S.P.G., it is not superfluous to give some special attention to the
person and the ideas of the man of whom Overton says: "It would
be difficult to point to any one who has done more real and enduring
service to the church". [53] Yet Bray was no brilliant figure, no deep
thinker, no leading prelate: he is "a striking instance of what a man
may effect without any extraordinary genius, and without special influence". [54] Perhaps the secret of Bray's influence lies in the fact that
in his person the various tendencies of his own time were combined
in a happy and harmonious way. He was English through and
through, [55] but not in a hide-bound way: called to go overseas in 1695,
he was quite prepared to change the quiet country life for the „greater
field for doing good". [56] He was a thorough Anglican, but at the same
time he was broad enough to correspond with Protestant Churches
on the Continent and to acknowledge the Independents of New
England as respected fellow-Christians. He had a strong antipathy
against Rome, but he was still prepared to listen to the missionary
teaching of Thomas a Jesu's *De conversione omnium gentium procuranda.* [57] He had affinities with High-Church ideals as well as with
the Low-Church group and with some of the intellectualist trends of

---

[51] See for a detailed description of the foundation of the S.P.C.K.: H. P.
Thompson, *Thomas Bray*, London 1954, pp. 36—42.
[52] K. Scott Latourette, *A. History* etc., III, 1939, p. 48, writes that the S.P.C.K.
"was formed chiefly by members of the Church of England". The word „chiefly",
however, has to be omitted: the S.P.C.K. was from its first beginnings fully Anglican.
[53] J. H. Overton in: *Dictionary of National Biography*, VI, London 1886,
p. 241.
[54] J. H. Overton, *in loco citato.*
[55] Cf. R. P. Stacy Waddy, *250 Years of S.P.G.*, I.R.M. XL (1951), p. 332.
[56] H. P. Thompson, *Thomas Bray*, op. cit., p. 14.
[57] See for the relative importance of this work: P. Charles, *Les Sources du*

the "Aufklärung". He expected much from his library-plans, and education was one of his watch-words, but he had also felt the influence of the Pietism that found nourishment in the Religious Societies. He was much impressed by Erasmus' *Ecclesiastes* without ever becoming an Erasmian in the full sense of the word: for that, he was too deeply steeped in the doctrine of his own Church! [58] With all this he combined the personal qualities of piety, activity and unselfishness. In this way he became the man who gave the impetus to the formation of those Societies which were the Anglican response to the challenge of the new age.

The personal influence of Bray, however, was not the only moving factor. The way had been prepared by the work of the Religious Societies, which had been instrumental in creating the substratum of a new spiritual interest that lay at the bottom of the awaking activity of the Anglican Church, while at the same time they had helped to shape the form in which the new ideals could find concrete realization. Besides, the new age was coming to knock at the Church's doors with urgent demands. The clergy had to be provided with weapons to meet the intellectual challenge of a period in which "the Laity of all Ranks do freely read the most poisonous Authors". [59] New methods had to be found of tackling the problems of ignorance and religious decay which were the evil fruits of the anti-puritan reaction of the Caroline period. The Church's neglect of the Anglican settlers in the American colonies would lead to disastrous results if no effectual measures were taken: as early as 1693 Patrick Gordon had issued his *Geography Anatomized or the Geographical Grammar,* a work in which he confronted the Church of England with its responsibility towards the inhabitants of the American plantations. [60] And with the broadening of horizons the pagan population at the frontiers of the realm once more came into sight —as men who had to be freed from the darkness of paganism: "it is far more honourable to overcome paganism in one than to destroy thousand pagans", [61] but also as tools in the struggle with the French in Canada: "another means to prevent the influence of the French missionaries upon them [*i. e.* the Indians belonging to the "Five Nations"], and thereby more effectually to secure their fidelity, would be, that two Protestant Ministers be appointed with a competent allowance to dwell amongst them in

---

"*De Procuranda salute omnium Gentium*", in: *Scientia Missionum Ancilla,* Nijmegen en Utrecht 1953, pp. 46—53.

[58] H. P. Thompson, *Thomas Bray, op. cit.,* passim.

[59] Bray in his *Bibliotheca Catechetica* (1699), quoted by H. P. Thompson, *Thomas Bray, op. cit.,* p. 8.

[60] See: W. K. Lowther Clarke, *Eighteenth Century Piety,* London 1944, pp. 91 ff. Gordon became one of the first missionaries of the S.P.G.K.

[61] Patrick Gordon, with: W. K. Lowther Clarke, *in loco citato.*

order to instruct them in the true religion and confirm them in their
duty to Her Majesty...". [62]

Moreover, there were foreign influences which have to be taken into
account. Two names deserve special mention: that of Leibniz, who
initiated the period of the "Aufklärung" and that of Francke, one of
the fathers of the pietist movement. Between these two men there
were more connections than the names of the movements which they
helped to initiate would lead us to surmise! In the preceding chapter
we have seen already the part which Leibniz took in the awakening
of the missionary idea. We also saw that this influence reached
accross to England, where his *Novissima Sinica* (1697) found a very
favourable reception; it came into the hands of a number of clergymen,
one of whom was the Archbishop of Canterbury, Thomas Tenison.
As an immediate result of this, in 1699 an expedition was sent to
China which, though its aim was chiefly mercantile, also combined
a weak missionary element, as appears from the fact that one of its
leader's tasks was, "ut...et rem Christianismi (si quo possit modo)
promoveat" [63]. But the indirect influence of Leibniz will have been
greater: without any doubt it has helped to open the eyes of many
leading churchmen to the wider task of the Church. This is the more
probable in that there were elements in Leibniz' thought which moved
in perfect harmony with some trends of British contemporary thinking.
His optimistic view of man, the importance which he attached to civilization and cultural expansion and the place which reason took in his
system—all this related him to the Latitudinarian wing of English
ecclesiastical life, which had—as we saw above—already experienced
something of the influence of the "Aufklärung". The Latitudinarian
Burnet even wrote of Leibniz: "whom we do all here reckon one of
the greatest men that has lived in any age". [64]

Francke, too, had been influenced by Leibniz. We touch here upon
the point of the rather paradoxical relation between Pietism and Rationalism. There is a direct contrast between the ideas of both thinkers.
Leibniz, in his perfectly sincere optimism, saw the consummation of
the Kingdom of God in harmony with the humanitarian efforts of
mankind, and he saw the shades of sin disappearing against the shining
background of the *harmonia praestabilita* of this world. Francke, on the
other hand, had eyes fully open to the dark recesses of the human
spirit, to the sinfulness and the brokenness of this world, and to the
demoniacal aspects of the human situation. [65] Here two worlds of

---

[62] From an "Order in Council", given by Queen Anne on the 3d April 1703:
C. F. Pascoe, *Two Hundred Years of the S.P.G.*, I, London 1901, pp. 66—67.

[63] J. Wallis to Leibniz, quoted by F. R. Merkel, *op. cit.*, SS. 192—193.

[64] G. Burnet in a letter to the Princess Sophia, also quoted by F. R. Merkel,
op. cit., S. 195, N. 3.

[65] Cf. H. Stahl, *August Hermann Francke*, Stuttgart 1939, S. 187: "Wie seht
Francke die Lage des natürlichen Menschen?: im Rachen des Teufels oder wie

thought, two totally different views of man, life and God stood over against each other. The cleavage between these two worlds is one of the most important determining factors of European Church history. And continental missions especially bore for a long time the mark of an emphatic rejection of the ideas of the "Aufklärung", although in the course of the eighteenth century Rationalism succeeded in slipping in through the back-door of the Danish-Hallensian mission, so contributing to the collapse of a splendid piece of work on the Indian field. [66] We can even ask ourselves how far Pietism and Rationalism have some fundamental issues in common. That they are both children of a new climate of thought appears already from the fact of the presence of anthropocentric elements in both currents. [67] We must not forget, however, that there is an element of continuity between the ideas of Erasmus and that of Rationalism on the one hand, and between the theology of the Reformers and the pietist world of thought on the other side. The great and abiding division between these two lines of thought appears from the totally different evaluation of the human situation with Erasmus and with the Reformers, with Rationalism and Pietism, with Leibniz and Francke. [68]

How to explain against this background the influence of Leibniz on Francke? Francke was deeply impressed by the *Novissima Sinica*. He appears to have read it as a testimony of genuine zeal for the spread of the Gospel [69] — and it will have made the more impression upon him, because such a testimony was a rare thing at a time when the missionary ideal in Germany was almost dead. And apart from the mutual respect of great spirits which marked the correspondence between both men, they had in spite of their differences still a number of points in common: both possessed a ready eye for the problems and the opportunities of the period in which they lived, both saw farther than the frontiers of seventeenth century Germany, and both expected much of education — and while for Francke new horizons revealed

---

einen Brand im Feuer. Daraus ergibt sich die brennende Notwendigkeit, zu retten, das ganze Leben dafür einzusetzen, "als Knechte des lebendigen Gottes vor den Risz zu treten und die Seelen dem Teufel in einem gewaltigen Glaubenskampf aus dem Rachen zu reiszen"".

[66] H. Frick, *Die Evangelische Mission, op. cit.*, SS. 191 ff.

[67] This fact receives too heavy an accent with E. Hirsch, when he writes: "Man sieht, wie der Pietismus selber ... die aufgeklärte Moralisierung des Heilsprozesses eingeleitet hat ... Franckes psychologische Bestimmungen leiten, ohne dasz er es will und ahnt, dazu über, den Glauben wesentlich als Frömmigkeit und Tugendkraft zu verstehen. Wie es dann in der Aufklärung geschehen ist.": *Geschichte der neueren evangelischen Theologie*, II, Gütersloh 1951, SS 159—160.

[68] "Dem wissenschaftlich-kulturellen Missionsziel (ad propagandam per scientias fidem) von Leibniz stand das religiöse Missionsziel A. H. Franckes gegenüber": C. Mirbt, *A. H. Francke und die Mission*, in F. Mahling, C. Mirbt, A. Nebe, *Zum Gedächtnis A. H. Franckes*, Halle 1927, S. 88.

[69] Cf. Francke's letter to Leibniz of 9th July, 1697, quoted by F. R. Merkel, *op. cit.*, S. 161.

themselves through the reading of the *Novissima Sinica*, Leibniz clearly saw that the men who would be prepared to take in hand the missionary work which he proposed would have to be found in the circle of the Pietists. [70]

In Germany the ways of "Aufklärung" and Pietism soon parted, but in England Francke's influence coincided with that of Leibniz in such a way, that it helped to awaken the Anglican Church to its missionary task. There runs an indirect line from German Pietism to the rise of the S.P.C.K. and the S.P.G. through the Religious Societies, which were themselves partly children of Pietism, while the S.P.C.K. in its turn has been called "the daughter of the Religious Societies". [71] But there is also a more direct relation: Francke soon became a corresponding member of the S.P.C.K., while Pietists from Halle who were present in London in the retinue of the Danish consort of Queen Anne strengthened the already existing ties. [72] And Miss Jones rightly sees a parallel between the educational ideals of Francke and those of the S.P.C.K.: " . . . there is no great difference between the Praxis Pietatis of German pietist and English puritan". [73]

It is the combination of pietist elements and rationalist ideals which his one of the characteristics of the newly-formed organization. [34] The form which the new enterprise took was not quite new: there was the precedent of the "New England Society", there was, further in the background, the example of the Roman Catholic *Congregatio pro Propaganda Fide*. Bray was inspired by the ideal to form a counterpart of this latter organisation. [75] At first he thought of a chartered society, which might be the instrument of the Church of England to fulfil its long neglected task on the other side of the ocean.He submitted to the Bishop of London a plan which contained already in nuce the idea of the later S.P.G. [76]—but when it appeared that the time was

---

[70]   F. R. Merkel, *op. cit.*, S. 161.

[71]   C. W. Lowry, *art. cit.*, p. 141, nt 54.

[72]   See for the relations between Francke and England, apart from the quoted article of E. Benz, also: M. Schmidt, *Das Hallische Waisenhaus und England im 18. Jahrhundert*, Theologische Zeitschrift VII (1951), SS. 38—55.

[73]   M. G. Jones, *op. cit.*, p. 38.

[74]   In view of the "Instructions for the Protestant Missionaries in the English Colonies at Madras, Cudulur etc.", given in 1734 by the S.P.C.K. and present in M.S. in the "Ostindische Missionsbibliothek' in Halle, of which he gives extensive quotations, M. Schmidt remarks: "Zugleich aber erweist die Missionsauffassung der religiösen societies durch ihren starken pädagogischen Zug ihre Verwandtschaft mit der Aufklärung. An diesem Punkte läszt sich sowohl eine Eigentümlichkeit der englischen Kirchengeschichte beobachten, die in der Kontinuität der einander ablösenden Bewegungen liegt, als auch ganz allgemein der innere Zusammenhang von Pietismus und Aufklärung wahrnehmen", *Der Missionsgedanke des jungen Wesley auf dem Hintergrund seines Zeitalters*, in: *Theologia Viatorum*, Jahrbuch der Kirchlichen Hochschule Berlin-Zehlendorf, I (1948—1949), S. 89.

[75]   H. P. Thompson, *Thomas Bray, op. cit.*, p. 36.

[76]   H. Cnattingius, *Bishops and Societies*, London 1952, pp. 9—11, has shown

not ripe for it, he turned his attention to an adjacent object: the forming of a private society which could at least partly fulfill his ideals
with regard to Christian education at home and overseas. So the
S.P.C.K. came into being, supported by several ecclesiastical leaders,
but regarded askance by another part of the clergy, especially in the
country, who feared a reawakening of puritan fanaticism. [77] Many
were the aims of the new society: libraries and schools were to be
founded at home and in the colonies, literature had to be provided,
and the idea of the reformation of manners was also included, while
real missionary ideals were present in a modest form, as we shall
see below.

Part of Bray's ideals had now found an instrument through which
they could be fulfilled. One great ideal, however, was still unfulfilled:
to have an agency which, with the *official support* of Church and
nation, could be instrumental in giving an honourable place to the
Church of England in the Colonies. Bray saw there a great field of
labour for the Church: a missionary task among their own colonists
and among the heathen—and the S.P.C.K. was not quite equal to
this task because of its non-official character. One possibility would
have been to try to obtain a charter for the S.P.C.K.; indeed such
a plan has existed. [78], but it was allowed to lapse because of a better
one: namely the formation of a new society, which with the background of a royal charter and the official support of the Church could
be the special instrument of the Church of England for the work on
its transatlantic frontier. So the matter was brought before the Lower
House of Convocation, after Bray had sought contact with Bishop
Compton of London, who had the American colonies under his jurisdiction, and with Archbishop Tenison; and a petition was sent to the
King. Bray received the charter on 16 June 1701 and laid it before
the S.P.C.K., which asked him to convene the first meeting of the
new society. [79] The *Society for the Propagation of the Gospel in Foreign Parts* was born, sponsored by the S.P.C.K., chartered by the
King, backed by the Church: it was "the nearest approach to an official
Church organ for missionary work that the circumstances of the time
allowed". [80] It had the sympathy of the highest ecclesiastical leaders:
Bishop Compton was one of its originators, Archbishop Tenison was
its first president, and Archbishop Sharp, too, proved himself a warm

---

that from the beginning it was Bray's intention to form a society like the S.P.G. —
such in correction of the general opinion that the original plan contained a combination of the ideas of the S.P.G. and the S.P.C.K.

[77] M. G. Jones, *op. cit.*, pp. 62 63.
[78] H. P. Thompson, *Thomas Bray, op. cit.*, p. 72.
[79] See: H. P. Thompson, *Into all Lands, The History of the S.P.G.*, London
1951, pp. 15—17.
[80] H. Cnattingius, *op. cit.*, p. 15.

friend of the S.P.G. [81] It is evident that these same influences which stood behind the origins of the S.P.C.K. also prompted the formation of the S.P.G.

b. The work and character of the new Societies

In the first years of its existence the S.P.C.K. found its main task in the field of education and philanthropy. A number of books was published, libraries were founded, grants were given to supply overseas ministers with books of study; the Societies for the Reformation of Manners were supported and the founding of Charity Schools was taken at hand. In all these activities could be seen the "new puritanism", typically English in its accent on the practical side of life and influenced by the spirit of the age in its attitude of "benevolence" and "charity" and its emphasis on knowledge and education. Yet the glow of Pietism was also present: the S.P.C.K. Minutes of March 1699 mention as one of the aims of the work "the salvation of the souls of our poor brethren" [82] And from the outset attention was also directed towards the heathen world: in the memorial which Bray presented to the Society two months after its first meeting, we read: " . . . in order to convert the Indian nations, it seems a likely method, could there be provision for the education of some of their youths in Schools . . ." [83] We must add, however, that at first his ideal did not come to be realized.

But the scene changed with the foundation of the S.P.G. This Society was destined for work in the colonies: the scope of its activities reached as far as the frontiers of the English possessions, and its objects were according to the royal charter "our loving subjects". [84] Were there among these "loving subjects" included also the negros and the Indians? Some have tried to prove this on the ground of the official documents. Jonathan Mayhew, a minister in Boston who, in the second half of the century, flamingly protested against the policy of the S.P.G. in America and who because of this wanted to show that it was the ultimate task of the S.P.G. to evangelize the heathen, not to proselytize among fellow-Christians, saw a proof of the Society's original missionary character in the following words of the charter:

---

[81] A. Tindal Hart, *The Life and Times of John Sharp, Archbishop of York.* London 1949, p. 278.

[82] M. G. Jones, *op. cit.*, p. 38.

W. O. B. Allen and E. McClure, *Two Hundred Years: The History of the S.P.C.K.,* London 1898, p. 24.

[84] To be found, among others, in: [J. Pratt], *Propaganda, being an Abstract of the Designs and Proceedings of the Incorporated S.P.G., by a Member of the Society,* London 1819, pp. 13—14. Josiah Pratt published this work anonymously for fear that otherwise the fact of his being one of the leaders of the Evangelical Revival might hinder the circulation of the book: C. F. Pascoe, *Two Hundred Years,* I, *op. cit,* p. XI.

" . . . and that such other provision be made as may be necessary for the Propagation of the Gospel in those parts". [85] H. P. Thompson follows him in this exegesis of the charter. [86] J. L. Trinterud, however, holds the view that the charter makes no mention of Indian missions at all. [87] It seems to us, that the passage to which Mayhew and Thompson appeal is no sufficient warrant for their thesis. The most evident paraphrase of this passage is: " . . . other provisions than the maintenance of an orthodox clergy"; read in this way, its meaning appears to be that of making it possible to include within the limits of the work such activities as were not directly connected with the ecclesiastical office. The seal of the Society affords no proof either: Mayhew may have seen "naked savages" in the people who stood on the coast, calling "Transiens adjuva nos", [88] and the image may recall that of Massachusetts Colony—according to Cotton Mather "a poor Indian having a label going from his mouth, with a Come over and help us" [89],—but are the people of the S.P.G. seal, "standing in the shore in a posture of expectation" [90] really "naked savages"? It is not so easy to discern their true identity! Then Mayhew and others appeal to the name of the Society, but this again is no proof: the objects of the "propagation of the Gospel" are not named. [91] Without any doubt the white settlers were in the foreground of the founders' thoughts, as Mayhew himself must concede; their spiritual needs were so great, that Humphreys could write in 1730: " . . . the very Indian darkness was not more gloomy and horrid than that in which some of the English inhabitants of the Colonies lived, [92] and not without ground Klingberg remarks that the main objective of the founders was "the equalization of Christian culture on both sides of the Atlantic". [93]

On the other hand, however, the expression „our loving subjects" does not explicitly exclude the negros and the Indians. The charter, the seal and the name of the S.P.G. give no decisive answer to the question whether the work among these two groups was one of the

---

[85]   J. Mayhew, *Observations on the Charter and Conduct of the Society for the Propagation of the Gospel in Foreign Parts*, Boston and London 1763, p. 17.
[86]   H. P. Thompson, *Into all Lands, op. cit.*, p. 17.
[87]   L. J. Trinterud, *The Forming of an American Tradition*, Philadelphia 1949, p. 28, cf. p. 322 note 16.
[88]   J. Mayhew, *op. cit.*, p. 27.
[89]   C. Mather, *op. cit.*, p. 503.
[90]   E. Clowes Chorley, *The Seal of the S.P.G.*, Historical Magazine of the Protestant Episcopal Church XII (1943), p. 253.
[91]   Archbishop Benson (1883—1896) saw in the name of the Society a sign that the element of ecclesiastical propaganda was paramount: he saw a difference between the original proposal of the Lower House of Convocation (to found a Society "pro christiana religione promovenda") and the official title; see: [An.], *The Spiritual Expansion of the Empire*, London 1900, p. 6.
[92]   D. Humphreys, *An Historical Account of the Incorporated Society for the Propagation of the Gospel in Foreign Parts*, London 1730, pp. 21—23.
[93]   F. J. Klingberg, *Contributions of the S.P.G. to the American Way of Life* The Church Historical Publication No 14, Philadelphia [1943], p. 37.

original aims of the Society, or the question whether the S.P.G. was a missionary society from its first beginnings. Still, we are inclined to give a positive answer on the grounds of what we know of the ideals of Bray, who already in his first plan, laid before Compton and other friends, made mention of "such ministers as shall most hazard their persons in attempting the conversion of the Native Indians". [94] This impression is confirmed by the "annual sermons". [95] Mayhew rigthly noticed that the preachers of those sermons had also the heathen in mind: "the sermons rather coincide with the ultimate than with the more immediate aim of the institution". [96] Already in the first "annual sermon" which was held for the S.P.G. the Dean of Lincoln, Dr Willis, remarked that it was the aim of the Society "to settle the State of Religion as well as may be among our own People there . . . and then to proceed in the best Methods they can towards the *Conversion* of the *Natives* . . ."; [97] Gilbert Burnet, in his sermon of 1704, treated at length of the way in which according to him the work of missions had to be performed, [98] and many preachers after him have given attention to the work among Indians and negros. [99] Besides, the missionary ideals found a clear expression in the resolutions, proposed to the S.P.G. by a commision, of which Archbishop Tenison was the chairman, and accepted in 1710: they stated, that the principal design of the Society was the conversion of the heathens and infidels, and that a stop had to be put to the sending of any more missionaries among fellow-Christians. [100] We must not lose sight of the fact that these resolutions, taken under the impression made by the visit of four Iroquois "Sachems" to the Queen, gave a one-sided picture of the real situation and that they only found a very defective realization— but at any rate they show that in 1710 the missionary element was at least recognized as an integral component of the Society's work.

Was it also recognized in practice? Was the money, was the manpower, were the activities of the Society really made productive in the service of the Kingdom on the mission-field? It has been denied by men who lived in the second half of the eighteenth century: Mayhew spoke sarcastically of the "pompous accounts" of the S.P.G. missionaries, who seemed "to have been less indefatigable, and sooner discouraged in their labours among the Indians, than among Us", and he contended that the Five Nations had been *"wholly* neglected by the

---

[94]   H. P. Thompson, *Thomas Bray*, op. cit., pp. 36—37.

[95]   F. J. Klingberg, *op. cit.*, p. 42: "The greatest honour that could be paid an eighteenth century clergyman was to be asked to deliver one of their sermons".

[96]   From this quotation it appears, that Mayhew did not attach much value to the missionary element which he thougt to be present in the charter (*op. cit.*, p. 27).

[97]   Quoted by H. P. Thompson, *Into all Lands*, op. cit., p. 20.

[98]   Quoted by F. R. Merkel, *op. cit.*, SS. 198 ff.

[99]   See, among others, the "Extracts from Sermons preached before the Society", given by Pratt in his *Propaganda*, op. cit., passim.

[100]   C. F. Pascoe, *Two Hundred Years*, op. cit., pp. 68—69.

Society", [101] while in a later period Melvill Horne (of whom more in Chapter IV) criticized the work of the S.P.G. in the following, rather disparaging, way: "Their money and their labours have been extremely unproductive". [102] These judgments however, are not quite fair— for, though the work was not performed on a large scale and though it often lacked vision, courage and Christian aggressiveness, yet there was done something for Indians and negros which had some real and visible results. We look first at the work among the Indians. In 1703 the cause of Indian missions came under the notice of the S.P.G. by the already mentioned order of the Queen, which pleaded that there should be taken in hand the work among the "Five Nations". [103] It was the first step of the Society to send a gift to the Dutch Reformed minister at Albany, Mr Lydius, who worked among the Indians. [104] But more had to be done: the Queen's order had asked for two full-time missionaries. So in 1704 T. Moore was sent out to the Iroquois — his career was a "chequered story of intermittent missionary activity". [105] In 1709 a second one followed, [106] while missionaries were also sent to the Indians in North Carolina and in other colonies. [107] It would be possible to multiply these examples—but they are enough to show, that the S.P.G.-leaders tried indeed to put their missionary ideals into practice. In the meantime, there were many hindrances. The fact that the missionaries were often seen against the background of the English garrison with which they had contact, could be a real barrier; there was opposition, not only from the side of Quakers and Dissenters, [108] but also from Anglican clergymen, who thought Quakers and heretics to be worse than infidels and Indians and who, consequently, would give priority to the recovering of the "lost sheep" of their own race and people; [109] and sometimes, there was also a lack of financial support. Moreover, the fact that America dit not receive Bishops appeared to be a negative factor: partly because of this, the Anglican community did not become so deeply rooted in the American soil as, e. g., the Independents and the Presbyterians, whose communities could become real "home-bases" for the missionary work—while

---

[101]   J. Mayhew, op. cit., p. 100.
[102]   Melvill Horne, Letters on Missions addressed to the Protestant Ministers of the British Churches, Bristol 1794, p. 32.
[103]   See above, pp. 41—42.
[104]   C. F. Pascoe, Two Hundred Years, op. cit., p. 67.
[105]   E. A. Payne, The Church Awakes, London 1942, p. 88.
[106]   C. F. Pascoe, Two Hundred Years, op. cit., p. 68.
[107]   H. P. Thompson, Into all Lands, op. cit., pp. 54 ff.
[108]   See D. D. Oliver, The Society for the Propagation of the Gospel in the Province of North Carolina, The James Sprunt Historical Publications IX (1909), pp. 19—20. The Quakers especially felt themselves menaced by the activities of the S.P.G., which were indeed particularly directed against them!
[109]   See: C. F. Pascoe, Two Hundred Years, op. cit., p. 17.

at the same time the difficulties of obtaining episcopal ordination made the growth of a native clergy almost impossible. [110]

Next to the Indians, the negros in the American colonies bespoke the attention of the Society. As early as 1680 a voice was raised within the Anglican Church to evangelize the negros: in a candid work, M. Godwyn pleaded the cause of the negros as much as that of the Indians by maintaining their *"equal Right* with other Men, to the Exercise and Privileges of Religion"; he refuted the idea that the negros would be cursed with Cham (only Canaan had been cursed!); he asked if the missionary command was not lawful for his own time, and he could not suppose "that God should damn so great a number of men, for the abominable Lucre of a few greedy Epicures and Mammonists". [111] The tone of his argument is Christian, simple and strong. It is difficult to ascertain in how far his voice found an echo among the slaveowners. The "owning" of slaves was not seen as sinful in itself: the most eminent Christians possessed "plantations, stocked with negros"—it would take almost a century before the immoral character of this attitude was generally recognized. But already in 1699 Bray was so interested in the cause of the conversion of the negros, that he was able to impart his enthusiasm to the King's secretary, Abel Tassin d'Allone, during a visit at Apeldoorn. [112] The ideals of Godwyn and Bray found a response in the S.P.G., which "looked upon the Instruction and Conversion of the *Negroes,* as a principal Branch of their Care; esteeming it a great Reproach to the Christian Name, that so many Thousands of Persons should continue in the same State of *Pagan* Darkness, under a Christian Government..." [113]

For one thing it was easier to plead the cause of the negros than that of the Indians: while there was a cleavage of fear and hostility between the Indians and the white settlers, the negros were not only within the sphere of Christian influence, but also within the range of direct national interest: "The Souls for which I am now pleading have a more particular Claim to our Regard, as they are truly a Part of our own Nation, ... and contribute much by their Labour to the Support of our Government, and the increase of the Trade and Wealth of this Kingdom" (the Bishop of London in an "Address to serious

---

[110] D. D. Oliver, *op. cit.,* p. 14.

[111] M. Godwyn, *The Negro's and Indians Advocate,* London 1680, pp. 6, 47, 71. Godwyn had been a clergyman in Virginia "in good liking" during several years; when he wrote his book, he was a minister in the neighbourhood of London: G. Goodwin in *Dictionary of National Biography,* XII, London 1890, p. 62.

[112] H. P. Thompson, *Thomas Bray, op. cit.,* pp. 98—100. The so-called "D'Allone Bequest", left by D'Allone for the work among negros, became for Bray the occasion to found a third institution, "The Associates of Dr Bray" (15 Januari 1723); in that period the relation between the S.P.G. and its principal founder had become very loose.

[113] D. Humphreys, *op. cit.,* p. 232.

Christians among ourselves", quoted by Humphreys; [114] their state roused a sense of pity and sometimes a feeling of guilt. But on the other hand there were the same hindrances as we met above in relation to the Indian mission, augmented by a new one: by the fear that baptism would annihilate the right of property—which fear the Bishop of London tried to dispel in his letter of May 1727: "The Freedom which Christianity gives, is a Freedom from the Bondage of Sin and Satan; but as to their *outward* Condition... their being baptized... makes no manner of change in it..." [115] His arguments had too much success: in 1749 the Rev. Th. Bacon, Anglican minister in Maryland, complained in the foreword of his "Sermons for Negro-slaves" that the white masters after every sermon remarked; "... If these poor creatures would but mind, and do as the minister told them today, they could make excellent slaves". [116]

The S.P.G. took the work in hand: men such as Neau in New York and le Jau in Goose Creek worked with enthusiasm. Their labours had more results than those of their colleagues who worked among the Indians [117]—though it is not without exaggeration that Klingberg remarks that the Christianization of the North American negros is "the monument to the Society's success". [118] Lastly it has to be mentioned that during the second half of the century the S.P.G. made a modest attempt to bring the Gospel to Africa itself: a converted negro, Quaque, became missionary on the Gold Coast, but the fact that he had been uprooted and estranged from his own people made his missionary career a tragedy! [119]

In the meantime, the S.P.G. was handicapped by the fact that the royal charter had limited the scope of its work within the bounds of the English colonies. When the German Pietist A. W. Boehm (or: Böhme), Danish chaplain in London, asked the S.P.G. to support the Danish-Hallensian missions, the S.P.G. had to hand over the matter to its sister-society, the S.P.C.K., which because of the fact that it was unchartered had complete freedom to work all over the world. [120] The

---

[114] *Op. cit.*, p. 255.
[115] From a Letter of the Bishop of London (Dr Gibson) to the Masters and Mistresses of Families in the English Plantations abroad, exhorting them to encourage and promote the Instruction of their *Negroes* in the Christian Faith; quoted by D. Humphreys, *op. cit.*, p. 265. See for the background of the "Letters" and the "Address": N. Sykes, *E. Gibson, Bishop of London*, London 1926, pp. 365—366.
[116] Quoted by W. K. Lowther Clarke, *op. cit.*, p. 26.
[117] H. P. Thompson, *Into All Lands, op. cit.*, p. 45.
[118] F. J. Klingberg, *art. cit.*, p. 35.
[119] See: S. P. Grover, *The Planting of Christianity in Africa*, I, London and Redhill 1948, pp. 171—176.
[120] W. O. B. Allen and E. McClure, *op. cit.*, p. 260. M. Schmidt asks: "Wie aber faszte man das gemeinsame Bemühen auf englischer Seite auf?... Unsere Quellen sind an diesem Punkte erstaunlich schweigsam. Sie erwecken den Eindruck, als habe sich die SPCK mit der praktischen Hilfeleistung und Organisation begnügt, geistig-theologisch aber willig der hallischen Führung untergeordnet", *Das Hallische Waisenhaus und England im 18. Jahrhundert*, art. cit., S. 53.

S.P.C.K. took the matter in hand, stimulated by Francke and by the Royal Consort: in 1710 a subscription was opened to assist the Danish missionaries at Tranquebar, while in 1728 the S.P.C.K. began its own mission in South India. [121] Only Lutheran missionaries were employed: obviously the English mind of that time was so familiar with the idea of the colonian empire and its claims, that no English missionaries "volunteered" for service on "foreign" ground [122]—an attitude not uncommon with colonizing nations! The use of foreign missionaries— who conferred ordination according to the rite of their own Church— remained practically unchallenged till the rise of the Tractarian Movement. [123] One of the main roots of the S.P.C.K.'s missionary activity was the feeling of ecumenical solidarity with the continental Churches— which in its turn was fed by the stream of Pietism on the one hand, and by the old idea of the "protestant interest", i. e. the common opposition against Rome, on the other. [124]

3. MISSIONARY IDEALS AND ACTIVITIES OUTSIDE THE CHURCH OF ENGLAND

a. The Quakers

When Frick in the missions of the Quakers sees at least a sign of a reawakening of the missionary ideal in its purest form, his judgment is certainly too much under the influence of the contrast which he sees between "Mission und Propaganda". [125] But still the missionary elements in Quakerism afford an interesting example of that type of spiritualism in the history of Protestant missions which we have also met at the margin of missionary thought in the time of the Reformation. In their first wave of enthusiasm the Quakers saw England as a "family of prophets which must spread over all nations"; [126] and the belief in the possibility of such an expansion was strong with them because they thought every man to be in the possession of a "seed

---

[121] *Op. cit.*, p. 125 and other places.
[122] H. Cnattingius, *op. cit.*, p. 41.
[123] N. Sykes in: *A History of the Ecumenical Movement, op. cit.*, p. 161.
[124] Speaking of Josiah Woodward, M. Schmidt remarks: "In seiner Vorrede zur Pietas Hallensis [i. e. the English translation of Francke's *Segensvollen Fusztapfen* etc.] spricht er im Sinne seines vereinsmäszig aufgebauten Kirchenbegriffes von einer "Protestantischen Union", die als Ziel über den hoffnungsvollen Bestrebungen gegen den Unglauben in beiden Ländern stehe", *Das Hallische Waisenhaus und England im 18. Jahrhundert, art. cit.*, S. 54.
[125] After having stated that, through the influence of Calvinism, missions had become propaganda of the whole of Christian culture, he remarks: "Eine Heilung aber dieser Schäden war erst dann zu erwarten, wenn aus religiösen Tiefen den Trieb zur Mission neu und ursprünglich hervorbrach, nicht mehr abgeleitet aus übergeordneter Zwecken, nicht mehr sekundär gefolgert aus primären Ueberzeugungen, sondern selber ein Urdatum, ein gewachsener Gewiszheit"; and the work of Fox pointed into this direction, according to Frick, *op. cit.*, S. 107.
[126] H. T. Hodgkin, *Friends Beyond Seas*, London 1916, pp. 14—15.

of God", through which he could give a response to the call of the Gospel. [127] Moved by his universalist outlook and by his humanitarian ideals George Fox visited negros [128] and Indians [129] in America, and the fact that the founding of Pennsylvania took place partly because of missionary motives shows that William Penn was of the same spirit. It was his ideal that his colony should be to "the glory of God in the civilisation of the poor Indians, [130] and their conversion by just and lenient measures to God's Kingdom", [131] and famous are his words to the Indians: "We are the same, as if one man's body were to be divided into two parts, we are all one flesh and blood". [132] A typical mark of the missionary attempts of the Quakers was the worth they attached to lay preaching: they saw every Christian standing under the missionary command—to limit it to office-bearers was "the very essence of Popery". [133] On the other hand their anti-institutionalism could lead — just as was the case with the sectarians of the sixteenth century—to a frustration of the missionary task: the historian Barclay mentions the opposition of an extreme separatist against the foreign mission work of the Quakers, because Fox c.s. had introduced "outward teachers", set apart and paid for the missionary work overseas! [134]

At the end of the seventeenth century Quakerism lost much of its "revivalist character": the Quakers became "a highly respectable and

---

[127] Cf. Fox's arguments in his dispute with Scottish Calvinists in 1657: "And doth not Christ say: "Go preach the gospel to all nations", which is the gospel of salvation. He would not have sent them out into all nations to preach the doctrine of salvation if the greatest part of men was ordained for hell. And was not Christ a propitiation for the sins of the whole world, for the reprobates as well the saints, and so died for the ungodly as well the godly: and died for all men ... and enlightens every man that cometh into the world that through him they might all believe ...": J. L. Nickalls (ed.), *The Journal of George Fox*, Cambridge 1952, p. 317.

[128] Fox was not opposed to slavery as such, but he admonished the masters and mistresses to instruct the negros in the faith: "And we set up meetings in every Friend's house, among the blacks, some 200, some 300, in their houses that the masters and dames of families might admonish their families of blacks and whites, as Abraham did, which is a great service", *Journal*, pp. 604—605, 609—610.

[129] Fox tried to prove that "the Light" was also in the Indians by asking one of them if, when he did wrong, there was not "'something in him that did tell him of it ... And he [*i. e.* the Indian] said there was such a thing in him ...": *Journal*, p. 642.

[130] Just as many others (cf. Zinzendorf). Penn, too, believed that they were the descendants of the lost tribes of Israel: W. I. Hull, *Eight First Biographies of William Penn*, Swarthmore (Pennsylvania) 1936, p. 26.

[131] H. T. Hodgkin, *op. cit.*, p. 19.

[132] See: J. Stoughton, *History of Religion in England*, IV, London[2] 1881, pp. 343—346.

[133] R. Barclay, *The Inner Life of the Religious Societies of the Commonwealth*, London[3] 1870, p. 207. Barclay sees a line running from Schwenckfeld to Fox, pp. 222—223.

[134] The separatist was William Rogers, who opposed the sending of paid preachers across the Atlantic in his *Second Scourge for George Whitehead*, 1685. quoted by Barclay, *op. cit.*, p. 470.

rather exclusive connection, not seeking to proselytize any more . . . [135] Though they still encountered a forceful opposition in the American colonies—how a man as Bray saw them appears from the fact that he wanted to 'reduce the Quakers to the Christian religion"! [136]—, their world of thought approached more and more the ideas of the Latidunarians: next to the spiritual factors, the moral element of the Gospel received from them a strong accent. [137] The historian of the Quakers' missions, Hodgkin, shows how in this period the world vision was lost. The evangelistic impulses were weak, but the ideals of love and humanity had retained something of their old flavour: the Quakers stood in the forefront of the battle against slavery—already in 1727 they saw the dangers and the immoral character of the slave-trade, in 1758 they prohibited the members of the Society from taking part in this horrible traffic, and at the end of the century they were the first to send a petition on this matter to Parliament. [138] But only when the waves of the Evangelical Revival had reached the shores of the island of Quakerism, were the world-wide view and the missionary spirit recovered.

b. The Dissenters

The main channel for the dissenting churches in England to fulfill their missionary task was the so-called "New England Company". Though at the time of its renewal, in 1661, it was definitely not a purely dissenting agency—the Anglican Boyle was its first president—, the work received its main support from the non-conformist side, [139] while the execution of it on the other side of the ocean was in the hands of the New England Puritans. The work was not without results —Crescent Mather wrote to the Dutch professor J. Leusden in 1687, that there were already twenty-four Indian preachers in New England [140]—and it continued in spite of the great losses which it incurred as a result of the Indian wars.

It is not easy, however, to find proofs of missionary fervour in the dissenting circles of our period. The Presbyterian climate will have been too cold for the survival of the evangelistic ideal; [141] the General

---

[135]   G. M. Trevelyan, *English Social History, op. cit.,* p. 267.

[136]   H. P. Thompson, *Thomas Bray,* op. cit., p. 39.

[137]   J. Stoughton *in loco citato.*

[138]   A. Plummer, *The Church of England in the Eighteenth Century,* London 1910, p. 206.

[139]   See: Ch. Hole, *The Early History of the Church Missionary Society,* London 1896, p. XXII.

[140]   „Ex Indis tunc fuisse XXIV qui Verbum *Dei* praeligerent et concionarentur": Crescens Mather in a letter to Prof. J. Leusden in Utrecht, published in 1699 and quoted by J. A. Fabricius, *Salutaris Lux Evangelii,* Hamburg 1731, p. 591.

[141]   Yet the missionary idea had not quite left the circle of Presbyterianism — so the Presbyterian minister Daniel Williams left a bequest for missionary work, from which among others a part of Sergeant's salary was paid: H. Hunter,

Baptists experienced in part the same difficulties as the Presbyterians, and the Particular Baptists formed so closed and rigid a community that they had no room for the broader vision. Only in the warmer climate of the Independent group—into which some evangelical Presbyterian congregations merged [142]—were there some signs of missionary interest. Though men such as Watts and Doddridge were only indirectly connected with the Methodist awakening and its counterpart on the other side of the Atlantic—we treat them here as representatives of the time between Puritanism and Methodism—, they still transcended the period of Latitudinarianism bij their evangelistic zeal and by the warmth of their spiritual life. Their evangelical spirit found its reflection in their attitude towards the cause of missions. In 1719 Watts wrote his famous hymn "Jesus shall reign where'er the sun does his successive journeys run . . ." [143]: a remarkably eschatological vision in a period in which Christian hope only played a very small part. We cannot call it a missionary hymn in the limited sense of the word: it does not call to missionary deeds, it does not even mention the factor of human activity in the realization of this vision. In a later period the expectance of far and distant things could even become the substitute for the active response to the actual challenge of the situation. But in the mouth of Watts these words are not symptomatic of an attitude of flight — on the contrary, they are the sign that the vision of the conversion of the nations had not altogether been lost, they prove that the promises of the Old Testament were applied to the relation between Jesus and those peoples who were still sitting in darkness. With the mystic Watts, these words are no shallow rhetoric, but the real and pious expression of a living hope. This positive explanation of Watts' hymn is in accordance with the fact that Watts had also a practical interest in the cause of missions; he followed in the steps of Baxter by collecting money for missionary work among the Indians, [144] he remained equally in the line of the older Puritans by looking at the great day of God which was breaking behind all the activities of little men. Watts' contemporary Doddridge was of the same spirit and, in this point, even more outspoken than his older friend: [145] the dissenting historians Bogue and Bennett mention that Doddridge "formed an extensive plan for the advancement of religion, in congregations in dark places of the country, and abroad"; [146] in a sermon, preached in

---

A Brief History of the Society in Scotland for Propagating Christian Knowledge in the Highlands and Islands, London 1795, p. 52.

[142] B. Manning, *The Protestant Dissenting Deputies*, Cambridge 1952, p. 54.

[143] To be found in the *Hymnary of the Church of Scotland* as Hymn 388.

[144] A. P. Davis, *Isaac Watts*, London 1948, p. 49.

[145] In Watts' work: *A Humble Attempt towards the Revival of practical Religion among Christians, and particularly the Protestant Dissenters*, I found no reference to the missionary task of the Church.

[146] D. Bogue and J. Bennett, *The History of the Dissenters from the Revolution to the year 1808*, II, London[2] 1833, p. 235.

1742, on "The Evil and Danger of neglecting the Souls of Men" he proposed the forming of praying and money-collecting societies. [147] Already it appears from this title that Doddridge was moved by soteriological motives. This was the period, in which Doddridge was influenced by his contact with the Moravians. In this context it is interesting to notice that Leslie Stephen sees a difference between the way in which Doddridge and that in which Jonathan Edwards speaks of the horrors of hell: while Doddridge is "an ingenuous special pleader", Edwards is "a seeer", a man "overpowered by an awful vision". [148] Yet it may be that the difference was smaller than Stephen supposes: Doddridge was deeply moved and impressed by the Diary and Journal of David Brainerd, who had worked and written fully in the spirit of Jonathan Edwards. [149]

c. Scotland

It seemed as if the missionary spirit, so strong in the Scottish Church of the early Middle Ages, had died away in the period of decay before the Reformation. And the great events of the sixteenth century brought an awakening on many sides, but not in the field of missionary activity. Only the confessions gave a weak witness of the Church's missionary character: the title-page of the "Scots Confession" bore the text Matt. 24. 14; the same confession ended with the prayer: "let all the nations cleave to Thy true knowledge", [150] and in a former Chapter we heard some missionary notes which originated from the Westminster assembly. [151] It is not difficult to explain from external circumstances the absence of the missionary view: in the time of John Knox Scotland itself was still a missionfield, while the serious political and ecclesiastical troubles of the next century absorbed almost all the energies of the Scottish nation. [152]

The last year of the seventeenth century witnessed a broadening of Scotland's horizon: we think here of the expedition to Darien which, however, finished such a tragic failure because Scotland had "not the power and resources needed to open markets and found colonies for herself alone." [153] In the meantime this expedition forms at least to a certain degree an interesting parallel with a venture in the Reformation period. In 1555 De Villegaignon went with a number of Huguenots to

---

[147] See: E. A. Payne, *Doddridge and the Missionary Enterprise*, in G. F. Nuttall (ed.), *Philip Doddridge 1702—1751*, London 1951, pp. 79—101.
[148] L. Stephen, *op. cit.*, II, p. 388.
[149] E. A. Payne, *in loco citato*.
[150] See: G. D. Henderson, *The Church of Scotland*, Edinburgh 1939, p. 121.
[151] See above, p. 24.
[152] See D. Mackichan, *The Missionary Ideal in the Scottish Churches*, London 1927, pp. 51—67.
[153] G. M. Trevelyan, *History of England*, London-New York-Toronto, 1947, p. 481.

Brazil in order to found there a free colony; ministers, sent through the mediation of Calvin, were among those who went out to seek a new country; the missionary ideal played a part in the venture, as we know from letters written to Calvin by some of the participants—but the story ends in utter tragedy: De Villegaignon proved to be a traitor, some of the emigrants were killed and the others had to return under the most miserable circumstances. [154] While the expedition of De Villegaignon was from the point of view of the partaking Huguenots an attempt to regain religious freedom, the Darien expedition was an endeavour to bring about economic expansion by way of colonization —but this expedition, too, witnessed a naive effort to convert the Indians. The Church of Scotland General Assembly of 1700 addressed a letter tot the participating ministers in which the following passage occured: "the Lord will yet honour you and the Church from which you are sent to carry the Name among the heathen". [155] From this wish, which the Church of Scotland conveyed to its servants overseas, it appears that the ecclesiastical leaders of this period saw the venture in a missionary light. One of the ministers of the expedition was the former Cameronian leader Alexander Shields, who wrote in bitter disappointment to the Moderator of the Commission of the General Assembly: "There might be some hope of doing some good among them if we had any that had their language and if our people's practices did not stumble them; but alas! we have reason to fear we shall do them more hurt than good, for the first of our language that they learn is cursing and swearing ..." [156] More even than the expedition of 1555 this venture proved that it leads to a complete frustration of missionary work when missions are considered as a subordinate appendix to colonization.

Of abiding importance, however, was the formation of the *Society in Scotland for the Propagation of Christian Knowledge*. It seems that the first origins of this Society are to be found in the circle of an Edinburgh praying society: one of its members, an Episcopalian minister, who was in correspondence with the English S.P.C.K. and who knew by experience the spiritual needs of the Highlands, took the initiative to form a Scottish daughter-society of the organization on the other side of the Border! [157] It speaks favourably of the spirit in the Church of Scotland, that it gave its support to an enterprise which was largely sponsored by Episcopalians. [158] The first aim of the new Society was

---

[154] See, among others, the article of G. Baez-Camargo, mentioned above on p. 8, note 24.
[155] D. Mackichan, *op. cit.*, pp. 68—69.
[156] H. Macpherson, *Alexander Shields*, in: Records of the Scottish Church History Society, VI (1938), p. 59.
[157] M. G. Jones, *op. cit.*, p. 176.
[158] D. Maclean, *Scottish Calvinism and Foreign Missions*, Records of the Scottish Church History Society, VI (1938), p. 5. Maclean even sees in this fact a

the work in the Highlands—then considered almost in the light of a mission-field, where lived "a heathenish race", which had to be christianized [159]—, and Rome was not sitting idle! But it appears from the first patent, granted by Queen Anne in 1709 at the intercession of the Archbishop of Canterbury, and from its constitution of 1710, that the idea of foreign missions wat not outside its scope. [160] Though not an official agency of the Church of Scotland, the Society had as its task to instruct the people "in the Christian Reformed Protestant Religion", and it moved thoroughly on presbyterian lines. It turned to the work of foreign missions in a later period than the English Society— but when it had once begun to look to the transatlantic territories, it initiated there a piece of work among the Indians, which has received a lasting place in the history of missions because of the excellent qualities of some of the missionaries. In 1732 the first steps were taken "to have the full light of the Gospel shine everywhere, and its teachings communicated to all who still sit in darkness", [161] but the work did not prove successful; hence a fresh start was made in 1741 with the help of a "Board of Correspondents", the members of which belonged to the "New Side" of American Presbyterianism, the group which was touched by the revival spirit. [162] The Board was able to enlist a number of enthusiastic young missionaries, among whom we mention as the most prominent figure: David Brainerd—but he belongs properly to the period that will be the subject of the next chapter.

Perhaps the most important example of Scottish missionary interest in this period is the work of Robert Millar, minister at Paisley: *The History of the Propagation of Christianity and the Overthrow of Paganism,* which appeared in first edition in 1723. [163] The design of his book is "to excite us to thankfullness to our gracious God, for being delivered from that miserable *Darkness* and *Idolatry,* under which we were sunk . . ., to set before us the wonderful steps of *Divine Providence* . . ., to move our Bowels of Pity for that slavery and thraldom to which the *Heathens* . . . are yet chained . . ., and to make *Christians* with fervour and zeal contribute their utmost endeavours, that the Salvation purchased by CHRIST may be known to the *Ends of the Earth".* [164] Millar shows himself as a warm Christian, who is moved by truly evangelical motives; he knows of the necessity of the Spirit's

---

proof of "the catholicity and superb denominational confidence of Reformed Scotland".

[159] H. Hunter, *op. cit.* p. 13; cf. p. 7: " . . . men in a state of total ignorance and barbarism; the very light that was in them, worse than darkness".

[160] *Op. cit.,* pp. 21, 56.

[161] D. Maclean, *art. cit.,* p. 6.

[162] L. J. Trinterud, *op. cit.,* p. 130.

[163] See the article of J. Foster, *A Scottish Contributor to the Missionary Awakening, Robert Millar of Paisley,* I.R.M. XXXVII (1948), pp. 138—145. The edition of which I made use, is that of 1731; it appeared in London in two volumes.

[164] Vol. I. p. III.

presence, [165] he knows, too, that prayer is an indispensable factor, he is looking forward to the day of the great advancement of the Kingdom and he is moved by compassion for "perishing souls". [166] With him we find already a parallel to the modern distinction between "propaganda" and "mission": "The zeal of the Church of *Rome*, in their College for propagating the Faith, ought to excite Protestants to the like endeavours: not to propagate their own opinions, to make proselytes to a party, . . . but to *turn sinners from darkness to light*". [167] He is, however , quite a child of his time in his view of the acceptability of the Christian religion for natural man and in his optimism with regard to man's natural possibilities: "The reasonableness of the Christian Religion gives one great hopes that it will meet a ready reception among the Heathen"; and: ". . . their acknowledgement of one true God and of a future state, and of the just notions they have of many moral virtues, gives us reason to believe, that they are already somewhat prepared for embracing the other precepts of the Christian Religion . . ." [168] He does not stand far from the Latitudinarians when he sees as the great design of the Gospel "to teach men the most perfect system of morality", [169] but on the other hand he is impressed and influenced by Francke and his missionary ideals, and he does not expect a missionary awakening unless there has taken place a revival of sincere piety at home. [170] So we find also with him that seeming *coincidentia oppositorum*, that blend of Rationalism and Pietism, which again and again has proved to be one of the main characteristics of the British missionary enterprise.

4. WHAT WERE THE MOTIVES?

a. Political motives

At the end of the preceding chapter we saw that the theocratic motive had played an important part in post-Reformation Protestant missions. There was a relation between the theocratic idea and the concept of the *corpus christianum*: theocratic ideals can only function within the framework of the integral unity of the political and the ecclestical sphere. In this chapter we saw, however, that after the Glorious Revolution new ideas respecting the relation between Church and State gained ground: the *corpus christianum* had broken and the old ideal of the complete mutual integration of Church and State only lingered on in the closed circle of some isolated communities. Yet the alliance

---

[165] See, *e. g.*, Vol. I, p. VI.
[166] Cee Vl. I, p. XII; Vol. II, pp. 354, 355, 388 ff.
[167] Vol. II, p. 370.
[168] Vol. II, p. 382, 384.
[169] *In loco citato*.
[170] Vol. II, p. 370.

between Church and State was not abruptly broken—it only entered into the sphere of political and ecclesiastical opportunity, where remnants of the corpus christianum-idea lived on in a secularized form. It is under such conditions that the political motive can play a part. In the sphere of the integral *corpus christianum* it is—at least *idealiter*—swallowed up by the theocratic motive, while where the Church has found a prophetically-critical attitude towards the State it disappears from the scene. But in the period of friendly alliance between Church and State with which this chapter occupies itself— a period in which the Church more than once became the tractable and even servile tool of the government—we meet it more than once, especially within the circle of the Established Church. This motive played a part when the S.P.G. started its mission among the Iroquois. Already in his Memorial of 1700 Bray spoke of the need to send twenty missionaries to the Indian tribes in order to counteract the French influence, [171] while in later years the same attitude found its expression in an "Annual Sermon" of Archbishop Secker (1741): " ... every single Indian, whom we make a Christian, we make a friend and ally at the same time ..." [172] It would be unfair to accentuate this motive unduly, but it has certainly exercised its influence alongside other, more sympathetic motives. A similar motive we meet in connection with the missionary work among the negros: speaking of their conversion, Archbishop Secker remarked in the same sermon: "Success in these endeavours will both be a security, and everyway an advantage, to their proprietors"! In this context it is significant to note that many negros, when they turned Christian, did not want to belong to their proprietors' church! [173] The negros were considered as useful instruments: they "contribute much by their Labour to the Support of our Government, and the increase of the Trade and Wealth of this Kingdom"; [174] when in the second half of the century schools were founded for negrochildren, the leaders had to see to it "that the great and necessary duties of obedience and fidelity to their masters, and humility and contentedness with their condition, were duly impressed on their minds". [175] In order to deal fairly with utterances like these, however, we have to keep in mind the fact that they were meant to break through the anti-missionary attitude of the slaveowners and to take away the grounds of their criticism in a time when only a very few Christians were persuaded of the immoral character of the slave-system.

---

[171]   H. P. Thompson, *Thomas Bray, op. cit.*, p. 57.
[172]   *Propaganda, op. cit.*, p. 177.
[173]   W. K. Lowther Clarke, *op. cit.*, p. 28.
[174]   From the "Address of the Bishop of London" in: D. Humphreys, *op. cit.*, p. 255.
[175]   *Public Spirit illustrated in the Life and Designs of the Rev. Thomas Bray D.D.*, London² 1808, p. 66.

b. The cultural motive

The old Puritans were not anti-cultural: they were culture-bearers of a very characteristic type — and though a certain negativism with regard to various cultural problems cannot be denied to them, [176], they tried at least to integrate such ideals as they had in the totality of their religious life: it was their weakness and their strength at once that the expansion of their culture virtually coincided with the spread of their religion. During the anti-Puritan reaction culture went its own wild ways, but the period after 1689 witnessed a partial return to the old position. Many attempts were made to bring cultural life again under the sway of Christian morality—but the accent had completely shifted, and the time of the complete integration of culture in religious life was definitely past: while one of the marks of the puritan way of life was the absorption of the cultural elements by the religious sphere, the Latitudinarians tended to see religion as one of the forms of their culture. It was the time of Leibniz's *propagatio fidei per scientias*. The "calm broadminded optimism, characteristic of the Eighteenth Century Briton", [177] saw no distance between civilization and the bringing of the Christian message, and it saw the Kingdom of God in alignment with the culture of Western Europe. So the cultural motive, which had always been present in British missions, received a new accent as a result of the general aspect of religious life in the period of the "Aufklärung". Yet the religious context was strong enough to prevent the cultural motive from becoming an independent factor in the missionary development. It was always in the background: the terminology pointed to it (Christian *knowledge* had to be spread, the "poor natives" had to be converted from *barbarism* [178]), a feeling of cultural superiority pervaded the whole attitude towards the heathen nations with which British missionary activity came into contact, and even a man like John Sergeant, missionary among the Indians in Massachusetts, saw as one of his motives "to cultivate humanity among a people naturally ingenuous enough, but who, for want of instruction, live so much below the dignity of human nature". [179] Not before the second part of the century, however, did the cultural motive find explicit mention among ecclesiastical leaders who were so deeply imbued with the rationalist spirit and had taken such a radical stand against all forms of "enthusiasm" that the pietistic strain was almost totally

---

[176]   See R. Bronkema, *op. cit.*, pp. 186—190.
[177]   G. M. Trevelyan, *English Social History, op. cit.*, p. 330.
[178]   See the sermon of Dr Willis, quoted by H. P. Thompson, *Into All Lands, op. cit.*, p. 21.
[179]   W. Brown, *History of the Propagation of Christianity among the Heathen*, I, London³ 1854, p. 59, in a quotation from Hopkin's *Memoirs relating to the Housatunnuh-Indians and to the Ministry of the Rev. John Sergeant*, 1753, p. 2.

erased. [180] That the cultural motive can become a menace to the purity and even to the continued existence of missionary work, appears with Bishop Watson of Llandaff, who declared that "he did not expect much success in propagating Christianity by missionaries from any part of Christendom, but he expected much from the extension of science and commerce". [181]

c. The motive of debt

The ascetic motive, which had played a part in post-Reformation Protestant missions with some of the men of the "Second Reformation", had almost totally disappeared in the period of the Latitudinarians: in their conception there was no room for "a call to renunciation and asceticism". [182] It reappeared only in individual cases, as in that of John Wesley, who went to Georgia in 1735 in the hope of saving his own soul. [183] It is, however, a proof of the complexity of the human situation, that in a period of self-complacency, in which the results of one's own efforts and strivings were eulogized to an abnormal extent, there was also present a feeling of recognition of the white man's debt. Here we find a slight and weak echo of some aspects of the old ascetic motive [184]: while England's prosperity grew in its contact with other parts of the world, it was felt at least by a few people, that something had to be done in return, that something had to be paid off to those who contributed to England's happy state. Godwyn had already addressed strong words to those who wanted to deny the means of salvation to negros due to the fact of their being slaves; his words contained an implicit confession of England's debt. [185] Some prelates who gave an "Annual Sermon" for the S.P.G. also gave expression to this feeling of debt—albeit in more inoffensive words—: " ... to them, whose strength is consumed in the service of your carnal things, some debt is contracted ..." (Dean G. Stanhope of Canterbury, 1714); "Planting of the Gospel seems, indeed, a debt of common justice ..." (Archdeacon Denne of Rochester, 1731). [186] It would, however, take

---

[180] Cf. Bishop W. Warburton of Gloucester in his "annual sermon" of 1766: "The method I presume to recommend ... is, first of all, to CIVILIZE the subjects of our Mission", and Bishop Th. Newton of Bristol in the sermon of 1769· „ ... do we not find in our Colonies and Plantations abroad, that the people grow less and less savage, and more and more humanized, in proportion as true Christianity is propagated and prevails among them?": Propaganda, op. cit., pp. 157, 179.
[181] N. Sykes, Church and State, op cit., p. 348, quoting from R. Watson, Anecdotes, I, p. 321.
[182] Op. cit., p. 258.
[183] See: J. S. Simon, John Wesley and the Religious Societies, op. cit., p. 126.
[184] In which the elements of renunciation and penance are almost always present.
[185] See above, p. 50.
[186] Propaganda, pp. 107, 109.

a long time before this feeling of debt would become the general property of British Christianity and before it would lead to an attitude
of self-denial and penance in which the old ascetic motive could re-
claim its rights in a new form!

d. The motives of love and compassion

Above we have seen how great was the place which the ideas of
benevolence and charity took in the mind of the eighteenth century
British Christian. His age was more deeply impressed by the love
than by the wrath of God, and it had a stronger belief in the natural
capacity of man to open his heart to this love than in the innate
resistance of fallen man to the call of God. It is not strange that the
idea of missions was taken up in the humanitarian movement of the
century: "Let us all consider one another to provoke one another to
Love and to good Works", said Burnet in his "Annual Sermon" of
1704, [187] and Bishop J. Wynne of St Asaph spoke in 1725 of "the
general duty of all Christians ... to be aiding and assisting in a work,
which of all others tends most to illustrate the infinite love and goodness of God...", [188] while we meet the same thought with Millar:
"Universal love and benevolence to all men, is also a duty which flows
from the same principles; for as God is just, so He is perfectly
good..." [189] Yet a general humanitarian ideal, however noble it might
be, was in itself not a sufficient stimulus to take the work of foreign
missions in hand: in eighteenth century England the objects of "benevolence" and "charity" could be found in the immediate neighbourhood,
and much was done indeed: "No period before the eighteenth century
had witnessed the creation of so many societies for associated efforts
on behalf of the ignorant and the helpless ...". [190] The humanitarian
striving only found its way to the transatlantic territories when eyes
were opened to the needs of that part of the world: the needs of the
white settlers first, and then the needs of the negros and the Indians.
Sometimes it was the this-wordly aspect of the need which attracted
the attention: under this aspect we meet the motive of pity with Godwyn, who was moved to "commiseration towards these people, the
Negro's" by the fact of their slavery [191] — but more often the appeal
to compassion pointed in the direction of the spiritual need of negros
and Indians. In his "Address to serious Christians" the Bishop of
London remarked that it was deplorable that so many negros did not
hear the Gospel: "every Christian who believes the Promises of th⌐

---

187 See: F. R. Merkel, *op. cit.*, p. 201.
188 *Propaganda*, p. 98.
189 R. Millar, *op. cit.*, I, p. 35.
190 M. G. Jones, *op. cit.*, p. 342.
191 *Op. cit.*, pp. 61—62.

Gospel, and is concerned in earnest for the honour of Christ, and the Salvation of Souls, must be sensibly affected with the thought of it ...": [192] Bishop E. Chandler of Lichfield remarked that the British people had been placed by God "where they must behold the thick darkness in which these natives live"; [193] Humphreys saw it as "a great Reproach to the Christian Name, that so many Thousands of Persons should continue in the same state of *Pagan* Darkness ...", [194] while with Millar the soteriological motive took the direction of a pronouncement—rare in that period!—on the eternal fate of the heathen: he was moved to pity those who "are in the path that leads to eternal ruin". [195] But the purely soteriological motive had no power to exercise a deep influence in a period, swayed by a theology in which the idea of the necessity of atonement had receded into the background because of the dominance of moralist and rationalist categories. "What are a family and a name", wrote Doddridge, "when compared with a regard to extending my Redeemer's Kingdom, and gaining souls to Christ?". [196] In these words we see that the pietistic fervour had not vanished—but it would be the Methodists in whose circle the soteriological motive would become a burning fire again!

e.   *The ecclesiological motive*

The S.G.P. has rightly been called "the Church in action" [197]: it was the agency through which the Church of England tried to reassert itself in those colonies in which Dissent had got so large a footing. It was this quality which was perhaps the strongest moving force behind all the activities of the young Society: the position of the Church of England had to be strengthened and the Anglican Community had to expand itself all over the newly-won territories. Often, however, its alliance with the interests of he Church diverted the S.P.G. from direct missionary work: at first the Quakers were one of the main objects of its activities, while in a later period Mayhew made bitter complaints of the Society's attitude towards the Dissenters—an attitude marked by the aim "to root out *Presbyterianism* etc. and to establish both *Episcopacy* and *Bishops* in the colonies". [198] The idea of the *plantatio ecclesiae* could not function as a missionary motive so long as the missionary character of the Church was not fully recognized. Only indirectly did the interests of the Church become a motive for

[192]   D. Humphreys, *op cit.*, p. 251.
[193]   Annual sermon of 1719: *Propaganda*, p. 112.
[194]   *Op. cit.*, p. 232.
[195]   *Op. cit.*, p. 390.
[196]   G. F. Nuttall (ed.), *Philip Doddridge, op. cit.*, p. 99.
[197]   H. P. Thompson, *Thomas Bray, op. cit.*, p. 74.
[198]   J. Mayhew, *op. cit.*, p. 91.

missionary action: "the combating of Roman Catholic propaganda was undoubtedly an important consideration for Dr Bray and the Anglican Church leaders of the time", [199] as appears from the fact that the Indian mission of the S.P.G. was partly undertaken to prevent activities from the Roman Catholic side and to counteract the influence of the Catholic missionaries—although political factors played as great a part as ecclesiological motives in this respect. [200] But the concept of the Church had to be deeply purified, the Church had to be liberated from the temptation to meet its opponents on the field of external power and to see the consolidation of its place in this world as its principal aim, the life of the Church had to recover once more the biblical openness towards the world, before the idea of the Church's expansion could become a positive factor in missionary development.

f. The eschatological motive

Eschatology was not the strongest side of latitudinarian theology. Yet we cannot say that the stimulus of the expectation of the coming Kingdom was altogether absent in this period. "And who can tell", said Dr E. Waddington in 1721, "whether, as dark and melancholy as the present face of things may be, yet that day may not even now be drawing on, when *the fulness of the Gentiles* is to *come in*". [201] It was the same idea which inspired Watts to his above-mentioned hymn, while with Millar the eschatological motive even gained a more apocalyptic character, when he saw the conversion of the heathen nations as a special means to advance the Kingdom of Christ in relation to the conversion of the Jews: „. . . after the conversion of the Jews, or about that time, there shall be a more generous and full conversion of the *Gentiles* than was ever before . . . and the time I hope is near . . .". [202] Lastly we find the eschatological motive in a mild form with Doddridge (in the third rule of the missionary society which he tried to establish in Nottingham): "We do hereby express our desire, that some time may be then spent, if God give an opportunity, in reviewing those promises of Scripture, which relate to the establishment of our Redeemer's kingdom in the world; that our faith may be supported, and our prayers quickened, by the contemplation of them". [203]

---

[199]   H. Cnattingius, *op. cit.*, pp. 11—12.
[200]   See above, p. 60.
[201]   In an "annual sermon" for the S.P.G.: *Propaganda, op. cit.*, p. 180.
[202]   R. Millar, *op. cit.*, II, 392—394.
[203]   G. F. Nuttall (ed.), *Philip Doddridge, op. cit.*, p. 89.

Chapter III

METHODISM, GREAT AWAKENING AND MISSIONS

This chapter covers the period from the beginnings of the awakening movements in Britain and the British transatlantic territories up
till the missionary revival that commenced when Carey issued his
famous *Enquiry*. Seen from the view-point of foreign missionary activity, the middle part of the eighteenth century is of but relative importance: this was no period of impressive undertakings, of surprising
initiatives, of new ways of approach towards the heathen world. But in
the same period, which contains such a scanty record of direct missionary work, the forces were resolved that only a short time afterwards
were to change the face of the world. In this chapter we intend to
give special attention to those movements, which through their inner
dynamics have helped to inaugurate the "Great Awakening" of Protestant foreign missions: the Methodist movement in Britain, the Awakenings in America.

On two points we shall have to overstep the chronological limits
of this chapter. Owing to of the fact that the missionary development
in Methodism between 1786 and 1813 is integrally related to the foregoing period, there is no sense in treating it in a separate chapter. At
the same time we shall deal in this chapter with the story of the American missions after 1783 only as an appendix to what will be said of
the missionary attitude in the circles which were influenced by the
Great Awakening: since the missionary development in post-war
America went its own way, in a great degree independent of the
development in Britain, a full treatment of it would not fit in with the
scope of this study.

1. THE MIDDLE EIGHTEENTH CENTURY IN ITS GENERAL ASPECT

a. The secular background.

According to Professor Trevelyan, the men who lived beten 1740
and 1780 were the most characteristic representatives of the spirit of
the eighteenth century. [1] They belonged to a period which was no

---

[1] G. M. Trevelyan, *English Social History, op. cit.*, p. 339.

longer disturbed by the passions that ran so high in the seventeenth century, and which was not yet shocked and shaken by the repercussions of the French revolution. Though this period witnessed the first dawn of the romantic movement, the sway of rationalist philosophy had not yet been broken: deistic authors still exercised their chilling influence, and so contributed to the moulding of the spirit of what has been called the glacial epoch in Church history; [2] a deep trust in reason sprang from "a pathetic belief in the fundamental goodness and rationality of man"; [3] natural religion was considered as fully equivalent to revealed religion; the "tragic sense of life" [4] had disappeared; in spite of disappointments, the myth of the "noble savage" had not yet lost its charm. [5] And the prevalent feeling of general harmony resulted in a spirit of satisfaction and complacency, which, though the eighteenth century did not fail to give rise to several philanthropic and charitable activities, [6] left no room for the revolutionary aggressiveness of the Christian reformer. [7]

When, however, we survey the social life of this period, it clearly appears that there was no reason for complacency, and that the spirit of rational harmony which was eulogized by enlightened thinkers had not yet permeated the relations of ordinary life. On the contrary: the same "classical period", which dreamt its charming dreams of harmony and perfection, witnessed a reality which was imperfect and disharmonious to such a degree that later generations, looking back upon the middle eighteenth century, could not but paint it in the darkest colours. The awakening movements of the same times were a reaction not only against the optimistic dreams of deistic philosophers, but also against that degradation of human life which the first Methodists and Evangelicals saw in slums and in prisons, in coal-mining districts and in neglected country-areas, on West-Indian plantations and on the frontier-line of the rapidly growing North American community. That their reaction had more a spiritual than a social character, does not alter the fact that they at least did not shun a realistic confrontation with

---

[2]   G. R. Balleine, *A History of the Evangelical Party in the Church of England*, London etc. 1908, p. 16.
[3]   L. E. Elliott-Binns, *The Early Evangelicals*, London 1953, p. 59.
[4]   Basil Willey, *The Eighteenth Century Background*, London 1946, p. 10.
[5]   R. N. Stromberg, *op. cit.*, p. 57.
[6]   Cf. N. Sykes in his *The English Religious Tradition*, London 1953, p. 59: "This age was by no means one of the ages of faith; but few epochs have given more convincing proof of their faith by works. If its favourite text was that upon which Archbishop Tillotson preached one of his best-known sermons ... "And His commandments are not grievous", it could plead in extenuation that charity covers a multitude of sins".
[7]   G. R. Cragg, *op. cit.*, p. 290, speaks of "a mood of dangerously complacent satisfaction"; R. N. Stromberg, *op. cit.*, p. 87, says that "to the great majority, Christianity meant a rather complacent creed of bourgeois morality"; Basil Willey, *op. cit.*, p. 48, remarks that eighteenth century optimism was in essence "an apologia for the status quo".

the real needs of their times. Recently it has been remarked that perhaps of all centuries the eighteenth century was nearest to the Kingdom of God, but that in the Evangelical Revival the experience came, with pain and terror, that this was not in fact and reality the Kingdom. [8] We have but to turn to England to find the confirmation of this thought. Today, temporal distance is great enough to see both aspects of these times, to recognize the strange alternation of charm, beauty and noblesse on the one hand and of corruption, egoism and moral laxity on the other. The scene is not so dark as some critics of the eighteenth century would make us believe! But it is an undeniable fact that in the upper classes religious indifference and moral decadence went hand in hand; university life in England was on a very low level; [9] the life of the poorer classes was marked by gross ignorance and by degrading habits: especially before the taxation of spirits in 1751, gin-drinking was a real scourge for the city-population, [10] and the experiences which Wesley recorded in his Journal reveal how raw and brutal could be the manners of the people in country-towns and villages; criminality was appallingly high, and the judicature often hit back with a hardness and relentlessness which in their turn were symptoms of the hypocritical severity that was to be found in the circles of the aristocracy. [11]

Conditions in Scotland were relatively better than in England: the eighteenth century witnessed there a new prosperity, fresh opportunities offered themselves as a result of the Union of 1707, [12] and in the midst of all this, Scottish public life possessed strong checks against moral decay in Puritanism, which was still a living force, and in the "Kirk", whose influence was still strong in the life of the population. But here, too, secularizing influences made themselves felt: R. Wodrow complained, perhaps with exaggeration but not quite without ground, that trade was put in the place of religion. [13] And America had its own problems, perhaps even more serious than those of the mother country: problems created by the amazing growth of the population. The great influx of people from various parts of Western Europe and the situation of the frontier, where the struggle for life was hard and merciless, created a religious and moral vacuum of considerable proportions: at the beginning of the eighteenth century the number of church-goers in Virginia was no more than one in twenty, while in other provinces the situation was still more unfavourable. [14] Apart

[8] A. A. van Ruler in: *Réveil en Revival*, Wending X (1955), p. 290.
[9] G. M. Trevelyan, *English Social History*, *op. cit.*, pp. 365 ff.
[10] G. M. Trevelyan, *English Social History*, *op. cit.*, pp. 342—343.
[11] See for these and other aspects of the life of the lower classes in this period: R. F. Wearmouth, *Methodism and the Common People of the Eighteenth Century*, London 1945, passim.
[12] G. M. Trevelyan, *English Social History*, *op. cit.*, pp. 450 ff.
[13] A. J. Campbell, *Two Centuries of the Church of Scotland*, *op. cit.*, p. 24.
[14] W. W. Sweet, *The Story of Religions in America*, New York-London 1930, p. 7.

from a reinforcement of Presbyterianism by the stream of Irish-Scottish emigrants, the immigration-waves of the years after 1740 did not improve the religious condition of the North American provinces — on the contrary! [15] And not only on the "frontier", but also in the cultural centres of New England, the old Puritan way of life was in serious decline. [16]

One other point calls for special mention: the complex character of Britain's attitude towards the possibilities of transoceanic expansion. While the Western hemisphere saw the building and the demolition of the "First Empire", in India Britain was reluctantly driven on the road of territorial expansion, and together with what happened in the South Sea, where exploring expeditions repeated the story of the voyages in Elizabethan times, this inaugurated the period of the so-called "Second Empire". We turn first to America. The peace of Paris (1763) brought under British control not only the Canadian provinces, but also the immense territory which formed the "Hinterland" of the British colonies along the Atlantic coast of North America. The favourable treaty, however, faced Great Britain with one of the most difficult dilemmas in its history. What was to be the function of the former French North America: had it to become a new empire, into which the ever growing stream of colonization could be led, or had it to remain in its present state as not much more than a reservoir for trade, a field for commercial contacts with the native population? Here the interests of colonization and commerce clashed with each other, and the strength of the collision was so great that it ultimately led to the downfall of the "First Empire". While England's leading circles were anti-expansionist and tended towards the protection of native interests at the cost of the possibilities of new colonization, the American colonists desired the opening of the boundary and of the road towards a new Eastward expansion. [17] The conflict ultimately led to the loss of all the North American colonies south of the Canadian frontier, twenty years after the peace of Paris! In the same period, however, Great Britain—represented by the East India Company—entered into a task in India which it had carefully sought to avoid: the assuming of territorial responsibilities. Britain was drawn into this task by the vacuum created by the decline of the Great Mogul's power. [18] And farther still, in the Pacific, pioneers who took up again the sea-faring tradition of Tudor times blazed the trail for a new expansion of the United

---

[15] See: W. W. Sweet, *Revivalism in America*, New York 1945, Chapter I (pp. 1—22).
[16] See: W. Burggraaff, *The Rise and Development of Liberal Theology in America*, Goes and New York 1928, pp. 31—32.
[17] V. T. Harlow, *The Founding of the Second British Empire 1763—1793*, I, London-New York-Toronto 1952, pp. 162 ff.
[18] See: L. H. Gipson, *The British Empire in the Eighteenth Century*, Oxford 1952, p. 4.

Kingdom. We must keep in mind that there, too, the aim was not colonization, but trade: one of the English slogans of this period was "we prefer trade to dominion". [19] But at any rate new perspectives opened up: with eager attention Britain followed Cook on his travels into unknown territories—and we can imagine the thrill of expectation which his voyages raised in the hearts of men and women who saw, with sorrow and regret, how on the other side of the Atlantic the demolition of the first British empire was in progress. The lethargy of the eighteenth century was broken—new times approached, and the repercussion of the expeditions of James Cook would be felt in circles which hitherto had lived in silent obscurity on the sidelines of British public life. But this story belongs to the next chapter!

b. The ecclesiastical background

In the Church of England of this period, Latitudinarianism was virtually dominant. Against the deistic attacks a barrier of rationalist theology was erected which cast its shadows upon the total life of the Church. Nothing was feared more than "enthusiasm": "True Christianity lies in the middle way", remarked Bishop Gibson in his Pastoral Letter of 1739, directed against the Methodists, [20] and thirty years later Bishop T. Newton of Bristol said in a sermon on John 10. 16: God "commits no violence upon our faculties, but addresses himself coolly to our understandings". [21] Even such an orthodox man as Archbishop Th. Secker, who had no wish to be classified as a Latitudinarian, was so afraid of all forms of enthusiasm that he "unconsciously helped to keep the Church at that dead level which so fatally crippled its energies in the eighteenth century". [22] The government of the Church lay firmly in the hands of Whig Bishops, who were often more interested in their political activities than in their spiritual duties: only during the summer months did the Bishop use to reside in his diocese [23]. Pluralism and absenteeism were not considered as moral evils: even conscientious ecclesiastics, who threw the whole weight of personality into the service of the Church, shared in the practice. We have no grounds for passing too hard a judgement on the Church of England of this period, and over against the often quoted words of Bishop Joseph Butler that he could not accept the primacy in 1747 because it was too late to try to support a fallen Church — words of which the authenticity is dubious [24] — other testimonies can be put, which show the eccle-

---

[19]   V. T. Harlow, *op. cit.*, p. 6.
[20]   N. Sykes, *E. Gibson, Bishop of London*, London 1926, p. 307.
[21]   *Propaganda, op. cit.*, p. 143
[22]   J. H. Overton and F. Relton, *The English Church from the Accession of George I to the End of the Eighteenth Century*, London 1906, pé 120.
[23]   N. Sykes, *Church and State, op. cit.*, pp. 93 ff.
[24]   See: A. Plummer, *op. cit.*, p. 113.

siastical life of the period in a much more favourable light. [25] But stronger forces than those, which took the lead in the Anglican Church of this period, were needed to stem the tide of religious decline and to lead the way towards a new task and a new perpective!

Among the Dissenters, the situation differed from group to group. The drift of Presbyterianism into liberal waters went steadily on: at the end of the century the once strong Presbyterian group had dwindled to a small number of congregations which maintained the old tradition, while much the largest section of the former Presbyterians had become Unitarian. [26] Some General Baptists, too, had gone over to the unitarian side. [27] On the contrary, the Particular Baptists were as rigid and sterile as in the beginning of the century: in the first years of ministry, before 1779, even a man such as Andrew Fuller was afraid to invite the unconverted to come to Jesus! [28] The Independents had remained, if not strictly Calvinistic, then in a broader sense evangelical, thanks to the influence of a leader like Doddridge; [29] the theological development in Congregational circles had gone into quite another direction from that of the Presbyterians, as appears from the fact that at the end of the century the prevailing spirit was even more distinctly Calvinistic than it had been in the foregoing period. [30]

The ecclesiastical situation in Scotland was rather complex. In the Church of Scotland, there was during the period of moderate ascendancy a group of Evangelicals who combined a warm piety with a firm stand for the doctrinal tradition of their Church; during the second half of the century their leader was John Erskine of Edinburgh; there were close connections between the Scottish Evangelicals and George Whitefield, [31] while some of their number also kept up a friendly correspondence with Jonathan Edwards. [32] The Secession group was divided by inner strife: in 1747 it was rent into two parts, the Associate Synod ("Burghers") and the General Associate Synod ("Anti-Burghers"), of which the second group especially took up a

---

[25] Cf. N. Sykes, *The English Religious Tradition, op. cit.*, pp. 62—63: "To a considerable degree, the lethargy both of the establishment and of the Protestant Dissenters has been exaggerated and even caricatured, in order to bring out more brightly the Methodist revival".

[26] B. Manning, *op. cit.*, pp. 54, 63.

[27] See: W. H. Whitley, *A History of British Baptists*. London² 1932, pp. 216—217.

[28] G. Laws, *Andrew Fuller, Pastor, Theologian, Ropeholder*, London 1942, p. 28.

[29] A. T. S. James, in: G. F. Nuttall (ed.), *Philip Doddridge*, op. cit., p. 45, calls Doddridge 'a man from whom others, at a time when religion seemed in decay, learned again the meaning of faith".

[30] Cf. D. Bogue and J. Bennett, *The History of the Dissenters from the Revolution to the Year 1808*, II, London² 1883, pp. 307—317.

[31] See: Sir H. Moncreiff Wellwood, *Account of the Life and Writings of John Erskine D.D.*, Edinburgh 1818, pp. 99, 105.

[32] See among others: O. E. Winslow, *Jonathan Edwards 1703—1758*, New York 1941, p. 365 note 20.

very rigid course under the leadership of Adam Gib; the Seceders were generally opposed to the revivalist work of Whitefield, while in the debates around the "Schism-Act" of 1766 Gib appeared to be as little moved by the religious needs of the growing Scottish population as was the moderate leader William Robertson. [33] Influenced by the Marrow-Men, by Doddridge, by Whitefield and by Jonathan Edwards was the sympathetic Thomas Gillespie, the founder of the Relief Church, in which the spirit of a broadminded Calvinism was to be found; [34] his group was too small, however, to have much influence in eighteenth century Scotland.

In America the Church of England was as weak as before — mainly due to the fact that no bishops could be ordained for transatlantic service. The fault lay not with the English bishops, who wanted to establish the episcopate. Archbishop Secker even made a proposal in this direction — but the Government was adamant to all demands, because it knew the strength of the opposition of the non-episcopal Churches in America. [35] Presbyterianism, however, became stronger in the course of the century as a result of the influx of Irish-Scottish emigrants, who transplanted their staunch Presbyterian faith into the new country. [36] In some cases the Presbyterians and the older Congregational group influenced each other in such a way, that practically no difference was felt (Connecticut); in other instances the two traditions remained separate, but still with much mutual contact (Massachussets); in some of the middle colonies (as New Jersey), Presbyterianism absorbed Congregationalism; Congregational ministers could serve Presbyterian congregations, and conversely. [37] But more important is the question: were the New England Churches still Calvinistic in doctrinal matters? The old Congregational Churches had lived, if not under the formal dominance of, then still in the sphere of Calvinistic confessional thinking. But they also had their typically Congregational traits: individualism and voluntarism, [38] while the practice of the so-called "half-way covenant", invented as a compromise between the strict Puritan ideals and the exigencies of practice, contributed to the lowering of the standards of ecclesiastical life and so helped to prepare,

---

[33]   A. J. Campbell, *op. cit.*, p. 126.
[34]   See for the principles of the Relief Church: G. Struthers, *The History of the Rise of the Relief Church*, Edinburgh-London 1848, pp. 289—321.
[35]   See: J. H. Overton and F. Relton, *op. cit.*, pp. 307—310; they even consider the dread of Secker's proposal as one of the most important secondary causes of the Rebellion!
[36]   See: A. A. van Schelven. *Het Calvinisme gedurende zijn Bloeitijd*, II, Amsterdam 1951, pp. 387 ff.
[37]   See: W. W. Sweet, *The Story of Religions in America*, op. cit., p. 95.
[38]   R. Boon, *Het Probleem der Christelijke Gemeenschap, Oorsprong en Ontwikkeling der Congregationalistisch geordende Kerken in Massachusetts*, Amsterdam 1951, p. 177.

in a negative way, the coming of the Great Awakening. [39] At the same time, English latitudinarian influences made themselves felt among some New England ministers and their congregations: a liberal movement arose that ultimately debouched itself into Unitarianism. [40] And though in the majority of congregations Calvinistic doctrine still prevailed, the form of Calvinism which put its stamp upon preaching was often one-sided in its rigidity: the sovereign character of God's free grace was emphasized at the expense of the factor of human responsibility, and man was taught to wait in complete passivity upon the saving work of God in his soul. [41] It is against this background that those awakening movements have to be seen which we shall consider more closely in the next part of this chapter.

2. STREAMS OF NEW LIFE

a. The historical development of the revival movements

The spiritual development of eighteenth century Britain differs from that of Germany in this respect, that while in Germany the first wave of Pietism was followed by a period in which the "Aufklärung" was dominant, the English-speaking countries witnessed in the same period "a reaction against all that the eighteenth century stood for", [42] a reaction which possessed such strength that it ultimately led to the overthrow of the once so powerful Deism. It is a remarkable fact that the three main streams of this reaction sprang up about the same time in different parts of the British commonwealth without genetic interdependence.

The first stream which we shall consider is that of Methodism. It took its origin from a group of younger members of the Church of England, who reacted against the spiritual luke-warmness and the moral laxity of their surroundings by pursuing the ideal of holiness in a way which they thought to be in conformity with that of the primitive Church. Methodism in its very first stage, in the period after Wesley's so-called first conversion, [43] can be called "a Tractarian movement avant la lettre". In this period we meet the figure of the non-juring mystic William Law: the idea of Christian perfection, which has played such an important part in the development of the Methodist movement, can be traced to his influence. Afterwards, however, the ways of Law and Wesley separated: while Law moved more and more in the direction of

---

[39] See: W. Burggraaff, op. cit., pp. 29—30.
[40] W. Burggraaff, op. cit., p. 56.
[41] W. Burggraaff, op. cit., p. 48.
[42] B. Willey, op. cit., p. 182.
[43] It took place in 1725, and it was a conversion from formal Christianity to a life in strict obedience to the commands of Christ.

a direct mystical communion with God, Wesley maintained the reformatory doctrine of justification by the redeeming work of Christ. [44]
Parallel with the impression made by Law, we meet the revived influence of Puritanism. Perhaps A. Lang goes too far, when he
sees in Methodism primarily a reawakening of puritan Pietism. [45]
Methodism was a new phenomenon, which cannot be measured ade-
quately by standards that are derived from a former period. But there
was undoubtedly a puritan vein in the attitude of the young men, who
in the Oxford of about 1730 desperately tried to bring their life and
that of their surroundings into conformity with the pattern of the
biblical commands. Law's influence alone does not account for this:
we are here merged in the stream of a genuinely reformed tradition,
though the deepest *motifs* of that tradition had not yet been discovered
by the young Methodists! [46]

A new stage in the history of Methodism began in 1738 and 1739
— the years of Wesley's contacts with the Moravians and of Whitefield's first contacts with the American Calvinists. Wesley's "great
conversion" took place in 1738, after he had learned to see by bitter
experience the necessity of finding peace with God through the meritorious work of Christ. [47] Three years earlier, Whitefield, faced with
the impossibility of finding peace along the road of ascetic life, had
undergone a similar experience. [48]

It was the Moravians, who opened Wesley's eyes to those elements
of the Christian faith which had receded behind his passionate quest
for holiness. He discovered the hidden secret of a life spent in the
service of Christ: "sola fide"—and in Herrnhut he saw the practical
effects of this belief: he met there "living witnesses to the power of
Christ". [49] No doubt his visit to Herrnhut helped to dynamize his
conceptions; in this way Moravianism contributed to the infusion into
Methodism of the fiery and electrical force which "was needed to
release the energy, generated and stored up in the Oxford Methodists". [50] The well-known remark of Bishop Warburton is true in-

---

[44]   See: E. W. Baker, *A Herald of the Evangelical Revival*, London 1948, pp.
5 ff., 84—85, 175 ff.
[45]   A. Lang, *op. cit.*, p. 349.
[46]   Wesley had been reared in a home in which the Puritan tradition was part
of the "family heritage", and Whitefield was an admirer of the Puritan authors:
he even declared himself to be "in love with the good old Puritans", L. E. Elliott-
Binns, *op. cit.*, p. 120.
[47]   Roman Catholic authors such as M. Piette (in his: *La Réaction Wesleyenne
dans l'Evolution Protestante*, Bruxelles 1925), place the great conversion of Wesley
in the year 1725; the leading Methodist authors on this subject, however, maintain
the year 1738 as the year of Wesley's conversion (see: H. Carter, *The Methodist
Heritage*, London 1951, p. 49).
[48]   See: J. P. Gledstone, *George Whitefield, Field-Preacher*, New York s. a.,
pp. 21—22.
[49]   See: H. Carter, *op. cit.*, p. 45.
[50]   C. W. Lowry Jr, *Spiritual Antecedents of Anglican Evangelicalism*, Historical Magazine of the Protestant Episcopal Church XII (1943), pp. 121—122.

deed, that Zinzendorf rocked the cradle of the Methodist movement—
and in spite of the differences between Hallensian Pietism and Moravianism, [51], we can say, that it was through the canal of Moravianism
also the German Pietist movement has influenced the revival of the
missionary spirit in Great Britain. [52] On the other hand, the journey
to Herrnhut also marked the beginning of the separation between
Wesley and the Moravians. Whitefield, too, took a stand some distance from them; but while Wesley complained mainly of Herrnhut's
quietism and antinomianism, it was Whitefield's great objection that
the universalism of the Moravians was incompatible with the doctrine
of predestination. [53]

But this meant also that a separation between Wesley and Whitefield was now within the horizon of possibilities! It is difficult to state
where and when Whitefield's predestinarianism found its origin; perhaps his own experience and his reading of Puritan authors had already
prepared him for the decisive influence, exercised by the American
Calvinists, while acquaintance with the works of contemporary Scottish theologians may also have played a part. [54] At any rate, it is
important to notice that, early in his career, Whitefield turned from a
rather vague mixture of High-Church ideals and pietist sentiments to
Calvinistic thinking. Henceforward the two main currents of English
Methodism went their own way!

In the meantime, Wesley as much as Whitefield was displaying
an amazing evangelistic activity: both preached to great crowds in the
open air, revival followed closely upon their preaching, they set ablaze
the mining districts of England and the Lowlands of Scotland; the
rough frontier population of New England came under the spell
of Whitefield's words, while in the saloons of the Countess of Huntingdon members of the English aristocracy listened to his unsparing
sermons. Perhaps of the two men Whitefield made the greater impression during his lifetime, but he lacked the organizing talent of
Wesley, who built up a system of classes and circuits that was to
make Wesleyan Methodism a strongly organized body. The Methodist

---

[51] Differences, at present overaccentuated under the influence of a dialectical
theological thinking, which sees in original Pietism a humanization of religion, while
Zinzendorf would have rediscovered the Pauline and originally Lutheran dimension
of a *gratia extra nos* (see among others: F. Gärtner, *Barth und Zinzendorf*, München 1953, passim). This view of Barth and others, though partially true, fails to
appreciate sufficiently the historical and theological relation between Pietism and
Moravianism!
[52] Cf. the remark of E. Hirsch, *op. cit.*, III, S. 247: "Unter den Einflusz des
deutschen, vor allem des herrnhutischen Pietismus war in England... die *methodistische* Erweckungsbewegung entstanden".
[53] See: A. Wauer, *op. cit.*, *pp. 109—113*.
[54] See: C. H. Lowry, *art. cit.*, pp. 125—126; Lowry calls Whitefield "a natural
Calvinist". L. J. Trinterud, *op. cit.*, p. 86, sees as the main cause of Whitefield's
change his contact with the so-called "Log College men", the "Tennent-group" in
American revivalism, of which more below.

leaders were—though each of them in a different degree—loyal
adherents of the Church of England; yet their work contained already
in nuce some elements, which after their death would effectuate the
separation of the Methodists from the Church of England. The first
separation took place in the circle of Whitefield's followers: in 1782,
almost twelve years after the death of the great leader, the Countess
of Huntingdon broke away from the Established Church and formed
what was called the Lady Huntingdon's Connexion, a small and uninfluential community, which in a later period passed almost totally
into Congregationalism. [55] Welsh Calvinistic Methodism also dates
from the times of Whitefield; by far the greater part, however, of
those who had been awakened by him remained in their respective
Churches: the "evangelical movements" in the Established Churches
of England and Scotland as much as the "New Light groups" in the
New England Churches owed much to Whitefield's activity. In the
Wesleyan group, the appointment of lay-preachers and the ordination
of "bishops" for America [56] widened the gulf between Church and
Methodism—and soon after the death of the brothers Wesley (John
† 1791, Charles † 1788) the Methodists came to stand outside the
Church of England, while some Methodists groups in their turn split
off from the main body, either in protest against the Wesleyan legacy
of an aristocratic Church-government or in search of the original glow
of the primitive revival-spirit.

We now come to the second movement which the spirit of awakening
called into life: the early evangelical movement. It is difficult to draw
a clear line of distinction between Methodism and early Evangelicalism:
in some cases both movements were merged into each other, in other
instances the border-line was almost indistinguishable, and especially
for outsiders the words "Methodist" and "Evangelical" were often
synonymous. [57] Still it is necessary to maintain the distinction: the
Evangelical Revival is not a direct offshoot of Methodism, but a parallel movement [58] which started even before the Methodist movement
began; Elliott-Binns mentions a number of evangelical Anglican clergy-

---

[55]   L. E. Elliott-Binns, *op. cit.*, p. 218.

[56]   That Wesley as an Anglican was an adherent of the idea of "presbyterian
ordination" was not as strange as it may seem to be in the light of present circumstances: in his times the difference between presbyterian and episcopal ordination
was only seldom felt to be important: N. Sykes, *Church and State, op. cit.*, pp.
394—395.

[57]   C. W. Lowry, *art. cit.*, p. 122.

[58]   This point is particularly accentuated from the Anglican side: see L. E.
Elliott-Binns, *op. cit.*, p. 133, and A. C. Zabriskie, *The Rise and Main Characteristics of the Anglican Evangelical Movement in England and America*, Historical
Magazine of the Protestant Episcopal Church XII (1943), pp. 85—96; N. Sykes,
however, sees the Evangelical Revival in the Church of England as "an offshoot
from the Calvinist movement of Whitefield": *The English Religious Tradition,
op. cit.*, p. 68.

men, who were "awakened" without being influenced by either Wesley or Whitefield. [59] The difference between the two movements lay in their attitude towards the Church and its order. While the Methodists —often in spite of themselves—were "virtual dissenters", [60] the Evangelicals abhorred everything which could lead to a separation from the Church. Symptomatic of the difference between these groups was the attitude towards "itinerancy" (the performing of spiritual work by ordained clergymen outside the bounds of their own parishes): though at the outset some evangelical clergymen shared in the practice, it found more and more disapproval in evangelical circles, while among the Methodists it became a standing custom. [61] On the other hand we must not overemphasize the difference: the Methodist leaders themselves stood on the verge; Charles Wesley in particular was perhaps more an Anglican Evangelical than a downright Methodist, and of considerable importance is the relation between Whitefield's action and the rise of the evangelical movement. [62] It is this relation which accounts for the Calvinistic element in the Evangelical Revival: though some Evangelicals such as J. W. Fletcher were on the "Arminian" side, by far the greater part was more or less Calvinistically-minded; like their Evangelical brethren in the Church of Scotland, they "had drunk deep of the well of Whitefield". [63]

The American movement of awakening took its beginning in the congregations of the Dutch Reformed minister Th. J. Frelinghuysen, called by his opponents a "Koelmanite" (a follower of the seventeenth century Dutch theologian J. Koelman): here we find an interesting connection with the Second Reformation in Holland! [64] Gilbert Tennent, Frelinghuysen's Presbyterian colleague in the Raritan Valley of New Jersey, carried the flame of the revival into the Presbyterian Churches. [65] About the same time, in 1734, the reactions on a sermon of Jonathan Edwards marked the beginning of the New England revival, an awakening movement which commenced within the circle of the Congregational Churches. It seems that there is no genealogical rela-

---

[59]   *In loco citato.*

[60]   This expression was used by the Evangelical clergyman John Berridge in a letter to the Countess of Huntingdon: J. H. Overton and F. Relton, *op. cit.*, p. 76.

[61]   See: C. Smyth, *Simeon and Church Order*, Cambridge 1940, p. 255, and G. R. Balleine, who writes: "All the Methodists, like their leader, claimed the world as their parish ... the Evangelicals were in danger of making the parish their world": *op. cit.*, p. 51.

[62]   This relation is to be seen as the interaction between two parallel movements: see above, p. 76, note 58.

[63]   A. J. Campbell, *op. cit.*, p. 37.

[64]   While Sweet emphasizes the fact that Frelinghuysen was a German, educated by his German Pietist father, Trinterud draws attention to his relation with the Dutch "Second Reformation": W. W. Sweet, *Revivalism in America, op. cit.*, p. 45; L. J. Trinterud, *op. cit.*, p. 54.

[65]   See: W. W. Sweet, *Revivalism in America, op. cit.*, Ch. III, pp. 44—70 (*The Log College Evangelists*).

tion between the movement of Tennent and that of Edwards: it was Whitefield who brought the two movements together. [66] The "Great Awakening" set New England on fire, and it also touched the other provinces. At the same time, however, it led to a conflict within the existing Churches: in 1741 the "New Side Presbyterians", the so-called "Log College men", were turned out by the "Old Side" Synod of Philadelphia, [67] while latitudinarian ministers like Jonathan Mayhew were opposed to Old Side and New Side alike. [68] The Great Awakening can be considered as a threefold reaction: against the frontier-conditions with their decline of morals and religion, against the liberal tendencies which had began to grow in strength, and against a "hyper-Calvinism" which by its one-sided emphasis upon the sovereign character of the grace of God threatened to darken the consolation offered in the promises of the Gospel. Political unrest and ecclesiastical troubles partly engulfed the results of the awakening, [69] but at the end of the century a new revival took place, the "Second Great Awakening", which strengthened and deepened the life of the Congregational and the Presbyterian Churches. [70] In the meantime, Wesleyan Methodism had made its entrance in North America; though it was unpopular during the War of Independence because of Wesley's pro-British attitude, it rapidly gained ground in the period of new expansion after the war, which saw the formation of the Methodist Episcopal Church in 1784. By the system of "itinerancy" and "circuit-riding" the Methodists were able to reach those who lived "in the highways and hedges"; the terms "preacher" and "missionary" were even used interchangeably! [71]

b. Some characteristic elements of the revival movements

It is difficult to reduce the three movements to the same denominator. Every definition is either too broad to convey any exact meaning, or too narrow to compass the awakenings of the middle eighteenth century in their totality. Still it is possible to discern some common elements. In a period in which a certain lukewarmness had invaded the domain of ecclesiastical life, a period which expressed a distinct preference for the safe middle road and a deep horror for all forms of enthusiasm, the Methodists, the Evangelicals and the men of the Great Awakening were characterized by a burning seriousness with regard to the ultimate issues of life. Their preaching marked a return from the

---

[66] See:' W. W. Sweet, The Story of Religions in America, op. cit., pp. 188 ff.
[67] L. J. Trinterud, op. cit., pp. 104 ff. Since 1745 the New Side formed the "Synod of New York", which reunited with the old group in 1749.
[68] See: W. Burggraaff, op. cit., p. 59.
[69] W. W. Sweet, The Story of Religions in America, op. cit., p. 200.
[70] O. W. Elsbree, op. cit., pp. 36—46.
[71] See: W. C. Barclay, Early American Methodism, I, New York 1949, pp. 100—104.

superficial moralism of the Latitudinarians to the deep notes of the full
biblical message. This imparted to every utterance a new sense of
urgency, which did not fail to make a deep impression. Naturally, this
attitude could lead to a one-sided accentuation of the emotional aspect
of religious life. In some respects, the awakening movements of the
eighteenth century were unable to escape the danger of an unhealthy
emotionalism: particularly during mass-meetings, strange phenomena
took place which gave some foundation for the criticisms that arose
from various sides. But as a rule, the leaders did not encourage an
excessive emotionalism: Wesley especially stressed time and again that
Methodism was no "enthusiasm", and though Whitefield and Edwards
were more emotional in their appeal to the "unconverted", we may not
hold them responsible for the excesses of their followers. [72] Personal
experience received a strong accent, indeed; but before we speak of
a man-centred form of religion [73] we have to realize that it was the
men of the revival-movements who began to take seriously again the
doctrine of the Holy Spirit and his work in man's heart: here, too,
we see a parallel with the "Second Reformation". In a period of cool
rationalism, a renewed emphasis on "feeling" was necessary: the qua-
lification "Church of Englandism felt" [74] brings down no disgrace
upon Methodism!

Did this feeling of urgency also involve what is sometimes called
"hell-fire-preaching"? Here we must make a distinction between
Wesley on the one side, and Whitefield and Edwards on the other
hand. In the works of Wesley we but seldom meet a reference to the
terrors of hell. The following question and answer are to be found
in the Minutes of the Wesleyan Conference of 1746:

Q. What inconvenience is there in speaking much of the wrath of
God and little of the love of God?

A. It generally hardens them that believe not, and discourages
them that do.[75]

---

[72] Jonathan Edwards wrote: "The weakness of human nature has always appeared in times of great revival of religion, by a disposition to run to extremes,
and get into confusion; and especially in these three things, enthusiasm, super-
stition, and intemperate zeal"; *Some thoughts concerning the present revival of
religion in New England, Works*, VI, London 1817, p. 25.

[73] A judgment, given by some very disparate theologians: F. D. Maurice thinks
that the Evangelical scheme of salvation made the sinful man and not the God of
all grace, the foundation of Christian theology: quoted by L. E. Elliott-Binns, *op.
cit.*, p. 387; J. D. du Toit writes that the standpoint of the Methodist *locus de salute*
is anthropological-soteriological, not theological: *Het Methodisme*, Amsterdam-
Pretoria 1903, p. 170; and Karl Barth sees in Pietist missions — and *mutatis
mutandis* we can apply his words equally to the activities of the Methodists — a
parallel to the work of the Jesuits, a form of "Barockchristentum" in which man
receives the central place: see his *Die Theologie und die Mission in der Gegenwart*, Zwischen den Zeiten X (1932), S. 204, and his *Kirchliche Dogmatik*, II 2,
Zürich 1945, S. 368.

[74] See L. E. Elliott—Binns, *op. cit.*, p. 382.

[75] As quoted by H. Carter, *op. cit.*, p. 199.

Here we find Wesley's point of view *in nuce*. In Wesley's *Works* there is only one sermon which explicitly speaks of hell; [76] it seems to be "an early academic exercise"; [77] its general tone is more rational than emotional, though the appeal to fly the terrors of hell is not wanting: "Suffer any pain then, rather than come in that place of torment"! Wesley was overwhelmed by the thought of God's love: H. Carter rightly remarks, that "the primary emphasis in John Wesley's teaching was not on the eternal punishment of sinful and sinning men, but on the love of God in Christ, love to the uttermost". [78] The same note of amazament at the love of Christ we meet in the hymns of Charles Wesley: "Jesus, lover of my soul"; "Love Divine, all loves excelling", and "O Love Divine, how sweet thou art! . . . Stronger His love than death or hell". [79]

Whitefield laid greater stress on the threat of hell and eternal judgment than Wesley did: "And I think, if any consideration be sufficient to awaken a sleeping drowsy world, it must be this, that there will be a day wherein these heavens shall be wrapt up like a scroll . . . and every soul, of every nation and language, summoned to appear before the dreadful tribunal of the righteous Judge of quick and dead . . .". [80] Yet a far stronger emphasis on this point is found with Jonathan Edwards: in his sermon "Sinners in the hands of an angry God" [81] he painted natural man as "held in the hands of God over the pit of hell", and in an almost medieval way he gave a vivid description of the horrors of hell. Yet his ultimate aim was soteriological: "The use of this awful subject may be for awakening unconverted persons in this congregation".

Not unrelated to the foregoing point is the attitude of the men of the awakening towards the general offer of the grace of God. From the beginning, Wesleyan Methodism was marked by an outspoken universalism: God's love was for all and sundry, Jesus died for all, "He spreads His arms to embrace you all" [82] — though at the same same time the indispensability of faith was strongly emphasized. [83] The ways of Wesley and Whitefield parted on the point of the uni-

---

[76] *Works*, ed. by Th. Jackson, VI, London 1829, pp. 381—391. The title of this sermon is: *On Hell*, the text Mark. 9. 48.

[77] See W. C. Barclay, *op. cit.*, p. XVIII.

[78] *Op. cit.*, p. 198.

[79] In the hymnary of the Church of Scotland resp. hymn 414, hymn 479 and hymn 428.

[80] Sermon on *The Wise and Foolish Virgins* (Matth. 25. 13) in: G. Whitefield, *Sermons on Important Subjects*, London 1841.

[81] *Works*, VI, pp. 450—464. The text was Deut. 32. 35; the sermon was preached in 1741 "at a time of great awakening".

[82] From the "conversion hymn" of Charles Wesley, as quoted by H. Carter, *op. cit.*, p. 31.

[83] See E. W. Baker, *op. cit.*, p. 88, who makes a distinction between the "unconditional universalism" of Law and the Moravians and the "conditional universalism" of Wesley.

versalism of grace: Wesley had an aversion to the doctrine of predestination—" ... this uncomfortable doctrine" [84]—, while Whitefield
came more and more under the impression of the sovereign character
of God's grace: "The doctrines of our election and free justification
in *Christ Jesus* are daily more and more pressed upon my heart". [85]
Historically, it was the influences of that Laudian tradition which had
made "Arminianism" dominant in High Church circles that, cooper-
ating with those of Law and the Moravians, brought Wesley to his
theological position. [86] Besides, the rationalist element in his thinking
shrank back from the mysterious depths of the predestination doctrine, [87] while his active spirit, striving for "perfect holiness", feared
the consequences of what he considered as a form of Antinomianism: [88]
this doctrine "tends to destroy our zeal for good works". [89] Wesley,
however, failed to see the distinction between "hyper-Calvinism" and
the form of Calvinism which was to be found with men such as Whitefield and Edwards. [90] In their thinking, the general offer of grace in
Christ to all men was not an inconsistency, [91] but a legal element —
in accordance with the general trend of Reformed theology. [92] In their
turn the Calvinistic Methodists feared an over-accentuation of the
human factor in Wesleyan circles, and recoiled at the thought of the
possibility of becoming perfectly free from sin. [93]

These points of controversy, however, must not make us shut our
eyes to the many points which are characteristic of the revival movement in its totality. We have seen already, that the preaching of the
revivalists was marked by a strong note of urgency. They had a real
"passion for souls", and in their methods they revealed a certain aggressiveness: while German Pietism tended to introversion, their work
had a distinctly extrovert and open character! Another common mark
of the revival movements was their individualism: they aimed at the
conversion of individual souls; its relative indifference to the doctrine
of the Church was one of the weak spots of Methodism, and Edwards
and his co-revivalists tended to neglect the reformatory doctrine of the
covenant of grace. [94] And though the after-effects of the revivals have

---

[84]   J. Wesley in a *Sermon on Free Grace* (Rom. 8. 32), *Works*, VII, p. 378.
[85]   In a letter, written from Philadelphia on 10 November, 1739: *The Works of
the Rev. George Whitefield*, I, London 1771, p. 79.
[86]   See C. H. Lowry, *op. cit.* p. 123.
[87]   See Wesley's *Sermon on Free Grace*, mentioned above.
[88]   See L. E. Elliott—Binns, *op. cit.*, pp. 199 ff.
[89]   *Works*, VII, p. 378.
[90]   The same misunderstanding plays a large part with H. Bett in his severe
judgment on Calvinism: *The Spirit of Methodism*, London 1937, pp. 147 ff.
[91]   So L. E. Elliott—Binns, *op. cit., in loco citato.*
[92]   See: H. Bavinck, *Gereformeerde Dogmatiek*, Kampen[4] 1930, IV, p. 4.
[93]   Wesley c.s. were called by Edwards "high pretenders to spirituality":
Works, VI, p. 44.
[94]   J. Ridderbos, *De Theologie van Jonathan Edwards*, 's Gravenhage 1907, pp.
289—290.

been of great importance for the general level of public life, the revivalists were no political or social reformers. The theocratic ideal lay outside their horizon: on this point they differed radically from the Puritans and from the Second Reformation in its initial stage! This difference finds a partial explanation in the fact that the revival movement was to a certain degree a result of the breaking of the *corpus christianum:* where the old, sheltering influence of a life in a community permeated by Christian ideals was falling away, an appeal was made to man as an individual; man, groping for new, experiential certitude amidst the disintegrating forces of his own times and circumstances. [95]

With both Wesley and Whitefield, eschatology only played a very small part. Their attention was so much absorbed by soteriological questions, that it is difficult to find in their works an explicit exposition of their opinions with regard to eschatological problems. Writing on the thought of Bengel, that the Millennium would begin in the year 1836, Wesley remarked: "I have no opinion at all upon that head. I can determine nothing about it. These calculations are far above, out of my sight. I have only one thing to do: to save my own soul and those that hear me". [96] And in the same year he wrote on the same subject: "I do not determine any of these things: they are too high for me. I only desire to creep on in the vale of humble love". [97] Still, he shared the belief of so many Evangelicals of these times in a Millennium, a period of a thousand years of peace and of general obedience to the Lord, which would prepare the second coming of Christ. In this period the reign of Christ would not take place by means of his corporeal presence, but in a spiritual way; it would be preceded by a period of great convulsions among the nations, and the signs of its beginning would be the fall of the antichristian powers and the conversion of the Jews to Christ. It was the idea of a *spiritual* Millennium, which distinguished the mild Chiliasm of the eighteenth century from the cruder forms of Millennarianism which were to be in vogue in some circles in the nineteenth century. [98] Wesley expected a gradual spread of the Gospel, until God would have given to his Son the uttermost

[95]   See: W. W. Sweet, *Revivalism in America, op. cit.,* pp. XI—XV.

[96]   In a letter, written in 1788: *The Letters of the Rev. John Wesley,* ed. by J. Telford, VIII, London 1931, p. 63.

[97]   *Op. cit.,* p. 67.

[98]   See: K. Dijk, *Het Rijk der Duizend Jaren,* Kampen 1933, esp. pp. 73—93. The millennarianism of eighteenth century Evangelicalism had been prepared by theologians of the Second Reformation in Holland, such as W. à Brakel and H. Witsius; in a later period we meet it with a Reformed theologian such as Charles Hodge, who expected a glorious state of the Church before the Second Coming of Christ, in which there would be a time of continued spiritual prosperity, a period in which all nations would be converted, the Jews would be brought in and knowledge would everywhere abound: *Systematic Theology,* III, London and Edinburgh 1884, pp. 857—859.

parts of the earth for his possession; [99] understood in this way, he saw
the doctrine of the Millennium as a "comfortable doctrine, of which
I cannot entertain the least doubt as long as I believe the Bible". [100]
With Whitefield, too, the eschatological element disappeared behind
the soteriological interest. Wherever we catch a glimpse of his eschatological expectations, we meet also the idea of a gradual approach of
the millennial period: "Surely JESUS CHRIST is about to set the
world in a flame. He is working powerfully at home; he is working
powerfully abroad. I trust he will continue working, till the earth be
filled with the knowledge of the *Lord*, as the waters cover the sea". [101]
Whitefield saw a relation between awakening and eschatology; in a
sermon on Zech. 4. 10 he remarked with reference to the promise that
the knowledge of the Lord would cover the earth: "Hasten o *Lord*
that blessed time! O let this Thy kingdom come! Come, not only by
the eternal preaching of the gospel in the world, but by its renovating,
heartrenewing, soul-transforming power, to awakened sinners!" [102]

The eschatology of Jonathan Edwards showed virtually little difference from that of the Methodists — but in his thinking as a whole,
eschatology performed a more important function than it did in the
thought-world of his English fellow-revivalists. Edwards, too, expected
a period of "glorious enlargement of the church of God in the *latter
ages* of the world", a period in which the Gentiles would come to the
Church and the Jewish nation would have an eminent and distinguished share. [103] But while Wesley and Whitefield made no calculations with regard to the exact time of these events, Edwards tried
to ascertain the time and place of the coming of the millennial period
by "ingenious observations on the prophecies". [104] In the time of the
Reformation, the destruction of Antichrist was begun, and the events
of Rev. 1. 7 belonged already to the past ; [105] "there is reason also to
think that the beginning of the great work of God's Spirit, in the
renewal of religion, which, before it is finished, will issue in Antichrist's ruin, is not far off"; [106] and lastly, Edwards expected the beginning of the "Latter-Day-Glory" in New England! [107]

In the Edwardian school, this millennial expectation remained an important factor. Samuel Hopkins, the representative of the so-called
"consistent Calvinism", dedicated his work on the Millennium "to the

---

[99]   See his sermon on Is. 11. 9, in: *Works*, VI, pp. 277 ff.
[100] *Works*, X, p. 228.
[101] *Works*, I, p. 293.
[102] *Works*, VI, p. 378.
[103] *Works*, II, p. 432 (in: *A Humble Attempt to Promote Explicit Agreement
and Visible Union of God's People in Extraordinary Prayer*).
[104] So the American editors of Edwards' *Humble Attempt*: *Works*, II, p. 427.
[105] *Works*, II, pp. 497, 502.
[106] *Works*, II, pp. 529 ff.
[107] *Works*, VI, pp. 55—59.

People who shall live in the Days of the Millennium", [108] and though his "chronology" of apocalyptical events was not quite concurrent with that of Edwards, he, too, saw the end of the reign of Antichrist drawing near now that "the Pope and the hierarchy of Rome" were "sinking with a rapid descent". [109] The men of the Second Awakening were eschatologically-minded to a high degree; some of them even expected the Millennium in the year 1866, so that for them the time was short indeed. They considered as signs of the times the supposed fall of the papal power, the "tottering of the pillars of Mohametan imposture", the activities of Napoleon and the interest in the world of the East, created by the formation of the Asiactic Society. [110] The "Old Calvinists" stood hesitatingly or even disavowingly aside, but their cool reasoning voice got lost in the general enthusiasm of the Second Awakening, which found expression in a pronouncement of the Presbyterian General Asssembly of 1809: "We have only to add our ardent prayer, that the angel flying through the midst of heaven, having the everlasting Gospel to preach to every kindred and tongue, may soon reach the bounds of his destination...". [111]

3. THE MISSIONARY ASPECT OF THE REVIVAL MOVEMENTS

a. The missionary aspect in general

Before we turn to a consideration of the activities of the Methodists and the men of the Great Awakening with regard to foreign missions, we have to occupy ourselves with two previous points. The first one is, that the period of Methodism saw no difference between what we distinguish as home and foreign missions. [112] In a certain sense this fact is bound up with the breaking of the corpus christianum and with the rise of new conditions as a result of the changing social situation. In the growing commercial and industrial centres of the old country the traditional parish system was unequal to the exigencies of new times, while in the transatlantic territories many people, uprooted in the rough and primitive life of the "frontier", lost the connection with their ecclesiastical background. The Methodists and the American revivalists saw the spiritual needs of the neglected masses in their immediate neighbourhood, and their answer to the challenge that came to them was an amazing evangelistic activity. Wesley saw it as his first

---

[108]   S. Hopkins, A Treatise on the Millennium, Edinburgh 1794, p. III.
[109]   Op. cit., pp. 117, 120.
[110]   See: O. W. Elsbree, op. cit., pp. 122—131, 138.
[111]   Op. cit., p. 46, quoting from The Panoplist of June 1809.
[112]   In Dutch ecclesiastical terminology the word „missions" (zending) is generally reserved for foreign missions, while for "home missions" is often used the word "evangelization" (evangelisatie).

task to go to the lost sheep of the Church of England, [113], and neither he nor the other revivalists saw any fundamental difference between the nominal Christians and the heathen who lived outside the circle of the Christian revelation. A clear distinction between the objects of home and foreign missions can only be made on the ground of the notion of the covenant of grace, which especially in Methodism played practically no part at all. [114] There can arise, however, a situation in which the boundary-line of the covenant of grace becomes almost invisible, because life in Christian countries shows the marks of a relapse into heathenism. Today we are facing such a situation in large parts of Europe, and Professor Hoekendijk has signalized the approach of the "fourth man", who lives in the post-Christian area. [115] It would be too much to say that the "fourth man" had already crossed the path of the eighteenth century revivalists: they were still confronted with the "third man", who had at least some knowledge of the traditional Christian pattern of life and some understanding of the Christian jargon. But yet there were strata of the British population which had drifted so far away from the Christian heritage that in the eyes of the Methodists they had approached the state of heathenism. When Whitefield was on the point of leaving England for his first voyage to America, his adherents in Bristol remarked that he might as well go among the Kingswood colliers, and find Indians enough there; [116] two years later, Wesley thought the inhabitants of Wales as utterly ignorant of the Gospel "as any Creek or Cherokee Indians", [117] and once on a visit to London he made the bitter remark: "O who will convert the English into honest heathens!" [118] The fact that he saw no essential difference between the revivals in Cambuslang, Kilsyth and Northhampton and the results of Brainerd's work among the Indians [119] also shows that he knew no real distinction between the missionary work among the heathen and the revivalist work at home.

The same truth is evidenced by the use of the well-known slogan "the world is my parish". It was used by Wesley — in a somewhat broader formulation — in order to defend the method of itinerant preaching. [120] Whitefield used almost the same words, when a new

---

[113] R. F. Wearmouth, op. cit., p. 124.

[114] See: J. D. du Toit, op. cit., pp. 139—141.

[115] J. C. Hoekendijk, Rondom het Apostolaat, Wending VII (1952), pp. 547—566.

[116] J. S. Simon, John Wesley and the Religious Societies, op cit., p. 253.

[117] The Journal of the Rev. John Wesley, ed. by N. Curnock, II, London 1938, p. 296.

[118] Journal, IV, p. 52.

[119] Journal, III, p. 449.

[120] "When John Wesley said 'I look upon all the world as my parish', he was defying the veto of the parish priest...": G. G. Findlay and W. W. Holdsworth, The History of the Wesleyan Methodist Missionary Society, I, London 1921, p. 32.

field of evangelizing activity opened itself in America as a result of his contacts with the leaders of the Great Awakening, [121] while in a sermon on Mark. 16. 16 he, too, applied the words "Go into all the world" in the first instance to the principle of itinerancy. [122] Though the Methodist leaders were men of a world-wide outlook, who were not blind to the needs of the heathen world, yet their first and primary interest lay in the evangelizing of the nominal Christians in England, Scotland and the colonies. They, as much as the American revivalists, wanted above all other things to bring about an awakening within the circle of Christianity — and in this way they tried to be obedient to the missionary command of their Lord.

The second point which we want to consider refers to the question whether there is a direct relation between Wesley's repudiation of the doctrine of predestination and the missionary fervour of Wesleyan Methodism. This question is answered emphatically in the affirmative by various Methodist authors who have occupied themselves with the missionary element in Methodism. Findlay and Holdsworth ascribe the Methodist interest in foreign missions to the universalist outlook, which in turn was a result of the "revolt from Calvinism"; [123] W. C. Barclay sees the missionary character of Methodism "as a natural and almost inevitable outgrowth of its fundamental doctrine of universal redemption", [124] and Carter, too, traces here a direct connection. [125] In this they only follow the example of Wesley himself, who said of the doctrine of predestination in his Sermon on Free Grace: " . . . it cuts off one of the strongest motives to all acts of bodily mercy, such as feeding the hungry, clothing the naked, and the like,—viz., the hope of saving their souls from death". [126] This viewpoint, however, is based upon a theological misunderstanding and leads to a reconstruction of the historical situation which is contrary to the real state of affairs. Theologically, it is based upon a confounding of original Calvinism with its caricature, the so-called "high Calvinism" or "hyper-Calvinism", which leaves no room for the general offer of grace and which limits salvation to the "happy few" who have received the certainty of their election by the way of mystical experiences. In this context, the doctrine of predestination gains a tyrannical dominance and spreads a sterilizing

---

[121]   See: J. D. du Toit, *op. cit.*, p. 42 note 2.

[122]   "Yes, yes, 'Go into all the world"; and though I will not pretend to say, that this enjoins ministers to go into every part of the world; yet I insist upon it, and by the grace of God, if I were to die for it, I will say, that no power on earth has power to restrain ministers from preaching, where a company of people are willing to hear...": sermon *"The Gospel a dying Saint's Triumph"*, in: *Sermons on Important Subjects, op. cit.*, p. 650.

[123]   *Op. cit.*, p. 31.

[124]   *Op. cit.*, p. XLI.

[125]   *Op. cit.*, p. 72.

[126]   *Works*, VII, p. 378.

influence. The Marrowmen as much as Jonathan Edwards, however, made room again for the offer of grace to all men, without which missionary work becomes indeed impossible. But if rightly understood, the mysterious doctrine of God's electing love gives to those who stand in the stream of missionary work the comforting certainty that the grace of God is able to break all resistance, and that the eternal fate of the nations is not dependent on man is his weakness, but on God "who showeth mercy". Election opens the gates of the unlimited possibilities of God's saving grace! [127] This is confirmed by history: in an important article on this subject E. A. Payne has shown that the missionary awakening of the eigteenth century is above all the fruit of "an Evangelicalism with a strong Calvinistic strain", and that, even more than Wesley, Edwards and Whitefield have influenced the rise of the modern missionary movement. [128] The missionary stimulus has not to be sought in the particular marks of Wesleyan Methodism, but in the common denominator of the awakening movements: the rediscovery of the note of urgency in the biblical appeal to conversion. [129]

b.   The actual service of the awakening movements to the cause of foreign missions

We have seen that the revival movements were marked by a strong evangelistic fervour which was mainly directed towards what we call at present the work of "home missions". But the question remains: have they also thought of the nations who lived outside the light of God's revelation in Christ, and if so, what was their part in the awakening of foreign missionary activity? First of all we turn to Wesley. The great leader of Methodism had been born and reared in a family in which an interest in the cause of foreign missions had been always present. Wesley's father, Samuel Wesley, in his younger days had made a plan for the evangelizing of India, China and Ethiopia. [130] Of Wesley's mother, Suzanna Wesley, it is known that she was deeply moved by the account of the work of the missio-

---

[127] See: G. Brillenburg Wurth, *Herorientering ten aanzien van de ontmoeting tussen Kerk en Wereld*, Kampen 1955, pp. 42—50.

[128] E. A. Payne, *The Evangelical Revival and the Beginnings of the Modern Missionary Movement*, The Congregational Quarterly XXI (1943), pp. 223—236.

[129] Cf. the remark of B. Citron, who writes that "the Evangelical doctrine of conversion inspired the modern missionary movement"; he also remarks: "Augustinian theology is always opposed to the accusation of Pelagians and Arminians, that their doctrine of conversion discourages the missionary approach. This fallacy is clearly rejected by all theologians who take their Evangelical commission seriously": B. Citron, *New Birth, A Study of the Evangelical Doctrine of Conversion in the Protestant Fathers*, Edinburgh 1951, pp. 60, 59.

[130] W. C. Barclay, *op. cit.*, p. XXXIX.

naries in Tranquebar, [131] while she rejoiced in her son's going to
Georgia in 1736. [132] One of the purposes of this voyage was the work
among the Indians: [133] already on board the ship which brought him to
Georgia he tried to learn, together with his friend B. Ingham, „the
Indian tongue", [134] and when, in Savannah, he met an Indian chief,
he hoped that "a door was opened for going up immediately to the
Choctaws . . ." [135] He considered the Indians as his real parishioners,
and when the English congregation of Savannah raised objections
to his plan of going to the Indians he emphatically declared, that he
would and could take charge of the English only until such time as it
was possible for him to go among the Indians. Nevertheless he
remained in Savannah, because he saw that the time was not come to
preach the Gospel of peace to the Indians, "all their nations being in a
ferment", while he did not want to become an instrument of what he
saw as an unjust policy towards them. [136]

After his return to England, his life took a new course; his evangelistic zeal was fed by deeper sources than before, and his attention
was absorbed by the religious needs of those who lived in his own
surroundings. Yet he remained interested in the cause of the Indians.
In 1776 he wrote in his *Journal,* on the occasion of a collection for the
Indian schools in America: "A large sum of money is now collected;
but will money convert heathens? Find preachers of David Brainerd's
spirit . . .," [137] and in 1787 he wrote a moving letter to Francis Asbury,
in which he said of the Indians: "Will neither God nor man have compassion upon these outcasts of men? Undoubtedly with men it is impossible to help them. But is it too hard for God? Oh that he would
arise and maintain his own cause!" [138] Negros, too, were within the
circle of his evangelistic interest: when in 1758 in the house of Natha-
niel Gilbert some "Negroe servants" had been among his audience, he
wrote in his *Journal:* "Shall not his saving health be made known to
all nations?" [139] And in later years his interest dit not fade: in 1784

---

[131]   By the reading of it in 1710 "her desire for the salvation of souls was
intensified": J. S. Simon, *John Wesley and the Religious Societies, op. cit.,* p. 80;
see also J. Wesley's *Journal,* III, p. 33. M. Schmidt presumes that Wesley himself
had already read the account of the work of B. Ziegenbalg and H. Plütschau, *Propagation of the Gospel to the East* etc., before his departure to Georgia: *Der Missionsgedanke des jungen Wesley* etc., *art. cit.,* S 89, A. 3.
[132]   See Th. E. Brigden, *John Wesley,* in: W. J. Townsend, H. B. Workman,
G. Eayrs, *A New History of Methodism,* I, London 1909, p. 190.
[133]   See his letter on this subject to Dr John Burton, one of the "Georgia Trus-
tees": *Letters,* I, pp. 188—191.
[134]   *Journal,* I, pp. 134—135.
[135]   *Op. cit.,* pp. 237—238.
[136]   *Op. cit.,* p. 298.
[137]   *Journal,* V, p. 226.
[138]   *Letters,* VIII, p. 24.
[139]   *Journal,* IV, p. 248: in the same year the two negros were baptized, on
which occasion Wesley wrote: "One of them is deeply convinced of sin, the other
rejoices in God, his Saviour, and is the first African Christian I have known. But

he wrote to one of the Methodist preachers of Nova Scotia: "The work of God among the blacks in your neighbourhood is a wonderful instance of the power of God", [140] and his attitude towards the temporal needs of the negros appears from his last letter, written to Wilberforce as a proof of his interest in the great cause! [141]

It is remarkable, however, that when it came to the point of giving concrete support to the work of foreign missions, Wesley showed some reluctance. The support was asked by Thomas Coke, undoubtedly the most important figure in the early history of Methodist foreign missions. In 1776 the first meeting between Wesley and Coke took place; under Wesley's influence, the Church of England curate became a Methodist, and, expelled from the parish where he worked, he received from Wesley the following advice: "Why, go and preach the Gospel to all the world!" [142] Coke became one of Wesley's most devoted assistants, and in 1784 he was even ordained as a "General Superintendent" for America — but even wider prospects still opened themselves to his mind's eye: in the year of his ordination he published a *Plan of the Society for the Establishment of Missions among the Heathen!* This *Plan* [143] was nothing more than a circular letter, that had as its first aim the collecting of a sum of money for missionary purposes. That in this period Coke's thoughts went out to the establishment of a mission in India appears from the fact that he had been in communication on this subject with Charles Grant, a member of the East India Company. [144] But in his *An Address to the Pious and Benevolent,* which had the cordial consent of Wesley, [145] he turned his attention towards other parts of the world, and when he had once come into living contact with the negro population of the West Indies [146] the whole of his active personality was set aflame for the cause of missions among them: "I confess, the interests of this work, particularly that part of it which relates to the myriads of poor Negroes who inhabit the British Isles in that great Archipelago, possess a large portion of my heart". [147] In the meantime, Wesley began to assume a somewhat critical attitude towards Coke's missionary enthusiasm; the old leader remarked in 1788: "The Doctor is often too hasty. He does not matu-

---

shall not our Lord, in due time, have these heathens also for his inheritance?": *op. cit.,* p. 292.

[140]   *Letters,* VII, p. 225.
[141]   *Letters,* VIII, p. 265.
[142]   C. J. Davey, *The March of Methodism,* London 1951, p. 4. Though at that time these words meant nothing more than: "become an itinerant preacher", they almost had a prophetic flavour!
[143]   Reprinted in: G. G. Findlay and W. W. Holdsworth, *op. cit.,* II, pp. 14—16.
[144]   See Editor's note in: J. Wesley, *Letters,* VII, p. 322.
[145]   In a letter to Dr Coke d.d. 12 March, 1786, he wrote: "I greatly approve of your proposal for raising a subscription": *Letters,* VII, *in loco citato.*
[146]   See: G. G. Findlay and W. W. Holdsworth, *op. cit.,* II, pp. 36 ff.
[147]   Th. Coke, *To the Benevolent Subscribers for the Support of the Missions . . . for the Benefit of the Negroes and Carribs,* London 1789, p. 17.

rely consider all circumstances", [148] and one year later he wrote: "... ought we to suffer Dr Coke to pick out one after another the choicest of our young preachers?" [149] Wesley agreed with Coke's missionary ideals in principle, but Coke's tempo was too fast for him, and the work on the home front had absorbed his attention to such a degree that it had quite superseded his old active interest in the cause of foreign missions. It seemed as if in the circle of Methodism Coke's voice was "crying in the wilderness". He stood alone in his interest in the work of the London Missionary Society, he stood alone when he pleaded for missions in Africa and Bengal, and almost alone he bore the burden of the work in the West-Indies. Between 1791 and 1797 Coke met with some distrust in Methodists circles. Were the British Methodists afraid that his forceful personality would exert too dominant an influence? Besides, the failure of the expedition to Sierra Leone, of which he had been the great promotor (1796), added to the Methodist hesitance with regard to foreign missions. [150] Political reasons also played their part. While especially in L. M. S. circles the missionary enthusiasm was partly fed by an optimistic valuation of the great political events in the initial stage of the French Revolution, the politically conservative Methodists [151] contemplated the same events with a horror that had a dampening influence on the interest in new missionary experiments. [152] And while Baptists and Congregationalists saw their own period as a time of the providential opening of doors, Wesley and many of his followers thought that the "times of the heathen" had not yet approached in such a fullness that the way for great missionary enterprises was already open. Perhaps this was connected with the fact that Wesley expected the conversion of the heathen after the general awakening of Christianity. He sometimes saw the need for direct and immediate work among what he called "the outcasts of men"—but at the same time he was afraid that the building up of a great missionary commitment would weaken the revival work at home and so not would hasten, but rather retard, the coming of the "times of the heathen", which he expected with the certainty of his great and living faith. [153] It must be added that Coke, too, was one-sided in his outlook: while he was active on behalf of the missionary work in the West and the East, he had but little interest in the cause of the mission among the Indians of North America, whose

---

[148]   *Letters*, VIII, p. 101.
[149]   *Letters*, VIII, p. 129.
[150]   C. J. Davey, *op. cit.*, p. 66.
[151]   „Methodism was heartily opposed to the French Revolution, and its opposition to the Dissenters was in part a reflection of this fear and hatred": E. R. Taylor, *Methodism and Politics 1791—1851*, Cambridge 1935, p. 13.
[152]   See: C. J. Davey, *op. cit.*, pp. 13, 16.
[153]   Cf. his sermon on *The General Spread of the Gospel*, Is. 11. 9, *Works*, VI, pp. 277—286.

conversion he saw lying in the far future. [154] And especially in its first stage his work was too personal and individualistic to be fully integrated into the whole of the Methodist community. Still, his appeals were not without result: when in 1804 the work was brought out of the purely personal sphere by the formation of a "Committee of Finance and Advice" [155] it became more solidly rooted in Methodist soil, and in 1813—the year in which Coke died on a missionary voyage to Ceylon—a surprising awakening of the missionary ideal took place in the Methodist circle. While the older leaders—for whom the method in which they had been trained had become a sacrosanct tradition— had almost vetoed Coke's expedition to Ceylon, the younger generation started the foundation of Methodist Missionary Societies in every district; and the eager response which they received from the Methodist people proved, that Methodism was still missionary in core and essence! [156]

Whitefield's attitude to foreign missions was not very different from that of Wesley. He, too, had seen the evangelizing of the Indians as one of his tasks in Georgia; [157] he, too, was interested in the work of Brainerd; he, too, collected money for an Indian school [158] — but his main interest lay in the sphere of the revivalist work. After his death, Lady Huntingdon sent out a "missionary party" to Georgia, but troubles of various kind caused the expedition end as a failure. [159] In later years, the missionary interest of the "Huntingdonians" found an outlet in the work of the L. M. S. [160]

Of more direct importance to the cause of foreign missions, however, was the figure of Jonathan Edwards. As we saw above, he came into contact with Whitefield during the initial stage of the Great Awakening, and between the two spiritual movements which they represented a cross-fertilization took place: while Whitefield's theology was deepened, he imparted to the men of the Great Awakening the full vigour of his fervent evangelism. There is a direct relation between Great Awakening and missions. The men of the Awakening not only turned their attention towards the white population, but also to the negros [161] and the Indians; Edwards himself worked among the Indians in Stockbridge, a mission in which, as a minister working in North-

---

[154]   For quotations from Coke see: W. C. Barclay, op. cit., pp. 201—202.
[155]   See: G. G. Findlay and W. W. Holdsworth, op. cit., I, p. 36.
[156]   See for a description of the meeting in Leeds Old Chapel, whence the movement started: G. G. Findlay and W. W. Holdsworth, op. cit., I, pp. 45 ff.
[157]   J. P. Gledstone, op. cit., p. 60; see also J. Wesley, Works, VII, p. 410: "In the year 1738 Mr Whitefield came over to Georgia, with a design to assist me in preaching, either to the English or to the Indians".
[158]   G. Whitefield, Works, II, p. 206.
[159]   E. A. Payne, The Church Awakes, London 1942, p. 101.
[160]   In loco citato.
[161]   Cf. K. Scott Latourette, op. cit., III, p. 225: "The Great Awakening spread to the Negroes. In their revivals, Presbyterians, Baptists and Methodists made a marked appeal to the blacks."

hampton, he had already shown a lively interest. [162] But a greater name as a missionary was acquired by Edwards' younger friend, protégé and prospective son-in-law David Brainerd, whose *Diary* is still one of the classics of missionary history. As a student, Brainerd was touched by the Great Awakening. Because of a tactless remark regarding his principal, he was expelled from Yale College—but as a minister of the (New Side Presbyterian) Synod of New York he found a splendid field of action among the Indians, especially the Delawares; he died, however, at an early age. The accounts of his travels, work and meditations, published by Jonathan Edwards, reveal to the fullest extent the spirit of the Great Awakening, with its light and shadows: they give evidence of a consuming passion for the glory of God and the salvation of man, but they also contain a self-analysis which sometimes tends to understate the liberating power of Christ's redeeming work. Brainerd's work was read with reverence by great spirits such as Wesley, John Erskine, Carey and Martyn, and in this way it exercised a powerful influence upon the missionary awakening. In the meantime, we have to realize that Brainerd was not the only son of the Great Awakening who became a missionary among the Indians: Scott Latourette gives the names of S. Occom—a converted Indian!—, E. Wheelock, J. Sergeant, J. Brainerd, and—in a younger generation— S. Kirkland. [163]

But even more important than the direct missionary results of the Great Awakening is the part which it played in the awakening of the missionary ideal in Scotland and England. We saw already something of the influence exercised by Brainerd's *Diary*. This influence was almost equalled, however, by one of Edwards' own works, published in America in 1748: *An Humble Attempt to Promote Explicit Agreement and Visible Union of God's People in Extraordinary Prayer*. In this work Edwards gave a description of the "Concert of Prayer", formed in 1744 by a group of ministers in Scotland who were strongly influenced by the "Cambuslang Work" and who had a deep interest in the Great Awakening in New England. [164] The hopes expressed in the prayers of the Scottish ministers were that God "would appear in his glory, and favour Zion, and manifest his compassion to the world of mankind, by an abundant effusion of his Holy Spirit on all the churches, and the whole habitable earth, to revive true religion in all parts of Christendom, and to deliver all nations from their great and manifold spiritual calamities and miseries, and bless them with the unspeakable benefits of the kingdom of our glorious Redeemer, and

---

[162]   O. E. Winslow, *op. cit.*, p. 270.
[163]   *Op. cit.*, III, pp. 220—221.
[164]   J. Foster, *The Bicentenary of Jonathan Edwards' "Humble Attempt"*, I.R.M. XXXVII (1948), pp. 375—381, gives the names of those, whom he thinks to be the originators of the "Concert".

fill the whole earth with his glory". [165] By giving publicity to this "Concert of Prayer" and by stimulating the praying interest in the spread of the Gospel, Edwards has rendered an important service to the cause of missions. There is a link between Edwards' book and the work of William Carey: in 1784 Dr John Erskine of Edinburgh sent the "Humble Attempt" to a group of leading Baptist ministers in Northhamptonshire, whom it excited to fervent prayers for the extension of God's Kingdom! [166]

In America also Edwards' call to prayer found a late echo: in 1795 a "Concert of Prayer" started in America; [167] some years later, the first American missionary society was founded (the New York Missionary Society), followed by a number of other societies, all of which entered the field of missionary activity with deep enthusiasm and great élan. [168]

4. THE MISSIONARY MOTIVES IN THIS PERIOD

a. Political motives

It is evident that in the circle of the awakening movements utilitarian motives could only take a very small place. When missions are taken in hand by reason of political interest or in order to keep intact the social *status quo*, a process of secularization has set in which is contradictory to the spiritual character of missionary work. The awakening movements, however, were a reaction against the secularizing tendencies in their period and a symptom of the longing for a form of religion in which the spiritual elements would be dominant. We can understand Wesley's indignation, when he suspected that the official policy towards the Indians in Georgia was not righteous: he did not wish to have his work made an instrument in their subjection. [169] The same attitude is evident among the later Methodists: no radical reformers themselves, they were all the less prepared to be the servile tools of the secular powers! And when we turn to the men of the Great Awakening, we see that Edwards defended the Stockbridge Indians against their exploiters, that Brainerd in his mystical passion was far removed from any political motivation and that Kirkland almost tried to identify himself with the Indians among whom he worked. Kirkland's political activity during the War of Liberation by keeping the Oneidas on the side of the colonists was accidental: the motives of his missionary work lay on another level! [170]

---

[165]   J. Edwards, *An Humble Attempt...* in: *Works*, II, p. 440.
[166]   See. E. A. Payne, *The Prayer Call of 1784*, London 1941, passim.
[167]   O. W. Elsbree, *op. cit.*, pp. 130—137.
[168]   *Op. cit.*, pp. 51—76.
[169]   *Journal*, I, pp. 237—238.
[170]   *Dictionary of American Biography, in loco citato.*

b. The cultural motive

This motive, too, played a greater part in circles which were influenced by the spirit of the "Aufklärung" and which consequently moved more or less along Erasmian lines, than in revivalist circles. Every revival movement has a tendency to keep a certain distance from the life of culture: especially in those periods in which the need of a revival movement makes itself felt, cultural life is often so much tinged by the spirit of the age, that it is seen as the "world" which has to be shunned by the Christian. The revivalist sees more the necessity of separation than of integration, and he is interested in conversion, not in compromise. It must be said that Methodism was not as bigoted as it is sometimes supposed to have been: the Methodists had respect for cultural values [171], and they could enjoy „the good things of life", such as music and poetry — but never without restrictions, never without scruples and reserves. [172] They were certainly not the people who could be set on fire for the mere ideal of the spread of a Christian culture!

In the circle of the New England missionary work the situation was somewhat different; there, the old Puritan tradition, which aimed at the reformation of the totality of life, was still a living force. The missionaries among the Indians saw a conversion towards the New England way of life as an indispensable concomitant of the conversion to Christ. [173] Edwards' work among the Indians of Stockbridge consisted partly in the teaching of the Christian commands: the Indian way of life had to be replaced by that of the New England Calvinists, and the Puritan Sabbath observance in particular was strictly enjoined upon the Indian community. [174] Yet the main motive of the New England missionaries lay elsewhere: there is some truth in the remark of Miss Winslow that they "had little interest in Indians except as souls to be saved". [175]

---

[171]   According to Wesley, clergymen had to possess "all the courtesy of a gentleman, joined with the correctness of a scholar": *Addres to the Clergy, Works,* X, p. 485.

[172]   See for Wesley's appreciation of music: L. E. Elliott-Binns, *op. cit.,* p. 81. His interest in poetry in contrast to that of the Methodists in general appears from a letter, written in 1788 to a poet who had asked Wesley's advice with regard to the publication of some of his poems; after having remarked that in the poems there is much to be found that has his appreciation, but that they are not so "tender or pathetic" as to attract the general attention, Wesley goes on: "And they lie utterly out of the way of the Methodists, who do not care to buy or even to read (at least the generality of them) any but religious books...": *Letters* VIII, p. 82. Interesting is the different attitude of John and Charles Wesley with regard to the musical inclinations of Charles' sons: see F. Baker, *Charles Wesley as revealed by his letters,* London 1948, pp. 110—114.

[173]   See above, p. 29.

[174]   O. E. Winslow, *op. cit.,* p. 275.

[175]   *Op. cit.,* p. 274.

c. The ascetic motive

In the former chapter we saw that during the first decades of the eighteenth century the ascetic ideal played practically no part in the awakening of the missionary spirit. In the period of the great revivals, however, we meet it more than once, though always incidentally: it remains confined to the personal sphere, it never becomes the dominant motive of a whole group, as was the case with the Iro-Scottish monks, who as "peregrini Christi" brought the Gospel to the most distant parts of Western Europe. [176] The first time we meet it in eighteenth century England is with the Wesley's on their first voyage to Georgia. They went out with the purpose of working among the Indians; but the deepest motive behind their zeal to shoulder the burden of a life in the wilderness was not so much the care for the souls of the Indians as the care of their own souls: [177] they thought that they would be led on the way to righteousness by the arduous, lonely task among the savages in Georgia. [178] Without any doubt, we are meeting here the influence of Law: "By reading the writings of Mr Law, and others of a similar kind, they were deeply impressed with the necessity of holiness. According to their apprehensions, true holiness is attained principally by means of sufferings, mentally and bodily; and hence they adopted this mode of life..." [179] The ways of Law and the Wesleys parted, however, not only in theological, [180] but also in practical respects: while Law became a mystic recluse, John Wesley especially

---

[176] See: J. H. Bavinck, *Inleiding in de Zendingswetenschap, op. cit.,* p. 288.
[177] Cf. John Wesley, *Journal,* I, p. 109: "Our end in leaving our native country was not to avoid want... but singly this — to save our souls, to live wholly to the glory of God"; in his letter to Dr. Burton of October 10, 1735, he wrote: "My chief motive, to which all the rest are subordinate, is the hope of saving my own soul", *Letters,* I, p. 188. Charles Wesley went to Georgia in a deep depression: "In vain have I fled from myself to America", letter of Febr. 5, 1736; later his thoughts became brighter, though the desire to find God in the solitude of Georgia remained: "But Georgia alone can give me the solitude I seek after. I cannot look for a long life there, but neither do I count that a blessing": see F. Baker, *op. cit.,* pp. 22 and 27.
[178] Wesley expected that his stay in the wild regions of Georgia would help to mortify the desire of the flesh, that it would deliver him from many occasions "of indulging the desire of the eye", etc.: *Letters,* I, pp. 189—190.
[179] Th. Jackson, *Memoirs of the Rev. Charles Wesley,* London 1875, p. 28, as quoted by E. W. Baker, *op. cit.,* p. 10.
[180] In his interesting and important study on the missionary idea with Wesley before 1738, M. Schmidt rightly calls attention to the fact that there is a relation between Wesley's asceticism and his desire of a return to the ideals of primitive Christianity: *art. cit.,* SS. 92 ff. We wonder, however, whether it is not an over-statement with regard to the importance of this period in Wesley's life, and at the same time an undervaluation of the influence which Law exercised upon Wesley in the years before 1738, when Schmidt remarks of Wesley's missionary idea: "Er trägt ... alle Kennzeichen der Ursprünglichkeit ... Dieses Missionsverständnis ... dürfte auch in der Missionsgeschichte einen besonderen Platz verdienen. Mission als Schlüssel zum Ursinn des Evangeliums...": *art. cit.,* S. 95.

became the active crusader, [181] excellently characterized by the description which Melvill Horne gives of the Methodist in general: "He feels himself in a pushing world, and pushes with the foremost". [182] Wesley's attitude towards the world became positively aggressive: he had made his peace with God through Christ, and the certainty of this experience engulfed the ascetic tendencies, which had played a part in his first missionary experiment! [183]

In Brainerd's *Diary* we meet another type of asceticism, akin to that which we came across in the work of a typical representative of the Second Reformation in Holland, J. Heurnius. [184] Brainerd wrote: "I rejoiced in my work as a missionary; rejoiced in the necessity of self-denial and still continued to give myself up to God . . . "; [185] earlier, he had already written: "It was delightful to give myself away to God, to be disposed of at his pleasure. I had some feeling sense of the sweetness of being a pilgrim on earth", [186] and: „. . . . my heart exulted in the thoughts of any distressses that might alight on him [*i. e.* his brother John] or me, in the advancement of Christ's kingdom". [189] Brainerd was a mystic with a Calvinistic background; his asceticism had not the aim of finding righteousness before God along the road of holiness, as was the case with Wesley before his second conversion. Brainerd wanted to make sure of his election by coming into closer communion with God along the way of self-denial. Ascetic traits are also to be found with other missionaries in the circle of

---

[181]   Charles Wesley's attitude, too, had changed: cf. the following hymn, as quoted by H. Carter, *op. cit.*, p. 30:

> Not in the tombs we pine to dwell,
> Not in the dark monastic cell,
> By vows and grates confined;
> Freely to all ourselves we give,
> Constrained by Jesu's love to live
> The servants of mankind.

[182]   Melvill Horne, *op. cit.*, p. 36.

[183]   J. D. du Toit, *Het Methodisme*, op. cit., p. 135, sees asceticism lying at the root of the Methodist movement. Prof. du Toit distinguishes two kinds of ascetics: those who withdraw themselves from the struggle in this world, and those who go into the world to take there their ascetic message; Wesley belongs to the second type of ascetics. It is, however, preferable to reserve the word "asceticism" for what is according to Prof. du Toit the first type of ascetic attitude: the world-flying attitude. This does not mean that asceticism always implies the seeking of solitude and loneliness. But the actions of the true ascetic are always determined by a negation of those aspects of life which he fears to be a hindrance on the road to full communion with God. Seen in this light, Wesley's first going to America had a definitely ascetic aspect, because it contained the elements of negation and flight; Wesley's later travels, however difficult they may have been and however many hardships they may have entailed, were not ascetic in the strict sense of the word, because they were not motivated by the element of negation, but by positive love to God and man!

[184]   See above, p. 20.

[185]   *The Diary and Journal of David Brainerd*, London 1902, I, p. 193: entry of 1 July, 1754.

[186]   *Op. cit.*, I, pp. 58—59: entry of 20 July, 1742.

[187]   *Op. cit.*, I, pp. 65—66: entry of 4 Sept., 1742.

the Great Awakening, such as Gideon Hawley, missionary to the Iroquois, who "by his own statement would have given up his labours among the Indians a hundred times, except for the glory of the sacrifice he knew himself to be making, and the "sanctity" of the missionary's character as he aspired toward it". [188] But on the whole, asceticism remained restricted to individual cases; the "pilgrim-idea" never won the place which it had, e. g., with the Moravians, [189] and the ascetic motive got no foothold in the totality of the thinking of the Methodists and the men of the Great Awakening. [190] Nor did the idea of the necessity of a certain form of collective self-denial, as penance because of "the white man's debt", take a place of any importance with the politically conservative Methodists or with those American Presbyterians and Independents who expected the beginning of the Millennium in happy New England!

d. The romantic motive

We now turn to the romantic motive, to the stimulus given to the awakening of the missionary ideal by the thrill of newly discovered areas, which are seen together with their population under the most romantic and fascinating aspects. It might seem an anachronism to speak of romantic elements in a period which was dominated by a naive belief in reason. We must not forget, however, that Methodism and its parallel movements were partly a reaction against the cool reasonableness of their century: to a certain degree they were a return to feeling, and in this way they helped to blaze the trail for the great romantic movement. [191] Furthermore, romanticism is so deep a human quality, that it is impossible to confine it within chronologically fixed limits. There was a romantic element in the expectance of the Wesleys, that they would find peace with God in the solitude of the Georgian woods, and we know that in the same period John Wesley had a romantic view of the Indians. [192] But he was too much of a realist to be carried away by romantic views: he soon started to look at the

---

[188]   O. E. Winslow, op. cit., p. 274.
[189]   They called their house in Little Wildstreet in London the "Pilgrim-House": A. Wauer, op. cit., p. 118.
[190]   According to Miss Winslow, there is neither a suggestion at any point that J. Edwards regarded the missionary's life as peculiarly saintly, nor the slightest hint of an ascetic attitude towards his own labours: op. cit., p. 276.
[191]   See: F. C. Gill, The Romantic Movement and Methodism, London 1937, passim.
[192]   In the summer of 1736 he considered the Choctaws as "the least polished, that is, the least corrupted of all the Indian nations": Journal, I, p. 238; during the same period he wrote of the Chickasaws, that they seemed to have "so firm a reliance on Providence, so settled a habit of looking up to a Superior Being in all the circumstances of life, that they appear the most likely of all the Americans to receive and rejoice in the glorious Gospel of Christ", Letters, I, p. 229.

Indians with a more critical eye; [193] Brainerd, too, did not see the Indians in a romantic light — in 1742 he wrote in his *Diary*: "Rode sixteen miles to Mantauk, and had some inward sweetness on the road; but something of flatness and deadness after I came there and had seen the Indians". [194] The general judgment of the Americans of that period on the Indians was hard and utterly unromantic: "a base, ungrateful people, with a blasphemous worship and with an ignorance, which could excite nothing but compassion". [195]

In a later period, when the idea of the "noble savage" received new momentum from the accounts of the voyages of Captain Cook and Captain Wilson in the Pacific, Wesley preserved his critical soberness: G. Keate's *Account of the Pelew Islands* he considered as a dangerous book because it exalted the virtues of natural man; [196] in his *Thoughts on a Late Publication* he wrote: "Nor therefore can I believe that there is, I will not say a nation but an individual upon earth, who are either born without shame, as Captain Cook affirms the nations of Otaheite to be, or to be wholly unblamable, both in their tempers and actions, as Captain Wilson affirms the nations of Pelew to be". [197] It may be that Wesley in his later years even evinced a certain lack of imagination with regard to the Church's missionary task: his attitude towards the plans of Coke was almost narrow-minded, and while other groups of Christians were carried away by the dazzling possibilities for missionary work which offered themselves as a result of the new discoveries, the majority of the second Methodist generation persisted in their unimaginative attitude. It must be said that this lack of romanticism was not altogether a disadvantage: it saved the Methodist missions from those deceptions and disillusions which accompanied the initial missionary ventures of other groups of British Christians, [198] and when once the missionary work of the Methodist community began to unfold, it appeared to be founded on the solid basis of a Christian realism. It is the same spirit of realism we meet in Calvinistic America during the period of the Second Awakening: with the young men who offered themselves for missionary work "there was nothing involved which could be termed a spirit of romance or adventure". [199]

e.   *The motives of love and compassion*

General Oglethorpe, the friend of Bray and the man with whom the Wesley's had so many contacts during their stay in Georgia, was

---

[193]   Cf. his view of the Indians in Georgia at the end of 1737: *Journal*, I, p. 407.
[194]   *Diary*, I, p. 94.
[195]   O. E. Winslow, *op. cit.*, p. 274.
[196]   *Journal*, VIII, p. 29 (entry of 1 December, 1789).
[197]   *Works*, XIII, pp. 374—375.
[198]   E. g. in the initial stage of the missionary activity of the L. M. S., as we shall see in the next chapter.
[199]   O. W. Elsbree, *op. cit.*, p. 141.

characterized by Pope in the following lines: „One, driven by strong benevolence of soul, shall fly, like Oglethorpe, from pole to pole". [200] No doubt the praise was deserved, but the good general was not the only one who was driven by "benevolence of soul": as we saw in the former chapter, the idea of benevolence was even one of the watch-words of the eighteenth century. At the end of the century, however, a man with a burning passion for the cause of God dared to ask whether the general acceptance of the idea of love in the eighteenth century was really in accordance with the deep tones of the Bible, and his answer was negative: "The richest fruit of our philanthropy has been a cold, ineffective pity". [201] Perhaps Melvill Horne's criticism was onesided and not quite fair: the pity of the men of the eighteenth century may have been cold, but it was certainly not always ineffective. It often missed, however, the deep background, the soteriological set-ting, which the words "love" and "pity" receive in the light of biblical revelation. Here lies the difference between the idea of "benevolence" which we met in the circle of rationalism, and the concept of love as we find it with the Methodists and the men of the Great Awakening: with them it has, as its background, "the love that passeth knowledge". When Wesley speaks of " a love of benevolence, — of tender good-will to all the souls that God has made", he knows that this love finds its source in another love, the love of Christ for sinners: " . . .this love sweetly constrains him to love every child of man with the love which is here spoken of . . .". [202] "Constrained by Jesus' love to live the ser-vants of mankind"! [203] The love of the Methodist is qualified by the words of the 116th Psalm: "What shall I render unto the Lord for all his benefits toward me?" We are reminded here of an event in the life of the Welsh Methodist, Howell Harris, who in 1735, the year in which "the fire of the love of God" fell upon him, after the use of the sacrament, saw Jesus, hanging on the Cross, and at the same moment "felt some insatiable desires after the salvation of poor sin-ners". [204]This event recalls the well-known experience of Count Zinzen-dorf, when he stood before a painting of the crucified Lord! We meet with the same spirit in Whitefield [205] and in Brainerd, [206] while in the period of the Second Awakening Shipping Townsend remarked in a sermon, preached at Boston in 1802, that "pure gratitude to God be-

---

[200]   As quoted by G. O. Trevelyan, *English Social History, op. cit.*, p. 347.
[201]   Melvill Horne, *op. cit.*, p. 13.
[202]   In: *Sermon on Charity* (text 1 Cor. 13. 1—3): *Works* VII, p. 47.
[203]   The growth of this concept of love has perhaps been influenced by the world of thought of Ziegenbalg and Plütschau, with whom the idea of love took a central place in the missionary motivation: see M. Schmidt, *Der Missionsgedanke dos jungon Wesley etc., art. cit,* SS. 89—90.
[204]   J. S. Simon, *The Revival of Religion, op. cit.*, pp. 140—141.
[205]   See: O. Riecker, *Das Evangelistische Wort, op. cit.*, p. 100.
[206]   "I feel much more kindness, meekness, gentleness and love towards all mankind than ever": *Diary*, I, p. 69.

cause of one's election ought to suffice as an incentive to propagate the Gospel among sinners everywhere". [207] Love as a grateful response to the love of God in Christ was a mighty motive in the missionary attitude of the revivalists!

The motives of pity and compassion, too, were abundantly present in the revivalist circle. Like the Moravians, the Methodists had a special sympathy for the "outcasts of men": "Sinners alone His grace receives: no need of Him the righteous have; he came the lost to seek and save". [208] The Methodist preacher knew: "We are all by nature children of wrath"; [209] it was the great passion of Methodists and other revivalists to save souls, to liberate men from the bondage of darkness, to bring them into communion with the fountain of life. What Elliott-Binns remarks of the Evangelical movement in the Church of England can be applied to the whole of the revival movement: "It was this intense hunger for souls and care for the salvation of individuals on the part of the promoters and agents of the movement which gave strength to their endeavours". [210] Wesley wrote in 1785, that his only end was to save sinners: "what other end could I possibly have in view? or can have at this day?" [211] and these words of the aged Wesley were in complete harmony with those of the young Whitefield, that are to be found in a letter of 1739: "Oh Rev. Sir, it grieves me to see people everywhere ready to perish for lack of knowledge. I care not what I suffer, so that some may be brought home to Christ". [212]

Brainerd reproached the Dutch settlers with the fact that they had "no regard for the souls of the Indians"; [213] he looked forward to the day that the Indians would be "delivered from the bondage of the powers of darkness . . .". [214] Indians and negros often received the epithet "poor": Wesley spoke of "these poor outcasts", Brainerd of "the poor Indians", Coke of "the poor slaves" — and they meant the word "poor" primarily in a spiritual sense: poor without Christ. And when the work of Methodist foreign missions had come to receive a place in the conscience of the Methodist people, these same chords were struck. At the famous meeting in Leeds of 6 October 1813, a layman remarked: 'Under such a ministry [i. e. the Methodist ministry]

---

[207]   O. W. Elsbree, op. cit., p. 139.
[208]   From the "conversion-hymn" of Charles Wesley, which begins with the following lines: "Outcasts of men, to you I call, Harlots, and publicans, and thieves!": as quoted by H. Carter, op. cit., p. 31.
[209]   See: J. Wesley, A Short History of Methodism, Works, VIII, p. 350.
[210]   Op. cit., p. 423.
[211]   Works, XIII, p. 373.
[212]   Works, I, p. 121; in the same way Wesley wrote in his letter to Dr. Burton of 10 October, 1735, that his "second motive to visit the heathens" was "the desire to impart to them what I have received — a saving knowledge of the gospel of Christ": Letters, I, p. 190.
[213]   Diary, I, p. 105.
[214]   Diary, I, p. 171.

we enjoy "feasts of fat things, of wines on the lees well refined"; and shall we see our heathen brethren famishing with hunger and not send them one dish of the dainties of the Gospel?" [215] The idea of the "hungry" heathen was perhaps an echo of the tidings which had come from the mission field; so years ago the widow of Francis Gilbert had written to Wesley, that the British at home "can hardly conceive the hunger and thirst experienced by a poor Negroe, when he has learnt that his soul is immortal and is under the operation of awakening influences". [216] It contained, however, the danger of a certain feeling of spiritual superiority: though *idealiter* the compassionate love of the Methodist was accompanied by a feeling of solidarity-in-guilt, already the repeated use of the epithet "poor" pointed in a dangerous direction. Besides, the idea of pity could bring the fulfilment of the missionary task into a subjectivist sphere: the missionary went out to those for whom pity was *felt*, who perhaps by incidental circumstances were considered as being pitiable. Here, too, lies a partial explanation of the fact that it was so difficult for Methodism to obtain a broad view of the "ends of the earth" in relation to the missionary task, while in the same way can be explained also the preference of the Methodists for missions among the negro slaves. We find a moving illustration of the Methodist's compassion of the negros in the *Journal* of F. Garretson, who wrote in 1777: "Many times did my heart ache on account of the slaves in this part of the country, and many tears did I shed, both in Virginia and Carolina, while exhibiting a crucified Jesus to their view... While many of their sable faces were bedewed with tears, their withered hands of faith were stretched out, and their precious souls made white in the blood of the Lamb". [217]

The motive of love took a special form in the period of the Second Awakening: Samuel Hopkins tried to escape the influence of a too anthropocentric soteriology in the missionary motivation by the idea of "disinterested benevolence", in which the soteriological motive is subordinated to the idea of the glory of God. [218] In the same period we hear the old Edwardian tones in a sermon of H. Kulloch's, preached in 1803 before the General Assembly of the Presbyterian Church in the U.S.A.: "Suppose in that dreadful day some miserable condemned pagan just ready to sink into the eternal flames should turn his despairing eyes upon you and exclaim in a voice that shall rend your heart: "Why, why did you not warn me of this day...?" [219]

Lastly, in Methodist circles the "hunger for souls" took an individu-

---

[215] G. G. Findlay and W. W. Holdsworth, *op. cit.*, I, p. 51.
[216] *Op. cit.*, II, p. 35.
[217] Quoted from W. W. Sweet, *Revivalism in America, op. cit.*, pp. 104—105.
[218] See: O. W. Elsbree, *op. cit.*, p. 148, and W. W. Sweet, *Revivalism in America, op. cit.*, pp. 154—155.
[219] O. W. Elsbree, *op. cit.*, p. 139.

alistic form: not peoples in their totality, but individual persons, were brought into contact with the Gospel message. We saw already that this individualism, which was as strong in the British [220] as in the American [221] revivalist circles, in a greater or lesser measure lost sight of the ideas of "Church" and "covenant". This explains much of the revivalist missionary methods; it explains also why the ecclesiological motive —the motive of the expansion of the Church as such—was present neither with the Methodists nor with the men of the Great Awakening. On the other hand, we have to acknowledge that, while in the Church-type in which the ecclesiological motive tends to take a place of importance—the "High Church type"—missions threaten to become a matter of interest for a group of ecclesiastical leaders or official Church organs only, the "Low Church type" is often better able to bring about a close integration between missionary interest and congregational life. [222]

f. The motive of inner compulsion

Methodism and revivalism meant a return to the belief in the immediate guidance of the Holy Spirit. For those who were "awakened", the idea of "guidance" began to function in an almost mystical way. [223] The man of the revival movement believed in direct communion with God — a communion which was not restricted to the inner room, but which was experienced in the service of the Lord in the midst of the full bustle of life. The history of Methodist missions records several examples of men and women who by direct inner compulsion were driven to missionary work or to a new attitude towards their surroundings. When John Baxter was sent as a ship-wright to Antigua, he felt that God was calling him to carry on the work of Gilbert. [224] When Coke had to appoint a missionary for St Vincent, he also had a strong consciousness of guidance: "It is impossible to have any doubt concerning the will of God in respect to the appointment of a missionary for this island . . . all is as clear as if it was written with a sunbeam". [225] Freeborn Garretson set his slaves free after he had heard a "voice" during his morning prayers: "It is not right for you to hold fellow-creatures in bondage. You must let the oppressed go free". [226]

---

[220]   L. E. Elliott-Binns, op. cit., p. 424.
[221]   R. Boon, op. cit., pp. 178—179.
[222]   See among others: G. G. Findlay and W. W. Holdsworth, op. cit., II, p. 58.
[223]   Charles Wesley sang: "Hangs my helpless soul on Thee" (in the hymn: Jesus, Lover of my soul) — and Elliott-Binns writes: "Knowing their weaknesses and acknowledging their failures, they [i. e. the early Evangelicals] depended utterly upon God. So close was their walk with Him that they sought His help and guidance in even the smallest details of life": op. cit., p. 429.
[224]   F. Deaville Walker, The Call of the West Indies, London s. a., pp. 30—31.
[225]   Op. cit., p. 41.
[226]   E. S. Tipple, The Beginnings of American Methodism, in: W. J. Townsend, H. B. Workman, G. Eayrs, A New History of Methodism, II, op. cit., p. 80.

Coke felt that it was God who guided him to Ceylon: "God Himself had said to me: Go to Ceylon". [227] And a converted Indian, John Stewart, had quite a remarkable experience in 1816: he declared himself to have been led to his missionfield, to his work among the Wyandotte Indians, by powerful voices which he heard during his prayers in the fields. [228]

Some of the above-mentioned examples of confidence and surrender are indeed moving. [229] Yet here, too, the danger of subjectivism is not imaginary: neither Asbury nor Coke felt themselves "guided" towards the work of the Indian missions — and this subjective view of the two leaders influenced the attitude of the whole of the American Methodist community towards the cause of the Indian missions. [230] And it is not impossible that Wesley's hesitation with regard to Coke's plans was partly caused by the fact, that he did not feel himself to have clear "guidance" in this matter!

g. The eschatological motive

Last of all, we come to the eschatological motive. We have observed already that, with the Methodists, the eschatological element disappeared behind the soteriological interest. They were moderate Millennarians, but their eschatological expectations played practically no part in the development of their missionary ideals. The salvation of souls absorbed their attention in such a measure, that they perceived no place for the work of missions in the context of the great drama of history. German Pietists and Moravians were inspired by the thought that the coming of the Kingdom was near at hand [231] — but with a "non liquet", the Methodists passed on to the order of the day: the salvation of souls whenever and wherever God was leading the way and giving them a opportunity. And if their eschatology played any part at all, it performed rather the function of a comforting background than of a strong stimulus! [232] They saw the Kingdom approaching along the road of the conversion of individual souls, [233] and they believed that

---

[227] C. J. Davey, op. cit., p. 19.
[228] J. A. Faulhoun, The Work of American Societies, in: W. J. Townsend, H. B. Workman, G. Eayers, op. cit., II, p. 364.
[229] Cf. J. H. Bavinck, Inleiding in de Zendingswetenschap, op. cit., p. 291.
[230] See: W. C. Barclay, op. cit., pp. 201—202.
[231] See: J. C. Hoekendijk, Kerk en Volk in de Duitse Zendingswetenschap s.l. [1948], pp. 19, 20, 44.
[232] Cf. the hymn of the Welsh Calvinistic Methodist William Williams (of Pantycelyn), Church of Scotland Hymnary Hymn 387:
        O'er those gloomy hills of darkness,
        Look, my soul, be still and gaze;
        All the promises do travail
        With a glorious day of grace...
[233] Perhaps the most "eschatological" utterance of Wesley in relation to the work of missions is that, which we find in a letter to Dr. D. Humphreys, the secre-

God himself would find the ways and show the times of the great conversion of the heathen: "Yea, he can find out a thousand ways to foolish man unknown. And he surely will..." [234] But while the Methodist leaders did not trouble themselves about the "chronology" of the coming events, Jonathan Edwards thought to hear in his own time the signals of the approach of the Kingdom; he "brought the people to the very threshold of the millennium, and he was obviously intoxicated with the prospect". [235] This was no new accent in American circles: already Cotton Mather had thought he saw in the work of the German Pietists the first signs of the great outpouring of the gifts of the Holy Spirit for the propagation of the *evangelium*. [236] But Edwards proclaimed his ideas with a certainty and a fervency, which made a deep impression, not only in his own surroundings, but also in Scotland and later on in England. [237] Eschatology became a positive factor in the missionary development: the missionary ideal was lifted up upon the waves of fervent expectations, and the times of resigned and almost passive waiting gave place to a period of new activity: "Great things might be done for the advancement of the Kingdom of Christ at this day by those who have ability, by establishing *funds* for the support and propagation of religion; by supporting some who are eminently qualified with gifts and grace in *preaching the gospel* in certain parts of the country, which are more destitute of the means of grace..."; [238] more even than Brainerd himself, Edwards saw in the "results" of Brainerd's work and of that of other missionaries among the Indians a sign of the approach of the "days of mercy". [239] And in the period of the Second Awakening the same eschatological expectations returned: J. C. Moore wrote in *The Panoplist* of November 1811: "Prophecy, history and the present state of the world seem to unite in declaring that the great pillars of the Papal and Mahometan impostures are now tottering to their fall... Now is the time for the followers of Christ to come forward boldly, and to engage earnestly in the great work of enlightening and reforming mankind". [240] The missionary

---

tary of the S.P.G., written from Savannah in 1737, in which he remarked that, when once the *sanguis martyrum* would have fallen, when once the first missionaries would have been murdered,"... praising God in the midst of flame with joy unspeakable and full of glory, — then the rest, waxing bold by their sufferings, shall go forth in the name of the Lord God, and by the power of his might cast down every high thing that exalteth itself against the faith of Christ. Then shall ye see Satan, the grand ruler of this New World, as lightning fall from heaven; Then shall even these lands be full of the knowledge of the Lord as the waters cover the seas": *Letters*, I, p. 225.

[234]   J. Wesley, *Works*, VI, p. 286.
[235]   P. Miller, *Jonathan Edwards*, s.l. 1949, p. 318.
[236]   E. Benz, *art. cit.*, p. 48.
[237]   See above, p. 92.
[238]   *Works*, VI, pp. 193—194.
[239]   *Works*, II, p. 481.
[240]   As quoted by O. W. Elsbree, *op. cit.*, p. 128.

enthusiasm of various American circles in the beginning of the nineteenth century is closely connected with the eschatological optimism
of that period!

In this context something has to be said about the place which the
missionary command took in the thinking of the revivalists. It does not
often occur among the Methodists — and where we meet it, it is considered as the self-evident background of all missionary work: its validity is not denied, but its function is very small because of the domi-
nating influence of the motives of love and compassion. In our introductory chapter, we saw that in Dutch Calvinistic circles the idea
that the missionary command had been fulfilled by the apostles had
gradually disappeared during the seventeenth century. The American
Puritans had a special theory: though it seemed as if the missionary
command had been fulfilled by the apostles, the devil had hidden some
nations in order to snatch them away from the influence of the Gospel
— but with the approach of the last days these nations also would
hear the sound of the Gospel message. [242] So the missionary command
would receive a new function, when the "great day of the Lord" would
approach: it was put in an eschatological context. In the same context
we meet it again during the period of the Second Awakening: the
"great commission" found a new actuality in the lives of young people
such as Adoniram Judson and J. S. Mills, because their hearts had
been kindled by the fire of a flaming eschatological expectation! [243]

---

[241] See Whitefield's Sermon on Mark. 16. 15—16, in: *Sermons on Important
Subjects, op. cit.*, especially p. 650; cf. also Francis Asbury, *Journal*, III, p. 23, as
quoted by W. C. Barclay, *op. cit.*, p. 102: "Go, says the command, go into all
the world — go to the highways and hedges. *Go out* — seek them. Christ came
seeking the lost sheep".
[242] E. Benz, *art. cit.*, pp. 48—49.
[243] See: O. W. Elsbree, *op. cit.*, pp. 140—141.

Chapter IV

THE GREAT BREAK-THROUGH OF THE
MISSIONARY IDEA

We have now come to one of the most important periods in the
history of the awakening of the missionary ideal in Great Britain.
In the short time between 1792 and 1813, several missionary societies
sprang into being, members of various Churches were brought to a
new consciousness of their missionary task, a number of writings was
published which tried to stimulate the missionary interest, more than
one missionary venture was started, and the missionary ideal received
a new impetus which made its influence felt during the whole of
what is called by Scott Latourette "the great century of missions".
When we try to find the motives behind this new interest in the
cause of missions, we come across a complex of factors which cooperated in making the long repressed idea of missions one of the
constituent elements in the development of British religious life. We
meet the fertilizing influence of the deepest motives of the Methodist
revival, we also see how Edwards' missionary attitude made its
influence felt through various channels; we have to take into consideration the reactions on the revolutionary events of the period,
because they were related to the eschatological expectations of these
times, while eschatology in its turn influenced the missionary awakening; and we see how romantic ideals which were not unrelated to the
"noble-savage" idea played a role in circles that were at the same
time deeply convinced of the depravity of human nature! So in this
chapter, too, we have to put the quest for these missionary motives
against the background of the development of British life in general
and of British religious life in particular, in the period which marks
the transition to a new epoch in the history of the world.

1. GREAT BRITAIN DURING THE PERIOD OF THE FRENCH
REVOLUTION AND ITS AFTERMATH

a. *New expansion and new responsibilities*

The series of cataclysmic events which rocked the foundations of
various European countries in the late eighteenth century had only

an indirect influence upon Great Britain. In fact, the main stream of
the Revolution left Britain undisturbed; the wars with revolutionary
and Napoleontic France were mainly fought out in the maritime sphere,
and they gave to England a fresh opportunity to gain the naval
ascendancy over the world seas; new markets opened up in America,
Africa and the Far East, and the acquisition of new colonial territories
in various parts of the world was at least a partial compensation for
the loss of the American colonies. Safe behind the shield of its navy, [1]
Britain was able to enter upon fresh transoceanic ventures in a period
when the rest of Europe was almost completely under the laming
influence of war-time conditions, while at the same time it could follow
the course of European events with the eyes of an interested onlooker.
This was the period in which the foundations of the Second Empire
were laid. In relations with Eastern countries, the emphasis shifted
from the maintaining of mercantile contacts to the assuming of
territorial responsibilities. In India, the imperialist policy of Clive was
continued by Warren Hastings. At the same time, the India Bill of
1784 opened the way for a more direct control of Indian affairs by
the British government. [2] The bill found its origin in a growing uneasiness which existed in British circles with regard to the state of
affairs in India—an uneasiness which played a part in the various
attacks on the monopolist position of the East India Company. [3] And,
in its turn, there was a relation between "an uncomfortable awareness
of the abuses of British rule in India and the growing humanitarianism
of the age". [4] At first, this humanitarianism was characterized by rather
vague ideals. The parliamentary spokesmen of the growing humanitarian sentiment—we mention here the names of William Pitt and
Edmund Burke—had a keen eye for the faults of the British administration in India, and they wanted to bring Anglo-Indian relations
within the sphere of justice and morality; but they had no clear
perception of the fact that the assuming of territorial responsibility
entailed a duty to open the doors for the introduction of Christianity. [5]
Yet some voices were raised on behalf of the freedom to propagate
the Christian faith in India: those of the Baptist missionaries, but also

---

[1] See: G. M. Trevelyan, *English Social History, op. cit.*, p. 466.
[2] The bill, introduced by Pitt, had the character of a compromise—but one of
its merits was that "it placed the political conduct of the Company in due subordination to the policy of the national Government": C. H. Philips, *The East
India Company 1784—1834*, Manchester 1940, p. 33.
[3] "Contemporary statesmen anticipated the danger of a great empire being
created and ruled by Britons independent from the authority of the British
cabinet": C. H. Philips, *op. cit.*, p. 23.
[4] Lucy S. Sutherland, *The East India Company in Eigtheenth Century Politics*,
Oxford 1952, p. 367.
[5] See: E. Marshall Howse, *Saints in Politics, The Clapham Sect and the
Growth of Freedom*, Toronto 1952, pp. 65—66.

those of a group of Anglican chaplains in India. [6] They found support in high circles: the brilliant politician Wilberforce and the influential director of the East India Company Charles Grant valiantly threw themselves into the struggle for opening up India to the work of Christian missions. The men of the "Clapham Sect" [7] repeatedly attacked the policy of cool and even hostile neutrality which the Company followed on this question. [8] They had to face a strong opposition: the general Briton of these times did not consider religion as an "article of import", [9] and the mutiny of Indian troops in 1806, though caused by factors which lay in the military sphere, was used in the debate on this point as an argument against the introduction of Christianity. [10] As a counter-argument they brought to the fore the humanitarian aspect of the matter: both Wilberforce and Grant directed the attention of Britain to the horrible custom of the burning of widows [11]—but at the bottom of their humanitarian views lay the conviction that only the full Gospel of Christ could bring real happiness to the millions of India. [12] The long and difficult struggle had a twofold aim: the establishment and official recognition of the Church of England in India and freedom for Christian missionaries to propagate their faith among the Indian population. As Churchmen, the leaders of the Clapham Sect expected much through the realization of the first ideal, [13] while as Evangelicals they were ready to cooperate with

---

[6]   It was under the influence of the Evangelical chairmen of the Company, mockingly called the "pious chairs", that in the years between 1793 and 1813 about twenty Evangelical chaplains were sent out to India: C. H. Philips, *op. cit.*. p. 159.

[7]   The "Clapham Sect" was a group of prominent Evangelical laymen who found their rallying-point in the village of Clapham, where many of them possessed a house; their leader was William Wilberforce, who led them in the fight for the application of Christian principles to the great political questions of those days. See for them and their influence: E. M. Howse, *op. cit.*, passim.

[8]   A policy, which could only take rise after the breaking of the *corpus christianum:* in its initial stage the Company gave active support to the propagation of the Christian faith in India. See: F. Penny, *The Church in Madras, op. cit.*, pp. 180—181.

[9]   E. M. Howse, *op. cit.*, j. 65, mentions an utterance of Lord Macartney's, made in 1763 at the Court of China: "The English ... have no priests or chaplains with them ...".

[10]   See: C. H. Philips, *op. cit.*, pp. 162 ff. Philips defends in his work the policy of neutrality: he even calls the advice of Dundas to the Bengal Government to base its religious policy on political expedience rather than on Christian principles "the saner view", p. 165.

[11]   See: E. M. Howse, *op. cit.*, pp. 66—67, and C. H. Philips, *op. cit.*, pp. 158—159.

[12]   "These reformers were reformers because of a religious urge", remarks E. R. Taylor in his *Methodism and Politics 1791—1851*, Cambridge 1935, p. 97.

[13]   Grant especially thought much of a mission under official patronage; even in 1784 he was in correspondence with Thomas Coke on this subject; while the Methodists had no faith in such a method, Grant was of the opinion that through the channel of the work of the Established Church a great service could be done to the cause of missions in India: E. M. Howse, *op. cit.*, p. 69.

Nonconformists in order to reach the second goal. [14] After many years of defeat and disappointment, at last the great break-through took place: in 1813, the year in which the Charter of the East India Company had to be renewed, Parliament opened the door for "the introduction of useful knowledge, and religious and moral improvement" in India; at the same time, the British possessions in India got the ecclesiastical status of an Anglican diocese. [15] Of course this did not mean that Parliament had come to an official recognition of the missionary obligation towards the natives: the first aim of the establishment of the Church of England in India was to promote the spiritual welfare of the white population—but at any rate the Church received official status in India, and in this way the conditions were created under which there could take place the proclamation of the Gospel in a circle wider than that of the white colonists. In addition, after some opposition a motion of Wilberforce was adopted, which asked the insertion of the clause "that the Board of Control should be empowered to give licenses of residence in India to persons improperly refused them by the Court of Directors": [16] this clause cleared a way for missionaries not belonging to the circle of the official representatives of the Established Church.

During these years of struggle when India's doors were opened to the missionary activity of the Christian Churches, another sphere of action was created which for more than one reason aroused the imagination of the British people. During the whole of the eighteenth century the mysteries of the South Sea had fascinated the British mind; from 1704 onward various collections of voyages in the South Sea had been published—but it was Cook who was the first to unveil in a scientifically justified way the mysteries of the Pacific territory. [17] The voyages of Cook afford a remarkable proof of the fact that British public life in this period was secularized to a large degree: while the expeditions of the sixteenth and early seventeenth century took their place within the framework of the *corpus christianum*, religion played a very small part in the eighteenth century expeditions into Oceania: the "Endeavour"—the ship with which Cook made his first great voyage in 1768—had not even a chaplain on board, and when during the stay on Tahiti one of the members of the expedition died, the body was buried at sea because Cook did not want to offend the religious feelings of the Tahitians. [18] It is no wonder that practically no attempt

---

[14]   During the agitation of 1812, it was Wilberforce who secured himself of the support of the Nonconformists by emphasizing the second aim: C. H. Philips, *op. cit.*, p. 169.

[15]   See: H. Gnattingius, *op. cit.*, p. 67

[16]   C. H. Philips, *op. cit.*, p. 191.

[17]   See: J. A. Williamson, *The Ocean in English History*, Oxford 1941, pp. 164 ff.

[18]   J. A. Williamson, *Cook and the Opening of the Pacific*, London 1946, pp. 114, 117.

was made to bring the inhabitants of Oceania into contact with Christianity! [19] Though Cook did not pass by in silence the dark sides
of the life of the Tahitians, his descriptions, and more still those
of J. Hawkesworth, who "pictured the natives as the sum of all earthly
charm and beauty", [20] contributed to the rise of the romantic view
of the population of Oceania. [21] This romantic view in its turn was
connected with the influence which the writings of Rousseau began to
exercise in England: Hawkesworth in particular was a great admirer
of Rousseau's world of thought. [22]

In the same period, however, the men of the "Clapham Sect" faced
the grim reality of the slave trade, and together with other groups
they tried to awaken the British conscience on this point. They had
to struggle against the opposition of vested interests and of lukewarm
conservatism. Their first aim was the abolition of the slave trade;
partly owing to their activity, the Abolition Bill passed on March 25,
1807 [23]—but as their ultimate goal they saw the extinction of slavery
itself. In the year of Wilberforce's decease that goal was reached;
one of his friends could remark: "The day which saw the termination
of his labours saw also the termination of his life". [24]

b.   *The impact of the revolution on the British mind*

One of the most interesting features of this period is the way in
which the British people reacted upon the revolutionary movement of
these times. While some of the older generation evinced an almost
hysterical fear for all that could possibly be associated with revolutionary strivings, a number of younger intellectuals saw in the French
Revolution the dawn of an era of universal rigtheousness. [25] This wave

---

[19]   One—clumsy—misionary attempt is mentioned: in May 1769, two Tahitians
were invited to attend "Divine Service" at the fort, in the hope "that it would
give occasion to some enquiries on their part, and some instructions on ours . . .
yet when the service was over, neither of them asked any questions": J. Hawkesworth, *An Account of the Voyages, undertaken . . . by Comm. Byrom, Capt. Wallis,
Capt. Carteret and J. Cook*, II, London 1773, p. 127.

[20]   L. B. Wright, *Religion and Empire, op. cit.*, pp. 160—161.

[21]   Cf. the paintings of William Hodges, who—in the true romantic way—
painted Tahiti as an earthly paradise. For a reproduction of one of these paintings,
see: *Engelse Landschapsschilders van Gainsborough tot Turner*, Catalogus Museum
Boymans, Rotterdam 1955.

[22]   Roddier remarks that since the publication of Hawkesworth's Accounts of
the South Sea voyages and the subsequent reaction of the *Monthly Review*, which
paper drew a parallel between Hawkesworth's description of the inhabitants of
Tahiti and Rousseau's *Second Discourse*, "le sauvage est tout à fait à la mode . . .
il est l'incarnation d'un idéal moral que l'on doit prendre pour modèle si l'homme
veut retrouver le bonheur primitif que l'évolution de la société lui a fait perdre":
H. Roddier. *J. J. Rousseau en Angleterre au XVIIIe Siècle*, Paris 1950. p. 131.

[23]   See: E. M. Howse, *op. cit.*, p. 64.

[24]   E. M. Howse, *op. cit.*, p. 165.

[25]   "To a great many young intellectuals in England, the Revolution was the
incarnation of ideal liberty, fraternity and justice. This romantic upsurge was more

of enthusiasm for what happened in France coincided with the origin of a number of voluntary associations. These were in essence an adaptation of British society to the emergencies of modern times and their rise can be considered as nothing less than a sociological necessity: they filled up "many of the gaps left by the limited scope of State action", [26] and, we may add, of ecclesiastical activity. They were no new phenomena: in the first instance their rise was connected with the breaking of the *corpus christianum;* the dissolution of the integral unity of Church, state and society left a vacuum which had to be filled by voluntary activity. But the fact that the number of these societies rose considerably in a period of great political ferment and that indeed some of them were meeting-points for sympathizers with the Revolution, made every new association suspect in the eyes of the politically conservative: speaking of the newly created missionary societies, the later Lord Justice-General David Boyle remarked in the General Assembly of the Church of Scotland on 27th May, 1796: "Observe, Sir, they are *affiliated,* they have a common *object,* they *correspond with each other,* they *look for assistance from foreign countries,* in the very language of many of the seditious societies. Above all, it is to be marked, they have a *common fund ...*". [27] It is evident that this almost hysterical fear of all that had only a superficial resemblance to revolutionary political activities did much harm to the cause of missions! [28] In the meantime we must not forget that the anti-revolution attitude did not always lead to a negative evaluation of the work of the missionary societies: the "Clapham Sect" was definitely conservative in politics—Wilberforce was a supporter of Pitt's "repressive acts"— while nevertheless its members rendered immense services to the cause of missions! As a rule the Anglican Evangelicals were as vehemently opposed to the French Revolution as their High Church brethren; the Evangelicals were on the side of the High Tories, [29] and a man such as Bishop Porteous, who sympathized with the Evangelical movement, saw in the Revolution the approach of the day of Antichrist. [30]

---

widespread in England than in Scotland; but in the latter country, young intellectuals were swept from their traditional moorings by the same tide": W. M. Kirkland, *The Impact of the French Revolution on Scottish Religious Life and Thought with special reference to Thomas Chalmers, Robert Haldane and Neil Douglas* (MS thesis of the University of Edinburgh), Edinburgh (New College) 1951, pp. 4—5.

[26] G. M. Trevelyan, *English Social History, op. cit.,* p. 497.

[27] [R. Heron], *Account of the Proceedings and Debate in the General Assembly of the Church of Scotland, 27th May 1796,* Edinburgh 1796, p. 55. This little work is further quoted as *Account:* see for the authorship of Robert Heron: D. Mackichan, *op. cit.,* p. 78.

[28] It would be interesting to draw a parallel between Boyle's denunciation of the missionary societies and the attitude of some adherents of the present American Senator Mc Carthy towards certain aspects of the ecumenical movement!

[29] Ch. Smyth, *Simeon and Church Order, op. cit.,* p. 296.

[30] S. C. Carpenter, *Church and People 1789—1889,* London 1933, p. 1.

The Methodists, too, were on the conservative side. [31] Quite different, however, was the attitude of the Dissenters: not only Unitarians, such as Dr. Richard Price, saw in the French Revolution the approach of the Millennium, [32] but also the Calvinist David Bogue, Independent minister of Gosport, thought to discern in the events in France the first signs of the coming of Messiah's great day; [33] Scottish Seceders, as much in the two Secession Churches as in the Relief Church, [34] welcomed the political changes of the new period, and the Haldanes, too, were not unresponsive to the call of the revolutionary movement. [35] This optimistic attitude in Dissenting circles with regard to the French Revolution can be explained from the coincidence of apocalyptic expectations with ideals of liberty, which both seemed to be realized by the possibilities which the Revolution opened up for "the spread of civil and religious liberty, accompanied also by a diminution of the spirit of popery". [36] A. Lincoln writes that "the Dissenters felt that they were living in one of those rare epochs, when history momentarily loses its natural uniformity, and responds directly and catastrophically to the will of God". [37] At the end of the century, however, the horrors of the French Revolution brought the greatest part of the Dissenters back to a more critical and reserved attitude; the influence of "Rational Dissent" waned, and the new evangelicalism of orthodox Nonconfirmity was more interested in evangelism than in political activity. [38] In this way, the cleavage between Dissenters and Evangelicals was lessened and the way was opened for a fruitful cooperation between both evangelistically-minded groups. [39]

---

[31] See: E. R. Taylor, op. cit., especially pp. 88—114.

[32] See: E. A. Payne, The Free Church Tradition in the Life of England, op. cit., pp. 90—93.

[33] J. Morison, The Fathers and Founders of the L.M.S., I, s. 1., 1839, p. 504.

[34] G. Struthers, The History of the Rise, Progress and Principles of the Relief Church, Glasgow 1843, pp. 378 ff.

[35] Kirkland writes that "the impact of the French Revolution aroused [Robert] Haldane from a life of ease and complacency", though on the other hand both he and Dr Bogue "steadfastly refused to commit themselves to social and political action": op. cit., pp. 110, 107.

[36] William Carey in his An Enquiry into the Obligations of Christians to use Means for the Conversion of the Heathen, reprinted in facsimile from the edition of 1792, London 1891, p. 79.

[37] A. Lincoln, Some Political and Social Ideas of English Dissent 1763—1800, Cambridge 1938, pp. 50—51.

[38] G. M. Trevelyan, English Social History, op. cit., p. 494: "While the war lasted the influence of the new type of Nonconformity was anti-French and on the whole conservative"; cf. E. Halévy, Histoire du Peuple Anglais au XIXième Siècle, I, Paris³ 1924, p. 462: "On peut suivre, de 1792 à 1815, à mesure que le temps passe, la décadence de l'esprit révolutionnaire dans les sectes".

[39] See: Ch. Smyth, op. cit., p. 266.

2. THE BRITISH CHURCHES AT THE DAWN OF A NEW ERA

a. *The ecclesiastical scene*

The Church of England was affected by the influence of the
Methodist movement in a twofold way. On one hand there was a
strong reaction against all forms of "enthusiasm": Latitudinarians such
as Bishop W. Warburton and more still Bishop R. Watson represented
an attitude of mind which found part of its strength in the negation
of all that Methodism stood for. [40] But on the other side, Methodism
exercised a fertilizing influence on a group of Evangelicals, who
wanted to remain loyal to the Church of England, but who at the
same time wished to share in the blessings of the rediscovery of the
elementary Biblical truths by the Methodist leaders. [41] During the
greater part of the eighteenth century the Evangelicals formed only a
small minority in the Anglican Church, but at the end of the century
the tide turned: Beilby Porteous, who became Bishop of London in
1787, was so much on the Evangelical side that he was sometimes
considered as a Methodist; [42] a number of younger clergymen joined
the Evangelical group, and under the guidance of able leaders such
as John Venn, Rector of Clapham, [43] Isaac Milner, president of
Queen's College at Cambridge, [44] and above all Charles Simeon,
curate-in-charge of Trinity Church, Cambridge, [45] the Evangelicals
became an influential group in the Church of England. A number of
leading Evangelicals, for the greater part clergymen, regularly gathered
at the meetings of the *Eclectic Society,* founded in 1783. The members
of the "Eclectic" discussed a variety of important and pertinent subjects, and more than once the necessity of Evangelical action was
pleaded at the meetings of this Society. [46] Yet the Society's tempo was
not so dynamic as that of some Evangelical dissenting circles, where
the "Eclectic" was considered by some as a "holy, but not heroic

---

[40] Warburton considered all forms of enthusiasm as "a viperous brood":
Watson was so much of a Latitudinarian, that he had only "a very general broad
belief': J. H. Overton and F. Relton, *op. cit.,* pp. 163, 259.

[41] "It is impossible to separate Evangelicalism from Methodism, even if their
relation to each other offers a problem that would also need closer investigation":
Y. Brilioth, *Three Lectures on Evangelicalism and the Oxford Movement,* London
1934, p. 6.

[42] J. H. Overton and F. Relton, *op. cit.,* p. 254.

[43] He was a son of Henry Venn, one of the leading figures among the early
Evangelicals. See for the father: L. E. Elliott-Binns, *op. cit.,* pp. 321 ff.; for the
son: M. L. Loane, *Cambridge and the Evangelical Succession,* London 1912, pp.
160 ff.

[44] See: G. R. Balleine, *op. cit.,* pp. 128 ff.

[45] See for him: H. C. G. Moule, *Charles Simeon,* London² 1948 (first edition:
1892).

[46] See: E. M. Howse, *op. cit.,* pp. 73 ff.

circle". [47] The gravity of the times led to a new seriousness in various strata of the population: in higher circles also the message of the Evangelicals found a response, [48] Wilberforce's *Practical View* made a deep impression, [49] and the activities of the "Clapham Sect" proved that the "practical view" of its members found its sequel in an attitude of life which combined the best traditions of the old Puritanism with the evangelistic fervour of the new revival movements. For the Church of England, the Evangelical Revival was a blessing in more ways than one: it brought many of its members to a deeper understanding of their spiritual heritage; it made Evangelical Anglicans feel "at home" within the circle of the Established Church who would otherwise perhaps have left to join an Evangelical dissenting denomination; and it infused the rather dormant Anglican community with a spirit of new vigour and enthusiasm. Other groups also shared in the salutary deepening of religious life: Bishop Samuel Horsley, a "High-Church-man", pleaded a return from moralistic preaching to the proclamation of the essential truths of the Christian message, [50] and the "Clapton Sect", a group of Anglicans who can be considered as the forerunners of the Oxford Movement, played a part in the awakening of the evangelistic ideal in the Church of England. [51]

The Dissenters also were carried along by the new tide. They, too, had reaped some of the fruits of the Methodist campaigns: in more than one instance, people who had been converted as a result of the work of itinerant preachers found a spiritual home in a Dissenting Church with an Evangelical ministry; quite a number of Calvinistic Methodists joined an Independent congregation, "where they seemed to pour young blood into an aged frame", [52] while the General Baptists witnessed a revival through the work of Dan Taylor, a former Methodist who had turned Baptist. [53] At the same time, there was the influence of Jonathan Edwards: leading Congregationals were strengthened in their Evangelical attitude through the contact with Edwardian Calvinism, [54] and we saw already how, in the circle of the Particular Baptists, it was the influence of Edwards which brought about a transition from a narrow "hyper-Calvinism" to a Calvinism

---

[47]   See: A. Haldane, *The Lives of Robert Haldane of Airthrey and of his brother James Alexander Haldane*, London 1853, p. 121.

[48]   See for a description of the change which took place in the life of the higher classes: G. M. Trevelyan, *English Social History*, op. cit., pp. 492 ff.

[49]   In 1797 William Wilberforce published his *A Practical View of the Prevailing Religious System of Professed Christians in the Higher and Middle Classes of this Country, contrasted with Real Christianity*; the work immediately attracted the attention of wide circles.

[50]   J. H. Overton and F. Relton, op. cit., p. 257.

[51]   J. McLeod Campbell, op. cit., p. 53.

[52]   D. Bogue and J. Bennett, op. cit. II, London² 1833, p. 576.

[53]   E. A. Payne, *The Free Church Tradition*, op. cit., pp. 80—81.

[54]   E. A. Payne, *The Evangelical Revival and the Beginnings of the Modern Missionary Movement*, art. cit., p. 233.

that was evangelically-minded and fit to become the spiritual substratum of Carey's missionary work. [55] The Congregationals as much as the Particular Baptists had excellent leaders: we mention only the names of David Bogue and Andrew Fuller, men of learning and ability, Calvinists touched by the spirit of the Evangelical Revival and missionary-minded to a high degree—and they did not stand alone! Only the Presbyterians stood outside the stream: their congregations had almost all turned Unitarian, and the gulf between orthodox and "rational" Dissent had widened because of the deepening of Evangelical convictions with the first group and the increase of radical ideas in the second. [56]

In Scotland we are confronted with the same phenomenon as in England: there, too, several circumstances cooperated in strengthening the influence of the Evangelicals. The Evangelical Party in the Church of Scotland regained much of its influence under the able leadership of Dr. John Erskine, minister in Edinburgh; as we saw above, it was through his mediacy that Edwards' *Humble Attempt* was introduced into Scotland and England. [57] At the same time it must be said that there took place a considerable change in Moderatism: while there have always been "shades of Moderatism and shades of Evangelicalism" and while there was always present a large middle group "of an indeterminate shade", [58] in the later period of Moderatism especially many Moderates returned to a more orthodox position: [59] they were still more or less Erastian with regard to ecclesio-political matters, but in doctrinal questions they were without doubt more Calvinistically-minded than their predecessors had been. On the other hand, a later generation of Evangelicals was at least formally influenced by the spirit of Moderatism: a recent study on Thomas Chalmers, one of the great leaders of Scottish Evangelicalism and one of the "fathers" of the Disruption of 1843, remarks that Chalmers himself always retained something of the suppleness and breadth of the Moderates. [60]

The spirit in the Relief Church is characterized by the fact that they bore the nick-name of "Scots Methodists". [61] Many Seceders were losing something of their old rigidity [62] and became active sup-

---

[55] See E. A. Payne's quoted article on p. 227.
[56] See: A. Lincoln, *op. cit.*, pp. 230, 234.
[57] See p. 93.
[58] H. Watt, *Thomas Chalmers and the Disruption*, Edinburgh etc. 1943, p. 6.
[59] J. de Bruijn, *Thomas Chalmers en zijn Kerkelijk Streven*, Nijkerk 1954, p. 16.
[60] J. de Bruijn, *op. cit.*, p. 2.2
[61] G. Struthers, *The History of the Rise, Progress and Principles of the Relief Church, op. cit.*, p. 254.
[62] In this respect there was some difference between the Associate Synod ("Burghers") and the General Associate Synod ("Anti-Burghers"): though even in the circle of the "Anti-Burghers" the spirit was not so narrow as it had been when Adam Gib was the undisputed leader, yet they were still less inclined to cooperate with Christians in other Churches than were the "Burghers"; moreover, "Burgher" preachers appealed frequently to the feelings, the "Anti-Burghers"

porters of a number of Evangelical enterprises; their force, however, was weakened by a continuing process of splitting. [63] One man deserving special mention is Robert Haldane, a layman who together with his brother James Alexander took an important part in the revival of religious life in Scotland. At first, Haldane had close contacts with English Congregationalists, to whom he felt akin in more than one respect; in a later phase, however, he turned towards Baptism and became the originator of Scottish Baptism. He was a typical representative of the type of "free-lance-evangelists", who, mistrusted by the ecclesiastical leaders and unable to get a clear view of the real meaning of the Church, have yet rendered an important service to the cause of the Kingdom by their missionary fervour. [64]

Established and Dissenting Churches, English Episcopalians and Scottish Presbyterians, old communities and younger groups—they all shared in the new life, which stirred both in and outside the ecclesiastical world during these important years of transition!

b. The theological background

This is not the place to give a full treatment of the theological background of the various religious groups in Britain about 1800: we only want to bring into prominence some traits which are characteristic of the new Evangelicalism that formed the substatrum of the missionary awakening. The first thing which attracts our attention is the fact that not only genetically but also with regard to their ideological background there is a close relationship between Methodism and the Evangelicalism of our period. Both movements had a strong soteriological interest, both movements put great emphasis upon the value of the individual soul, both movements had a place for the elements of feeling and experience. [65] Last of all, both movements also possessed some

addressed chiefly the intellect: D. Scott, *Annals and Statistics of the Original Secession Church*, Edinburgh [1886], p. 595.

[63]   A split took place in the two Secession Churches on the ground of a different view of the task of the Government, as it related to the interpretation of Chapter XXIII, 3, of the *Confession of Westminster*, which is parallel to Article 36 of the *Confessio Belgica*: in 1799 the "Old Light" group separated from the Associate Synod, while in 1806 a similar separation took place in the more conservative General Associate Synod. See J. McKerrow, *History of the Secession Church*, II, Edinburgh 1839, pp. 108—167, 300—352.

[64]   See: A. Haldane, *op. cit.*, passim.

[65]   "The whole genius of early Methodism was experimental... The religious contribution of Methodism was, therefore, the recovery of the evangelical witness and the evangelical experience—the spiritual fact that real penitence, real faith, a real surrender of the heart and life to Christ, brings an assurance of the pardon and the grace of God... which leads directly to an intimacy of religious fellowship and a zeal of passionate evangelism": H. Bett, *The Spirit of Methodism*, London 1937, pp. 127—128; William Wilberforce defended the admission of the passions into religion on the ground of the fact that in Christianity all the faculties of our nature are brought "into their just subordination and dependence; that so the whole man, complete in all his functions, may be restored to the true ends of his being, and be devoted, entire and harmonious, to the service and glory of God... My son, give me thine *heart*": *A Practical View* etc., London^2 1797, p. 84.

weak spots in common, of which the most prominent was perhaps their lack of a clear doctrine of the Church. [66] With regard to this point, however, the difference which existed between Wesley and his followers repeated itself in the circle of Evangelicalism in the inverse direction: while Wesley's followers were less "Church-minded" than their leader, the later Evangelicals saw more of the value of the Church and its order than their predecessors did. Some of the early Evangelicals did not care very much about parish boundaries and sat loose in their relation to the Church of England; Simeon, however, was a real Churchman, who brought home to his followers the great significance of the idea of the Church. [67]

A second point which invites our attention is the fact that the theological background of a great part of the Evangelicals in our period was formed by a more or less moderate Calvinism. This holds true in the first place for the Independents: the deepening of the cleavage between liberal and orthodox Dissent had made the last group more conscious of its theological heritage; the necessity of a policy of irenic compromise was not felt as strongly as in the times of Doddridge; the prominent Independent leader David Bogue was a convinced Calvinist, and a remarkable light is thrown on the convictions of the average Independent by the fact that the L.M.S. missionaries, going out on board the "Duff" in 1796, excommunicated two of their brethren who had some doubts about the doctrine of limited atonement! [68]

During the eighteenth century the Particular Baptists were the most consistent Calvinists of English Protestantism. At the end of the century their theological leader was Andrew Fuller, who in his *The Gospel Worthy of all Acceptation*, written in 1781, took leave of the "hyper-Calvinism", to which he, too, had once adhered. His eyes were opened by the fact that Eliot, Brainerd and other missionaries "appeared to him, in their addresses to these poor, benighted heathens, to have none of those difficulties with which he felt himself encumbered", [69] while the combined influence of the theology of the "Marrowmen" [70] and of Jonathan Edwards [71] made him a champion of the free offer of grace to all sinners. In due time he became one of the leading Evangelical theologians of his period, [72] a man whose

---

[66] "Their weakness was... that in their devotion to St Paul's Epistle to the Romans they forgot St Paul's Epistle to the Ephesians... It was in the ultra-personal conception of Christianity that the essential defect of Evangelicalism lay...": S. C. Carpenter, *op. cit.*, pp. 40—41.

[67] See: Ch. Smyth, *op. cit.*, passim.

[68] R. Lovett, *The History of the London Missionary Society*, I, London, 1899, pp. 48—49.

[69] A. Fuller, *The Complete Works*, II, London 1831, p. 1.

[70] *Op. cit.*, p. 12.

[71] "The greatest, though not the only instruction that I have received from human writings in these subjects, has been from *President Edwards's Discourse on Justification*": Fuller in a letter to Dr Ryland, 22 January, 1803, *op. cit.*, p. 553.

[72] Fuller considered himself as a "strict Calvinist" in distinction from the

influence reached far across the boundaries of his own "denomination". [73]

It needs no special mention that the Scottish Evangelicals, who
belonged to Churches in which the Westminster Confession of Faith
was still a living part of their spiritual heritage and who were almost
all of them influenced by Edwards' theology, were convinced Calvinists.
More remarkable is the revival of Calvinism in the circle of Anglican
Evangelicalism. There is no direct connection between original Anglican
Calvinism and the Calvinism of the Evangelicals: the Arminian-
Laudian world of thought had fully superseded the older traditions.
The revival of Anglican Calvinism is rather due to the influence of
Whitefield; it was the chaplains of the Countess of Huntingdon, too
"Church-minded" to leave the Anglican Church after Lady Selina had
made her group a dissenting denomination, who formed the nucleus
of the rising Evangelical party within the Church. Theology was not
the strongest side of Evangelicalism, [74] yet the thoughts of the
Evangelicals moved within the framework of Calvinistic theology,
though they did not strongly emphasize its specific points. [75] Their
attitude towards the problem of the extension and the character of
the offer of grace is to be found in Basil Woodd's answer to the
question whether redemption was general or particular, put at the
April meeting of the Eclectic Society in 1800: "Not general as to be
available to all, but so far as the ransom-price sufficed to save the
whole world...".[76] The most typical representative of Anglican
Evangelicalism in this period, Charles Simeon, had been in contact
with John Erskine and other Scottish Evangelicals, and had been
influenced by Henry Venn of Huddersfield, who also belonged to the
Calvinistic wing of the Evangelical group; [77] sometimes he called himself a Calvinist, but his Calvinism was more an accentuation of the
element of grace in theology than an emphasis upon the specific marks

---

"high Calvinism" of men as such G. Bryne, a Particular Baptist who carried supra-
lapsarianism to its ultimate consequence, and from the "moderate Calvinism" of
the Baxterians: cf. E. A. Payne, *The Evangelical Revival and the Beginnings of the
Modern Missionary Movement*, art. cit., p. 227.

[73]   See for Fuller's contacts with Scottish Seceders and with Evangelicals within
the Church of Scotland, for his influence on Thomas Chalmers and for the respect
which he commanded even in Anglican circles: G. Laws, *op. cit.*, pp. 87—95.

[74]   Cf. some remarks of Ch. Smyth, *op. cit.*, pp. 6 and 106: "The history of the
Evangelical Revival is essentially a history of personalities, rather than of
opinions", and "The Evangelical Revival was conspicuously unintellectual"; V. F.
Storr writes: "They were no theologians, they were religious reformers": *The
Development of English Theology in the Nineteenth Century, 1800—1860*, London
etc. 1913, p. 70.

[75]   "Their Calvinism was of a very moderate type", V. F. Storr, *op. cit.*, p. 72.

[76]   From Josiah Pratt's notes of the meetings of the Eclectic Society, MS in the
Library of the C.M.S., London.

[77]   M. M. Hennett, *Henry Venn of Huddersfield*, The Churchman LXVIII
(1954), p. 99. Hennett warns against an overstatement of Henry Venn's Calvinism:
art. cit., p. 94.

of the Calvinistic heritage. He believed in election, not in reprobation; [78] he recognized the depth of the corruption of human nature: "the uniform testimony of revelation is, that men are all in a lost and perishing condition", [79] and he knew that man can only be saved by God's saving grace, But in 1825 he could write to a friend: "Sometimes I am a high Calvinist, at other times a low Arminian"; [80] he saw the truth not lying in one, but in two extremes, and when Wesley declared to Simeon during a meeting in 1784: " ... I have no hope but in Him", Simeon replied: "... This is all my Calvinism ... therefore we will cordially agree in those things wherein we agree". [81] Still less specifically Calvinistic was the Evangelicalism of Wilberforce: he, too, emphasized the corruption of human nature and the saving grace of God in Christ, [82] but in his later days he became more and more opposed to "the system of Calvin". [83]

The last point which we have to consider in the context of the present study is the eschatological element in the theology of the Evangelicals. We have noted already the relation between the political ideas and the eschatological expectations of some Evangelicals, especially in Dissenting circles. A general belief was that in a Millennium, a period of spiritual government by Christ at the end of the times before Christ's Second Coming. [84] Even Unitarians shared this belief to a certain degree: Joseph Priestley expected the dawn of the Millennium in 1814, [85] and this expectation gave to his thinking an optimistic flavour: "... whatever was the beginning of this world, the end will be glorious and paradaisical, beyond what our imagination can now conceive". [86] How far, however, the conceptions of some "rational Dissenters" on this point were secularized, appears from what Attorney Nash remarked in his answer to Burke's *Reflections*

---

[78]   See: A. W. Brown, *Recollections of the Conservation Parties of the Rev. Charles Simeon*, London 1863, p. 270.

[79]   Ch. Simeon, *Horae Homileticae*, XI, London 1820, p. 377.

[80]   H. C. G. Moule, *op. cit.*, pp. 77—78.

[81]   H. C. G. Moule, *op. cit.*, p. 80.

[82]   *A Practical View*, *op. cit.*, pp. 20, 50.

[83]   See: E. Halévy, *op. cit.*, pp. 413—414; Halévy even writes of the Evangelicals: "Ce ne sont pas des théologiens, mais des hommes d'émotion et d'action; leur Calvinisme, si tant est que l'on puisse encore parler de Calvinisme, est de Calvinisme sentimental et pratique, on serait tenté de dire: un Calvinisme sans doctrine", *in loco citato*.

[84]   We have already met with this belief in the foregoing chapter, with the Methodists and, more emphatically, with the Edwardians. The Reformers were no "chiliasts": what is sometimes called the "third wave of Millennianism" (the first wave is then placed in the period of the apostolic fathers, the second one is found among the sects of the Reformation period) began about 1700; it was prepared by Coccejus, and widely propagated by Johann Albrecht Bengel: see R. B. Evenhuis, *De biblicistisch-eschatologische Theologie van J. A. Bengel*, Wageningen 1931, pp. 155, 161—102, 183.

[85]   E. A. Payne, *The Free Church Tradition*, op. cit., p. 84.

[86]   In his *Essay on Government* (1768), as quoted by Basil Willey, *op. cit.*, p. 199.

on the French Revolution: "As I am a believer in Revelation, I, of course, live in the hope of better things; a millennium (not a fifth monarchy, Sir, of enthusiasts and fanatics), but a new heaven and a new earth in which dwelleth righteousness; or, to drop the eastern figure and use a more philosophic language, a state of equal liberty and equal justice to all men". [87]

Among orthodox Dissenters, the eschatological expectation had a deeper background. Their eschatology is strongly reminiscent of that of Jonathan Edwards, with this difference that they thought to see the partial fulfilment of what Edwards had expected at a farther distance. No doubt there was an interaction between their view of the political circumstances and their explanation of "prophecy", though the general scheme of their eschatology was not dependent on external circumstances. The first thing which attracts our attention is the fact that the expectation of a Millennium was the common property of all Evangelical Dissenters of this period. A second point of importance is that they saw the Millennium—just as some theologians of the Second Reformation and as Edwards had seen it—as a period of *spiritual government of Christ.* They were "post-millennarians": they emphatically rejected the idea of a double coming of Christ. Further: they considered the Millennium as a period of great spiritual blessings, a period in which the knowledge of the Lord would cover the earth and in which Jews and Gentiles would accept the call of the Gospel. And lastly, they supposed that the signs of the Millennium's dawning, apart from convulsions in nature and on the political field, would be the break-down of "the papal power" and the opening up of the world for the spread of the Gospel. As examples we take Andrew Fuller and David Bogue. In his *Prophecies relating to the Millennium* (written in 1815), Fuller described the sequence of apocalyptic events as follows: first, there would be great calamities; these would be followed by the "overthrow of the Papal Antichrist", and then the Millennium would be introduced, [88] of which the character would be spiritual—we now quote his *Expository Discourses on the Apocalypse* (also written in 1815)—: "... a time in which the Gospel will be spread over the whole earth, and cordially embraced both by Jews and Gentiles; when those prophecies will be fulfilled which speak of the cessation of wars—of the stone cut without hands becoming a great mountain ...". [89] David Bogue saw the Millennium in the same way: he, too, did not consider it as a period of the corporeal presence of Christ on earth, but "there will be far more eminent measures of divine knowledge ... and these will not be the attainments of a few Christians only, but of the general mass. The

---

[87]   As quoted by A. Lincoln, *op. cit.,* p. 3.
[88]   A. Fuller, *Complete Works,* op. cit., III, pp. 501—502.
[89]   *Op. cit.,* pp. 408—409.

boundaries of the kingdom of Christ will be extended from the rising to the going down of the sun ... Universal harmony will prevail ...", and, lastly, the way in which the Millennium would come would be one of "gradual growth". [90] An interesting parallel with Edwards is that, while the American theologian expected the Millennium to begin in New England, Bogue wrote: "As the Millennium will probably begin in some particular country, what an honour will it be, should it begin in ours!" [91] During the first years of the revolutionary period, waves of fervent eschatological ideals spread through Dissenting circles, and the speedy dawn of the Millennium was expected. The orthodox Dissenters would not have agreed with Price, who said in a sermon: "I could almost say, Lord, now lettest thou thy servant depart in peace, for mine eyes have now seen they salvation", [92] yet they also were touched by the almost apocalyptic enthusiasm which was to be found in Britain during the initial stage of the revolutionary period. [93] In the post-Napoleonic period, however, the utterances with regard to the coming of the Millennium were cautious and restrained in the circle of the Evangelical Dissenters: they had a strong feeling that they lived in the times preceding the Millennium, [94] but they did not give a detailed determination of the beginning of the millennial period: ".... it appears almost certain that the dispensations of Providence for the last twenty-five years, form a part of those awful events which are connected with an introduction of the Millennium. But how large or how small a part, who can say!"; and: "... I cannot but consider the commencement of the Millennium to be more remote (than fifty years)"; "let it be granted that nearly two hundred years must yet revolve before the Millennium begins ...". [95]

In fact, the eschatology of Evangelical Anglicans was virtually little different from that of Evangelical Dissenters: they, too, were post-millennarians, who expected a gradual approach of the millennial period. Their expectation, however, was not linked up with an optimistic view with regard to the French Revolution: on the contrary, the events in France were, to them, rather symptoms of an outburst of Antichristian power than the first signs of the millennial reign of Christ! Political events did not play a part in kindling the fire of eschatological expectations among the Church of England Evangelicals; besides, however little they might be inclined to accentuate the "Catholic" character of their ecclesiastical community, they were

---

[90]   D. Bogue, *Discourses on the Millennium*, London 1818, pp. 18, 152, 606.
[91]   *Op. cit.*, p. 304.
[92]   S, C. Carpenter, *op. cit.*, p. 5.
[93]   See above, pp. 110 ff.
[94]   Writing on Isaiah 25. 26, 27, Fuller remarked: "Now it is in these prophecies, referring to the times which *precede* the Millennium, that we shall find the events of our own times": *Complete Works*, III, p. 499.
[95]   D. Bogue, *Discourses on the Millennium*, *op. cit.*, pp. 306, 606—609.

nevertheless members of a Church which to a greater or lesser degree belongs to the "Catholic type", which always tends to fall into "the error of subordinating the eschatological to the historical". [96] Perhaps the combination of these two factors accounts for the fact that in the Anglican Evangelical circle the eschatological expectation took a quieter form than in that of Evangelical Dissent. Still it was not wholly absent: Simeon, who was vehemently opposed to the Irvingite "pre-millennarianism", [97] expected a spiritual Millennium in which it would "appear as if all the saints who have ever lived upon earth had risen again, and as if Christ himself had come down again to reign over them . . .". [98] He, too, was very cautious with regard to the exact time of the day when the Millennium should break: "To prevent misapprehensions, I repeat, that of "the times and seasons which God has reserved in his own power" I presume not to speak". [99]

British Evangelicalism of this period had essentially one and the same background of eschatological thinking. The differences which existed on this point between the various Evangelical groups were but gradual: they did not lie in the purely theological sphere, but in the intensity of the eschatological expectations and in the way in which they functioned amid the political tensions of their times.

3. THE DEVELOPMENT OF THE MISSIONARY IDEAL

a. Some general aspects of the missionary awakening

In the foregoing chapter we have seen that the religious awakening in Great Britain and North America, which had such an important influence on the revival of the missionary idea, was not unrelated to the parallel movements of Pietism and Moravianism, but that it would be wrong to explain the British missionary revival primarily from foreign influences: above all, it was conditioned by the development of British theological and ecclesiastical life, which proved responsive to the call of new times, and which appeared able to adapt itself to the spiritual exigencies of a new period in the history of human thinking and striving. Now we have arrived at the treatment of another phase in the history of British missions, we have to ask ourselves anew whether there is a possibility that the awakening of the missionary ideal was caused either directly or indirectly by the missionary development in other countries.

In the first place, we turn to America. We have already noticed

---

[96]   L. Newbigin, *The Household of God*, *op. cit.*, p. 82.
[97]   A. W. Brown, *op. cit.*, pp. 315 ff.
[98]   Ch. Simeon, *Horae Homileticae*, VI, London 1820, p. 252.
[99]   Ch. Simeon, *The Conversion of the Jews, Two Discourses preached before the University of Cambridge*, London 1821, p. 52.

the extent of the influence which Jonathan Edwards exercised upon Calvinistic circles in Scotland and England: without any doubt, the British missionary awakening owes a great deal to the stimuli given by this great Reformed theologian. [100] It does not seem probable, however, that the later missionary development in America influenced to any marked degree the development in the mother country. On the contrary, since the foundation of the new American missionary societies did not take place before that of the societies in Great Britain, there is no reason to assume a dependency of the British missionary revival from that which commenced during the so-called "Second Awakening" in America. Besides, in the documents relating to the awakening of the missionary interest in England and Scotland no special reference is made to the activities of the new American societies, while on the other hand the missions of Eliot and Brainerd receive ample attention. [101] The development in America has rather to be seen as a movement running parallel to that in Great Britain. It is notable that the resemblance between the atmosphere of the L.M.S. missionary activity and that of the New York Missionary Society with its daughter-organizations, is conspicuous in more than one respect, and can but partly be explained from the fact that the New York Missionary Magazine often borrowed from the London Missionary Magazine and other British missionary reviews; [102] a spiritual affinity and relationship was present between both movements.

On the Continent of Europe the situation was quite different. This was partly due, of course, to the political circumstances of this period: while Britain and America had free opportunity for expansion, Continental activities were haltered by the great convulsions and drastic changes in the political field. But already, before the French Revolution, the glow of German Pietist missions had begun to wane. The work of the Danish Hallensian mission, once so splendid, had collapsed under the pressure of the flood-tide of Rationalism; [103] leading rationalists had uncompromisingly attacked the missionary ideals of the Pietists; [104] a younger generation of missionaries, who had found an entrance into the rationalist world of thought at the German universities, had lost its enthusiasm for the purely missionary task, and a cold moralism had taken the place of the fervent evangelism of half a century before. Only the missions of Herrnhut had tided over the period of rationalist ascendency as a result of the isolated

---

[100]   See above, p. 92.
[101]   See, e.g., W. Carey, An Enquiry, op. cit., p. 36.
[102]   O. W. Elsbree, op. cit., p. 55.
[103]   See: M. Richter, Der Missionsgedanke im evangelischen Deutschland des 18. Jahrhunderts, Leipzig 1928, SS. 138 ff.
[104]   W. Oehler, Geschichte der Deutschen Evangelischen Mission, I, Baden-Baden 1949, SS. 51—52.

position which they took in the totality of German spiritual life. [105]
We cannot say that the "Aufklärung" as a whole was hostile to every
form of religious propaganda among non-Christian nations—but it
was definitely opposed to the pietist form of missionary work, which
aimed at religious conversion. Frick remarks that the fault did not lie
exclusively on the rationalist side: he sees in the lack of independent
theological reflection on the side of old Pietism one of the main causes
of the fact that Rationalism could penetrate so easily into the circle
of pietist missionary work. [106] In Britain the situation was quite
different: not an extreme deistic Rationalism, but a more mild and
moderate Latitudinarianism had gained the ascendency in eighteenth
century British spiritual life— an ascendency, threatened and ultimately
broken by a vigorous Evangelicalism, that at the end of the century
had succeeded in gaining a strong foothold in almost every British
religious denomination. Another remarkable feature of the development
in Great Britain is to be found in the fact, that the cleavage between
Latitudinarianism and Evangelicalism was not by any means as great
as that which ultimately came to exist between Rationalism and
Pietism. Though Frick certainly goes too far when he sees in the
British missionary awakening an alliance between Rationalism and
Pietism, yet it is true that British Evangelicalism tried to absorb the
positive elements of the rationalist-latitudinarian influence. While
German Pietism tended to become "other-wordly" and so lost its grip
on a rising generation. British Evangelicalism blended in a fruitful
way its spiritual purposes with the humanitarianism of the new age.
In this way it could take the lead in several enterprises of humanitarian
interest and become the rallying-point for those members of a new
generation who wanted to combine a deeply religious attitude of life
with an open and positive approach to the problems of their own day.
Perhaps it is possible to explain this ..comprehensiveness" of British
Evangelicalism partly from some deeply rooted qualities of British
spiritual life with its distinctly synthetic character, partly also from
the Calvinistic background of the evangelical movement: Calvinism
has always had a lively interest in the task on "the broad front of life".

In the meantime, the influence of Pietism had not quite disappeared
in the period of rationalist dominance in Germany. When the missions
which had been inaugurated by the fathers of "old Pietism" had
reached a very low level, the first signs announced themselves of the
missionary activity of "new Pietism". We think here of the work of
the "Deutsche Christentums-Gesellschaft", a society founded by the
German Pietist J. A. Urlsperger: it formed a link between old and
new Pietism and it prepared the way for the work of the "Basler

---

[105]   H. Frick, *Die Evangelische Mission*, op. cit., S. 192.
[106]   See: H. Frick, *Vom Pietismus zum "Volkskirchentum"*, Gütersloh 1924,
SS. 21 ff.

Mission". [107] We think also of the work of J. Jänicke at Berlin, that exercised a lasting influence on German missionary life. These men stood directly in the line of pietist tradition; at the same time, however, they were deeply influenced by the missionary development in Great Britain. Urlsperger's father, S. Urlsperger, was a corresponding member of the S.P.C.K.; it became his life's task to "translate into German" the basic ideas of the older British Societies; his son, too, was impressed by the example of the S.P.C.K., [108] and some years later it was the new British Societies, particularly the L.M.S., which exercised a fascinating influence upon such Germans as were—in Bengel's footsteps—eschatologically-minded and at the same time deeply interested in the cause of missions. [109] There were some contacts between the missionary awakening in Britain and in Germany: K. F. A. Steinkopf especially, for some time a secretary of the British and Foreign Bible Society, [110] played a part as intermediary which recalls that of Dr. Horneck, one of his predecessors at the Savoy Church in London; these personal contacts, however, do not entitle us to see in what happened in Germany one of the causative factors of the British missionary awakening. We must rather speak of a simultaneity, which is a striking sign of the fact that the time had become ripe everywhere for a new development in the history of missions. With regard to the missions of the Moravians, here also we cannot speak of a direct influence on the British missionary awakening, though the heroic work of Herrnhut did not fail to awaken the admiration of the spiritual leaders in Britain: Wilberforce held up the zeal of the Moravians as an example to his English fellow-Christians, because they had "perhaps excelled all mankind in solid and unequivocal proofs of the love of Christ, and of the most ardent, and active, and patient zeal in his service". [111]

We may also eliminate as a positive factor in the development of British missionary life the influence of Roman Catholic missions. In the second chapter we saw that the example of the Roman Catholic *Propaganda* had played some part in the formation of the S.P.G. During the eighteenth century, however, the Church of Rome did not display any such missionary zeal as to attract the attention of other circles: the revival of Roman Catholic missions would only take place after the Napoleonic era. [112] It is the impulses, given by Methodism

---

[107] E. Schick, *Vorboten und Bahnbrecher*, Basel 1943, S. 228.
[108] E. Schick, *op. cit.*, SS. 195, 217.
[109] See among others: J. C. Hoekendijk, *Kerk en Volk in de Duitse Zendings-wetenschap, op. cit.*, p. 21.
[110] See: E. Schick, *op. cit.*, SS. 229—230, 263—264.
[111] W. Wilberforce, *A Practical View, op. cit.*, pp. 79—80.
[112] The reawakening of Roman Catholic missionary activity in the beginning of the nineteenth antury was closely connected with the "Restoration" on the Continent of Europe and with the romantic movement in the second stage of its development: "Dieselbe Kraft, welche im Zentrum die durch Häresie oder Un-

and Edwardian Calvinism, which in the first place account for the rise of a new Evangelicalism in Britain—and the coincidence of this new religious feeling with a favourable and even stimulating socio-political situation resulted in the amazing spread of the missionary ideal in Great Britain about the turn of the century. Before we turn to an examination of the motives of this missionary awakening, we have first to give a survey of its historical growth. In this survey we shall meet with a variety of missionary organizations; we have to pay attention to their special character, to the reasons for their separate existence and to their particular contribution to the awakening of the missionary idea. But in doing so, we have to realize that, in spite of their differences, the various societies were interdependent and integrally related to each other: Carey was influenced by John Erskine, Fuller stimulated the missionary awakening in Scotland; the roots of the C.M.S. lay as much in the L.M.S. as in the work of the Anglican chaplains in India, and in their turn the Anglican Evangelicals contributed to the reawakening of missionary fervour in the circle of the S.P.G. There was variety, indeed; but underlying this variety there was a deeper unity which makes it possible to see the various branches of British missionary life in this period as branches of one great movement. That there was in these days already a living consciousness of this deeper unity appears from the fact that Carey in 1806 proposed to Fuller to summon "a meeting of all denominations of Christians at The Cape of Good Hope somewhere about 1810"! [113]

b.   The awakening in the Baptist circle

With the beginning of modern Protestant missions the name of William Carey is indissolubly connected: he was the pioneer, who blazed the trail for a new form of missionary activity. Yet it would be wrong to see him even in his own circle as an isolated figure. Early in his career, he came into contact with a group of prominent Baptist ministers, of whom we mention here only the names of A. Fuller, J. Ryland and J. Sutcliff: together with Carey and R. Hogg they constituted the Baptist Missionary Society in October, 1792. [114] Now we know that at first these men looked with some hesitance on the idea of undertaking practical missionary work: they had been reared in a hyper-Calvinist circle which, if it did not reject the idea of missions in general, yet stood aloof from its actual realization on the ground of

glauben abgetrennten Glieder wiederzugewinnen trachtete, bekundete sich im Umkreis dadurch, dasz man sich mit wachsendem Eifer der Heidenbekehrung zuwandte", J. Schmidlin, *Katholische Missionsgeschichte*, Steyl 1924, S. 426.

[113]   See: R. Rouse, *William Carey's "Pleasing Dream"*, I.R.M. XXXVIII (1949), especially p. 181.

[114]   A. H. Oussoren, *William Carey, especially his Missionary Principles*, Leiden 1945, p. 34.

their belief that man had to bide in a spirit of passive expectation the time when it would please God to convert the heathen. [115] But under the influence of Jonathan Edwards' theology they had learned to see the greatness and value of God's offer of grace to all men, and Edwards' *Humble Attempt* had led them to issue a call to pray regularly for "the general revival and spread of religion". [116] It was Carey who opened their eyes to the immediate urgency of the missionary task; [117] but that, after some understandable hesitation, they were prepared to follow his lead was not only a result of the impression which Carey's strong personality made upon them, but also of the fact that they lived already in a spiritual climate which was favourable to the development of the missionary idea. There was a spiritual congeniality between Carey and his future supporters, which Fuller felt from the moment of their first meeting: when Carey descended from the pulpit after his first sermon for the association at Nottingham, Fuller "grasped his hand, and described in the warmest language the delight he felt at finding so exact a coincidence in their sentiments". [118] The circle of ministers into which Carey entered after he had become a Baptist preacher was at heart mission-minded, but it needed Carey's world-wide outlook to transform the latent ideal into a burning passion. In his broad outlook, too, Carey did not stand alone: the new discoveries attracted wide attention, the travels of Cook became immensely popular, the world-wide interest was "in the air". But in Carey's highly gifted personality the world-wide outlook of his times coincided with the new Evangelicalism of his period; his cultural interest was made subservient to his religious ideals, and the result was an outburst of missionary zeal which continues to make its influence felt up to these present times. Carey was not a solitary meteor: Eliot and Brainerd, Ziegenbalg and the Moravian missionaries were among his examples, [119] the Anglican Evangelical Thomas Scott [120] and the Baptist Andrew Fuller among those who guided him in the spiritual and theological sphere—but yet we see something of the mysterious guidance of God in the fact that exactly this man should become the pioneer of modern missions.

The B.M.S. was founded shortly after the publication of Carey's

---

[115]   Cf. the (alleged) remark of J. C. Ryland (the father of Dr J. Ryland): "Young man, sit down, sit down. You're an enthusiast. When God pleases to convert the heathen, he'll do it without consulting you or me. Besides, there must first be another pentecostal gift of tongues!", in: S. Pearce Carey, *William Carey*, London[8] 1934, p. 54.

[116]   E. A. Payne, *The Prayer Call of 1784, op. cit.*, pp. 1 ff.

[117]   S. Pearce Carey, *op. cit.*, p. 56.

[118]   See: J. C. Marshman, *The Life and Times of Carey, Marshman and Ward*, I, London 1859, p. 9.

[119]   See: *An Enquiry, op. cit.*, pp. 36—37.

[120]   S. Pearce Carey, *op. cit.*, pp. 34—36. Speaking of the influence of Anglican

Enquiry; it was restricted to the Particular Baptist community (the Missionary Society of the General Baptists was only founded in 1816), but at the same time it set the example for the foundation of other missionary societies. [121] In the course of the next year Carey set out for India, where he started missionary work which would grow into one of the most important missionary undertakings of modern history. At first, Carey had thought of going to the South Sea Islands; [122] his going to India was not inspired by a distinct preference for missionary work among a more civilized nation, but was simply a result of a combination of "fortuitous" factors, behind which the believer knows to be present the guiding hand of God. [123]

c.   The London Missionary Society

There is a direct relation between the activity of William Carey and the foudation of the L.M.S. In 1794 a meeting took place between J. Ryland and Mr. Wills, an Independent layman, who had brought with him his friend Dr. Bogue: Ryland had invited Mr. Wills to hear "an interesting letter just received from William Carey". The letter made such an impression on Bogue and his friend, that on returning home they expressed the wish to form a similar society. Here lies the inception of the L.M.C. [124] But its basis had already been laid by other events, of which deserves special mention the appearance of Melvill Horne's *Letters on Missions* in the same year. [125] Horne was an Anglican clergyman, who had served as a chaplain in Sierra Leone; because of the health of his wife and children he had to leave his African post; [126] while still in Africa, he wrote his *Letters,* which contain a passionate and sometimes even upbraiding appeal [127] to his fellow-clergymen to give practical support to the cause of missions. Horne felt lonely in his missionary enthusiasm: "As a minister of the establishment I did not dare hope to find ministers to act with me"; only Carey "has given to his precepts the force of example". [128] It

---

Evangelicals H. P. Thompson remarks in his *Into all Lands, op. cit.,* p. 105: "It was one of these, Thomas Scott, who first lighted the spark in the heart of William Carey which . . . flared up at last in the formation of the B.M.S.".

[121]   E. A. Payne has given a number of short biographies of the leaders of the B.M.S. in its initial period in his: *The First Generation,* London [1936].

[122]   G. Laws, *op. cit.,* p. 63.

[123]   See: A. H. Oussoren, *op. cit.,* pp. 36—37, 186—187.

[124]   R. Lovett, *The History of the London Missionary Society 1795—1895,* I, London 1899, p. 802.

[125]   M. Horne, *Letters on Missions addressed to the Protestant Ministers of the British Churches,* Bristol 1794.

[126]   *Op. cit.,* p. IV.

[127]   'I wish . . . that the whole breathed more affection, and had less spirit": *op. cit.,* p. XI.

[128]   *Op. cit.,* p. V, XII.

was this book, which attracted the special attention of the Anglican clergymen John Eyre, the editor of the *Evangelical Magazine,* and of Thomas Haweis, Rector of Aldwinkle, who gave a review of it in the same magazine. [129] In Horne, Eyre and Haweis we meet with the contribution of Anglican Evangelicalism to the formation of the L.M.S. About the same time a group of Independent ministers in Warwickshire, influenced by the *Prayer-Call* of the Northampton Baptist ministers, considered at one of their conferences the question: "What is the duty of Christians with respect to the spread of the Gospel?" The results were: monthly prayer-meetings, the forming of a fund and the issuing of a circular letter to the various associations of Independent ministers. [130] Once again, we meet here the influence of Jonathan Edwards, from whose *Humble Attempt* the prayer-meetings for the extension of the Kingdom took their inspiration; some years afterwards, it was published in an abridged edition by George Burder, the secretary of the L.M.S. [131] All this activity resulted in the formation of "The Missionary Society", as was its official title, at a meeting in "The Castle and Falcon" in London on 21 September, 1795; this meeting had been prepared by a number of previous informal meetings and by some articles in the *Evangelical Magazine.* The most important of these articles was a letter to "the Evangelical Dissenters who practise Infant Baptism" by the hand of David Bogue, who accused his fellow-Dissenters of a lack of interest in the cause of missions: "*We alone* are idle"; "If we have never thought of these things, there is much reason to lament our criminal unconcern for the honour of God, and for the perishing souls of men". [132]

The spiritual background of the L.M.S. was that of Calvinistic Evangelicalism. [133] It was designed as an interdenominational organization; the participants were not only Independents, but also Anglicans, Scottish Churchmen and Scottish Seceders. William Carey, broadminded as he was, had still thought it better to work on a denominational basis [134]—but the founders of the L.M.S. held a different view. Bogue declared during one of the foundation meetings in 1795: "We are called together this evening to *the funeral of bigotry*", and in 1796 it

---

[129]   R. Lovett, *op. cit.,* pp. 11—12.
[130]   R. Lovett *in loco citato.*
[131]   E. A. Payne, *The Prayer Call of 1784,* op. cit., p. 11.
[132]   *The Evangelical Magazine,* 1794, pp. 378—380.
[133]   The first missionaries of the L.M.S. were convinced of the fact that "the Missionary Society was quite Calvinistical": R. Lovett, *op. cit.,* pp. 48—49.
[134]   "But in the present divided state of Christendom, it would be more likely for good to be done by each denomination engaging separately in the work, than if they were to embark on it conjointly: *An Enquiry,* op. cit., p. 84; cf. R. Rouse, *Voluntary Movements and the Changing Ecumenical Climate,* in: *A History of the Ecumenical Movement,* op. cit., pp. 311—312. We must add, that for Baptists it is more difficult than for other groups of Christians to engage in common missionary action because of the controversy on the question of infant baptism.

was accepted as a fundamental principle "that our design is not to send Presbyterianism, Independency, Episcopacy, or any other form of Church Order and Government, ... but the glorious Gospel of the blessed God to the Heathen". [135] The L.M.S. sought to realize a unity that would bridge the differences in Church order between the various groups of the one Calvinistic Evangelical family: this was no ecumenicity in the modern sense of the word, but more a relativism with regard to forms of Church government which was in conformity with the Low-Church tendencies in the Evangelical movement. The deepest and most lasting roots of the L.M.S. lay in the circle of Independency, which as a result of its inherited character could adapt itself without much difficulty to this form of interdenominationalism.

The "Low-Church-character" of this Society also appears from the fact that in this first stage it worked mainly with lay missionaries. It was not deemed necessary that every missionary should be "a learned man"; "godly men who understand mechanic arts may be of signal use to this undertaking ..; [136] behind the L.M.S. stood a popular movement, which was carried forward by a mixture of genuine religious enthusiasm and romantic ideals, [137] though David Bogue in particular retained a more sober judgment: his heart sank when he saw the faces of those who went out with the "Duff" in 1798; he had wanted a higher standard of selection, and after the disappointments which were the result of the "hasty methods of selection" he was appointed as a tutor of the future missionaries. [138]

In 1796 the "Duff" made for Tahiti with thirty missionaries, of which only a small number proved really valuable in missionary service; in 1799, it sailed a second time, but it was captured by a French privateer. This expedition ended in utter failure. The question arises: what made the L.M.S. leaders choose the South Sea Islands as their first field of missionary action? We know that Bogue's thoughts went out to India: in 1796 he was even on the point of going to Bengal together with Robert Haldane. [139] But it was Haweis, who pleaded with success the cause of a mission to Tahiti; his choice was partly inspired by romantic motives, but behind these a deeper incentive is discernible: "I have always been convinced that the heathen, who are in an inferior state of knowledge and civilization, are to be preferred to those who are more advanced. This view coincided with those of the London Missionary Society". [140] In the meantime, other fields also

---

[135]   R. Lovett, op. cit., pp. 38, 49—50.
[136]   R. Lovett, op. cit., p. 46.
[137]   The first meetings of the L.M.S. were considered by some as "a new Pentecost": R. Lovett, op. cit., p. 38.
[138]   R. Lovett, op. cit., pp. 56, 66, 74.
[139]   A. Haldane, op. cit., pp. 101 ff.
[140]   Th. Haweis, An Impartial and Succinct History of the Rise, Declension and Revival of the Church of Christ, III, London 1800, p. 347.

came within the range of vision. In 1796, a mission to Africa was contemplated: "To this benighted and oppressed country we are desirous of sending the Gospel of Christ", [141] and in 1797 it was resolved to send missionaries to India and Jamaica. [142] The "Missionary Society" certainly had its defects, but on the other hand it was marked by a fervent enthusiasm and by an intrepid pioneer spirit, both of which have exercised a salutary influence far beyond Britain's frontiers. [143] It combined the fervour of the Evangelical Revival with a dynamism that was a reflection of the dynamic times in which it had its origin!

d.   Missionary awakening within the circle of Anglicanism

In the period which saw the rise of the B.M.S. and the L.M.S., the wave of the missionary awakening had as yet but lightly touched the Church of England. The circles which supported the work of the S.P.G. stood quite aloof from the new revival movement; the number of its members had dwindled down to a few hundred, and one of the historians of the S.G.P. writes that the Society had been infected with the lethargy of the official Church. [144] On the other hand, the group of Anglicans which stood behind the L.M.S. was relatively small and uninfluential: it consisted of a number of isolated Evangelicals who, contrary to the general stream of Anglican feeling, saw no objection in a far-going cooperation with Dissenters. The scene changed, however, when Evangelicalism gained a footing within Anglican circles which up to that time had been resistant to Evangelical influences: it was no longer a few scattered individuals, but a whole group which embraced the ideals of Evangelicalism and which became sensitive to the stimuli of the missionary awakening. We think here in the first place of the "Clapham Sect", whose members were men of a broad vision as well as of a deep religious life. In more than one way they had connections with the cause of missions. They were deeply interested in the propagation of Christian religion in India: as early as 1792 Charles Grant had written a pamphlet in which he championed on humanitarian grounds the introduction of Christianity into India; [145] the men of the Clapham Sect followed the work of Carey with deep attention, as appears from the fact that they belonged to the circle of

---

[141]   R. Lovett, op. cit., p. 477, quoting from the Evangelical Magazine of Dec. 1796.
[142]   R. Lovett, op. cit., pp. 102—103.
[143]   So the Society directed itself to the "religious inhabitants of the Netherlands" by means of an address, translated by J. T. van der Kemp: Adres van het Zendeling-genootschap te Londen aan de godsdienstige ingezetenen der Verenigde Nederlanden, Dordrecht etc. 1797. In the same year the "Nederlandsch Zendeling Genootschap" was founded!
[144]   H. P. Thompson, Into All Lands, op. cit., p. 104.
[145]   C. H. Philips, op. cit., pp. 158.

readers of the B.M.S. *Periodical Accounts,* [146] and though Grant was
not blind to some of the mistakes made by the Serampore missionaries,
yet he was their champion when their work was attacked in the Court
of Directors. [147] But Grant and his friends not only were the "missionary conscience" of Anglican laity, they also actively contributed to
the cause of Christian missions. This contribution was a twofold one.
In the first place, Charles Grant and Edward Perry, both chairmen
of the Company—the "pious chairs"!—succeeded in having a number
of Evangelical clergymen sent as chaplains to India. [148] Among these
were Claudius Buchanan and Henry Martyn, two men who each in
his own way rendered an invaluable service to the awakening of the
missionary ideal. In 1809 and 1810, Buchanan gave some brilliant sermons, bundled under the title of the first sermon: *The Star in the East,*
in which as well as in his *Christian Researches in Asia,* published in
1811, he made a major point of the humanitarian value and the civi-
lizing influence of Christianity. [149] He is a typical representative of
that strain in English missionary tradition in which a combination is
to be found between the "Erasmian" and the "Reformatory" lines; this
strain we also met in a man such as Thomas Bray. Although an Evangelical—Thomas Newton was his spiritual father—Buchanan had a
keen eye for the positive values of humanity and civilization, of which
in the foregoing century the Latitudinarians particularly had been
the advocates. Once more, British Christianity showed its generic
inclination towards comprehension and synthesis and its dislike for
that type of radical and antithetic thinking which we so often meet in
continental theology, from the days of Luther with his outburst against
"die Hure Vernunft" to those of Barth with his criticism of the Anglo-
American missionary methods. [150] Buchanan met the opponents of
Christian missionary activity in India on their own ground. In his
notorious article in the *Edinburgh Review* of 1808, Sydney Smith had
attacked the Indian missions from the high bastion of "respect for
the religion of the Hindoos", from his consideration of the "duties
of general benevolence" and from his care for the happiness of the
inhabitants of India. [151] Buchanan tried to disarm his opponent by
taking his citadel from within, by showing that the Christian mis-

---

[146]   E. A. Payne, *The Church Awakes, op. cit.,* p. 36.
[147]   C. H. Philips, *op. cit.,* pp. 162—165.
[148]   Philips states that between 1793 and 1813 about twenty chaplains were
sent by their influence to India: *op. cit.,* p. 159 note 3.
[149]   See for the impression which these writings made: E. M. Howse, *op. cit.,*
p. 82.
[150]   See his: *Die Theologie und die Mission in der Gegenwart, op. cit.,* ss.
208—212.
[151]   "The duty of conversion is less plain, and less imperious, when conversion
exposes the convert to great present misery"; "Conversion is no duty at all, if it
merely destroys the old religion ..."; "As the duty of making proselytes springs
from the duty of benevolence, there is a priority of choice in conversion": *The
Works of the Rev. Sydney Smith,* London 1850, pp. 115—116.

sionary does not destroy the old religion but finds his point of contact in the "general and systematic analogies" between the Hindu and the Christian religion, [152] and by pleading a missionary method which would avoid the dangers of force and personal injury. [153] We find similar thoughts with Henry Martyn in his sermon on *Christian India* (Galat. 6. 10), in which he reduced the duty towards India to the general duty of universal benevolence: "look at the nations of the earth, and be a philanthropist". [154] Martyn was a different type from his friend Buchanan: he took a more sober view of religion in India and of the work which could be done there: after the appearance of Buchanan's *Star in the East* he wrote to Lydia Grenfell: "I tremble for every thing our dear friends publish about our doings in India, lest shame come to us and them..." [155]

The Evangelicalism of the "chaplains" had some points of contact with the humanitarianism of their age, while at the same time some of their ideals had a remarkable congeniality with the world of thought of the S.P.G. It was in particular David Brown, since 1787 chaplain at Calcutta, who pleaded a state-sponsored mission to India, which had to be carried out by the Established Church. In 1787 he published *A Proposal for Establishing a Protestant Mission in Bengal and Bihar*: in this work he advocated the idea that the Company and the Government should become responsible for the work in India. [156] Similar ideas were favoured by his friends Buchanan and Martyn. In his *Memoir of the expediency of an Ecclesiastical Establishment for our Empire in the East* Buchanan wrote: "Let us first establish our own religion amongst *ourselves,* and our Asiatic subjects will soon benefit by it. When once our national Church shall have been confirmed in India, the members of that Church will be the best qualified to advise the State as to the means by which, from time to time, the civilization of the natives may be promoted..." [157] What Martyn expected from the lending of political support to the work of missions appears from some utterances in his *Journal* with regard to Persia: "It does not appear how the Gospel can be preached in Persia, till a Christian nation conquers the country, which probably will soon be the case; how marvellously is India put into the hands of a Christian nation for

---

[152] In his *Christian Researches in Asia:* see *The Works of the Rev. Claudius Buchanan,* New York 1812, pp. 158—162; cf. *The Star in the East,* Sermon on Matt. 2. 2, in which Buchanan remarks that the East again is bearing witness to the truth of Messiah's religion "by affording luminous evidence of the divine origin of the Christian faith", *op. cit.,* p. 293—294.

[153] *Op. cit.,* p. 164.

[154] H. Martyn, *Sermons,* Calcutta 1822, p. 406.

[155] H. Martyn, *Journals and Letters, edited by S. Wilberforce,* II, London 1837, p. 321.

[156] Ch. Hole, *The Early History of the C.M.S.,* London 1896, p. 10; cf. [Ch. Simeon], *Memorial Sketches of the Rev. David Brown, With a Selection of his Sermons, preached at Calcutta,* London 1816, p. XIV—XV.

[157] C. Buchanan, *Works, op. cit.,* p. 163.

a short time... [158] The chaplains had a twofold end in view: first the establishment of the *Ecclesia Anglicana* in India, and then the evangelizing of India from the bridgehead of the Establishment. Their ideals were shared by Grant—but when the idea of a state-sponsored mission proved to be impracticable, Grant and his friends turned towards the idea of a voluntary society in the spirit of the existing Missionary Societies. [159]

The missionary idea also came to the fore during one of the meetings of the *Eclectic Society*. As far back as 1796 Simeon had opened a discussion on the subject of missionary activity in general; [160] three years later, in 1799, the matter was brought to a head by the question: "What methods can we use most effectually to promote the knowledge of God among the heathen?" It was John Venn, son of Henry Venn, [161] who formulated the principles, of which we mention the following: "God's providence must be *followed, not anticipated",* [162] and: "Better that a missionary society should proceed from small beginnings... rather than enter upon a large scale at first". [163] Possibly this last point was obliquely directed against the L.M.S. with its initial outburst of activity; [164] the pronouncement of the "Eclectic" that the mission had to be founded upon "the Church-principle, not the high-Church principle" was directed against the L.M.S. as much as against the S.G.P.; it was quite in the spirit of Simeon, who did not feel at liberty to apply the principle of interdenominationalism to the work of missions: "We cannot join the Missionary Society; yet I bless God they have stood forth. We must now stand forth..." [165]

In this way the Church Missionary Society came into being as an Evangelical Anglican missionary organization, and it has retained its original character up to present times. Its original name, which it received on April 12, 1799, was: *The Society for Missions to Africa*

---

[158]   *Journals and Letters, op. cit.,* p. 56.
[159]   See: M. L. Loane, *Cambridge and the Evangelical Succession, op. cit.,* p. 198; cf. E. Stock, *The History of the Church Missionary Society,* I, London 1899, p. 50, who writes: "It was the Dutch method of missions, and it had been tried and found wanting".
[160]   Cf. E. Stock, *op. cit.,* p. 60—62.
[161]   See above, p. 113.
[162]   A typically Calvinistic remark, which in another form was repeated by the Dutch Calvinistic theologian Abraham Kuyper in his lecture at a Missionary Congress, held at Amsterdam in 1890: the missionary, sent by Christ, must follow the trail, blazed by the Lord; if God in his election does not precede, the word of the missionary can bear no blessing: *Acta van het Zendingscongres, gehouden te Amsterdam,* Amsterdam 1890, p. 5. It is a pity that Kuyper himself did not clearly see these very ideas reflected in British Evangelicalism—his description of the Missionary Societies that were formed in Britain at the end of the eighteenth century verged on caricature and elicited a strong protest from one of the members of the Congress, the Rev. F. Lion Cachet: *op. cit.,* p. 7.
[163]   See MS notes of the Eclectic Society.
[164]   Thomas Scott considered the first expeditions of the L.M.S. as "over-sanguine and hasty, though well meant, proceedings": Ch. Hole, *op. cit.,* p. 33.
[165]   See Ch. Smyth, *op. cit.,* p. 294.

and the East. To Africa: the "dark continent" had come into the spot-
light through the unwearying struggle against slave-trade and slavery,
carried on by those who were also the supporters and even the spiritual
fathers of the new Society. To the East: the chaplains and the Evangelical directors of the Company were moved by the vision of a christianized India. But the great difficulty was how to find in the Anglican
circle the labourers for the newly-planned tasks. Here we touch upon
the weak spot of the C.M.S. in its initial stage: its lack of "manpower".
How to explain this, especially when we think of the quantity of
missionaries which the L.M.S. had at its disposal? In the first place,
the C.M.S. did not want to make use of lay missionaries, though even
Simeon had pleaded for sending out "catechists" because it would
be "hopeless to wait for missionaries". [166] Some members of the C.M.S.
had fundamental objections against lay-missionaries, [167] while acquain
tance with the difficulties with which the L.M.S. had met due to the
defective quality of some of their missionaries will not have augmented
the enthusiasm for this solution of the problem. [168] So the candidates
for missionary work had to be sought among the settled or prospective
clergy. Now the number of Evangelical clergymen was still relatively
small, and such Evangelical clergy as there were felt deeply the urgent
need of their presence in England itself. [169] Another factor may have
been, that the more "catholic" type of Church—and those who sympathized with the C.M.S. were Anglicans as much as Evangelicals—
tends to instill into its members a form of ecclesiological thinking which
in its turn creates a certain reluctance to enter upon tasks that lie
outside the bounds of the typically ecclesiastical work. While more
than one Evangelical clergyman with fervent missionary ideals went
to India as a regularly appointed chaplain, no one offered himself for
direct missionary work in the service of the C.M.S. [170] In addition the
mobility and dynamism of even the Evangelical sector of the Church
of England was no doubt not so great as that of the Evangelical

---

[166]   E. Stock, *op. cit.*, p. 64.
[167]   E. Stock, *op. cit.*, p. 72.
[168]   From the outset, the C.M.S. demanded a high standard of admission into
missionary service. Brown and his friends wrote to Simeon in September 1787:
"We are much concerned that the Missionaries sent out to this country may be
of the right sort", H. C. G. Moule, *op. cit.*, p. 87; John Venn remarked in 1799
that "a missionary should have heaven in his heart and tread the world under
his foot", E. Stock, *op. cit.*, p. 63.
[169]   "Ardent young clergymen there were at that urging juncture who, though
warmly interested for missions, did not offer their personal services... but while
such as they felt the motive to stay irresistible, it is clear that the Church of
England... had hardly yet begun to awake to the missionary call", *Proceedings
of the Society for Missions to Africa and the East*, I, London 1801—1805, p. 68.
[170]   Balleine's remark that the chaplains offered themselves for the work among
white men, but that there was no preparedness to work among the heathen is
not quite correct: the "chaplains" were also prepared to take a part in direct
missionary work, but they wanted to be missionaries in official ecclesiastical status.
See: G. R. Balleine, *op. cit.*, p. 161.

Dissenters, who had thrown themselves into the full stream of the dynamic life of their times! These various reasons made it necessary for the C.M.S. to start its work with missionaries from Germany and Switzerland; [171] even in 1813 Buchanan had to complain, when the East India Bill had passed: "Now we are all likely to be disgraced. Parliament has opened the door, and who is there to go in? From the Church not one man". [172]

At the end of this period, the old Anglican Societies also revived to new life and new activity. In this context the question can be put why the men who formed the C.M.S. did not make use of the existing missionary agency of the Anglican Church, the S.P.G.: why was it necessary to form a second missionary society within the Church of England? The answer is clear: because the founders of the C.M.S. wanted to form an Evangelical Society, while the S.P.G. during that period was definitely opposed to Evangelical influences; it represented more or less the "High Church tendency" in the Anglican Church. The cleavage between the two groups was too great to make possible a hearty cooperation of the Evangelicals with the S.P.G., though some of them gave a financial contribution to the old Anglican Society. [173] Compared with the missionary fervour of the Evangelical leaders, the spirit of the S.P.G. of those days leaves an impression of coldness and aloofness: Bishop J. Randolph of Oxford remarked in the S.P.G. Sermon of 1803: "I do not pretend to prescribe what can be done, or to say that any thing can be done hastily, for eradicating the super-stition of the various tribes and nations which compose it [i. e. "the Eastern Empire"]; one year later, Bishop H. W. Majendie of Chester declared: " . . . yet, however questionable the success of attempts at eradicating the ancient and inveterate superstition of the Hindoo . . . there can exist no doubt whatever of the fitness, nay of the duty, of making public provision for the public exercise of our Religion among our own people in that country". [174]

Yet in the long run the example of the C.M.S. and the indirect influence of the Evangelical leaders did not fail to offer a fresh stimulus to the S.P.G. The ideas of Buchanan in particular found a response in their midst: his thoughts with regard to the function of the Anglican Establishment in India were more in line with the ideals of the S.P.G. than with the "Low-Church attitude" which the C.M.S. adopted in this matter. While the C.M.S. during the first half of the eighteenth century showed considerable distrust towards the idea of

---

[171]   See for the contacts between the C.M.S. and "Basel": A. Streckeisen, *Die kirchliche Missionsgesellschaft von England (C.M.S.) und die Basler Mission*, I—II, E.M.M. VIC (1950), pp. 76—96, 114—128.

[172]   E. M. Howse, *op. cit.*, p. 93.

[173]   E. Stock, *op. cit.*, pp. 64 ff.

[174]   *Propaganda, op. cit.*, pp. 116—117.

episcopal supervision, [175] the leaders of the S.P.G. wanted a full integration of all missionary work in the "Establishment". Another factor which contributed to the awakening of the missionary ideal in S.P.G. circles was the religious deepening which resulted from the activity of the "Clapton Sect". The missionary work of the S.P.C.K. was gradually taken over by the S.P.G., which was considered by the High Church group as the missionary agency of the Church of England; the S.P.C.K. returned to the position of Bible- and Tract-Society.

e. Other activities in England

Of the other religious activities in England which were in one way or another related to the missionary awakening we mention in the first place the *Religious Tract Society,* which took its origin from the same circle as the L.M.S.: the Society was formed after the L.M.S. anniversary of 1799; its purpose was to provide Evangelical tracts to be used in the work of home missions, as appears from what Bogue wrote on the contents of these tracts in his *On the Distribution of Religious Tracts:* "The Tract should contain *pure truth.* There should be *some account of the way of a sinner's salvation* in every tract . . ." [176] Of more importance for direct missionary work was its younger sister, the *British and Foreign Bible Society,* founded in 1804 by the same group which supported the Religious Tract Society. That from its inception there was a consciousness of the relation between the Bible Society and the work of foreign missions, appears from what the correspondent of the Society in Wales wrote in 1804: "Great joy prevails universally at the thought that poor heathens are likely soon to be in possession of a Bible; and you will never have a prayer put up, without a petition for the Bible Society and Heathen Nations". [177] Schick even calls the unity of Bible-, Tract- and missionary movement characteristic of the Evangelical Revival in England. [178]

A third organization which deserves special mention is the *London Society for the Promotion of Christianity among the Jews,* founded in 1808 by a converted German Jew, S. C. F. Frey. In the eschatological expectations of many Evangelicals of those times the idea of the conversion of the Jews played a more or less important part, but it would be wrong to assume a direct connection between certain eschatological views and the foundation of this Society. In its second Report the Committee of the Society expressly declared:

---

[175] In 1841 a rapprochement took place between the Episcopate and the C.M.S.: H. Cnattingius, *op. cit.,* pp. 196 ff.
[176] As quoted by S. W. Green, *The Story of the Religious Tract Society,* London 1899, p. 6.
[177] See: J. Owen, *The History of the Origin and First Ten Years of the British and Foreign Bible Society,* I, London 1816, p. 161.
[178] E. Schick, *Vorboten und Bahnbrecher, op. cit.,* p. 264.

"If nothing peculiar appeared in the aspect of the times—if neither Jews nor Christians believed the future restoration of Israel—if no exposition of prophecy had awakened attention or excited expectation in men's mind—if it were possible to place things as they stood many centuries ago—still your Committee would urge the importance and propriety of establishing a Jewish Mission". [179]

f.   Missionary awakening in Scotland

We bring our historical survey to a close by giving consideration to the missionary development in Scotland. In doing so, we must first of all give some attention to the work of the first Scottish missionary society, the *Society in Scotland for the Propagation of Christian Knowledge*. [180] As we saw in the foregoing chapters, the S.S.P.C.K. rendered a real service to the cause of missions by supporting the work of David Brainerd and other American missionaries. But just like the S.P.G. and the S.P.C.K. in England, the S.S.P.C.K. lost much of its missionary dynamism during the second half of the eighteenth century: a decline proportional to the increase of Moderate influence in the Church of Scotland. It cannot be said that the Moderates were absolutely opposed to missionary work: in 1762 the General Assembly of the Church of Scotland granted to the S.S.P.C.K. at its request a collection on behalf of the missionary work of the Society. [181] But there was no real enthusiasm: in his sermon, preached before the Society in 1755, Principal William Robertson, one of the leading Moderates, apologized for the missionary lethargy of the Society; [182] twenty years later, Robertson declared: ". . . the conversion of distant nations is not the chief care of the Society for Propagating Christian Knowledge: an object nearer at hand [*i.e.* the Society's work in the Islands and Highlands] demands their more immediate attention". [183] This preference for educational work at home was founded on the fundamental attitude of the Moderates: though they painted in well-chosen words the—distant—future, in which the whole earth would be filled with the glory of the Lord, they deemed it necessary that first of all a "removal of superstition in the Christian world" [184] should take place. Educational ideals superseded the old

---

[179]   See: W. F. Gidney, *The History of the London Society for Promoting Christianity among the Jews*, I, London 1908, p. 35.

[180]   In the rest of this chapter abbreviated as S.S.P.C.K. It must be kept in mind, that this Society was quite independent from the S.P.C.K. in England: see above, pp. 57—58.

[181]   D. Mackichan, *op. cit.*, p. 7.

[182]   See: D. Mackichan, *op. cit.*, pp. 72 ff.

[183]   W. Robertson, *The Situation of the World at the Time of Christ's Appearance, A Sermon preached before the S.S.P.C.K.*, Jan. 6, 1775, on Col. 1.26, Edinburgh 1818, p. 34.

[184]   Th. Hardy, *The Progress of the Christian Religion, A Sermon preached before the S.S.P.C.K. . . .*, 30 May 1793, on Hebr. 2.8, Edinburgh 1794, p. 45.

missionary fervour; the Erasmian line was accentuated to such a degree as to become a hindrance to the accomplishing of the missionary task! [185]

But other forces were stirring. The contact between Jonathan Edwards and the Scottish Evangelicals proved to be fruitful for the cause of missions, [186] the rising tide of Evangelicalism was accompanied by a growing missionary enthusiasm, and with great interest the Scottish Evangelicals followed the course of missionary events on the other side of the border: the foundation of the L.M.S. especially made a deep impression in Scotland. In 1797 the aged John Mill, minister of Dunrossness on the Shetland Islands, who had personally known Whitefield and who had officiated at the celebration of the Lord's Supper during the Cambuslang revival, wrote down in his diary: "It has pleased God also to stir up in the hearts of ministers and people of all ranks and denominations to have the gospel propagated among the heathen in all parts of the globe ..." He then went on to give a description of the foundation of the L.M.S. and the sending out of missionaries to "Ottahittee". [187] "Of all ranks": possibly Mill was not thinking only of the plain English Congregationalists who gladly offered up their money for the cause of missions, but also of the Scottish nobleman Robert Haldane, who, as Mill knew, had planned to go out to Bengal together with Bogue and some other Scottish ministers [188]—a plan stranded on the fact that he could not receive permission to go to India because of his progressive political inclinations. [189] "Of all denominations": alas this goes too far, but it is true that the L.M.S. in its initial stage afforded a good example of ecumenical cooperation in which Scotsmen of various denominations also participated—ministers of the "Burgher" Secession group even played an important part in the foundation of the L.M.S. [190]

In Scotland, the L.M.S. not only met with sympathy, but became a model for imitation: in 1796 the *Edinburgh Missionary Society* (from 1819: *Scottish Missionary Society*) and the *Glasgow Missionary*

---

[185] At the end of the century, the S.S.P.C.K. "gave little or nothing to Foreign Missions except the interest of the money devoted to that purpose", as appears from the Report of a committee of inquiry, appointed in 1796 on the motion of Dr Erskine: R. W. Weir, *A History of the Foreign Missions of the Church of Scotland*, Edinburgh 1900, p. 10.

[186] See above, pp. 92—93.

[187] *The Diary of the Rev. John Mill, edited by G. Goudie*, Edinburgh 1889, pp. 107—108.

[188] See: J. Mill, *op. cit.*, p. 112; Mill even sent a petition to Parliament in favour of Haldane's admission into India!

[189] Haldane's plans had the support of Wilberforce and the sympathy of Bishop Porteous: A. Haldane, *op. cit.*, pp. 114—116; but the opposition was so strong that even the Missionary Societies did not dare to move in his favour; G. Struthers, *The History of the Rise, Progress and Principles of the Relief Church, op. cit.*, p. 389.

[190] R. Lovett, *op. cit.*, p. 25, and J. McKerrow, *History of the Secession Church*, II, Edinburgh 1839, p. 296.

Society were founded, followed, among others, by the *Northern Missionary Society* (Inverness 1800).[191] But what was the attitude of the Churches towards the missionary awakening? The Associate Synod ("Burgher" Seceders) wholeheartedly supported the newly-formed Societies, but the General Associate Synod ("Anti-Burghers") had some objections: it was feared that the Societies were "too latitudinarian in their constitution" and that they would help to break down "the comely order of church government which Christ had appointed". Consequently, the Synod judged "that neither their own members, nor the people under their inspection, can, in a consistency with their distinguished profession as Seceders, and without danger of falling from it, publicly cooperate with these societies in their present state".[192] The fact, however, that several protests were launched against this decision and that some Anti-Burgher congregations even supported the Edinburgh Missionary Society, proves that here, too, the climate was changing.[193] The Synod of the Relief Church—a community in which the offer of grace to all sinners was strongly emphasized[194]—expressed itself in favour of "the laudable spirit of zeal which has been excited in various parts of this kingdom, to send the knowledge of salvation to the heathen nations"; at the same time, however, it resolved not to take a direct part in the work of foreign missions, but "to water the wilderness and solitary places at home".[195]

Though the two Secession Churches—on the eve of a new split in their own circle—and the Relief Church each adopted another course towards the practical realization of the missionary command, it is clear that these three Churches, all members of the "Evangelical family", at least fundamentally recognized the missionary duty of the Church. The situation becomes more complex, however, when we look at the Church of Scotland, in which the Moderates were still supreme, though the swelling tide of Evangelicalism already threatened their once strong position. The matter of the Missionary Societies was

---

[191]   J. Macinnes, *op. cit.*, p. 141.
[192]   J. McKerrow, *op. cit.*, II, pp. 48—50.
[193]   See also: D. Maclean, *Scottish Calvinism and Foreign Missions*, art. *cit.*, p. 7.
[194]   P. Hutchison wrote in his *A Compendious View of the Religious System taught by the Relief Synod* (1779), quoted by G. Struthers, *The History of the Rise of the Relief Church*, Edinburgh and London 1848, p. 316: "All men, as they are the sinful and perishing descendants of Adam, have a right to hear the gospel, because Christ himself gave his apostles, and in them, all ordinary ministers after them, a commission to go into all the world, and preach the gospel unto *every creature*. This *unlimited commission*, given by the chief Shepherd, to *all* his under shepherds, joined with his own *general invitation*, ... gives all men a right to hear the gospel, and to believe in him, high and low, rich and poor, learned and unlearned, wise and foolish, sober and profane, Barbarian, Scythian, bond and free, sensible and insensible sinners".
[195]   G. Struthers, *The History of the Rise, Progress and Principles of the Relief Church*, *op. cit.*, (Glasgow 1843), p. 394.

brought up at the General Assembly of 1796: the Synod of Fife overtured to the General Assembly, "that the Assembly may consider of the most effectual methods, by which the Church of Scotland may contribute to the diffusion of the Gospel among the Heathen Nations". [196] From the beginning, it was clear that on this issue the Moderates and the Evangelicals would be sharply divided. [197] The overtures found able defenders. W. Macbean urgently appealed to the ministers, "who, every Lord's Day in public, offer up their fervent prayers, and those of their congregations, for the speedy and universal diffusion of the Gospel..." [198] Robert Heron, the ruling elder from Galloway, made a big point of the favourable circumstances: the amazingly increased extent of commerce and the general diffusion of knowledge; in addition, by promoting the cause of missions, the Church of Scotland could prove itself innocent of the charge laid by David Hume, that the Scottish Established Church was more favourable to the cause of Deism than any other religious establishment. Cautiously, he moved that a committee be appointed by the Assembly, to inquire into and to deliberate upon the overtures—a proposal seconded by Dr. Erskine. [199] Then followed a strong attack by an outspoken Moderate, G. Hamilton. After some expressions of rather platonic love for the missionary cause in general, Hamilton went on to argue that civilization must precede evangelization: "Men must be polished and refined in their manners, before they can be properly enlightened in religious truths... Our Saviour himself we find instructing the inhabitants of the villages and populous cities of Judea, instead of collecting crowds of barbarians to listen to his doctrine". [200] Paul, too, would not have been prepared to preach to "the Barbarians of Malta", but this contention of Hamilton's was splendidly refuted by Erskine. An unknown eye-witness tells us: "When in the General Assembly the cause of foreign missions was opposed on the ground that Paul did not preach to the rude people of Malta, Dr. Erskine said: "Rax me that Bible", and read the account of that visit, and said, Paul prayed, and surely it would be in the name of Jesus, and he would tell them why he did so, etc."; Principal Hugh Watt supposes that Erskine opened the Bible at the last chapter of Acts, and read first Acts 28.2, then, on the page in front, Rom. 1.14! [201] In a brilliant speech Erskine tried to keep the door open for

---

[196] *Account, op. cit.* (see p. 111, note 27), pp. 3—4.
[197] D. Maclean writes in his *Scottish Calvinism and Foreign Missions, art. cit.,* p. 8: "To ask the Assembly, at such a period in world history, to identify the Church with an enterprise promoted by Societies even unjustly suspected, and go to the ends of the earth with a religion that was apparently collapsing elsewhere, and might, according to some, collapse in Scotland, was a severe test to determine whether faith or fear prevailed in the Church of Scotland".
[198] *Account, op. cit.,* p. 7.
[199] *Account, op. cit.,* pp. 11—16.
[200] *Account, op.cit.,* pp. 18, 22.
[201] The unknown eye-witness was the editor of the 1740 edition of James

the acceptance of the overtures—but he pleaded in vain: neither his able confutation of some charges, lodged by Hamilton, nor his eloquent defence of missionary work to non-civilized people—". . . I have always considered it the peculiar glory of Christianity, that it is adapted alike to the learned and the unlearned; to the citizen, and to the savage: to the bond and to the free..."[202]—could break through the barrier of Moderate resistance to the missionary proposals. Even Evangelicals [203] were influenced by the contention of some Moderates—Principal G. Hill and David Boyle—that there was a connection between the missionary movement and "the political aspect of the times", a contention the more obnoxious because it contained an insinuation in the direction of a link between the missionary Societies and the revolutionary agitation of the period. [204] Yet the speech of Principal Hill [205] was couched in a tone different to that of the other Moderates: his objections were only directed against the Missionary Societies in their actual form, not against the missionary ideals themselves; his motion, which, though it asked the General Assembly to judge the overtures in question "highly inexpedient", nevertheless held open the door for future missionary action—"that they will embrace with zeal and thankfulness, any future opportunity of contributing, by their exertions, to the propagation of the Gospel of Christ, which divine providence may hereafter open"—was carried by a majority of 58 against 44 votes. [206]

The result may have been disappointing at the actual moment, but it offered some brighter aspects too: the cause of missions had been brought to the notice of the Church of Scotland in its highest representative court; the debate had circled around the fundamental issues; it appeared that a large minority was for immediate missionary

---

Robe's *Narration of the Revival of Religion at Kilsyth etc.*; Principal Watt came into contact with this work after he had formed his opinion on this matter—so it afforded a proof *a posteriori* of his supposition. See: H. Watt, *"Moderator, Rax me that Bible"*, in: Records of the Scottish Church History Society X (1950), pp. 54—55.

[202] *Account, op. cit.*, p. 34.

[203] Such as Hugh Mackay, in later times member of the Northern Missionary Society: D. Maclean, *art. cit.*, p. 11.

[204] See above, p. 111. A striking example of this anti-mission attitude is also to be found in a letter of Dr. W. Porteous to the Lord Advocate of Scotland, dated on 24 January, 1797: "You have no doubt heard a great deal of this missionary madness, and of Mr. Haldane's intention of going to Indostan ... Many of us have reason to believe that the whole of this missionary business grows from a democratical root ...": see W. M. Kirkland, *op. cit.*, pp. 237—238. Dr. Porteous, Church of Scotland minister in Glasgow, combined a rigid orthodoxy with a sterile conservatism: "Strongly orthodox in his views, he resisted the smallest innovations", E. G. Hawke in *Dictionary of National Biography*, XLVI, p. 169.

[205] A Moderate theologian, who in his teachings had kept closer to the Calvinistic heritage of his Church than many other members of his party, see D. Maclean, *Aspects of Scottish Church History*, Edinburgh 1927, p. 93; but "his more orthodox beliefs were too little under the influence of an evangelical spirit to come forth in any tangible form against prevailing errors", writes R. Buchanan in his *The Ten Years' Conflict*, I, Glasgow 1852, p. 167.

[206] *Account, op. cit.*, pp. 53, 65.

action, and that among the majority which had voted against the overtures there were influential figures who were not without sympathy for the cause of missions as such. The door had been set ajar, and it would not be long before it was opened wide. Sons of Scottish manses were sent out by the Missionary Societies. [207] Prominent Scotsmen were confronted with the greatness of the missionary task. [208] Scotland took its part in the action of 1813 to secure the right of missionaries in the new Charter of the East India Company. [209] A Scottish Presbyterian chaplain, Dr. J. Bryce, was sent out to India, and became, on the spot, an enthusiast for direct missionary action. In consequence he sent a memorial on this subject to the General Assembly of 1824, and when the cause of missions was brought up at this General Assembly in the form of a number of overtures asking the Church to take steps towards accepting the responsibility for a missionary task of its own, it was one of the leading Moderates, Dr. J. Inglis, [210] who, referring to the pledge given in 1796, moved to accept the overtures, which were indeed unanimously accepted. [211] This meant that the Church as such recognised its responsibility for the missionary task. It also meant that the two main currents in the Scottish Church were one in their support of the work of foreign missions. The more or less Erasmian line of the Moderates—still evident with Inglis, though in a weakened form [212]—joined with the reformatory line of the Evangelicals. Alexander Duff, one of the greatest Scottish missionaries of the nineteenth century, combined in his person and work the two lines: himself a downright Evangelical, reared in the sphere of the Evangeical Revival, [213] adherent of the Free Church, he yet put into practice Inglis' ideas on the preeminence of educational mis-

---

[207] D. Mackichan, op. cit., pp. 107 ff.

[208] Thomas Chalmers turned Evangelical under the influence of—among others— the Reports of the Baptist Missionary Society: E. A. Payne, The Evangelical Revival and the Beginning of the Modern Missionary Movement, art. cit., p. 231.

[209] The first petition that was lodged was from the General Assembly of the Church of Scotland! R. W. Weir, op. cit., p. 27.

[210] J. Macleod writes: "Inglis, in view of his soundness of doctrine, might be spoken of not as a Moderate, but as an Evangelical Erastian", op. cit., p. 197.

[211] D. Mackichan, op. cit., pp. 112 ff.

[212] In a sermon of 1818, Inglis declared: "Till the human mind be, to a certain extent, cultivated and enlightened, it may be fairly regarded as, in one respect, incapable of entertaining the faith of the gospel ...; ... faith ... can be produced only in those, who are more or less qualified to estimate the excellence of the gospel doctrine ..."; schools have to be founded "to lay a foundation for the success of all other means": J. Inglis, Sermon preached before the S.S.P.C.K. in the High Church of Edinburgh on Is. 49.6, Edinburgh 1818, pp. 16, 17, 19. The same ideas, promulgated by Inglis at the General Assembly of 1824, called forth a protest from the Evangelical side: R. W. Weir, op. cit., p. 33.

[213] Duff's parents came to conversion under the preaching of Rev. A. Stewart of Pitlochry, who in his turn had been "awakened" under the influence of Charles Simeon; the parents "brought up their child in the full faith of the Gospel, and with a special dedication of his life to the service of Christ": H. C. G. Moule op. cit., p. 117.

sionary work. [214] But though it must be said in honour of the Scottish Moderates of this period that they gave a valuable contribution to the development of the work of missions, it was the (Calvinistic [215]) Evangelicals who were the most active supporters of the missionary cause. After his transition to the Evangelical side, Chalmers became an ardent advocate of foreign missions: the B.M.S., the L.M.S. and the Moravians found in him an able defender, the Scottish missionary work and above all the Bible Society a devoted cooperator. [216]

4. THE MOTIVES OF THE GREAT MISSIONARY AWAKENING

a. *Political motives*

We have seen that in a former period the work of missions sometimes threatened to deteriorate into a useful means of supporting Britain's colonial policy. A late example of this utilitarian view of missions is to be found in a communication of the S.S.P.C.K., made in 1772: "It is with particular pleasure we lay before the public any accounts of the success of our attempts to spread the gospel among the heathens in America, as nothing can tend more to secure our Colonies in that part of the World, from the ravages and desolations of Indian wars . . .", [217] though in this quotation the utilitarian argument (missionary work serves the security of our colonies) is closely connected with the humanitarian argument (missionary work creates a better condition of life). The political argument lost its strength after the emancipation of the American Colonies and the resultant change of the political situation on the other side of the Atlantic. Besides, the new Evangelicalism brought with it a certain purification of the missionary motives: the religious factors were again made central. David Bogue remarked in 1792: "And I frankly acknowledge that it would give me infinitely more delight to hear of a few solitary missionaries crossing the Ghauts, than a well-appointed English army". [218] And of the first missionaries to the Pacific Islands it has been rightly remarked: "Politics, or any political relation of their newly acquired flocks to Britain, was not in all their early thoughts". [219] Among the Evangelical chaplains also, who, on account of their function in the

---

[214]   See: D. Mackichan, *op. cit.*, p. 113 note 1.
[215]   No doubt the greatest stimulus as well as the most substantial support was given by the Evangelicals, who in this period were still fully Calvinistic: it is due to a misunderstanding, when O. Dibelius in his *Das Kirchliche Leben Schottlands*, Gieszen 1911, p. 40, considers as one of the causes of the Scottish missionary awakening a supposed weakening of the doctrine of predestination.
[216]   See among others: H. Watt, *Thomas Chalmers and the Disruption, op. cit.*, pp. 38—39.
[217]   H. Hunter, *op. cit.*, p. 55.
[218]   J. Morison, *op. cit.*, p. 507.
[219]   J. N. Ogilvie, *Our Empire's Debt to Missions*, London 1924, p. 29.

community of the "Establishment", no doubt had a stronger feeling for the relation between Church and State than had the Dissenters, we never meet political motives as the real background of their missionary zeal and activity, though in their vindication of the right of missions we sometimes hear sounds which point into a wrong direction: "Our religion is therefore inculcated ... 2ndly Because it attaches the governed to their governors". [220] We find an example of a utilitarian argument of another kind in a speech, given by the L.M.S. missionary, John Williams, before his departure to the Pacific in 1817: "Thus we see that the nation at large is interested, and that everyone, who is concerned to promote the commercial welfare of his country, is bound to exert himself on behalf of the missionary cause". [221] We must not forget, however, that an utterance such as this was rather a motivation than a motive; besides, it belongs already to a later period, in which again the "usefulness of missions" began to be emphasized; in the period covered by this chapter, utilitarian motives are only to be found at the margin of the thinking of the Evangelicals, of whose true spirit we find a good specimen in Melvill Horne, who emphatically, even with indignation, rejected "the stimulus of interest". [222]

The Evangelicals were not prepared to consider their missionary work as nothing more than a concomitant of the colonizing work of the State. At the same time, the politicians felt more strongly than before the existence of a certain cleavage between missions and colonial policy. While during the period of the First Empire the colonial authorities also considered the work of missions as a valuable contribution to the stabilization of the political situation, the attitude of the first builders of the Second Empire was sometimes even hostile towards the missionary cause. They saw the work of the missionaries as a de-stabilizing factor in the whole of their colonial policy and consequently they opposed the introduction of missions into their territory with all their might. In this negatieve attitude they were supported by anti-Evangelical clergymen. S. Butler, later the Bishop of Worcester, wrote in 1811: "Unless our Government act cautiously, these methodistical proselytisers, by their absurd enthusiasm, will bring about the loss of India"; [223] not less sharp were the utterances of Sydney Smith, who wrote in the *Edinburgh Review* of 1808: "Upon the whole, it appears to us hardly possible to push the business of proselytism in India to any length, without incurring the utmost risk of losing our empire"; the leading Evangelicals "would deliberately, piously and conscientiously expose our whole Eastern

---

[220] In the *Memoir of the Expediency of an Ecclesiastical Establishment for our Empire in the East, The Works of the Rev. Claudius Buchanan, op. cit.*, p. 206
[221] L. B. Wright and M. A. Fry, *Puritans in the South Seas*, New York 1936, p. 109.
[222] Melvill Horne, *op. cit.*, p. 28.
[223] Quoted by R. W. Weir, *op. cit.*, p. 22.

empire to destruction, for the sake of converting half a dozen Brahmans, who, after stuffing themselves with rum and rice, and borrowing money from the missionaries, would run away . . ." [224]

On the Evangelical side, the awareness of a certain distance between mission and colonial policy found its source in a twofold cause. Evangelicalism was to a certain degree a reaction against that secularized combination of the interests of Church and State, which had been the Latitudinarian counterpart of the Puritan theocratic concept and which had brought the Church into an Erastian position; however great the difference might be in political attitude between the more radical Evangelical Dissenters and the more conservative Evangelical Churchmen, they were all prepared to keep their distance from the State and its official policy. Besides, the interests of the Evangelical Revival were fully and directly religious; primarily, the Evangelicals aimed at personal conversion, and though they were not so "otherwordly" as to forget the needs of their own times, the ultimate goal of their activities was not the promotion of the glory of the British Empire, but the expansion of the Kingdom of God. [225] We must add that this "purification of the missionary motive", though it had a hidden relation with the deepest *motifs* of Evangelicalism, was not intentionally thought out by the Evangelicals, nor was it a purification all along the line. It was rather a result of a coincidence of circumstances, religious as much as secular, in which a part was also played by the isolated position of Evangelicalism and the distrust of many leading persons against all Evangelical activities. The scene would change in the Victorian age, in which Evangelicalism became a respected power in a State that tried to regain its religious aspect: during that period a rapprochement took place between empire and missions, [226] which has exercised its positive and negative influence up to these times! [227]

---

[224] *The Works of the Rev. Sydney Smith, op. cit.,* pp. 112—113.

[225] Cf. E. Williams in an *Address to the Missionaries* (of the L.M.S.): the motive had neither to be "your own reputation", nor "the glory of the British name", in: *A Sermon and Charge delivered on Occasion of the Designation of the First Missionaries,* London 1796, p. 37.

[226] Cf. the Second Draft of the *Royal Proclamation* on the occasion of the taking over of the administration of India by the Crown: "Firmly relying ourselves on the truths of Christianity, and acknowledging with gratitude the solace of our religion, We disclaim alike the Right and the Desire to impose Our convictions on any of Our subjects . . .": the first part of the sentence was inserted under the personal influence of the Queen. See: J. N. Ogilvie, *Our Empire's Debt to Missions. op. cit.,* p. 21.

[227] When in more than one instance during the first half of the nineteenth century British missionaries tried to bring the territory in which they worked under the aegis of the British Empire, their attitude was not inspired by imperialist motives, but rather by the desire to protect the natives against oppression and exploitation by white settlers, who had a "free hand" in those districts where no judicial system could take effectual measures against the offenders: E. A. Walker, *The British Empire, its Structure and Spirit,* London-New York-Toronto 1943, p. 37.

b. Humanitarian-cultural motives

From what has been said above it can be easily deduced that the cultural motive, too, did not play an independent role with the Evangelicals. To a certain extent this deduction is correct. On this point also a marked difference was evident between the Evangelicals on one hand and the Latitudinarians and the Moderates on the other. The latter group accentuated the this-wordly aspect of the Christian message to such a degree, that for them the propagation of Christianity and of Christian culture practically coincided. In our second chapter we quoted Bishop Watson, who expected more from the extension of science and commerce than from the propagation of Christianity by missionaries; [228] the same Bishop wrote to David Brown in 1806: "The commerce and colonization of Christian states have civilized America, and they will in process of time, civilize and christianize the whole earth . . ." [229] Other examples can be added: that of Sydney Smith, who saw "the duty of making proselytes" spring from "the duty of bene-volence", and who consequently judged the work of missions by the measure of its effectiveness with regard to the conferring of "present happiness" and *"human* comfort" to the Hindus; [230] that of Bishop S. Pelham, who remarked that the Christians had to instil into the Hindus "the mild precepts and social duties, which our Saviour taught us . . ." [231] or of Bishop Th. Burgess, who considered it as the Christian duty "to enlight and reform a people oppressed by intellectual and moral darkness". [232] Again, such Scottish Moderates as still stood on the line of the rationalist tradition could ony appreciate a missionary activity that would let "philosophy and learning . . . take the pre-cedence" [233] and that would not go out with "the teachings of meta-physics", but only with " . . . the rational and attractive theology of the New Testament," [234] which meant in fact the reduction of the biblical message to a system of morality!

At first sight it seems as if the Evangelicals virtually adopted the same attitude. They, too, "pleaded the cause of humanity" in their motivation of the missionary task. William Carey remarked in his *Enquiry* with regard to the "uncivilized state of the heathen": "Can we hear that they are without the gospel, without government, without laws, and without arts and sciences; and not exert ourselves to introduce amongst them the sentiments of men, and of Christians? Would not the spread of the gospel be the most effectual mean of

---

228 See p. 62.
229 See: *The Works of the Rev. Claudius Buchanan, op. cit.,* p. 173.
230 *Works, op. cit.,* pp. 116, 112, 119.
231 In a sermon, preached in 1807:*Propaganda, op. cit.,* p. 122.
232 In a sermon, preached in 1808: *Propaganda, op. cit.,* p. 123.
233 G. Hamilton in the debate of 1796: *Account, op. cit.,* p. 18.
234 Th. Hardy, *The Progress of the Christian Religion, A Sermon, op. cit.,* p. 18.

their civilization? Would not that make them useful members of society?", [235] and at the end of his *Christian Researches in Asia* Buchanan remarked, speaking of himself in the third person: "The object of his Work, and of his Researches, has been to deliver the people of Hindustan from painful and sanguinary rites ...". [236] Similar arguments were used by Wilberforce in his defence of the missionary cause in Parliament: " ... a regard for their temporal well-being would alone furnish abundant motives for our endeavouring to diffuse among them the blessings of Christian light and moral instruction". [237]

Quite plainly, cultural and social "uplift" of the non-christianized nations did not lie outside the scope of interest of the Evangelical missionary leaders. They had the cultural interest in common with their Puritan predecessors—Carey recognized himself on this point also to be in alignment with Eliot and Brainerd. [238] At the same time, they shared the philanthropic enthusiasm with their non-Evangelical contemporaries: in this they did not disown the "synthetic" character of English piety, which has always left an opening for the values of God's "common grace". It was out of humanitarian interest that the Evangelicals fought their grand campaign against slavery and their minor battles against other forms of injustice and inhumanity. But with them the cultural and philanthropic interests never absorbed the religious motives: Carey made his remarks on the duty of civilization in a defence against the charge of impractability, directed against missionary work; Buchanan knew that the Christian religion had also to be "inculcated" because of its "eternal sanctions", [239] and in his *The Star in the East* he remarked: "Every man, who hath felt the influence of religion on his own heart, will desire to extend the blessings to the rest of mankind"; [240] Wilberforce preceded the passage which we quoted by the words: "Not, Sir, that I would pretend to conceal from the House, that the hope which, above all others, chiefly gladdens my heart, is that of being instrumental in bringing them into the paths by which they may be led to everlasting felicity". [241] "Chiefly gladdens my heart ..."—the main motives of these Evangelicals lay in a sphere other than that of cultural or philanthropic interests: the centre of gravity of their missionary work lay in the proclamation of the redemption through the saving work of Christ, which was the solid foundation of all other activities. "If the human and social virtues

---

[235]   *An Enquiry, op. cit.*, p. 70.
[236]   *Works, op. cit.*, p. 164.
[237]   From his speech in the parliamentary debate of June 22, 1813: E. M. Howse, *op. cit.*, p. 89.
[238]   *In loco citato.*
[239]   *Works*, p. 206.
[240]   *Works*, p. 314.
[241]   *In loco citato.*

were recommended, it was on considerations founded on the scheme of salvation through Christ, ... every thing else was preached in reference to him", remarked John Erskine in a discourse on the preaching of Christ to the Gentiles, in which he drew a line from the apostolic preaching to the actual task. [242] Professor Moore reverses the situation when he writes: "It is easy to see that, of this enthusiasm for humanity which marked the end of the eighteenth century ... the outbreak of missionary zeal was but a part". [243] Not every humanitarian reformer was pro-missionary—on the contrary: the missionary awakening sprang from other sources, and though in some instances humanitarian motives have played their part in the missionary awakening, the Evangelicals themselves were quite aware of the fact that cultural motives only took a subordinate place in the revival of the missionary idea. Fuller remarked in his answer to the attacks of the *Edinburgh Review:* "We had no interst to serve but that of Christ. It was in our hearts to do something for his name among the heathen; and, if it might be, to enlarge the boundaries of his kingdom". [244]

c. The ascetic motive

Especially in the case of Henry Martyn we meet the ascetic motive as a factor in the personal dedication to the work of missions: in him we see the continuation of Brainerd's line. No doubt Martyn was one of the most saintly figures in the missionary circle of our period. In his *Diary* we find his personal reflections, the story of his spiritual struggle, the tale of his disappointments and the description of the rise of the light, again and again, through dark clouds of despondency and uncertainty. Brainerd was his shining example; on his birthday in 1810 he wrote: " ... today I completed my twenty-ninth year; how much had D. Brainerd done at this time of life"; [245] also on the question of celibacy he was sometimes inclined to follow Brainerd: "When I think of Brainerd, how he lived among the Indians, travelling freely from place to place: can I conceive he would have been so useful had he been married ...? But yet voluntary celibacy seems so much more noble and glorious, and so much more beneficial in the way of example, that I am loth to relinquish the idea of it"; [246] the same thoughts occurred to him when he read the life of Francis Xavier: "I was exceedingly roused at this astonishing example of that great saint, and began to consider, whether it was not my duty to live, as he did, in

---

[242] J. Erskine, *Discourses preached on Several Occasions*, Edinburgh 1798, pp. 403 ff. (Discourse XIII).
[243] E. C. Moore, *The Spread of Christianity in the Modern World*, Chicago 1919, p. 43.
[244] A. Fuller, *Complete Works*, V, London 1837, p. 204.
[245] *Journals and Letters, op. cit.*, II, p. 283.
[246] *Journals and Letters, op. cit.*, I, pp. 259—260.

voluntary poverty and celibacy". [247] Martyn was filled with a fervent desire for saintliness, a longing for a life which would burn out for God, though his asceticism was free from any association with the idea of the meritoriousness of good works. [248] It was rather connected with his spiritual disposition: while on one hand he had a cheerful character [249] yet he felt strongly that Christ considered "the ease and comfort" of his disciples in this world "as a mere trifle"—"He says to them: "Go through the world, while your young life lasts, and prepare men for that eternal world which is close upon them"; [250] he worked under the shadow of death [251] and he could never talk as cheerfully about missionary things as Carey and Marshman did. [252] Martyn's asceticism—pure and spiritualized as it was—was of a very personal character; and even with him it was not the main motive, and it was in no way characteristic of the prevailing tone of the missionary awakening in his times!

d.   The motive of debt

In the personal sphere, ascetic tendencies only played a limited part during the period of the great missionary awakening. But on the other hand there was in the same period a growing sense of collective debt and of the necessity of "penance" for all the faults and wrongs perpetrated by the "Christian" nations in their colonial and mercantile policy. The presence of this feeling is remarkable: this was a period of "empire-building" and of new expansion for the Western world, and in periods of dynamic activity man's spirit is but seldom open to the demand of self-inquiry concerning the legitimacy of the course which he is taking. We must not forget, however, the following facts: the failure of the "First Empire" made possible a more critical view of the preceding period; the faults of the British administration in India had been made public property through Court of Law and Parliament, and above all the public mind had been stirred to a recognition of the horrors of the slave-trade. In the Evangelical circle—though not exclusively there—the voice of the Christian conscience was heard, and it found its echo in a striving towards restitution for the wrongs inflicted upon other races, by bringing them into contact with the source of life and peace. While, after the abuses of British rule in

---

[247]   *Journals and Letters, op. cit.,* I, p. 470.
[248]   The "way of salvation by the righteousness of Christ" took a central place in his thinking: *Journals and Letters, op. cit.,* II, p. 101.
[249]   One of the high officials in Bombay wrote of him: "He is altogether a learned and cheerful man, but a great enthusiast in his holy calling...": H. C. G. Moule, *op. cit.,* p. 104.
[250]   From Martyn's Sermon on Matth. 28.18—20, in: *Sermons by the Late Rev. H. Martyn DD,* Calcutta 1822, p. 399.
[251]   In April 1806 he wrote: "Feeling myself very unwell, I was reminded of my no long continuance in this world": *Journals and Letters, op. cit.,* I, p. 436.
[252]   *Journals and Letters, op. cit.,* I, p. 457.

India had become known, there were to be heard "expressions of regret (to become common among the humanitarians of the nineteenth century) that Europeans had ever set foot on these distant shores...", [253] the Evangelicals felt that they had a positive task in the overseas territories. They recognised the guilt of their country: Carey saw it as a melancholy fact "that the vices of Europeans have been communicated wherever they themselves have been; so that the religious state of even heathens has been rendered worse by intercourse with them". [254] "Oh, turn your eyes to Afric's injured shore, Mourn o'er your nation's guilty traffic there...", [255] remarked Th. Beck in a poem, dedicated to the Directors of the L.M.S. In the same year these Directors wrote in the *Evangelical Magazine:* "Africa, that much-injured country, has been visited by Europeans, not for the communication of benefits, but to carry on a commerce which inevitably inflicts on its inhabitants the wounds of slavery and death...". [256] Wilberforce wrote in his diary in 1805, after a parliamentary defeat in the "great struggle": "The poor blacks rushed into my mind, and the guilt of our wicked land ', [257] and about the same time Martyn. speaking of the slave trade, reminded Wilberforce of the biblical words: "Shall I not visit these things". [258] This "pang of sympathy" became a motive for Christian deeds, born out of a deep feeling of debt, and as the most important deed the Evangelicals considered the proclamation of the gospel: "Ah! should not England earnestly begin/Her blood-recorded mischief to efface/With shame to put away her nation's sin... It is begun—the Messengers arise...", continued Beck. The Directors of the L.M.S. remarked, immediately following their complaint of Europe's guilt against Africa: "To this benighted and oppressed country we are desirous of sending the Gospel of Christ", and they wanted to direct their attention especially to the Western part of Africa, because "it is here where the guilt of Europeans has inflicted the deepest wounds". Robert Cecil mentioned the guilt of Christianity (its tolerance of the slave-trade) as a missionary motive in his C.M.S. Sermon of 1803, [259] and, to quote finally from a sermon preached for the S.P.G., Bishop Ryder remarked in 1819: "We shall be then, as Englishmen, amazed and confounded at the thought of our own *past* insensibility and negligence... and, to our deep remorse for the past, we shall add our strenuous resolution for the future". [260] There is enough here to show that the awareness

---

[253]   Lucy S. Sutherland, *op. cit.,* p. 367.
[254]   *An Enquiry, op. cit.,* p. 64.
[255]   Th. Beck, *The Mission, A Poem,* London 1796, p. 12.
[256]   As quoted by R. Lovett, *op. cit.,* p. 477.
[257]   E. M. Howse, *op. cit.,* p. 60.
[258]   *Journals and Letters, op. cit.,* I, p. 142.
[259]   E. Stock, *op. cit.,* I, p. 78.
[260]   *Propaganda, op. cit.,* p. 175.

of the "white man's debt" functioned as a motive in the missionary awakening! [261]

In this context one objection has to be faced. It is sometimes remarked that the missionary awakening was in fact a flight. Tr. K. Jones writes in an article on *The Missionary Vocation*: "There is perhaps some truth in suggesting that the modern missionary movement began two hundred years ago as an attempt to escape the difficult problems of industrial England". [262] Of course it is possible that incidentally the motive of flight has played a subconscious part in the decision to enter into the missionary task—but subconscious motives are difficult to indicate. It is not probable, however, that this motive has influenced the missionary awakening in its collectivity. Evangelical Dissenters were ardent champions of a more radical policy at home, and though the men of the Clapham sect did not always see clearly the urgent need for drastic social reforms, they were yet as deeply interested in British philanthropic activities as in the struggle for the oppressed negros. [263] Did they feel the full burden of the problems of the industrial revolution when they started their missionary activities? Probably not: here we meet one of their limitations. But in that case it is not logical to explain the missionary awakening partly from a feeling of reluctance to shoulder a task of which the full weight was not even surmised. On the contrary, the same spirit of responsibility for the souls of other people, which was such a mighty stimulus behind the missionary work of the Evangelicals, brought them to a renewed activity in the slums of the British cities and in the new industrial areas, where often it was only the Evangelical minister who cared for the "souls" of the inhabitants. Perhaps their activity was sometimes too individualistic, perhaps they had more an eye for the difficulties of the individual than for the collective problems—but before we accuse them of an escapist attitude with regard to the problems created by the industrial revolution, we do well to listen to Professor Trevelyan. After remarking that in the cause of the slave trade the Church Evangelicals were prepared to cooperate not only with their fellow-Evangelicals outside the Church of England, but also with free-thinkers and Unitarians, he continues by stating: "The same combination of forces . . . worked for the education of the poor in the

---

[261] The motive of debt is also present in the *Adres van het Zendeling-genoot-schap te London* etc., *op. cit.*, pp. 4—5: "Wij zijn bewust, hoe lang, en hoe beledigende wij onachtzaam geweest zijn omtrend de belangen van het Koninkrijk van onzen Verlosser, en hoe wij, terwijl wij met oogmerk om winst te doen, of Koophandel te drijven . . . zeeën en landen omtoogen . . . zielen, gekogt met het bloed van den in het vleesch verscheenen God, verwaarloost hebben. Wij buigen ons met diepe verootmoediging wegens ons voormaalig plichtverzuim voor zijne voeten . . .".

[262] Tracey K. Jones, *The Missionary Vocation*, in I.R.M. XL (1951), p. 403.

[263] See: E. M. Howse, *op. cit.*, pp. 124 ff.

British and Foreign School Society, and in the following generation for Shaftesbury's Factory legislation". [264]

e. Romantic motives

In the period which witnessed the rise of the romantic movement, the lack of romantic motives would be more remarkable than their presence. We have seen how a wave of romantic enthusiasm spread all over Britain as a result of the accounts, given by the explorers, of the South Sea territories, and how, especially through the influence of Hawkesworth, the ideas of Rousseau were introduced into Britain. The myth of the "noble savage" came to new life—and though some doubts regarding to the truth of this "myth" arose after the visit of Omai, a native of one of the South Sea Islands, to Britain, [265] romantic views still lingered on for a long time in British popular imagination.

The pioneer of modern British missions, Carey, had read with more than ordinary interst the accounts of the South Sea voyages: they found an echo with him because, no doubt, he had been touched by the romantic spirit which was in the air; partly through them, his eyes were opened to the problems of the wider world. [266] But though without a certain disposition for romance and adventure Carey would perhaps never have become the man whom history honours as a missionary leader of broad vision and admirable courage, it would be quite wrong to see in him a romantic dreamer. His clear and sober judgment guarded him against an unrealistic view of the heathen world, and his belanced mind did not fall into the errors of either a too bright or a too pessimistic view of the situation of the world "in pagan darkness". [267]

The same balanced view was not always possessed by some of the leaders of the L.M.S. It is as if they hesitated between their Calvinistic conception of the total depravity of man and the romantic views with which they had been imbued through their acquaintance with Hawkesworth's description of the Tahitians. L. B. Wright goes too far when he depicts the pioneers of the L.M.S. as men who "read about the Tahitians" and who consequently "felt a call to go to this island Macedonia, where dwelt a race of gentle and perfect people, destined to perdition simply because they had not heard the gospel message". [268] Their view of the Tahitians was not so naive as that! It had rather an ambivalent character: in the same sermon, in which Haweis pictured

---

[264] G. M. Trevelyan, *English Social History*, op. cit., p. 495.
[265] See: R. N. Stromberg, *op. cit.*, p. 57.
[266] S. Pearce Carey, *William Carey*, op. cit., pp. 12–13.
[267] Cf. *An Enquiry*, op. cit., p. 63: "Barbarous as these poor heathens are, they appear to be as capable of knowledge as we are; and in many places, at least, have discovered uncommon genius and tractableness".
[268] L. B. Wright, *Religion and Empire*, op. cit. p. 161.

the life of the inhabitants of the South Sea Islands with the darkest colours, he remarked: "No region of the world ... affords us happier prospects in our auspicious career of sending the Gospel to the heathen lands; now here are the obstacles apparently less, or the opportunities greater ..." [269] The noble Thomas Haweis was the great advocate of a mission to the South Seas on the ground of his optimistic views with regard to the possibility of a mission there: [270] "The ignorance, the levity, the stupidity, the perverseness of the heathen, we expect to meet, and overcome". [271] It looks as if Bogue was more sober in his judgment; he saw the situation of the heathen world as unfavourable, but added firmly: "Were it not bad, it would not require our aid". [272] We have no grounds for considering the romantic ideal as the dominant stimulus behind the missionary awakening in those circles that sympathized with the London Society—even with Haweis the deepest motives lay elsewhere—, but it cannot be denied that a certain amount of romanticism was not altogether strange to the rise of the great wave of enthusiasm which accompanied the first activities of the L.M.S. The applications of men and women who wanted to go out to Tahiti were "innumerable", [273] and it is stated in the biography of Bogue that "some of those who embarked on the second voyage to the South Seas had been allured by the flattering accounts given of the first". [274]

In other circles also we meet some romantic tendencies. Sometimes they coincided with a *theologia naturalis* which saw in heathenism "general and systematic analogies" to the Christian religion: Buchanan saw in Hinduism parallels to the doctrines of "the Trinity, the Incarnation (Jesus the Messiah is the true *Avatar*), the atonement and the work of the *Spirit*"; [275] in some cases they resulted from a naive spontaneity, as with Martyn, who wrote in his diary in July, 1806: "My romantic notions are for the first time almost realized,—for in addition to the beauties of sylvan scenery may be seen the more delightful object of multitudes of simple people listening to the words of eternal

---

[269] Th. Haweis, *The Apostolic Commission*, Marc. 16.15,16, in: *Sermons, preached in London at the Formation of the Missionary Society*, 22, 23, 24 Sept. 1795, London 1795, pp. 12—13.
[270] Cf. the 1798 Report of the Directors of the L.M.S.: "The islands of the South Seas were recommended to you, not as the most important objects of evangelization, but as the most accessible and favourable to our early efforts", in: *Thanksgiving Sermons, preached before the Missionary Society*, London 1798, p. 11. R. Lovett, *op. cit.*, p. 101, writes: "The powerful personality of Dr. Haweis, strengthened by his generous contributions, controlled the movement".
[271] Th. Haweis, *An Impartial and Succinct History, op cit.*, III, p. 349.
[272] D. Bogue, *Objections against a Mission to the Heathen stated and considered, Hagg. 1.2*, in: *Sermons, preached in London at the Formation of the Missionary Society, op. cit.*, p. 126.
[273] L. B. Wright and M. A. Fry, *Puritans in the South Seas*, New York 1936, p. 5.
[274] As quoted by R. Lovett, *op. cit.*, p. 66.
[275] In his *Christian Researches in Asia*, in: *Works, op. cit.*, pp. 158 ff.

life". [276] The Evangelicals did not live in isolation—and we may be thankful that they knew how to transform their share in the spirit of their times into positive gain. But they were by no means carried away by the waves of contemporary thinking. We know that Wesley retained his sober judgment when he read an enthusiastic account of the life of the inhabitants of the Pelew Islands. [277] And Wilberforce, too, was so deeply convinced of the corruption of human nature as to write on heathen life: "Surely, among these children of nature we may expect to find those virtuous tendencies, for which we have hitherto looked in vain. Alas! our search will still be fruitless!" [278] The Evangelicals who gathered round the C.M.S. especially were afraid of a too romantic attitude: in 1801, Thomas Scott gave a warning against "disreputable and romantic zeal". [279] Romanticism may sometimes have acted as a stimulus, but it is utterly wrong to try to explain the missionary awakening as a whole from the influence of the romantic movement.

f.   The theocentric motive

The idea of the "glory of God" has always taken a great place in Calvinism: "what is the chief and highest end of man? . . . to glorify God, and fully to enjoy him for ever". [280] As there were strong Calvinistic influences present behind the missionary awakening, it is quite natural that we meet with this motive more than once in our period. We may give some examples. Carey ended his *Enquiry* by remarking: "Surely it is worth while to lay ourselves out with all our might, in promoting the cause, and kingdom of Christ". [281] „The giving *glory to God in the highest,* and the spreading of *peace and good will among men on earth* are the only motives, which should influence these attempts", wrote Melvill Horne in his *Letters on Missions.* [282] Wilberforce remarked that there are "many passages of Scripture, wherein the promoting of *the glory* of God is commanded as our supreme and universal aim, and wherein the honour due unto *Him* is declared to be that in which he will allow no competitor to participate". [283] Bogue wrote in his *Letter to the Evangelical Dissenters who practise Infant Baptism:* "We all know that it is the supreme end of our existence to glorify God", and he added that we can only do that by leading "our brethren in pagan lands to glorify him also". [284]

---

[276]   *Journals and Letters, op. cit.* I, p. 476.
[277]   See above, p. 98.
[278]   W. Wilberforce, *A. Practical View, op. cit.,* p. 30.
[279]   E. Stock, *op. cit.,* p. 77.
[280]   *The Larger Catechism of Westminster,* Q. and A. 1.
[281]   *Op. cit.,* p. 8.
[282]   *Op. cit.,* p. 31.
[283]   W. Wilberforce, *A Practical View, op. cit.,* p. 157.
[284]   In: *The Evangelical Magazine,* Sept. 1794, p. 379.

Another L.M.S. man, E. Wiliams, also saw as the great motive: "the glory of God our Saviour". [285] These few examples could be multiplied —but they are sufficient to show that the theocentric motive played a great part in the thinking of the mission-minded Evangelicals. On the other hand we see that this motive practically never occurred in isolation: almost always we meet it in conjunction with other motives; in most cases the theocentric and the soteriological motive were so closely integrated, that they were seen as two different aspects of one and the same matter!

g.   The motive of love and compassion

The idea of love was one of the main components of Evangelical religious life. The Evangelicals saw in the concept of love more than a human quality, more than a virtue on the level of common humanity: for them, love was a quality which was closely connected with their relation to Christ; just as the Methodists knew themselves to be "constrained by Jesus' love to live the servants of mankind", the Evangelicals knew that only by "looking unto Jesus" they could "learn to grow in the love of God". [286] This expression contained more than a call to imitate the example of Jesus: [287] it supposed an existential relationship with Christ, by means of which the love of Christ could become a force in the life of his disciples. So Melvill Horne painted the apostles as men who "warmly felt" the love of Christ: "His blood had bought them, and his love *constrained* them to do and suffer all things for his sake". [288] The Evangelicals saw the factor of love in Christian action as a result of, and at the same time as a grateful response to, the love of Christ. They felt that a strong love was an indispensable element in the missionary attitude. Particularly with Melvill Horne we find a strong emphasis on the idea of love as the great stimulus of missionary action: "Reverend Brethren . . . you cannot be ungrateful for the blessings of revelation; and, whilst you rejoice in those blessings, you must have a benevolent desire to communicate them to a people, *who know not the only true God and Jesus Christ whom he hath sent . . . Do we love God . . .?* How does this love, this

---

[285]   In: *A Sermon and Charge delivered on the Occasion of the Designation of the First Missionaries, op. cit.,* p. 37.
[286]   W. Wilberforce, *A Practical View, op. cit.,* p. 337.
[287]   Yet the idea of Jesus' example was also present: *"Thou shalt love thy neighbour as thyself,* is a precept enjoined by authority, and illustrated and enforced by the example of the Redeemer", remarked Bogue in his *Address to Christians on the Distribution of Religious Tracts,* quoted by G. H. G. Hewitt. *Reflections on the Early History of the R.T.S.,* I.R.M. XXXIX (1950), p. 89. We find the same thought with Simeon, who saw the humiliation of Christ "as a pattern to be imitated", in: *Sermon on Phil. 2.5—8, preached before the C.M.S. in 1802, Proceedings of the Society for Missions to Africa and the East,* I, London 1805, p. 125.

reverence, this approbation, this conviction, accord with the astonishing coldness, with which we look upon a world, full of cruel habitations . . . ?" [289]

Love was a powerful incentive in the missionary awakening: love as gratitude for God's love in Christ, love as dedication to him who "so loved the world that he gave his only begotten Son". A fine example of the meaning of this love for the Christian cause is to be found in a remark of Wilberforce's in his diary: "Simeon with us—his heart glowing with love of Christ. How full he is of love, and of desire to promote the spiritual benefit of others". [290] Indeed, it was the love towards God which found its realization in love towards those who were in misery and need. This love, however, had more than one aspect and could even take more than one form. The first aspect under which we meet the motive of love is that of pity with the temporal needs of mankind, with the this-wordly aspect of human misery, a love which wanted to promote what used to be called "the present welfare" of the heathen nations. This aspect of the motive of love verged upon the cultural-humanitarian motive to such a degree, that it is often impossible to make a separation between the two. Yet it is still reasonable to maintain the distinction: the motive of love, as it found a place in the Evangelical circle, transcended the purely cultural and social interest by virtue of the fact that the this-worldly needs also were seen against their other-worldly background and were considered as—ultimately—religious problems. Speaking of those who "have no Bible, no written language, . . . no ministers, no good civil government . . .", Carey remarked: "Pity therefore, humanity, and much more Christianity, call loudly for every possible exertion to introduce the gospel amongst them". [291] In the first sermon, preached before the L.M.S., Haweis exclaimed, after having painted the social situation of the inhabitants of the South Sea Islands: "Ye untutored offspring of fallen nature, how are ye to be pitied!", and in the same context he remarked: "Yes, my dear friends, it is because we believe the wrath revealed from heaven against all ungodliness and unrighteousness of men . . . we are thus earnest to pluck some brands from the burning . . ." [292] Equally strong was the motive of pity with David Brown: "Utter disgust, intermingled with deepest pity, seemed to be the result in Mr Brown's mind of the knowledge he had acquired, in his investigation of the obscene and sanguinary frivolity of this debased religion". [293] And we saw above how Wilberforce, in his great speech

---

[289]   *Op. cit.*, pp. 4, 12.
[290]   As quoted by E. M Howse, *op. cit.*, p. 75.
[291]   *An Enquiry, op. cit.*, p. 13.
[292]   In: *Sermons, preached in London at the Formation of the Missionary Society, op. cit.*, pp. 12, 20—21.
[293]   [Ch. Simeon], *Memorial Sketches of the Rev. David Brown, op. cit.*, p. 150.

in Parliament on June 22, 1813, traced a direct connection between his humanitarian and evangelistic interests. [294]

It cannot be denied that the form which the motive of pity took among those Evangelicals who sponsored the missionary awakening was not always free from feelings of cultural superiority, while other religions were more often judged by their epiphenomena rather than by their deepest meaning. [295] But amidst a variety of all-too-human considerations we always find in the background the purely soteriological motive, which aimed at bringing the heathen to the salvation in Christ, to "everlasting felicity". In Evangelical circles the *soteriological* interest was prominent. V. F. Storr rightly remarks: "In the doctrinal teachings of the Evangelicals, Soteriology occupies the central place... Their passion was for saving souls...". [296] Here the question arises: did the Evangelicals believe that every heathen who died without "saving knowledge of Christ" would be lost? Perhaps their position on this point is best stated by Martyn: "... when I affirm my belief that those who reject the Triune Jehovah will perish, of course I mean those who do this deliberately and notwithstanding opportunities. I leave to God Almighty, the application of general threatenings to every particular case". [297] They were too deeply convinced of "the wrath of God" and "the depravity of human nature" to be able to concur with the latitudinarian view, that, because "a man is to be judged according to what he hath", "the gracious declaration of scripture ought to liberate from groundless anxiety, the minds of those who stated, in such moving language, the condition of the heathen". [298] From the Evangelical side it was remarked: "... the anti-scriptural sentiment, that heathens ... may be saved by their religions, if sincere in them ... has cut the very sinew of exertion". [299] On the other hand, the Evangelicals had seen too much of the overwhelming greatness of God's free grace to state bluntly that every man who lived outside the light of special revelation would be damned: "I am far from saying that God may not save some from among all nations, even though they have not a distinct knowledge of the Gospel: for God *may* do whatsoever seemeth him good...". [300] But they did not move along the road of speculation: they kept to "the

---

[294] See above, p. 148.

[295] Cf. Wilberforce's judgment on "the moral condition of the Hindoos" and on Hindu religion—"one great abomination"—, which called from him the exclamation: "And now, Sir, I am persuaded, that in all who hear me, there can be but one common feeling of deep commiseration for the unhappy people whose sad state I have been describing to you": see E. M. Howse, *op. cit.*, p. 91.

[296] V. F. Storr, *op. cit.*, pp. 67, 70.

[297] *Journals and Letters, op. cit.*, I, p. 10.

[298] G. Hamilton in the Church of Scotland General Assembly of 1796: *Account, op. cit.*, p. 19.

[299] Th. Scott in a sermon on Marc. 16.16, preached before the C.M.S. in 1801: *Proceedings, op. cit.*, I, London 1805, p. 26.

[300] Ch. Simeon, *Horae Homileticae*, XI, London 1820, p. 377.

uniform testimony, that men all need a Saviour, and that there is no other name given under heaven whereby any man can be saved, but the name of Jesus Christ [301]—and it was this knowledge, which filled them with a compassionate "love of souls", expressed with sober humour by Carey: "... we should have as much love to the souls of our fellow-creatures, and fellow-sinners, as they [i.e. the commercial men] have for the profits arising from a few otterskins...", [302] and in passionate words by Martyn: "...o may I so realize the day of judgment, that I may now pity and pray for those whom I shall then see overwhelmed with consternation and ruin!" [303]

h. The ecclesiological motive

It has been remarked that the Evangelicals preached "a Gospel without a Church" [304]—but this indictment is not quite fair. Especially in the second stage of the Evangelical Revival, when the distinction between Evangelicalism and Methodism became clear, there were many Evangelicals who had a deep respect for the Church and its order. [305] It was because of their ecclesiological attitude that the Anglican Evangelicals proceeded to the foundation of the C.M.S. "on the Church principle", and we have already seen that with some of the Evangelical chaplains—in particular with Buchanan—the idea of the establishment of the Anglican Church in India took a prominent place. [306] Yet the idea of the *plantatio ecclesiae* was certainly not the main stimulus of the missionary awakening: the Evangelicals went out "to save souls", and the formation of a Church on the mission-field was a corollary of their labours, but not their primary target. Interdenominational action does not necessarily involve a certain indifference towards the idea of the Church, but in the circumstances of these times it unavoidably entailed a lesser emphasis on the notion of the *plantatio ecclesiae* and a greater stress on the idea of individual salvation. Apart from the (Particular) Baptists, the non-Anglicans worked on an interdenominational basis—and Carey apologized for the fact that the Society whose formation he proposed would be restricted to his own group: "I wish with all my heart, that every one who loves our Lord Jesus Christ in sincerity, would in some way or another engage in it". [307] In C.M.S. circles the ecclesiological

---

[301]   Ch. Simeon *in loco citato*. We find the same line of thought with Bishop H. Ryder in his S. P. G. Sermon of 1819 on Acts 4.12: *Propaganda, op. cit.*, pp. 89—90.
[302]   *An Enquiry, op. cit.*, p. 69.
[303]   *Journals and Letters, op. cit.*, II, p. 32.
[304]   S. C. Carpenter, *op. cit.*, p. 40.
[305]   See for the influence of Simeon on this point in particular the work of Ch. Smyth, *Simeon and Church Order, op. cit.*, passim.
[306]   H. Cnattingius, *op. cit.*, pp. 64 ff.
[307]   *An Enquiry, op. cit.*, p. 84.

interest was small: its leaders gladly cooperated with Christians of other denominations, they had no difficulty in recognizing the validity of the office of such missionaries as had not been ordained in an Episcopal Church, they could—if absolutely necessary—dispense with episcopal sanction for their work, and "the great thing to the C.M.S. was personal piety, not office". [308] The only circle in which we meet ecclesiological ideals as real stimuli to missionary action is that of the old Anglican Societies: there the denominational character of missionary work received a strong emphasis as a result of a firm belief in the indispensability of episcopal ordination; there the idea of the *plantatio ecclesiae* could come to function as a powerful incentive for the missionary task. [309]

i. The eschatological motive

There exists an important connection between the missionary awakening and the eschatological expectations of the group in which the awakening took its beginning. In a period in which many Evangelicals thought to distinguish the first signs of the final break-through of Christ's Kingdom, they were more than ever inclined to accompany the second supplication of the Lord's Prayer by deeds of active missionary work. Carey's well-known slogan "expect great things from God, attempt great things for God" [310] was an extension of what Fuller had remarked eight years earlier: "By these prophecies the Christian Church is encouraged to *look for great things*—to look for a time when *the earth shall be full of the knowledge of the Lord as the waters cover the sea . . .*". [311] The expectation of great things was in the air: as we saw above, events in the field of world-politics seemed to point to the times in which Jesus would reign from sea to sea, and theologians such as Edwards and Bengel had helped to direct the attention of the Evangelical sector of Protestantism to the category of the coming Kingdom. Eschatological speculations are not always favourable to the right reception of the missionary ideal: Carey had to refute the thought that the time of the heathen had not yet come because a number of prophecies had not yet been fulfilled, [312] and among the Scottish Moderates the expectation of far-off things more than once became a substitute for immediate missionary action. [313]

---

[308]   H. Cnattingius, *op. cit.*, pp. 61—63.

[309]   The first Bishop of Calcutta, Thomas Fanshaw Middleton, a man with strong leanings to the side of the S.P.G., declared in 1819 that he wanted to remain in alignment with the Old Church, which saw the work of missions simply as "an expansion of the Catholic Church": H. Cnattingius, *op. cit.*, p. 92.

[310]   The theme of his famous sermon, given at Nottingham on May 30, 1792: see S. Pearce Carey, *op. cit.*, p. 84.

[311]   See: G. Laws, *op. cit.*, p. 46.

[312]   *An Enquiry, op. cit.*, p. 12.

[313]   So G. Hamilton proposed at the General Assembly of the Church of

But as a whole, contemporary eschatology worked in favour of the missionary awakening: the ground-work was prepared by it, and a new enthusiasm took possession of men and women all over Britain, who saw in the incipient missionary work one of the most important signs of the dawn of the Millennium. Carey—whose thoughts on this point had been fundamentally influenced by Edwards' *Call to Prayer*, which he knew in Sutcliff's edition—remarked: " ... we have the greatest reason to suppose, that the glorious outpouring of the Spirit, which we expect at last, will be bestowed". [314] With Melvill Horne we meet the expectation of the coming Kingdom as a direct stimulus to missionary action: "The night is far spent, and the day is at hand. The latter ends of the world are fallen upon us, and we have many considerations to excite us, if it were possible, to more than apostolic labours". [315] He, too, had to oppose the thought that the time had not yet come, because certain prophecies had not yet been fulfilled; apart from an appeal to the missionary command he further remarked that those servants would be pronounced blessed, "whom the Lord shall find so doing". [316] The idea that they were standing on the threshold of the millennial period was very strong in the circle of the L.M.S.: there the reserve which we find with Carey and other missionary leaders with regard to the interpretation of prophecy [317] gave place sometimes to an almost naive enthusiasm. Bogue remarked cautiously: "we are to be guided by what God enjoins as a duty, not by what he delivered as a prediction". [318] But others were not equally careful: John Hey declared in a sermon on Eph. 1.10: "What a pleasing change now takes place! How solemn is this time! How eventful is this period! ... the powers of darkness grim horribly ... But let us take courage: ... we may be confident of success". [319] Three years later, J. Cochin delivered a sermon (also before a L.M.S. meeting) on Is. 2.2, 3 under the significant title: "God's declared designs a motive to human endeavours"; he remarked: "The last days will be distinguished by very remarkable events ... These commotions will end sooner or later in the total ruin of Popery and Mahometanism. After this it is probable the gospel will find its way into the east". [320] During the same meeting, J. Brewer preached a sermon on Hab. 2.3, in which he remarked: "What reasons have we to expect that the vision, which presents so favourable an aspect to the souls of men,

---

Scotland in 1796 to await patiently the period of the propagation of the Gospel: *Account, op. cit.*, p. 19.

[314] *An Enquiry, op. cit.*, pp. 78—79.
[315] *Letters on Missions, op. cit.*, p. 20.
[316] *Op. cit.*, pp. 99—100.
[317] See: E. A. Payne, *The Church Awakes, op. cit.*, p. 74.
[318] D. Bogue in his sermon on Hagg. 1.2, in: *Sermons preached in London at the Formation of the Missionary Society, op. cit.*, p. 126.
[319] *Op. cit.*, pp. 88—90.
[320] *Four Sermons preached in London*, London 1798, p. 58.

is now drawing near its end? ... Consult the state of Europe: when were the signs of the times so portentous? ... we trust that the present storm, ... will usher in that splendid season, when the light of the moon shall be as the light of the sun ...". [321] These quotations are sufficient to show that there was a direct relation between the eschatological expectations and the missionary enthusiasm among supporters of the L.M.S. Its leaders appealed to the promises of Scripture in their missionary propaganda: "... every promise is a call and a motive to enter on the service without delay". [322] We must add, however, that even the most fiery Millennarian expected the Kingdom to come in a *gradual* way, that none dared to give speculations on the exact time of the coming of the Millennium, and that, moreover, the eschatological motive was never the exclusive stimulus to missionary action. It was generally felt that even when "the appointed time" was still far away, the duty to evangelize the heathen nations remained. It is interesting to notice that after the Napoleonic period we find proofs of a more tempered expectation, though the fundamental scheme of eschatology remained unaltered: "Those who think that the Millennium will commence in fifty years, do not perhaps consider, that on an average almost twenty millions of souls must in each of the intervening years be purified from Antichristianism, and converted from Mahometanism and Paganism to the faith of Christ? ... I cannot but consider the commencement of the Millennium more remote". [323]

In other circles also eschatological expectations played an important part. In his *The Star in the East* Buchanan saw the revolution of nations and the signs of the times "as indicating that the period is come for diffusing the light of Revelation". [324] Simeon writes that Brown's belief "was strengthened by the signs of the times, that the great purposes of God were about to be accomplished in the conversion of the nations to the faith of Christ". [325] Martyn, too, was filled with great expectations, though on "the scene of action" his faith was severely tested: "Here I am called to exercise faith ... My former feelings on this subject were more agreeable, and at the same time more according with the truth; for if we believe the prophets, the scenes that time shall unfold, "though surpassing fable are yet true". While I write, hope and joy shall spring up in my mind. Yes, it shall be; yonder stream of Ganges shall one day roll through tracts adorned with Christian Churches ... All things are working together to bring on the day". [326] Yet it is a remarkable fact that in those sermons

---

[321] *Op. cit.*, pp. 103—104.
[322] In a *Letter to the Evangelical Dissenters who practise Infant Baptism*, in *The Evangelical Magazine*, 1794, p. 380.
[323] D. Bogue in his *Discourses on the Millennium*, *op. cit.*, p. 606.
[324] *Works*, *op. cit.*, p. 311.
[325] In his: *Memorial Sketches of the Rev. David Brown*, *op. cit.*, p. 75.
[326] *Journals and Letters*, *op. cit.*, II, p. 272.

which were given at the meetings of the C.M.S. we meet only scanty allusions to the coming of the Millennium.

Scottish Evangelicalism was closely connected with the L.M.S. group. The leaders of the Edinburgh Missionary Society lived in the hope, engendered by the "tokens" which they saw around them, that "the set time is come". [327] Rev. J. Dun of Glasgow, a minister of the Relief Church, thought on the eve of the French Revolution that some of the predictions of prophecy were receiving fulfilment, and "his benevolent heart rejoiced over the brightening prospects which were beginning to dawn upon the world in the nascent religious institutions which were springing into existence". [328] Sober, reserved Robert Heron remarked during the General Assembly of 1796: "Prophecy, in clear language and at various periods, has predicted the conversion of the Gentile Nations", and he saw a relation between the fulfilment of those prophecies and the recent missionary awakening. [329] And Erskine, who as a student had already written his *The Signs of the Times,* in which he had uttered the supposition that in the *Cambuslang Work* "some indications of the predicted glory of the latter days might be found", [330] wrote in 1798: ". . . let none employed in preaching the gospel, despair of success . . . The happy day shall dawn, when, in every corner of the earth, Christ shall be preached to the Gentiles, and believed in the world". [331] In Scotland, too, it was the general belief that the Christian dispensation would "pass insensibly into the millennial state by gradual increase of the preaching of the Gospel"—a belief, opposed some time afterwards by men like H. Drummond and E. Irving, who advocated the idea of a sudden and apocalyptic approach of the Millennium. [332]

One other factor has still to be dealt with: the relation, which in these times also was reckoned to exist, between the conversion of the Jews and that of the Gentiles. Simeon—of whom one of his biographers says that the conversion of the Jews "was perhaps the warmest interest of his life" [333]—remarked in 1821: "The commencement of a work among the Gentiles will introduce the ingathering of the Jews; and in like manner, when once the Jews shall begin generally to be converted to the faith, they will be the means of awakening the great body of the Gentiles". [334] Similar ideas already occupied the minds of

---

[327]   In a *Letter of the Edinburgh Missionary Society,* appendix to the *Account, op. cit.,* p. 68.

[328]   G. Struthers in *The History of the Rise, Progress and Principles of the Relief Church, op. cit.,* p. 419.

[329]   *Account, op. cit.,* p. 14.

[330]   Sir Henry Moncreiff Wellwood, *op. cit.,* pp. 125—126.

[331]   *Discourses, op. cit.,* pp. 425, 428.

[332]   See: H. C. Whitley, *Edward Irving* (MS thesis of the University of Edinburgh), Edinburgh, New College, 1953, p. 56.

[333]   H. C. G. Moule, *op. cit.,* p. 95.

[334]   Ch. Simeon, *The Conversion of the Jews, Two Discourses preached before the University of Cambridge,* London 1821, p. 54.

Martyn [335] and Brown; [336] in a later period they played a part in the
impressive revival of the missionary ideal in the Scottish Evangelical
circle, which manifested itself above all in the love of missions that
was evinced by the Free Church of Scotland. [337]

k. The command of Christ as a missionary motive

Already from the full title of Carey's *Enquiry* it appears that with
him the *missionary command* took a dominant place: he spoke of the
obligation of Christians to use means for the conversion of the
heathen, and in the first section of his work he put the question,
whether the commission of Christ was still binding for the Church
of his times. In this chapter Carey combated the views of those who
thought that "the commission was sufficiently put in execution by what
the apostles and others had done" and "that because the apostles were
extraordinary officers and have no proper successors, and because
many things which were right for them to do would be utterly
unwarrantable for us, therefore it may not be immediately binding on
us to execute the commission...". [338] Now we know that this opinion
existed in the period of the Reformers, and that—confining ourselves
to the circle of the Calvinistic Reformation—more even than Calvin
himself it was Beza who defended this remarkable theory. But we
have also seen that in Anglican circles this idea has never been
accepted, that among Dutch Calvinists it died away during the course
of the seventeenth century, and that the American Puritans, though
they made no explicit use of the missionary command, certainly never
disputed its validity. Why, then, did Carey devote so much attention
to a practically extinguished idea? We have to see this against the
background of that "hyper-Calvinism" that lived on in the community
of the Particular Baptists. It was no doubt the ultra-Calvinists who
opposed Carey's missionary plans with an appeal to the "reformatory"
view of the missionary command—this explains why Carey in
particular gave so much attention to the right meaning of this command. A. H. Oussoren's statement that not charity but obligation was
Carey's main argument for the propagation of the Gospel [339] is
partially correct—but we must not lose sight of the fact this
accentuation of the command was not a direct result of Carey's
Calvinism: it was rather inspired by the historical situation in which
he stood. Carey was a pioneer of the missionary idea in a community
which was practically the last stronghold of "ultra-Calvinism" in

---

[335] *Journals and Letters, op. cit.,* p. 365.
[336] [Ch. Simeon], *Memorial Sketches of the Rev. David Brown, op. cit.,* p. 76.
[337] See: G. M. den Hartogh, *De Secession in Schotland van 1843 en het
Schotse Seminarie in Nederland,* in: Vox Theologica XIV (1942—1943), p. 85.
[338] *An Enquiry, op. cit.,* p. 8.
[339] A. H. Oussoren, *op. cit.,* p. 140.

England. On this point we quite agree with H. Boer, who portrays Carey's special emphasis on the great commission against its historical perspective. [340] Boer goes too far, however, when he states that since Carey wrote his *Enquiry* the main emphasis was laid on the missionary command, "working powerfully in its own right", while its background faded out of sight. In the first twenty years after the publication of Carey's *Enquiry* the missionary command continued to play only a very modest part: it was never the one and only motive, dominant in isolation, it always occurred within a special context. With Melvill Horne, who combated "the cold approbation of a duty" on one hand and "a cold, ineffective pity" on the other, it was closely integrated with the motives of love and expectance: "according to the spirituality of the commandment we are chargeable with the perdition of all the poor heathens whom our diligence might have saved ... The latter ends of the world are fallen upon us". [341] Thomas Scott saw the missionary command as a duty to zeal and compassion, [342] and in Martyn's sermon on the great commission the duty of obedience was partly motivated by the deep compassion we ought to have for those who are "involved in everlasting perdition". [343] A *Letter of the Edinburgh Missionary Society* also placed the missionary command within the context of soteriological and eschatological motives. [344] In Evangelical circles the missionary command was generally recognized, and obedience to it was seen as "a duty, highly incumbent upon every Christian"; [345] an appeal to it was made when its validity was denied or attacked on the ground of theological misunderstandings, as, *e.g.*, a wrongly applied eschatology; [346] a feeling of obligation was always present—but it never functioned as a separate stimulus, it was always connected with other motives, and in this way it affords a strong proof of the proposition that it is only in organic integration with the biblical motive *in toto* that a special missionary motive can render a real service to the awakening of the missionary ideal!

---

[340]   H. Boer, *Pentecost and the Missionary Witness of the Church*, Franeker 1955, pp. 20—24.
[341]   Melvill Horne, *op. cit.*, pp. 11—20.
[342]   In a sermon on Mark. 16.16, in: *Proceedings of the Society for Missions to Africa and the East, op. cit.*, I, p. 51.
[344]   Sermon on Matth. 28.18—20, in: *Sermons, op. cit.*, esp. pp. 382, 399.
[344]   *Account, op. cit.*, p. 67.
[345]   From the resolutions, taken at the "Castle and Falcon meeting" of the C.M.S. on April 12, 1799: E. Stock, *op. cit.*, p. 68.
[346]   Cf. D. Bogue in his sermon on Hagg. 1.2, *Objections against a Mission to the Heathen stated and considered*: "... I beg you to consider that in aiming to propagate the Gospel, we are to be guided by what God enjoins as a duty, not by what he delivered as a prediction", *Sermons preached in London at the Formation of the Missionary Society, op. cit.*, p. 126.

Chapter V

HUMAN MOTIVES AND THE DIVINE MOTIVE

Up to this point, our inquiry into the motives of the British missionary awakening has been mainly historical: it was the empirical motives, distinguishable by means of historical research, that bespoke our attention. We have tried to disentangle the various factors which have contributed to the growth of the missionary ideal from the complex background of the missionary awakening, and in this way we have found a variety of motives which, each according to its own character, helped to quicken the practical interest in the cause of missions. We have grouped those motives in a systematic way according to their basic characteristics, but at the same time we were fully aware that the distinctions which we made sometimes forced an artificial separation between motives essentially belonging together: time and again we saw that the boundary between the various motives was fluid, and more than once we had to point to the integral unity which existed between motives that our method of treatment required us to deal with separately. Therefore it is first of all necessary to make a recapitulation in which these various motives are seen in their wider context and in their integral relationship. For the sake of clearness, we shall bring them under four heads, each denoting a special aspect of the missionary motive, while at the end of our survey we intend to show that these four groups, too, are correlated to each other and have to be seen in the perspective of their complex unity. But even then our inquiry has not come to its end. Missionary science transcends the limits of purely historical research by the plain fact of its theological character. Missionary history has to be seen in the context of God's plan for his Church, which stands under the marching orders of her Lord as they are revealed in the Bible. The great question is: How far did the human motives of the missionary awakening correspond with the divine motive of which the Bible gives testimony? History has to be seen in the critical light of revelation. This brings with it the task of confrontation: a task which is difficult owing to the fact that this very confrontation points to a judgment which is deeper and more serious than any human criticism, yet at the same time a liberating influence, because it opens the door to a

166

justification which transcends all forms of human appreciation by placing the broken work of men in the dimension of the grace of God.

1. THE MISSIONARY MOTIVES IN THEIR HISTORICAL CONTEXT

a. In the sphere of the Corpus Christianum

It is impossible to gain a clear view of the historical development of the missionary idea without taking into account the concept of the *corpus christianum*, which from the days of Constantine onwards has played its part in the history of the Church. The roots of this idea have to be sought in the period of the Primitive Church: though before Constantine the Church was *ecclesia pressa*, her message was totalitarian from the outset, [1] and in a period of oppression and persecution the proud consciousness of belonging to the *triton genos* made some of the Fathers dream of a time in which the Christian religion would have permeated the life of state and culture. [2] This dream became reality after Constantine's conversion to the Christian faith. The Christian emperorship was seen as the consummation linking together the ideas of the *imperium romanum* and the kingship in the line of David. [3] Christianity was considered as the official form of religion, and the theocratic consciousness began to take form. [4] So the way was prepared for the *corpus christianum* of the medieval period, in which state and culture were seen in integral relationship with the Church of Christ, the visible form of the *civitas Dei* on earth. In the sphere of the *corpus christianum* it is difficult to discern between political, cultural and purely spiritual missionary motives: political expansion was at the same time an extension of the sphere of influence of the Church, and transmission of cultural values simply could not be thought of apart from the transmission of the Christian faith; in the conversion of the Germanic tribes as much as in the crusades, secular and religious imperialism went hand in hand, and medieval monasticism was as active in the spread of culture as in the propagation of Christianity. [5] What was the motive of Augustine's expedition to Britain, why did the Knights of the Teutonic Order extend their influence in Prussia, what brought the Christian nations to take up

---

[1] „Die christliche Religion ist von Anfang an mit einer *Universalität* aufge-treten, kraft deren sie *das ganze Leben* in allen seinen Funktionen ... mit Beschlag legte. Diese Universalität sicherte ihr den Sieg ... Von Anfang an umspannte sie die Menschheit ...": A. von Harnack, *Die Mission und Ausbreitung des Christen-tums*, I, Leipzig[4] 1924, SS. 527—528.

[2] A. von Harnack, *op. cit.*, SS. 276—281.

[3] A. J. Rasker, *Christelijke Politiek, Gesprek over de Theocratie*, Nijkerk s. a., p. 25.

[4] See: H. Berkhof, *De Kerk en de Keizer*, Amsterdam 1946, pp. 109 ff.

[5] See for concrete examples: J. Thayer Addison, *The Medieval Missionary*, London and New York 1936, passim.

arms against the power of the Islam, what was the aim of the foundation of monasteries on the frontier-line of Christian culture? It is impossible to give an unequivocal answer: though in some instances the political interests fully superseded the spiritual motives, while in other cases the process of Christianization meant not much more than the laying of a thin layer of Christianized culture on a substratum of heathenism, yet the political, the cultural and the ecclesiastical spheres of action overlapped each other to such an extent that the making of a clear-cut distinction lay outside the horizon of the medievalist. [6] Of course, this view of the medieval *corpus christianum* has all the drawbacks of a generalization: during the period between Constantine and the Reformation the relationship between Church, state and culture went through several phases, and from both sects and saints the voice of criticism made itself heard against a too massive unity of the various spheres of life. Yet. medieval life took more and more the form of a theocracy, of a culture, guided by the Church, [7] and the missionary motives of the Christian community in the Middle Ages have to be seen in this theocratic context.

Then came the Renaissance and the Reformation—and with them a rupture in the idea and the reality of the *corpus christianum*. This did not entail a sudden breakdown of the theocratic ideal: on the contrary, those ideals not only lived on in the circle of Roman Catholicism, but were also present with the Reformers, and in a special form with Calvin. It is true that Calvin did not adhere to the idea of the *corpus christianum* in its medieval form, as J. Bohatec righthly remarks, [8] but on the other hand we wonder whether it is really necessary to abandon with Bohatec the word "theocracy" in relation to Calvin's ecclesiastical and political ideals: [9] it cannot be denied that the idea of a complete separation between Church and state was far from Calvin's world of thought; [10] the Genevan Reformer

---

[6] K. D. Schmidt writes, speaking of Boniface: „Die Anpassung an die politischen Verhältnisse darf man doch nicht nur als „staatliche Umklammerung" werten, auch noch nicht einmal als missionstechnische Anpassung an die gegebenen Gelegenheiten, sondern dahinter steht das Ideal der Kongruenz des politischen und religiösen Prinzips, das die ganze Zeit erfüllte, ganz besonders aber die Angelsachsen": *Neue Zuge im Bild des Bonifatius*, E.M.Z. XI (1954), S. 99.

[7] Cf. the portrait of the „kirchliche Einheitskultur", given by E. Troeltsch in his *Die Soziallehren der Christlichen Kirchen und Gruppen: Gesammelte Schriften*, I, Tübingen 1919, SS. 221—226.

[8] „Indem Calvin der Reichsgottesgedanken das eschatologische Vorzeichen gibt, rückt er *prinzipiell* von dem Mittelalterlichen Einheitsenthusiasmus ab, der den Spannungscharacter nicht kennt, das Eschatologische in das Historische umdeutet und die anstaltliche-hierarchische Kirche die ecclesia militans, der Gemeinschaft der Erwählten gleichsetzt": J. Botatec, *Calvins Lehre von Staat und Kirche mit besonderer Berücksichtigung des Organismusgedankens*, Breslau 1937, S. 632.

[9] *Op. cit.*, S. 625.

[10] Cf. W. Pauck in *The Idea of the Church in Christian History*, Church History XXI (1952), pp. 211—212: "Calvin's theories imply a much clearer distinction between the church and the state than Luther had been able to make ... But this

and his followers in the sixteenth and seventeenth century were convinced that to a certain extent Church and state had a common task and a common charge, and though Calvin did not propagate the idea of a Church-governed state, yet much less would the modern idea of a neutral state have received a place in his thinking. [11] This theocratic tendency was transplanted to Britain, [12] where it became rooted in the circle of Puritanism, and, from there, to New England. Quite apart from this, the whole of British life still bore the marks of the idea of the *corpus christianum* as a heritage of the Middle Ages, with which the rupture had not been as complete as on the Continent. During the late sixteenth and early seventeenth centuries we meet the influence of the *corpus christianum* idea in the relation that, at least in theory, existed between imperialistic and ecclesiastical expansion; this connection seems to us to be naive and hypocritical, until we realize that we have to see it in the context of the belief of those days that these two spheres of life were knit together in a deeper unity. [13] The period of Cromwell witnessed a short-lived revival of the theocratic ideal, in which the missionary ideal received a place, while the Puritan missionaries in America, too, were partly driven by the same ideal to bring the whole of life under the dominance of the Lord. The revival of the missionary idea in early eighteenth-century Britain was certainly not influenced by theocratic motives, but still we can discern some remnants of the idea of the *corpus christianum* in the fact that there was still a feeling of the unity of life: missions were seen as a corollary of the expansion of British influence, and political and missionary interests were seen in alignment with each other. [14]

But the *corpus christianum* did not only stand for a unity between Church and state; it also entailed a close integration of Church and

---

insistence upon the distinction did not prevent him from advocating a Christian commonwealth subordinated to the sovereign will of God. In this regard (as in others) he followed the example of his teacher and friend, Martin Bucer of Strassburg, who in his last work, *De Regno Christi*, ... proclaimed the Christianization of all political, social, economic and cultural life in terms of a *respublica Christiana* which for him was identical with the Kingdom of God".

[11] See above, pp. 14, 15; cf. also: J. H. Langman, *Moet Artikel XXXVI der Nederlandse Geloofsbelijdenis gewijzigd worden?* in: *Schrift en Kerk, op. cit.*, esp. pp. 286—288.

[12] Cf. the remark of C. D. Cremean—to a certain extent an overstatement, but yet containing an element of truth—: "The aims of English Calvinists were primarily religious, but their chief aim and goal, a true theocratic state, had tremendous political implications which were to make themselves felt in English history", in: *The Reception of Calvinistic Thought in England*, Urbana (Ill.) 1949, p. 117.

[13] It is this factor which K. E. Knorr does not take sufficiently into account when he accuses the propagandists of missionary action in the period of the first British expeditions to America of a deficiency in sincerity and of lip-service to a duty which was acknowledged but not performed: *British Colonial Theories*, Toronto 1944, pp. 28 ff.

[14] See above, pp. 59, 60.

culture. Some remnants of this aspect of the *corpus christianum* lived on in the circle of such Protestants as were more or less influenced by the world of thought of Erasmus. Though they did not advocate a Church-guided culture, their view of the unity of life had its result in their consideration of the spreading of Christian culture as a form of missionary activity. With the rise of the Methodist movement, however, the lines of secular and spiritual interests parted: imperialism became a secular concern, culture was seen as a more or less dangerous field, and the full emphasis fell upon the "salvation of souls". A secularizing state was not inclined to give active support to the cause of missions, while a spiritual Christianity did not seek its missionary stimuli in motives that lay in the sphere of this world. On the one hand this meant a purification of the missionary motive, but on the other side it was not an imaginary danger that in this way the work of missions should become isolated from the broad context of the public form of life. Missionary work was deepened by its interest in the problems of the heart of man, but at the same time its frontier-line was narrowed by its almost exclusive concern with man's "soul".

In the meantime, the many-sided activities of the "Clapham Sect" inaugurated a certain change in this development. During the first half of the nineteenth century the two lines which had separated, began once more to draw nearer to each other. In political circles, as a result of the personal influence of leading Evangelical statesmen,[15] and—in a broader context—of the changing tone of British national life as a whole during the Victorian era, there was a growing conscious-ness of the value and significance of missionary work. This period witnessed a strange mixture of idealistic and utilitarian motives: from the side of the representatives of British public life, missions were again considered as useful components in the building up of the British empire—this at a time when it was generally felt that the imperial idea entailed a mission towards the (Eastern) world: "the idea of the providential destiny of Great Britain to carry the white man's burden was to grow into an extremely powerful movement in the course of the nineteenth century".[16] At the same time we see also, that while in the initial stage of the missionary awakening the missionary leaders at home as much as the missionaries themselves were absolutely free from imperialistic tendencies, it was felt in a later stage of the development that official support could be of great importance for the development of the missionary cause. We mention a few examples. The L.M.S. missionaries who went to the Pacific were no imperialists—on the contrary. In his study on this subject,

---

[15] "Nowhere was missionary influence more powerful than in the Colonial Office": K. L. P. Martin, *Missionaries and Annexation in the Pacific*, London 1924, p. 4.
[16] K. E. Knorr, *op. cit.*, p. 247.

A. A. Koskinen rightly emphasizes the fact that "missionary societies generally strongly opposed the political activities of the missionaries working under them". [17] They were Puritan Calvinists, and to a certain extent they had a predisposition for theocratic ideals—but we have no reason to suppose that they went out with the express purpose of founding theocratic communities in the South Sea Islands. They were driven on the road to "theocracy" by external circumstances: because the primitive communities in the islands in which they worked were already in a state of decay, they were called upon to lay the foundations of a new form of life in conformity with the new religion which they had brought—and only when their fragile theocratic creations were threatened by forces from outside did they seek protection under the British or the American flag. *Nolens volens* they became pioneers of Western imperialistic expansion. Another example is that of David Livingstone, who went out as a missionary from purely religious motives. His cultural activities were closely related to his missionary ideals: Western cultural and political influence were to him means for attaining the greater goal, the introduction of Christianity into the dark continent. He was a child of his own times, and his "confidence in Western culture seemed naive to a later generation which, after 1914, saw the havoc wrought by the unmet colossal ills born of the nineteenth-century Occident". [18] But behind this seemingly imperialistic attitude stood an intrinsically religious conviction; he was, as Frick rightly points out, the Calvinist who stands with a burning sense of vocation on the broad front of life. [19] And to a certain extent we can say, that in his weaving together of national and spiritual interests he still stood under the—vanishing— influence of the idea of the *corpus christianum*.

In our modern world, the last remnants of the *corpus christianum* are breaking down. [20] Imperialistic motives no longer threaten the puritiy of Protestant missionary work. We are wont to connect the adjective "theocratic" with the substantive "dream", and the cultural ideals with which men such as Troeltsch [21] and the authors of

---

[17]   A. A. Koskinen, *Missionary Influence as a Political Factor in the Pacific Islands* (Annales Academiae Scientiarum Fennicae B 78 ¹), Helsinki 1953, pp. 48 ff; cf. also K. L. P. Martin, *op. cit.*, p. 7: "The missionary did not go out to foreign lands as the ally of the trader and the colonist. Religious zeal was his sole motive".

[18]   K. Scott Latourette, *op. cit.*, V, p. 347.

[19]   H. Frick, *Die Evangelische Mission*, op. cit., SS. 274 ff.

[20]   See: H. Kraemer, *The Christian Message in a Non-Christian World*, London² 1947, pp. 27 ff.

[21]   See: E. Troeltsch, *Die Mission in der modernen Welt, Gesammelte Schriften* II, Tübingen 1913, SS. 780 ff, and his *Missionsmotiv, Missionsaufgabe und neuzeitliches Humanitätschristentum*, Zeitschrift für Missionskunde und Religionswissenschaft XXII (1907), SS. 129 ff., a defence of his thoughts on missions against the attacks of Warneck. Here the "Erasmian" and the reformatory line in missionary thinking came into collision with each other: over against Warneck, Troeltsch took up his position on the idea of a „modernes Humanitätschristentum".

Rethinking Missions, [22] each in their own way, linked up the missionary task, have lost much of their attraction for a generation that after the experience of two world wars has been thrown back upon the primary questions, a generation that stands in the grim reality of a disintegrated time. Yet these times desperately need healing, integration, a new sense of the unity of life. The Church of our days has still a task on the broad front of life, in the field of cultural problems and social needs. We shall return to this point below—but we do not want to conclude this part of our chapter without having remarked that in the idea of the "comprehensive approach" the Church of our days tries to reserve and to bring to reality at least something of the positive values of the old idea of the *corpus christianum.*

b. Around the idea of love

Before we try to recapitulate what we have found with regard to the idea of love as a missionary motive, we must first get a clear view of the different connotations of the concept of love as we meet it in the history of missions. In the first place, we meet love as an inner attitude, engendered and determined by the knowledge of the love of God in Christ, to which the love in the heart of man is nothing but a grateful response. The object of this love is above all: God. But love towards God receives form and actuality not only in the direct contact with God, in prayer and praise and liturgy, but also in love towards men, towards the "neighbour" in whom God meets his children. In its turn, this connotation of the idea of love—love as a continuance of and an answer to the love of Christ in inter-human relations—has two aspects. The first one is that of love towards man in his spiritual need, towards man who stands in need of salvation, towards man in his broken relationship to God. There is present a strong soteriological element in this aspect of the idea of love: in this context, love takes on the meaning of compassion with man because he is threatened by eternal damnation. It is clear that the intensity of the soteriological emphasis depended on the view of the human situation, on the depth of the feeling of sin and on the part which was played by the concepts of God's wrath and grace. The other aspect of the idea of love is that of love towards man in his temporal need, towards man in the brokenness of his daily life, towards

---

[22] *Re-thinking Missions, A Laymen's Inquiry after One Hundred Years,* by the Commission of Appraisal, W. E. Hocking, Chairman, New York and London 1932. This undoubtedly important, but at the same time very one-sided report, speaks of the rise of "the religion of the modern man, the religious aspect of the coming world-culture", p. 21; an "evangelizing by living and by human service" is propagated, p. 65, and in the foreword it is stated that for some of the members of the commission the missionary motive "would best be called the spirit of altruistic service, the desire to share with all mankind the benefits and the ideals of a Christian community", p. XIV.

man in the misery of his social and cultural existence. The strength of the humanitarian aspect of the idea of love is closely related to the valuation of other cultures and forms of social life and to the knowledge of the real needs in spheres which lay outside the circle of daily contact.

In the period of the Primitive Church, love was a mighty factor in the outward movement of the Christian community. The idea of love was still undifferentiated: the Church saw the spiritual as much as the temporal needs of her surroundings, and she considered herself as a *statio medicinae,* a hospital in which the great physician would heal the many wounds of human life. [23] Harnack characterizes the missionary preaching of the Christian message as a "Predigt der Liebe und Hilfsleistung", and he shows in an impressive chapter of his work on the mission of primitive Christianity, how the central truth that God is love stimulated the Church to demonstrate the love of Christ and to invite man to move into communion with that love in deeds of help and service. [24] If we take into account further that Harnack in his description of the life of the early Church was no doubt influenced by his own views respecting the centrality of the ethical emphasis in Christianity, we cannot deny that without a burning love the Church would never have been able to reach the many whom she has brought into the peace of Christ, in the face of opposition and persecution, during the first three centuries of her existence. During the Middle Ages the flame of love kept on burning: monks and missionaries went out to the frontiers of culture and Christianity, driven by an inner fire of love to God and men. [25] But the flame was sometimes threatened with extinction through the chilly draught of a theocratic ideal which in its very massiveness had lost the spontaneous warmth of primitive Christianity: during these times, the missionary ideal vaccillated between the motives of love and power. As in the period of the primitive Church, the idea of love was still undifferentiated: no separation had taken place as yet between soteriological and humanitarian ideals.

---

[23]   See: A. von Harnack, *op. cit.,* SS. 137—143.

[24]   *Op. cit.,* SS. 170—220.

[25]   By way of illustration we give a few isolated examples. Otto of Bamberg is reported to have said before going to Pomerania: "...the love of Christ constrains me to attempt immediately the difficult task of going as a messenger to the Pomeranians...": J. Thayer Addison, *op. cit.,* p. 20. And behind the work of the famous missionary Raymundus Lullus stood the strong desire of demonstrating and representing the love of Christ in the midst of this world: "Denn er, dem der Gekreuzigte erschien, begnügt sich nicht damit, wie andere Mystiker, das Abbild der Liebe Gottes in seiner Seele zu suchen und zu kultivieren, sondern seine Liebe, als Darstellung und Abbild der göttlichen Liebe, wendet sich nach auszen einer Welt zu, die in ihrem ganzen Umkreis eine Darstellung der göttlichen Liebe und Wahrheit werden sollte": M. A. Schmidt, *Thomas von Aquino und Raymundus Lullus, zwei Grundtypen missionarischen Denkens im Mittelalter,* E.M.M. IIIC (1953), S. 41.

In the world of thought of the Reformers, soteriology played an important part. Luther saw the finality of the work of God in the victory of his love—God's *opus proprium*[26]—, and though Luther himself did not see a direct relation between his soteriology and the idea of missions, yet we cannot explain the strong emphasis on the idea of love in German Pietistic and Moravian missionary work without taking into account the soteriological interest which was inherent to Lutheranism from its inception onward. With Calvin we have met the idea of love in both its aspects: he put the idea of love to man in the great context of eternal life and death, while at the same time he gave place to the idea of love as "humanité". [27] And with Bucer we meet the idea of love in the same aspects as with Calvin—only more closely related to the practical fulfilment of the missionary task. [28] In the missions of the Second Reformation in Holland and of Puritanism in Britain and America we find come back both aspects of the idea of love, though the first aspect received the heavier accent: seventeenth century Calvinism was not blind to the needs of the heathen world, but yet it was mainly their "passion for souls" which drove out men such as Heurnius and Eliot to the preaching of the saving gospel of Christ.

It was partly under the influence of the German Pietistic movement, that love in its quality of concern for the souls of perishing heathen acted as a missionary stimulus among such Anglicans as came together in the Religious Societies that formed the matrix of the S.P.C.K. and the S.P.G. But in fact this aspect of the motive of love was superseded by the other aspect: that of love as humanity, as benevolent charity towards man in his social and cultural needs and definciencies. This was not a result of a continuance of the Puritan spirit. There was, indeed, a point of contact in the common interest in the *form of life*, but while Puritanism had as its background the reformatory way of thinking, the background of the new attitude of mind was the spirit of the early "Aufklärung", of which Leibniz was the spiritual father. It will be due partly to the suppleness of British religious life, and partly to the Calvinistic heritage of a certain openness towards humanitarian interests, that the reformatory and the "Erasmian" lines could run parallel in the field of missionary activity—in this period certainly at the cost of a definite weakening of the soteriological motive. Besides, the combination of the purely religious motive with the ideal of the transmission of cultural values led to a certain feeling of superiority, which is a weak spot in the history of the missions

---

[26] See for the relation between *opus proprium* and *opus alienum* with Luther: J. T. Bakker, *Coram Deo, Bijdrage tot het Onderzoek naar de Structuur van Luther's Theologie*, Kampen 1956, esp. pp. 62—111.

[27] See above, p. 11 note 50.

[28] See above, p. 10.

of Western Christianity. And the shifting of the emphasis from "salvation" to "benevolence" was a real danger to the urgency of the missionary appeal.

The missionary attitude of Methodism, early Evangelicalism and the Awakening Movements in America was characterized by a revival of the soteriological passion. Love was a mighty stimulus in the activity of the revival groups, but this time the soteriological aspect prevailed over the humanitarian one. We can trace some external influences: in the circle of the Moravians the love of Christ, experienced in an almost mystic way, led to a deepened love of man, [29] while in the account also of the work of the pietistic missionaries Ziegenbalg and Plütschau, known to Wesley in English translation, the idea of pure love towards God and man took a central place. [30] But the main reason is to be found in a certain change of the respective views of God and man: in the revivalist circles, God was not primarily seen as the upholder of the moral order, but as the God of judgment and grace, the God who had brought about atonement through the blood of Christ, and man was not primarily seen as a being, gifted with the light of natural revelation, a mixture of evil and good, but as standing in the darkness of sin and guilt, with a soul which had to be saved from eternal death. This gave to the idea of love the element of urgency: come to Christ and his love, before it is too late.

The motive of inner compulsion, which of course was never totally absent, but to which we have given special attention in our third chapter because it was particularly strong in the Awakening circles, stands in relation to the totality of the revival attitude, in which the elements of feeling and experience received a special accent: the flame of love burned in the inner sanctuary of the heart. Meanwhile the missionary activity of this period did not quite escape the danger of an anthropocentric attitude with regard to the idea of love: in the missionary motivation there was a shifting of emphasis from the depth of God's love to the depth of fallen man's pitiable state.

During the period of the great missionary revival in the circle of British Evangelicalism the pendulum of missionary motivation in a certain sense came to a standstill. The humanitarian aspect of the idea of love was not denied or neglected—we think especially of the struggle against slavery—but it was seen as no more than a corollary to the dominant soteriological interest. In the meantime, the background of the missionary attitude of this period is too complex for the various aspects of the idea of love to be reduced to one common denominator.

---

[29] See for the missionary motive in the circle of the Moravians: J. M. van der Linde, *Het Visioen van Herrnhut en het Apostolaat der Moravische Broeders in Suriname, 1735—1863*, Paramaribo 1956, pp. 79—83.

[30] See M. Schmidt, *Der Missionsgedanke des jungen Wesley*, art. cit., SS. 89—91.

The Evangelical of about 1800 heard humanity and Christianity calling together for missionary action; his view of the heathen world vaccillated between pessimism and romanticism, and a consciousness of debt towards the heathen world because of the wrongs, inflicted upon other races by Western exploitation and injustice, alternated with a feeling of Western superiority. To a certain extent the third wave of missionary enthusiasm in eighteenth-century Britain was a synthesis between the fundamental characteristics of the first aspect (emphasis upon humanity) and the second one (a heavy accent upon the soteriological element). But the later development of Anglo-Saxon missions clearly shows that the two lines were not so closely integrated as to form a harmonious unity. On the one hand we see in the nineteenth century the rise of a form of missionary work in which the Christian concept of love broadened itself into vague humanitarian ideals, which in a subtle way linked up the notion of the superiority of Western culture with a sincere admiration for the religious and and cultural heritage of the East. The result of this attitude was that in the beginning of the twentieth century the missionary message was seemingly widened, but in reality narrowed, to the proclamation of the "Social Gospel". [31] On the other hand, a one-sided emphasis upon the soteriological aspect of the motive of love could lead to a convulsive form of missionary work, that in its deep concern for the eternal fate of perishing heathen [32] neglected the confrontation with human life in its totalitarian aspect; to a certain extent the "Social Gospel movement" is a—regrettable—reaction against this one-sided accent-uation of the soteriological element in the idea of love.

c. Joyful obedience and the hard road of asceticism

In the present study we have given little special attention to the theocratic motive, the motive of the *gloria Dei*. The reason for this omission is not that the idea of the honour of God would have played no part at all in the development of the missionary cause: on the contrary, we may suppose that the idea of the *gloria Dei* was almost always present, constituting the silent background of the work of the Christian community: the Primitive Church dedicated its worship and its deeds of love, its inner and its outer life as an offering to the Lord, and medieval Christianity sought the glory of God in the growth of the *corpus christianum* and in the expansion of the Catholic Church as well

---

[31] The change from "soteriological" to "humanitarian" motives was most clearly distinguishable in America: see P. A. Varg, *Motives in Protestant Missions 1890—1917*, Church History XXIII (1954), esp. pp. 74, 80.
[32] Cf. a pronouncement of Hudson Taylor in 1894: "There is a great Niagara of souls passing into the dark in China", as quoted by P. A. Varg, *art. cit.*, p. 71.

as in those silent works of love and service, performed by dedicated servants of the Lord in isolation from the great high-roads of life. After the Reformation, the theocentric principle became a mighty stimulus to action and activity in different spheres of life, especially in the Calvinistic circle. [33] The fact that this motive, though always present in the background, only incidentally received explicit mention in relation to the missionary task can be explained from its self-evidency: was not the whole of Christian life seen as a glorification of the name of God?

The same factor has to be taken into consideration with regard to the motive of obedience to the command of Christ, which is closely related to the theocentric motive because obedience is one of the central forms in which the glorification of God is realized. The Church stood under the marching-orders of Christ, given after his Resurrection in the "great commission" of Matt. 28.19, which we accept as an authentic testimony of the words spoken by our Lord himself in the period before his ascension. [34] Now it is a remarkable fact that not only during the first century of the Church's existence, but also afterwards, the divine command in its explicit form played only a very limited part in the motivation of the missionary task. The idea of standing under the Lord's marching-orders kept its hold, and the concept of the *militia Christi*, which brings it within the sphere of command and obedience, was present in the Primitive as well as in the Medieval Church. But we cannot say that the command of Christ functioned as the one great and overruling stimulus of missionary activity. [35] In the period of the Reformation it was an unhappy accident that the recognition of the validity of the missionary command for the post-apostolic Church was linked up with a dispute about the apostolic succession. This complication, however, could only temporarily confuse the view of the validity of the command of Christ: by the period of the Second Reformation, the two unhappily related issues were loosened from each other; Pietism, too, protested against the maintenance of an untenable view of the command by the Lutheran orthodox theologians, and in Britain the ideas of the Reformers on this point, and even more of their immediate successors, played practically no part. We must make one exception: it seems that in the group to which Carey belonged there was still present a reminiscence of those ideas, a reminiscence that could be used as an anti-mission argument: it is against this background that the functioning of the command as a missionary motive with Carey has to be seen. It is clear from the whole context

---

[33]   So Voetius remarked: "causa finalis ultima et suprema est gloria et manifestatio gratiae divinae", quoted by H. A. van Andel, *op. cit.*, p. 143.

[34]   For a fuller discussion of this point, see below, pp. 198 ff.

[35]   See: H. R. Boer, *Pentecost and the Missionary Witness of the Church*, Franeker 1955, pp. 13, 36—37, 39—40.

in which the notion of obedience to Christ's command occurs with Carey and his contemporaries that it never possessed the connotation of legalism. It had rather the meaning of joyful duty: the Evangelicals of this period saw the missionary task not as a heavy burden, but as a God-given opportunity to give an affirmative answer to the call of their Master. And their Calvinistic sense of duty coincided with all the other motives which contributed to the reawakening of the missionary ideal. The presence of a motivation to mission on the ground of the "great commission" in British, American and Dutch missionary thinking during the nineteenth and early twentieth century [36] can be explained as an effect of the missionary motivation of such British Calvinists as first sounded the trumpet of the missionary awakening. On the other hand, we must not overlook the fact that a motivation on the ground of the missionary command is also to be found in German Lutheran missionary circles during the same period: reflection on the missionary task of the Church simply cannot pass by the commandment, given by Christ himself.

The motive of obedience entailed a joyful affirmation of the command of Christ: "onward, Christian soldiers"! But there have always been individuals and communities who had a deeper understanding of the *multae afflictiones* (Heurnius), which attend the *militia Christi*. Now these two accents do not exclude each other: every "soldier of Christ" knows of the risks of service, and the true ascetic has a sense of happiness even amid his hardships. But we can only speak of asceticism as a missionary motive when missions are seen as a component of the ascetic attitude, when missionary service is sought for as a means to come nearer to God along the road of self-denial, penance and sacrifice: then there takes place a change between goal and means in the sphere of missionary work. Already the Early Church had seen the combination between ascetic tendencies and missionary ideals: as strangers in this world, the early Christians proclaimed the coming Kingdom. [37] In the Middle Ages we meet with the *peregrinatio* of the Iro-Scottish monks, which was mainly of an ascetic character, [38] while the attitude of the mendicant orders also was marked by an ascetic element. [39] A special aspect of the ascetic idea of these times is that it was taken up into the sphere of the meritoriousness of good works, into the sphere of redemption of one's own self through the cooperation of grace and works. [40]

---

[36] See E. Jansen Schoonhoven, *Critische Bespreking van enige Zendings-motieven*, N.Th.T. V (1950—1951), pp. 221 ff.

[37] A. von Harnack, *op. cit.*, p. 127.

[38] J. Thayer Addison, *op. cit.*, p. 7: "... in a sense not ignoble the *peregrinus* was much more concerned to save his own soul than to save the souls of others".

[39] P. Drews, *Mission und Askese*, art. cit., SS. 537 ff.; see also the scheme, given by J. Foster in his *World Church*, London 1945, p. 39.

[40] Cf. I. Klug, *Het Katholieke Geloof* (Nederlandse Bewerking), Heemstede 1939, p. 307.

It is clear that in the thought-world of the Reformers there was no place for the ascetic idea in this form. This does not mean, however, that the notion of asceticism was altogether absent. Troeltsch has coined the expression "innerweltliche Askese", which he uses in relation to the ethics of Calvin: while Lutheran ethics are marked by a "metaphysisch-gefühlsmäszige Entwertung der Sündenwelt", with Calvin the ascetic idea takes the form of a "methodische Disziplinie-rung der Sinnlichkeit"; Calvin's attitude is "innerweltlich" because he teaches the use of all the legal means which this world can procure in order to promote the glory of God, while nevertheless it remains ascetic because the ultimate goal does not lie in the enjoyment of the things of this world, but in the strengthening of the ties with Him to whom is due all glory. [41] This view of Troeltsch's has been cor-rected by Bohatec, who shows that Troeltsch has wrongly linked up the "innerweltliche Askese" with the certitude of faith (the idea of the so-called "Bewährungsethik) [42]; but Bohatec, too, gives ample attention to the presence of the ideas of *mortificatio* and *abnegatio* in Calvin's thought and of their relation to the positive idea of a struggle for the glory of God in the midst of this world: [43] "haec ergo mortificatio tum demum habebit in nobis locum, si charitatis numeros impleamus". [44] In the period of the Second Reformation, the ascetic element in Calvinism was connected with the missionary ideal (Heur-nius), while at the same time in Pietistic-Lutheran circles a relation was supposed to exist between asceticism and missions (Von Welz). The ascetic attitude of this period was not quite free from the element of flight: though in essence Heurnius' exposition on this point does not differ from the attitude of Calvin, yet the accent has shifted; it is as if, in order to counterbalance the sometimes too massive theocratic idea, some of the men of the Second Reformation were inclined to emphasize more strongly than Calvin had done the elements of nega-tion and mortification. The Second Reformation vaccillated between a world-affirming Calvinism and a world-denying Mysticism, and the same traits are to be found in British and American Puritanism. This was no return to the ideas of Roman Catholicism: never did the ascetic ideal come to mean a cooperation between grace and works in order to attain eternal salvation, though the work of heathen missions with its hardships and its call to total dedication to the service of Christ was seen indeed as one of the most favourable conditions for entering

---

[41]   E. Troeltsch, *Die Soziallehren der christlichen Gruppen und Kirchen, Ge-sammelte Schriften*, I, *op. cit.*, SS. 648—649.

[42]   „Eine eingehende Analyse der einschlägigen Stellen wie Inst. III, 14, 18 ff, 24 4 über die signa posteriora ... musz zu der Resultat gelangen, dasz Christus allein die Quelle unserer Heilsgewiszheit ist und bleibt ...": J. Bohatec, *Calvins Lehre von Staat und Kirche, op. cit.*, S. 710.

[43]   See: J. Bohatec, *Budé und Calvin, Studien zur Gedankenwelt des franzö-sischen Frühhumanismus*, Graz 1950, esp. SS. 395—438.

[44]   *Inst.* III, 7, 7.

into the purity of an undisturbed communion with and an undivided allegiance to the Saviour.

In the nineteenth century missionary revival in Britain we find only some isolated examples of an ascetic attitude. As we saw above, [45] it is M. Schmidt who has called special attention to the fact that during his stay in Georgia Wesley wanted to return to the pure sphere of primitive Christianity by means of the work of missions: he considered the work of heathen missions as the nearest approach to the original Christian situation. [46] Here a burning desire for the purity of Christianity in its original form joined itsef with asceticism, romanticism and idealism. This, however, was a passing phase in Wesley's life: later on, this aspect receded into the background, and in the later period of his life we can only call Wesley an ascetic in that he was prepared to accept difficulties, hardships and incidental persecutions as corollaries of his total dedication to the service of Christ. But the accent had shifted from the world-flying attitude to the aggressiveness of the "Christian soldier", who joyfully fulfils the *militia Christi* on the highroads of life. The asceticism of Brainerd and Martyn was closely related to that of Heurnius, and, in a certain sense, to that of the younger Wesley, though in their world of thought the consciousness of God's free grace was infinitely greater than it was in Wesley's before his "second conversion". Both Brainerd and Martyn tried to realize something of the pilgrim-character of true Christianity on the hard road of self-denial which their missionary work demanded: do we possibly meet here with an echo of Calvin's ideal of *mortificatio?* But this aspect of asceticism was subordinated to the great goal of their labours: the glorification of God through the salvation of sinners. They are shining examples of a genuinely Christian attitude in that they were prepared to take seriously the meaning of the word "sacrifice" in the context of their missionary work. Apart from some incidental exceptions, the later development of Protestant missions was certainly not ascetic—unless we see in the part which the motive of debt has played in the development of the missionary ideal a revival of the old concept of "penance".

d. The Church and the Kingdom

It would be possible to treat the whole development of ecclesiology in the light of the problem of the relation between Church and Kingdom. Of necessity such a treatment would be one-sided—but on the other hand it would give a clear view of the ever-present tension between the more institutional and the more eschatological view of the

---

[45]   On p. 95, note 180.
[46]   See: M. Schmidt, *Der Missionsgedanke des jungen Wesley ...*, art. cit., S. 95.

Church, the tension between the Church as "Anstalt" and the Church as "Ereignis". Such a treatment would no doubt reveal that in the period of the Primitive Church these two aspects of the idea of the Church still formed an undifferentiated unity and that the disintegration of this unity did not fully manifest itself until a later period in Church history. The early Church was a Church in the full sense of the word: a community of believers, held together by Word and Sacraments and guided by a ministry that was conscious of a direct calling by Christ. This Church felt the impulse of expansion not only from soteriological motives, but also from its character as a universal community, to the essence of which it belonged that it should expand to the ends of the earth. At the same time, internal and external factors, the echo of the words of the prophets, the apostles and above all of Jesus himself as well as the persecutions which brought the Church back once and again to the position of *ecclesia pressa,* kept alive a salutary eschatological tension. Some of the early Fathers were rather naive millenarians, while others, less "fundamentalistic" in their approach to the biblical data, yet looked forward with eager expectancy to the *Parousia* of Christ. [47] By and by, however, the accent shifted from the eschatological attitude to a dominant interest in the institutional aspect of the Church. Medieval Christianity also knew its periods of fervent eschatology, and not only among various sects, but also within the Church, the expectance of a speedy return of Christ could become a stimulus to missionary action. [48] But a dynamic eschatology was only to be found on the margin of medieval thinking: much of the future was already deemed present in the glory of the Church. Professor Torrance rightly remarks that the *Eschaton* was domesticated and housed within the Church. [49] This had its influence upon the missionary work of the Church: though the massive institutionalism of the medieval Church was several times broken by the apostolic dynamism of several of the monastic orders, yet it can be said that much of the work of missions in the Middle Ages was undertaken for the sake of the enlargement of the this-wordly power and influence of the Church. And this form of the ecclesiological missionary motive was legitimized by the fact that the empirical Church and the Kingdom of God were seen as coextensive, linked together through the mystery of the continued incarnation of Christ in his Church: the *basileia* was believed to be present in the *ekklesia* to such a degree, that expansion

---

[47] See: G. W. H. Lampe, *Early Patristic Eschatology,* in: W. Manson and others, *Eschatology, op. cit.,* pp. 17—35.
[48] So Pope Gregory III asked Boniface to proclaim the Gospel to the Saxon people with a strong note of urgency in view of the fact that the end of all things was fast approaching: see J. H. Bavinck, *Bonifatius de Missionaris,* De Heerbaan VII (1954), p. 90.
[49] *Eschatology, op. cit.,* p. 37.

of Church and Kingdom could be identified and that the Church could be considered as *Corredemptrix*. [50]

It was the Reformers who rediscovered the distance between Church and Kingdom. To a certain extent they recognized the value of the Catholic concept of the Church, and their attitude was far from that of such sectarians and spiritualists as in their apocalyptic enthusiasm, had no eye for the continuity and the catholicity of the visible Church. But at the same time they gave back to the concept of the Church the eschatological character which it had also possessed in the earliest period of the Church, but which it had seen recede into the background after the great change of the fourth century. The Church recovered what Bohatec calls "das eschatologische Vorzeichen", and the idea of the expansion of the Church lost something of its massive character: a consciousness of the interim-character of the Church in the period of expectancy combined itself with a new dynamism, engendered by the knowledge that the expansion of the Church was no goal in itself, but a means to attain the greater end, the full revelation of the royal dominion of Christ. These ideas were only present *in nuce* with the Reformers themselves, and there were considerable differences between Luther on the one hand, and Bucer and Calvin on the other. [51] But the later development of Protestant missionary thinking proves that the germs of a combination of eschatological and missionary ideals were present in the soil which had been prepared by the Reformation. Historically, the point of contact between eschatology and missions lies in the first place in the fact that on the ground of Matt. 24.14 the mission was seen as one of the *signa praecursoria*. We have met this idea already with Calvin, [52] though not in an apocalyptical sense, as if the mission could only find a place in the days which immediately precede the Second Advent of Christ. Calvin knew that the walls of the history of this world are kept apart [53] by the preaching of the Gospel, as appears from the fact that he saw in the *katechoon* of II Thess. 2.7 the *universalis gentium vocatio*. [54] The relation between eschatology and missions, however, received a special accent because of the rise of millennarian ideas in the circle of Protestant Christianity. Already in the Reformation period these ideas were to be found with the sects, but by and by they obtained a foothold with the Churches. Some of the theologians of the Second Reformation were millennarians, in German Pietism the same ideas were

---

[50] So also a modern Roman Catholic missiologist: "Itaque Ecclesia simul ac *redempta* a Christo, Eius *Corredemptrix* effecta est", O. Dominguez, *Theologia Adaptationis et Praxis Missionaria*, in *Scientia Missionum Ancilla*, op. cit., p. 74.

[51] See above, pp. 8 ff.

[52] See: R. H. Bremmer, *Enkele karakteristieke trekken van Calvijn's Eschatologie*, Gereformeerd Theologisch Tijdschrift XXXXIV (1943), p. 77.

[53] The expression is of J. C. Hoekendijk, *Kerk en Volk, op. cit.*, p. 223.

[54] R. H. Bremmer, *art. cit.*, p. 78.

prevalent—there Bengel was their protagonist—, and they were also present in Britain and America, where the influence of Jonathan Edwards partly accounts for their rapid spread in Calvinistic circles. [55] The millennianism of this period was of a "mild" character: a *gradual* approach of the Millennium was expected, and the Millennium itself was visualized as a period in which the *spiritual* dominion of Christ would spread all over the earth. By the spread of these millennarian ideas, the relation between eschatology and missions became more complex. This relation was seen in a threefold way: first of all, the missionary activity was visualised as a sign of the approach of the Millennium, then it was also considered as a preparation for the Millennium, while thirdly the events which were supposed to announce the breaking of the millennial age in their turn became a stimulus for taking in hand a more vigorous missionary activity. Now the signs of the times pointed in the direction of great eschatological events, God was opening the door for the conversion of the Gentiles. Here the idea of the "door-opening", of the "destined time", which since Calvin had played a part in Reformed circles, was linked up with the "chronology" of millennarian eschatological thinking. At the same time a connection was supposed to exist between the conversion of the Jews and that of the Gentiles in the context of the millennarian expectation. This connection also had a complex character: on one hand it was believed that the general conversion of the heathen would be preceded by the coming of the Jewish people to Christ, [56] while by others it was assumed that the conversion of Israel would be prepared by the general spread of the Gospel among the heathen nations; [57] all this would take place during the gradual approach of the Millennium. We meet these ideas in Britain during the whole of the eighteenth century, from Robert Millar to William Shrubsole, [58] but they came to full maturity during the beginning of the nineteenth century, when Charles Simeon in particular defended them with the full force of his burning conviction. And however complex may have

---

[55] An early proof of the presence of post-millennarian ideas in British Calvinism is to be found in the (Congregationalist) *Savoy-Declaration* of 1658. Ch. XXV, V: see D. H. Kromminga, *The Millennium in the Church*, Grand Rapids 1945, p. 178.

[56] More than one theologian of the Second Reformation expected a general conversion of the Jews and even a return of the Jewish people to Palestina: J. van Genderen, *Herman Witsius, op. cit.*, p. 127; cf. the Synod of Westminster's *Directory for the Publick Worship of God*, which, in the prayer before sermon, placed the coming in of the "fulness of the Gentiles" between the „conversion of the Jews" and "the fall of Antichrist": see above, p. 24.

[57] This was also the thought of Ch. Hodge, *Systematic Theology*, III, *op. cit.*, pp. 800—807.

[58] Shrubsole was one of the first secretaries of the L.M.S.; he wrote the well-known hymn: "Arm of the Lord, awake! awake!" (1795): see E. A. Payne, *The Growth of the World Church*, London 1955, pp. 84—85. I was only able to make use of this work of Payne's—an enlarged edition of his *The Church Awakes*— during the writing of the last chapter of the present study.

been the relation between eschatology and missions—the mission announces, prepares and hastens the millennial events, while these events prepare a still greater missionary activity—one thing becomes clear: the missionary work of the Churches was seen again in the light of the coming Kingdom.

This does not mean, however, that in the circle of Protestantism the eschatological element had totally absorbed the ecclesiological aspect: the idea of the Church as at least a broken and partial realization of the Kingdom of God had not disappeared behind the eschatological expectations. So we meet the idea of the *plantatio ecclesiae* as a missionary motive in the circle of the Second Reformation: missionary activity was necessary, not only because perishing souls had to be saved or because the coming of the Kingdom had to be prepared, but also because the Church in which the Kingdom became partly made manifest had to expand to the ends of the earth. This ecclesiological motive received a special form when it was taken up in the struggle against Rome: the expansion of the Roman Catholic Church had to be emulated and counterbalanced. In Britain we meet with the idea of the expansion of the Church as a missionary motive especially in the Anglican circle: in a more secular form around 1700 (a combination of High Church ideals with latitudinarian tendencies) and with a dominantly spiritual character in the circle of the "Clapton Sect" (a preparation for the Oxford movement). In the circles of Anglican and Church of Scotland Evangelicalism it played but a small part, while it is clear that Methodism and Congregationalism were no good soil for a development of high ecclesiological ideals.

The ecclesiological and the eschatological motives are not mutually exclusive. But history shows that a heavy accent on the expansion of the empirical Church is not always attended by a burning eschatological expectancy, while on the other hand a fervent eschatology sometimes leaves but little room for the idea of a steady and continuous expansion of the Christian Church. During the ninenteenth century, the ecclesiological motive played its most important part in the circle of High Church Anglicanism, which wanted to plant the *Ecclesia Anglicana*, the Catholic Church, standing in the full apostolic succession, all over the world. [59] Neo-orthodox Lutheranism also returned to a stronger accentuation of the idea of the Church, [60] while we find the same deveopment in more than one Calvinistic group. [61] The eschatological motive received a very heavy accent in fundamentalist circles,

---

[59] See for the tensions between (High Church) S.P.G. and (Evangelical) C.M.S.: H. Cnattingius, *op. cit.*, passim.

[60] Cf. Wilhelm Löhe, in whose missionary thinking the idea of the Church received a central place: J. C. Hoekendijk, *Kerk en Volk, op. cit.*, p. 71.

[61] Cf. the fact that already in the nineteenth century, in Scottish Calvinism and in some sectors of Dutch Calvinism, missions were seen as a task of the Church in its institutional form.

where it was often combined with a form of crude Millennialism which differed considerably from the Millennialism of the Evangelicals of a former period. [62] On the other hand, under the influence of liberal thinking the old idea of a gradual approach of the Millennium could be transformed into more social categories: the "Social Gospel" is in part a liberalized form of the Millennialism of the early Evangelicals!

In our present day, we have come to a new recognition of the value of the idea of the Church in the context of missionary thinking, while at the same time the eschatological factor, loosened from millennarian speculations, is once more going to play a very important part. Is it possible that we are returning to an integration of the ideas of the *ekklesia* and the *basileia* in a missionary theology that is Church-centred and eschatologically-minded all in one? [63]

e. Background and correlation

Several times we have had to point to the relation between theology and missions: certain theological views could either be a hindrance or a stimulus with regard to the fulfilment of the missionary task, while on the other hand certain phases of the missionary awakening were marked by the characteristic features of contemporary theology. In this context, the question arises whether it is possible to establish the fact of a connection between a particular form of theology and the presence of a special motive or complex of motives. To a certain degree, this question has already found its answer in the foregoing part of this chapter. But by way of resumé we may state that in more than one case the existence of such a relation is established beyond any doubt. Theocratic ideals have to be seen against the background of a theology which was deeply conscious of the unity of life and the royal dominion of Christ over every sphere of life alike: such a theology was Calvinistic theology in its original form. [64] In the dominant place held by the cultural motive during certain phases of the missionary awakening, we recognize the influence of a latitudinarian theology, which in its turn was a combination of reformatory and humanistic thinking. [65] The strong accent which the motive of love received during the middle part of the eighteenth century is due to the influence of

---

[62]   As we saw above (cf. also: D. H. Kromminga, *The Millennium in the Church*, *op. cit.*, pp. 250—252), it was under the influence of Irving and others that the thought arose of a double Advent of Christ, before and after the Millennium: the approach of the Millennium would be sudden and apocalyptic, and missionary activity had to be carried out in great haste, in order to prepare a speedy Advent of Christ.

[63]   See: W. Andersen, *Towards a Theology of Mission*, London 1955, passim.

[84]   It is via Puritanism that the theocratic element in Calvinism could influence some sectors of British spiritual life.

[65]   We are here on the line of Erasmus and Leibniz, who both were strongly interested in the cultural-humanitarian aspect of missionary work.

Reformed and Lutheran Pietism, which resulted from an emphasizing of the soteriological line in Calvinism and Lutheranism. [66] The fact that the motive of obedience to God's command could come to weigh heavily with Carey and his contemporaries was not unrelated to the Calvinistic background of their thinking; on the other hand, the quality of the ascetic element with some Calvinistic missionaries shows that there was a relationship between their world of thought and that of the Second Reformation in Holland. The ecclesiological motive was strongest in such circles as had retained more than the outward form of the "catholic" heritage of the ecclesia Anglicana, while the wave of eschatological enthusiasm had one of its origins in the theology of Jonathan Edwards, who in this respect was, however, no isolated figure, as a comparison with Bengel's "Reichstheologie" clearly shows.

From all this it appears that it is impossible to reduce the missionary awakening to the influence of one type of theology: various theological trends have contributed to the growth of the missionary ideal. Nor is it possible to make one common element in those theologies responsible for the missionary awakening itself or for the special form which this awakening took during the eighteenth century, such as, e. g., the anthropocentric element which was present in Pietism, [67] or the individualism which was a mark of eighteenth century spiritual life. [68] Over against the anthropocentric elements in the awakening movements one can put the theocentric emphasis which was present in some sectors of the same movement as a heritage of Puritanism; over against the care for the salvation of individual souls the idea of the coming Kingdom. Generalizations are of no use, and an over-simplification of the questions which engage our attention tends to blind the eye to the fact that the remarkable missionary awakening of the eigtheenth century was due to a coincidence of several factors, which together acount for the great events of this period.

On the other hand, we should not like to give the impression that the missionary awakening was the result of a fortuitous combination of various disparate factors. On the contrary: a closer study of the missionary motives of this period reveals the fact of their mutual correlation and integration. Again, in the period before 1700, the

---

[66] It is not necessary to explain the soteriological line only from Lutheran influences, though these influences were indeed present: by means of men such as Dr Horneck, Pietism exercised a fertilizing influence, while we must also take into account the personal influence of Francke and the general acquaintance with the work of Ziegenbalg and Plütschau. The Moravians made a deep impression on Wesley, and Scottish Calvinism was strongly influenced by The Marrow of Modern Divinity, in which Lutheran elements are traceable: see H. Watt, The Influence of Martin Luther on Scottish Religion in the Eighteent Century, art. cit., passim.

[67] See: K. Barth, Kirchliche Dogmatik I, 2, S. 368.

[68] W. Holsten, Das Kerygma und der Mensch, op. cit., S. 62.

various motives which we have met with were either latently or openly present—but the more they became integrated with each other, the stronger became the impulses which led to the great awakening of the missionary ideal. We take some examples. In the theocratic ideal was present a latent stimulus to extend the dominion of Christ all over the earth—but only the coincidence of this motive with the motive of love could guard it against a cold and formal imperialism of the Christian spirit, which had no eye for the needs and problems of man in his individuality. On the other hand: only when the soteriological motive was taken up in the sphere of the expectation of the coming Kingdom was it freed from a one-sided individualism which threatened to lose sight of ,,the ends of the earth". And the motive of obedience was actualized by other motives, which in their turn received a new strength through their being confronted with the command of Christ. We can go further: there was also a correlation between the outward circumstances and the inner motives. The opening up of unknown territories brought "the ends of the earth" within the circle of interest; the events of the French revolution contributed to a revival of the eschatological tension, and even romantic ideals had a useful function in so far as they helped to break through the wall of disinterestedness in the fate of lands and peoples which lay outside the horizon of immediate knowledge. At the end of our historical survey, we conclude that no one isolated motive or single factor can explain the growth of the missionary ideal: it is through a fulness of motives that the Church was thrown back upon its primary task: to proclaim the Gospel of Christ over all the earth.

2. THE EMPIRICAL MOTIVES CONFRONTED WITH THE BIBLE

a. *The necessity of this confrontation*

As yet, one great question has remained unanswered: were the motives which contributed to the awakening of the missionary ideal in conformity with the motive which is enshrined in the Word of God? It might seem superfluous to inquire after the legitimacy of motives that have powerfully contributed to the rise of a work which can only be considered by posterity with awe and gratitude. Is not the fact of their influence, are not their effects a sufficient legitimation? Here we are confronted with a double danger. The first one is, that we proclaim ourselves judges of former generations who, guided by the Spirit of God and living from a deep faith in Christ, have done indeed "great things for God". We have to be conscious of the fact that, if it is true that without the Spirit no one can say that Jesus is Lord, it is the more true that without the Spirit no man, no community, no Church can proclaim among risks and perils the name of the Lord to the ends of the earth. The knowledge that ultimately the work of missions does not lie in the hands of men but in those of Christ—the great missionary—must give to our critical judgment that quality of reserve without which all criticism unavoidably takes on the flavour of *hybris* and haughtiness. [69] Even if we see the limitations of missionary leaders in the past, we yet know that without their work we would have been unable to reach that point from which we can give a balanced judgment on the inner quality of the activities of former generations. Our judgment has to be a criticism-in-gratitude and a criticism-in-solidarity: what we have, we have received through their hands, while on the other hand the impure elements which have crept into their missionary motivation are the mirror in which we detect the impurity in our own motives.

But it is exactly on this point that we are confronted with the second danger: the danger of an uncritical attitude, which proceeds either from a feeling of admiration or from the thought that we have no right to judge the bygone past. An uncritical attitude does not sufficiently take into account the brokenness of all human work. Besides, the past is not dead: there is an undeniable continuity between our motives and those of the pioneers of Protestant missionary activity. A confrontation of their motives with the divine motive is none other than a piece of missionary self-scrutiny, a self-criticism which, according to Professor Kraemer, is a sign of health and an indispensible life-necessity. [70]

Every missionary motive is, in a greater or less degree, ambiguous. On the one hand, it is a response to the call of God. Sometimes, the response is clear, in other cases it is so much veiled in purely human considerations that it is difficult to distinguish the element of answer to God's voice. But always it possesses at least something of the religious quality without which no missionary work can exist. On the other hand, however, it is a response on the human level—which means that it shares in the impurity of all human thoughts and deeds. Even the purest motive is but an approximation of the ideal motive. Here the necessity of a confrontation becomes clear: it follows from the duty to set over and over again even the deepest roots of our work under the judgment of God.

But now the question arises: what is the norm of our criticism? This norm cannot be the contemporary situation, though from the fact that God acts in history it follows that we have to draw the development of the concrete historical situation within the circle of our considerations when we try to give a judgment of the missionary motives within a certain period. Neither is this norm our own theology, though it is

---

[69] Cf. W. Andersen, *op. cit.*, pp. 47—48.
[70] H. Kraemer, *The Christian Message in a Non-Christian World, op. cit.*, p. 32.

clear that, when theology is not a "play without engagement" but a serious effort to repeat in our own language the contents of the Bible in living communion with the Church of all ages, it is not unlawful to treat the problem under consideration in theological categories. But the ultimate norm is the Bible, the Word of the living God: the empirical motives have to be put in the light of biblical revelation.

In doing so, we have to stand clear of a fundamentalist view of the Bible on the one hand and of a liberal interpretation on the other. Over against the fundamentalist method, which on the ground of isolated texts tries either to criticize or to support a certain empirical reality, we put our view of the Bible as a unity which is centered in Him who is the Word of God in its most special sense: a confrontation with the Bible is nothing else but a confrontation with Christ. But over against the liberal view, which sees the Bible as the human record of an interaction between divine and human thoughts and deeds and which delivers the contents of the Bible to the arbitrariness of human judgment [71] we maintain the divine authority of the Bible as *norma normans* of faith and life: we have to surrender ourselves to the full testimony of Scripture. This means that we stand with the "fathers" before the bar of the Gospel in a condemning and liberating judgment. To the missionary idea can be applied the idea of *simul peccator et justus*. In spite of all the impurity of human motives, God accepts them by the fact that he inserts them in his royal work. But this does not release us from the obligation to enquire after the question on which concrete points the motives of the missionary awakening were in conflict with the purity of the biblical motive: it is on these points that the process of purification has to begin.

In the context of this study a total confrontation is impossible: we can only accompany the results of our historical inquiry with some critical questions. We want to put those questions together with such theologians of our day as are also reflecting upon the deepest roots of missionary work, while we listen with them to the voice of the Bible, in the knowledge that only in this way are we able to contribute to the ever necessary "purification of the missionary motive".

b. Corpus Christianum and dominion of Christ in this world

We have seen that the idea of the *corpus christianum* has played an important part in the missionary activity of the Church—not only in the Middle Ages, but also in a later period, when Puritanism was conscious of a relation between missions and the "public face of life", while the after-effects of this idea were still to be seen in the circle

---

[71] Cf. W. Holsten, who is critically suspicious of the Book of Acts on the ground of his—Bultmannian—view of the Pauline kerygma: *Das Kerygma und der Mensch, op. cit.*, S. 123.

of Latitudinarianism, which saw a connection between ecclesiastical expansion and the extension of the sphere of influence of Christian culture. The idea of the *corpus christianum* has an equivocal character: it has a negative aspect in so far as it is an attempt to adapt the life of the Christian Church to the forms of this world, but it has also a positive aspect in that it tries to give form to the totalitarian dominion of Christ in the "time between the times". From this it follows that missionary work has the same ambiguous character, when it is prompted by motives that lie in the sphere of the *corpus christianum*-idea. The history of missions shows that theocratic ideals easily deteriorated into a secular imperialism, and that the ideal of the christianization of culture almost always led to a transmission of the faults and limitations of the missionaries' own culture, which was still far from being integrally Christian. So the close connection between colony and missions made havoc of the missionary activity of the Second Reformation; many of the American Puritans changed the spiritual "war of the Lord" for a devastating warfare against the Indian tribes; Latitudinarianism at the last seemed to be more interested in the spread of European culture than in the propagation of the pure Gospel of Christ; even the Evangelicals did not always make a clear distinction between the *pax Brittannica* and the *pax Christi;* nineteenth century missions were marked by a too intimate relationship between Christian expansion and Western imperialism, and the recent events in China are the grim illustration of the dangers of a missionary policy which to a certain degree combined the Christian and the Western-cultural motives. These examples—which could be multiplied—show each in its own way the danger of that form of anticipation of the Kingdom which adapts the dimensions of God's eternal realm to the forms of this world. Since the days of Constantine, this form of adaptation has constantly threatened the purity of the life of the Church and its mission. It has infringed upon the principle of religious freedom, it has made the missionary activity of the Church subservient to secular purposes, it has contaminated religious issues with matters that lay outside the sphere of religion, and it has linked up the Gospel of God's peace with wordly power-politics. It was the fundamental fault of this form of anticipation, that it did not take sufficiently into account the passing character of the structure of this world. We live in the period of the "not yet", the period in which it is impossible to give a lasting and massive form to the Kingdom of God within the "scheme" of this world: "for the fashion—*schèma*—of this world passeth away" (I Cor. 7.31). The Christian mission bears the burden of the brokenness of this world— and when it ignores this fundamental brokenness and tries to overcome it by anticipating upon a form of life that cannot be realized within the dimensions of the world of to-day, the anticipation of the coming realm of God turns into the reverse and leads to a secularization of the idea of the Kingdom.

The concept of the *corpus christianum*, however, has also a positive aspect in so far as it takes seriously the idea of the dominion of Christ over the totality of life. The theocratic ideal and the attempts to christianize "the face of the earth" are an anticipation—but one of the motives of this anticipation is the urge to protest against a narrowing of the message to the territory of the soul, a resistance against a Hellenistic spirituality on the ground of the Israelitic-realistic character of biblical revelation. [72] The Old Testament knows of no salvation for the soul only: the prophets of Israel had the mighty vision of "an *earth*, filled with the knowledge of the Lord", and the fulfilment of their messianic prophecies has been realized in principle by the Messiah, whose Incarnation shows that he has come to redeem the world in the most concrete form if its existence—"the Word was made flesh, and dwelt among us" (John 1.14). His Cross and Resurrection do not only mean the liberation of the inner side of human life, but the redemption of life in its totality. The New Testament concept of peace has to be seen in the light of the *shalom*-idea of the Old Testament. [73] From this it follows that the missionary motive does not lie only in the sphere of the salvation of individual souls: the Christian missionary is driven by the urge to bring the whole of life—the life of state and culture, the life of man in the complex totality of his existence—under the royal dominion of Christ. [74] The

---

[72] In his important article *The Call to Evangelism*, I.R.M. XXXIX (1950), pp. 162—175, in which he gives a trenchant criticism of some aspects of the *corpus christianum* idea ("... in this way of thinking Christendom becomes a protective shell of the Church. The Church tends to be built into the vast realm of Christian-influenced society. Christendom becomes a shock-breaker"), Professor Hoekendijk also calls attention to the fact "that the aim of evangelism can be nothing less than what Israel expected the Messiah to do, i.e. He will establish the shalom". He fails however to form a connection between the biblical *shalom*-idea and the (broken and corrupted) attempts to realize the *shalom* in the *corpus christianum*.

[73] „So wird εἰρήνη auf der Grundlage des at.lich-rabbinischen Sprachgebrauches erst mit dem unfassendsten und tiefsten Inhalt gefüllt, indem es das eschatologische Heilsein des ganzen Menschen bezeichnet, das hier schon als Macht Gottes wirksam ist und den Zustand der καινὴ κτίσις als Zustand abschlieszender Erfüllung bezeichnet. In diesem Sinne ist las Heil offenbar geworden in der Auferstehung Christi": W. Foerster in *Th.W.N.T.* II, S. 413.

[74] It is this positive element of the theocratic ideal which has been brought to the fore in a brilliant way by Professor van Ruler in several of his works, of which we mention especially his essay *De Kolonie* in his *Visie en Vaart*, Amsterdam 1947, pp. 129—199, and his *Theologie van het Apostolaat*, Nijkerk s.a. Here we meet with a strong reaction against a spiritualizing thinking that has no concern for the concrete realization of the dominion of Christ in state and culture. In its turn, this reaction bears the mark of one-sidedness in so far as it fails to take seriously enough the fact that, because of the interim-character of this dispensation, the ideals of the Old Testament regarding the dominion of God over state and culture can only find a partial and broken realization in the period before the Second Advent of Christ. See for a critical exposition of Van Ruler's ideas in

urgent necessity of this aspect of the missionary attitude is illustrated by Canon Warren, when he quotes the words of an African student who remarked, speaking of such young Africans as find it difficult to bridge the gap between their Christian schooling and the full life in which they stand: "To them God is the God of the Church: He is not the God of politics and social life. They need help to see Him as one God: to see that the Church is concerned with the whole of life". [75] This exactly is the positive aspect of the *corpus christianum* idea: the knowledge that God is the God of the whole of life. The attempts of the Puritans to give to the work of missions a theocratic character, the cultural aspect which missions received during the period of Latitudinarian ascendency and the way in which the Evangelicals linked up the missionary task with their humanitarian ideals have at least this positive value, that they confront us with the duty of being concerned with life in its wholeness, the duty of showing that the God whom the Church preaches is indeed the God of politics and culture and social life. We may smile at the naive way in which Jonathan Edwards and his contemporaries tried to bring the life of the Indian tribes into conformity with the Puritan pattern of life, and we may be astonished at the ease with which such Evangelical leaders as Carey and Wilberforce bracketed together "civilization" and "the spread of the Gospel", „moral instruction" and "the diffusion of the blessings of Christianity". [76] But, within the limitations of the contemporary world of thought, they tried at least to realize something of the restoration of the unity of life under the dominion of Christ.

The *corpus christianum* has broken. [77] The great reduction of the sphere of influence of Christianity has brought the Church back to a new consciousness of the fact that she has only a place in this world under the shadow of the Cross. [78] The period of theocratic dreams and cultural visions belongs to the past. The Church has to learn again the hard lesson that she is treated as a stranger in this world—together with her Lord. But yet she knows that to the Christ whom she proclaims has been given all power in earth. And during the time in which she looks forward to the full revelation of his glory, she not only proclaims the coming of the Kingdom: she also tries to „restrain the chaos" [79] and to advance into the concrete needs of

---

relation with the missionary problems: A. J. Rasker, *Christelijke Politiek, op. cit.,* passim.

[75] M. A. C. Warren, *The Christian Mission,* London 1951, p. 9.

[76] See above, p. 147 ff.

[77] See: H. Kraemer, *The Christian Message in a Non-Christian World, op. cit.,* pp. 27 ff.

[78] See: J. de Graaf, *Het Apostolaat in een gereduceerde Kerk,* N.Th.T. VII (1953), esp. pp. 260 ff.

[79] A term, often used by Van Ruler, passim in his works; cf. also Canon

this world with a comprehensive approach. [80] This aim is modest in that it does not attempt to anticipate the future glorious state of the Kingdom, but is at he same time realistic in that it tries to bring life in its fulness and its unity under the healing dominion of Christ.

Rasker speaks of a relative theocracy. [81] Indeed, the theocratic and cultural motives have to be seen in their relative importance. But still they represent an essential aspect of the biblical missionary motive, if they are only integrated with the other motives of the Bible. Without a soteriological passion, they threaten to lose sight of the fact that the dominion of Christ takes its beginning in the heart of man who is taken up in the liberating grace of Jesus. Without an element of asceticism they are prone to forget the distance between the Kingdom of Christ and the "fashion of this world". Without an eschatological emphasis they lose sight of the truth that the work of the Church is only "preparatory in character", holding "the presence of better things to come". [82] But where in a comprehensive approach life is brought to a new integration and a deeper unity, a sign becomes visible of the realization of the vision which inspired the prophets of the Old Testament: "He shall have dominion also from sea to sea . . . and let the whole earth be filled with his glory" (Ps. 72.8, 19).

c. Human compassion and divine love

The motive of love is one of the most central and one of the most evident stimuli to missionary action. But this motive, too, has an ambivalent character. We give first attention to its negative aspects, which can be epitomized in one small word: the epithet „poor", used times without number in connection with the word "heathen". It has already become apparent from this little word that again and again the motive of love was brought within the anthropocentric sphere, that sometimes it was even practically identified with compassion on the purely human level. In our historical survey we gave some attention to the seal of the S.P.G., which bears the words "Transiens adjuva nos", a remembrance of the vision of the Macedonian man. Apart from the question of whether, in the particular case of the S.P.G. seal, the men who called "come over and help us" were really meant to represent the heathen population of America, it is clear that in this period the thought was current that the heathen in their helplessness and poverty were calling upon the benevolent help of the

---

Warren's study on "the theology of imperialism" in his Caesar, the Beloved Enemy, London 1955, pp. 10—41.
[80] See: A. G. Honig, Bijdrage tot het onderzoek naar de fundering van de zendingsmethode der comprehensive approach in het Nieuwe Testament, Kampen 1951, passim.
[81] A. J. Rasker, op. cit., p. 41.
[82] M. A. C. Warren, Caesar, the Beloved Enemy, op. cit., p. 27.

Christian nations. It is further evident that, even if the call did not come from the heathen world itself, still within the circle of Christianity the patent needs of the heathen world could be used as one of the strongest missionary arguments. From the Christian side, this argument inevitably brought with it the *beati possidentes* attitude, *i. e.* a feeling of superiority, which with the Latitudinarians received a more cultural accent (the heathen have to be brought into contact with the blessings of our Christian culture) and with the Revivalists a more spiritual connotation (the heathen have to be lifted up to the level of our religious existence). The heathen are the cultural and spiritual have-nots, who have to receive from the hands of Western Christians the treasures of Christian culture and Christian religious life. This leads to a form of missionary propaganda, in which heathen life is painted with the darkest colours, as a life of permanent unrest and unhappiness; the light of the Christian world is contrasted with the darkness of the heathen world, and lastly the darkness of heathen life is put against the grim background of the last darkness: that of eternal damnation.

It is not difficult to point out the deficiencies of this form of missionary motivation. In the first place, it is subject to the danger of a purely *anthropocentric foundation* for missions, in which the foundation of missionary work has shifted from God to man, and in which the stimulus to missionary action is sought in the view of the heathen world—a view which in its turn is determined by subjective and emotional factors and which consequently lacks the stability which is necessary for a solid foundation of the missionary task. In this sphere, a "Herabsetzung" of the heathen world combines itself in a remarkable way with a romantic attitude (Haweis!). Love becomes charity, benevolence, condescension—though it must be added that with the wisest and profoundest representatives of the missionary aim, this aspect of the idea of love was strengthened by a feeling of debt towards the heathen world which gave to their love a greater depth. Our second objection is, that in this way the consciousness of *solidarity* with the heathen world recedes into the background, that knowledge of being ourselves heathens by nature, standing under the same judgment and only existing by the grace of God's justification. Once again, the wisest and deepest were conscious of this solidarity, [83] and in the revivalist circle the feeling of superiority was made relative by a deep sense of sin and guilt. But in spite of this the attitude of the *beatus possidens* has had a tenacious existence in the sphere of Protestant missions. In the third place we would remark that when

---

[83] Cf. M. Schmidt on Wesley's attitude towards the Indians during his stay in Georgia: „Die pädagogische Überlegenheit des Missionars über die Heiden, die im Missionsgedanken der religious societies so stark hervortrat, in den dänisch-hallischen Berichten wesentlich eingeschränkt wurde, fällt hier ganz dahin ... Es ergibt sich eine letzte geheime Solidarität zwischen dem Bringer und dem Empfänger der Botschaft", in: *Der Missionsgedanke des jungen Wesley. art. cit.*, S. 96.

heathen life is seen against the background of eternal damnation, the danger of a speculative attitude with regard to the problem of the ultimate state of the heathen is more than imaginary. E. Jansen Schoonhoven rightly reminds [84] of the Pauline exhortation, "not to think [of men] above that what is written", and H. Bavinck remarks in his Dogmatics, with an appeal to Christ's answer to the question concerning the number of those who would be saved (Luke 12.23), that these things are only known to God, and that for this exact reason the Reformed confession gives to the salvation of lost humanity a broad foundation, because it does not seek the ultimate ground of salvation in man's attitude, but in the free grace and the boundless compassion of God. [85] This was also the attitude of the greater spirits in the missionary awakening (e. g. Martyn and Simeon) towards this problem. But some of their followers were not always free from unbiblical speculations on this point.

To summarise, we see as the negative aspect of the motive of love in the missionary awakening a certain humanization of the idea of compassion: a strong accent on human pity could lead to a missionary philanthropy which remained below the measure of the biblical demand of love. In the New Testament especially, love is seen in its relation to the source of love as a direct continuation of the love of God in Christ. It is this love which "is shed abroad in our hearts by the Holy Spirit" (Rom. 5.5) and of which it can be said that "the love of Christ constraineth us" (II Cor. 5.14). In this last verse, the genetive "tou Christou" has primarily to be seen as a *genetivus subjectivus*— love which proceeds from Christ—, but Professor Grosheide rightly remarks that the other meaning—that of a *genetivus objectivus:* love towards Christ—is not excluded, but rather follows from the first meaning. [86] In the Pauline testimony, love is the direction of the sovereign will of God towards the world of men and their salvation, and with John love is the love of God which descends into the *kosmos,* where it is realized in the deed of love. [87] The work of missions receives a place in the movement of this love towards the world: as the sending of the Son proceeds from this love (John 3.16), so the fact that men are sent out into this world finds its deepest motive in the impelling force of the love of Christ. This love is a gift, while at the same time it is a command: thou shalt love—but the fulfilment of this command is nothing but the responsive movement of this love, which transforms itself by the way of gratitude into love of fellow-man, in whom God meets us.

---

[84]   E. Jansen Schoonhoven, *Critische Bespreking van enige Zendingsmotieven,* *art. cit.,* p. 221.

[85]   H. Bavinck, *Gereformeerde Dogmatiek,* IV, Kampen⁴ 1930, p. 709.

[86]   F. W. Grosheide, *De Tweede Brief van de Apostel Paulus aan de Kerk te Korinthe,* Amsterdam 1939, p. 199.

[87]   So E. Stauffer in *Th.W.N.T.* I, SS. 49—55.

This means in the first place that the anthropocentric element is transcended: the heathen is not to be loved because of his pitiable state, but because he is an object of the love of Christ. We have not to see him through our own eyes, but through the eyes of Jesus. It is not the heathen world which calls us, but God calling in Christ. [88] In the second place this means that we are brought to the knowledge of a new solidarity. We are not the givers, standing over against spiritual "have-nots", but we all partake in the same mercy, which has come to us and which flows through us into the heathen world: "for all have sinned, and come short of the glory of God, being justified freely by his grace . . . Where is boasting then? It is excluded" (Rom. 3.23, 24, 27). The *beati possidentes* attitude can only be broken through when we are prepared to pass on what we have received by grace and to share our spiritual "possession" with others in a spirit of love, humility and solidarity. And thirdly, we leave the problem of the eternal state of the heathen in the hands of Him who is free in the bestowing of the gifts of his mercy.

But from this it follows that in the biblical context there is also a place for a positive evaluation of the motive of love. The anthropocentric aspect is transcended, but not in such a way that man in his need disappears behind the horizon. On the contrary: through the eyes of Christ we learn to see the real needs of mankind. We cannot say that because missions find their ultimate ground in God the situation of man is a matter of no importance and pity is quite out of place. Christ had compassion with man in his temporal and spiritual misery, he was moved with compassion on seeing the multitudes, he healed the sick and had mercy on sinful man who cried to Him for help. When we see man through Jesus' eyes we hear in man's social misery and his religious need the call of God. The anthropocentric aspect of the motive of love has its worth, if it is seen in direct connection with the theocentric aspect: the circle of God's love widens itself into an ellipse, in which man—through grace— becomes a focus. This view leads to deeds of love which transcend the humanitarian level because they are a continuance of the healing work of Christ (the comprehensive approach—cf. the struggle against slavery). But above all it leads to the most important deed of love: the "saving of souls", *i. e.* the bringing of the most central point of human existence into contact with Christ's redeeming love. [89] Though we are not allowed to make speculations with regard to the *numerus electorum* and the problem of the salvation of the heathen, we know

---

[88]   J. H. Bavinck, *Inleiding in de Zendingswetenschap, op. cit.,* pp. 62—63.

[89]   In his *The Christian Imperative*, London 1955, Canon Warren gives a fine exposition of the unity between the healing of the many wounds of mankind and the healing of its deepest wound: "Salvation according to the Bible is the restoration of man to his true harmony with God, with his neighbour and with himself", p. 63.

that outside Christ man is lost, [90] a sheep in the wilderness, threatened by the danger of being separated for ever from healing contact with the source of life. Over against the remark of Tillich that "such an interpretation of the meaning of missions is unworthy of the glory and of the love of God" [91] we put that of Bishop Newbigin: "The individual is brought by the preaching of the Gospel face to face with his Creator and Lord, and is compelled to face the issues of his life. The offer to him in Christ of complete and final salvation is inevitably at the same time a revelation to him of the possibility of complete and final damnation". [92] This gave to the missionary work of the Evangelicals, as it also has to give to our present missionary labours, the note of urgency! [93]

Lastly, it has more than once been suggested that the Reformed doctrine of election has been a barrier against the full break-through of the idea of love towards all men. Historically, this holds true only for the caricature of this doctrine in the so-called "hyper-Calvinism". The Reformed doctrine itself, however, leaves ample room for the preaching of the Gospel to all men and for the general offer of grace: it does not identify election and determinism, and in the knowledge of the free compassion of God it finds its broadest scope. [94]

Without the motive of love, the work of missions becomes sterile and cold. But this motive can only function in the right way if it is integrated with a number of other motives. We think here of the theocratic motive, which can save the motive of love from a narrowing of the missionary front to the problems of the "soul" only. We also think of the motive of obedience, which can save it from the unstability of an emotional attitude: there is a "duty of love" which gives to the motive of love its constant and stable character. [95] The ascetic element, too, has to be present: it guards the motive of love

---

[90]   In a weakened sense, the idea of man's "lostness" even occurs with Hocking (man is "lost", when he is without a sure direction of action): see R. Pierce Beaver, *North American Thought on the Fundamental Principle of Missions during the Twentieth Century*, Church History XXI (1952), p. 351.

[91]   P. Tillich, *The Theology of Missions*, Occasional Bulletin of the Missionary Research Library, V (1954), p. 3.

[92]   L. Newbigin, *The Duty and Authority of the Church to preach the Gospel*, in: *The Church's Witness to God's Design* (The Amsterdam Assembly Series II), London 1948, p. 34.

[93]   In the same way, Professor H. N. Ridderbos remarks in his *Zending in het Nieuwe Testament*, De Heerbaan VII (1954), pp. 138 ff., that what he calls the „anthropological motive", the motive which is determined by the consciousness of the necessity of faith and conversion, plays a great part in the New Testament: missionary work is not an objective proclamation of the salvation in Christ, but a struggle with the souls of men (II Cor. 5 : 11).

[94]   See for this problem: G. C. Berkouwer, *De Verkiezing Gods*, Ch. IV, Verkiezing en Prediking, pp. 250   308.

[95]   Cf. Niels F. S. Ferré: „Duty subordinates the all-seeking self to an unbending objective order", in: *Fear, Duty and Love as Ultimate Motives for Christian Missions*, I.R.M. XXXVII (1948), p. 397.

against a cheap sentimentality by placing it within the sphere of sacrifice. And it is the ecclesiological motive which can bring the motive of love out of the sphere of individualism: because the Church is the fellowship of love, participating in Jesus Christ and through Him in the full love of God, "the interpenetration of being and mission constitutes the nature of the Church, so that the Church *is* Church as it participates in the active operation of the divine love". [96] This gives to the idea of love its wide dimension: it is an act of the Body of Christ, and through this love man is brought into communion with the corporate expression of the love of Christ on earth.

d. Command and sacrifice

When we try to see the motive of obedience in its biblical context, we meet with the remarkable fact that the missionary command which we find in its most explicit form in Matt. 28.19 not only played a very slight part in the later history of the Church, but even in the apostolic period was relegated to the background. We might expect that the Apostles would have appealed frequently to the command of the Lord when they impressed on the congregations the greatness and importance of the missionary task. But instead of this we are confronted with a deep silence on this point. It is as if the command, given to the apostles between Resurrection and Ascension, had disappeared behind the horizon. The easiest solution of this problem—the denial of the authenticity of the missionary command—is no real solution: there is no internal evidence which makes it impossible to consider Matt. 28.19 as a word of Jesus himself, [97] while in addition the command of Matt. 28 stands in alignment with many other utterances of Jesus, made either before or after his Resurrection, and with the whole of his teaching on the *basileia*. [98] But why then is it not mentioned in the writings of the apostles, who knew that they stood under the vigour of a divine imperative: "necessity is laid upon me, yea, woe is unto me if I preach not the gospel" (I Cor. 9.16)? Yet it is this last point precisely which gives us a clue to the solution of this problem. In his study on the relation between Pentecost and missions, H. Boer

---

[96] T. F. Torrance, *Royal Priesthood*, Scottish Journal of Theology Occasional Papers No 3, Edinburgh-London [1955], p. 30.

[97] In his *De Komst van het Koninkrijk*, Kampen 1950, pp. 331 ff., H. N. Ridderbos convincingly shows that neither the use of the trinitarian formula, nor the fact that after the giving of the command a struggle could still arise on the missionary task of the Church (Acts 15), are sufficient grounds for denying the authenticity of this word. The trinitarian "formula" is not used here as a fixed baptismal formula, but as an indication of the nature of baptism which does not fall outside the scope of Jesus' teaching, and the quarrel in Acts 15 did not find its origin in a difference of opinion on the necessity of heathen missions in general, but in a disagreement with regard to the manner of admitting Gentiles into the Church.

[98] So H. N. Ridderbos *in loco citato*.

has convincingly demonstrated that since Pentecost the commission of Christ has become an organic part of the essence of the Church as an *inner law* which carried within itself its own effectuation. [99] We can also say that since the outpouring of the Spirit the command worked from within, it was transformed into an inner urge which was the result of an existential relationship between the Giver and the receivers of the command. In the Spirit, Christ had returned to his Church in order to fulfil by his own indwelling in the hearts of his followers the command which He had laid upon them. As the missionary command was nothing but the consequence of the self-revelation of the risen Messiah, the missionary duty did not need to be founded upon any one isolated utterance of Jesus: it simply resulted from his spiritual presence in the midst of his Church.

Does that mean that we are not entitled to make an explicit appeal to the missionary command, and that Carey was wrong when he used as one of the main arguments for missionary work Christ's great commission? Quite definitely not: there are circumstances in which it is even necessary to make use of this command. But when this necessity arises there is something wrong in the life of the Church—just as in marriage there is something wrong when the duty of mutual love has to be emphasized. The need to underline the missionary command indicates that the consciousness of the full implications of the victory of Christ as the Saviour of this world is below the mark. In such a case, the accentuation of the command of the Lord has to be attended by attempts to deepen the spiritual life of the Church.

This brings us to the negative aspect of the motive of obedience. When the missionary task is considered as a matter of cool and formal obedience, it has been drawn within a legalistic sphere which threatens to extinguish the joy and gladness essential to the right functioning of the missionary ideal. During the period of the missionary awakening, however, the fire of the Spirit burned so strong that there was no place for a legalistic approach to the missionary task. On the contrary, the motive of obedience can be seen in its most positive aspect, as when Carey tried to break through the apathetic attitude of a group of "hyper-Calvinists" by laying stress upon the plain duty of every Christian to carry the Gospel of Christ to the ends of the earth. It is in this sense that the missionary command has a lasting place in the life of the Church. In times of spiritual decline, in periods when the missionary task is no longer seen as the self-evident consequence of the bearing of the name of Christ, it can be necessary to confront the Church with the ineluctible duty which is founded in the imperative of the risen Lord. But equally when the missionary attitude in general is present it can be necessary to

---

[99] H. R. Boer, *op. cit.*, esp. pp. 111 ff.

emphasize the world-wide scope of the missionary command: "Go ye therefore, and teach *all nations*". In the meantime, it is clear that this motive, too, needs to be integrated with other motives, of which we mention here in particular the motive of love and the eschatological motive. Obedience without love stands under the Pauline judgment: "though I speak with the tongues of men and of angels, and have not charity, I am become a sounding brass, or a tinkling cymbal" (I Cor. 13.1), while obedience without expectance lacks the invigorating stimulus of direction upon the great *telos* of which Christ spoke after he had given his command: "Lo, I am with you alway, even unto the end of the world" (Matt. 28.20).

In this context we can speak of "joyful obedience". [100] But, on the other hand, the Bible also teaches that obedience entails the enduring of hardness: "Thou therefore endure hardness, as a good soldier of Jesus Christ" (II Tim. 2.3). This is the biblical background of the relation which Heurnius saw between the *multae afflictiones* and the *militia Christi*. The ascetic idea has certainly a place in the biblical world of thought: the Bible shows that the road to the glorification of God leads through pains and sufferings. This follows immediately from the centrality of the Cross in the biblical message. Back in the Old Testament we meet with the idea of "redemptive suffering": the sufferings of the Servant bring salvation to mankind, [101] and this thought is intensified in the New Testament—through his death Jesus has become the life of the world. The New Testament also teaches that there is a double relation between the Cross and the life of the Church. The Church may "glory" in the Cross, she may know that through the Cross she has been given a new freedom, which exists in the knowledge of forgiveness and liberation and through which she shares in the forces of the Kingdom. But at the same time the Cross has become the pattern of her life. There is a mysterious relation between the sufferings of Christ and those of his servants: Paul knows that he fills up that which is behind of the afflictions of Christ (Col. 1.24), and there exists a sym-pathy in the deepest sense of the word between Christ and his disciples. [102] This does not mean that the aspect of suffering is the only one under which the Church in the New Testament dispensation has to be seen, or that the message of the New Testament is so much determined by the idea of sharing in the afflictions of Christ that its total outlook becomes world-denying. On the contrary, because the Cross is followed by the

---

[100]   See: E. Jansen Schoonhoven, *Critische Bespreking van enige Zendings-motieven, art. cit.*, p. 222.
[101]   See: H. H. Rowley, *The Missionary Message of the Old Testament*, London [1944], pp. 61 ff.
[102]   „Das πάσχειν der Christen ist deshalb ein συμπάσχειν, weil Christus sie zum Leiden führt": W. Michaelis in *Th.W.N.T.* V, S. 925.

Resurrection there rings through the New Testament message a strong note of hope and victory which leaves room for a positive attitude towards this world. The new aeon has begun, which is marked by the virtual dominion of Christ, and the Church also shares in the conquering life of her Lord. We live in the period of the "not yet", and from this "not yet" it follows that the Church has to keep a certain distance from the forms of this world in which Christ has been crucified. But we also live in a time which stands under the sign of the Resurrection, of the break-through of the new life: this knowledge gives to the attitude of the Christian the accent of world-affirmation. [103] In the context of the New Testament message the ascetic element has a place, [104] and there is also a tangent-plane between this asceticism and the missionary task of the Church [105]—but this element is immediately counterbalanced by the joyful affirmation of Christ's total victory.

In the course of missionary history, however, the ascetic element has more than once slipped out of its place: instead of a corollary to the work of missions, it became the all-governing goal to which the work of missions was made subservient. The danger of this attitude is that it threatens to confound the two ways in which we are related to the sufferings of Christ, that it puts co-redemption in the place of sympathy and in this way it infringes upon the all-sufficient character of the redeeming work of Christ. [106] In the meantime we must not lose sight of the fact that there are transitions from one form of asceticism to another. So the asceticism of the younger Wesley is as much an intermediary form as that of Brainerd, and though these two forms of the ascetic attitude also differ from each other, they yet have a common point of contact with some remarks of Paul: "And this I do for the Gospel's sake, that I might be partaker thereof with [you] ... But I keep under my body, and bring [it] into sub-

---

[103] "Der Gläubige lebt in einer Welt, von der er weisz, dasz sie vergehen wird, aber dasz sie jetzt noch im Rahmen der Heilsgeschichte gottgewollt und von Christus beherrscht ist. Insofern er weisz, das sie vergehen wird, verneint er sie; insofern er weisz, sie ist der gottgewohlte Rahmen der heilsgeschichtlichen Gegenwart, bejaht er sie": O. Cullmann, *Christus und der Zeit*, Zürich 1946, S. 188.

[104] „Paulus hat das Wort ἀσκεῖν auszen Ag. 24.10 nie. In der Sache aber ist solche „Übung" in körperlich-geistiger Selbstzucht, Selbstkasteiung und Enthaltsamkeit schon bei ihm vorhanden: 1 K 9, 15—27 ...": H. Windisch in *Th.W.N.T.* I, S. 493.

[105] See: R. Liechtenhan, *Die urchristliche Mission, Voraussetzungen, Motive und Methoden*, Zürich 1946, SS. 66—67.

[106] T. F. Torrance rightly remarks in his *Royal Priesthood, op. cit.*, p. 17: "That sacrificial act of Christ once and for alle performed and enduring in His endless life in the presence of God, is realized in the life of His people, not by repetition of His substitutionary sacrifice, but by their dying and rising with Christ in faith and life, and by His worship of self-presentation to God (Rom. 12. 1; I Pet. 2. 5). This sacrifice of the Church in worship, ministry and life is entirely non-propitiatory, non-piacular."

jection: lest that by any means, when I have preached to others; I myself should be a castaway" (I Cor. 9.23, 27). But Paul's suffering in the
service of Christ was not the condition of his salvation, but the proof
of his knowledge of Christ's saving grace [107] (cf. Brainerd and others),
while at the same time it created that sphere of inner communion with
God which John Wesley tried to recreate during his stay in Georgia.

This brings us upon the positive value of the ascetic idea. What
Canon Warren remarks with regard to the healing ministry of the
Church we can apply to the whole of missionary work: "To share
in the healing ministry of Christ involves "the fellowship of his sufferings" ... It is with that in our minds, as the standard of our ministry,
that we must seek to grasp what it means for the Church and for the
Christian to "go heal" in the world to-day". [108] Without an element
of sacrifice, of self-denial, of preparedness to share in the sufferings
of Christ, missionary work is impossible in a world in which Christ
is still in agony (Pascal). [109] Especially in our own times, in which
so many of the old defences and protections are falling away, it becomes necessary for the Church to realize that the way of missions
is the way of the cross. The deepest ground of the Church's preparedness to travel that road must be the remembrance of the way
her Lord has gone. But next to this, the consciousness of the great
debt owed by Western Christianity can help the Church to recover
the attitude of humiliation which is indispensable for its living and
working under the sign of the Cross—especially when she sees the
debt to other peoples as a debt to God himself. [110]

The ascetic element is important—but only when it is saved from
isolation and taken up within the sphere of influence of other motives.
Without the counterbalance of the theocratic ideal, asceticism can lead
to a world-denying attiude. Outside the sphere of the motive of love,
it is in danger of receiving an egocentric direction and of being taken
up into the idea of self-salvation. If it does not remain open to the
companion truth of an eschatology which knows of the consolation of

---

[107]   See: D. van Swigchem, *Het missionair karakter van de Christelijke Gemeente
volgens de Brieven van Paulus en Petrus*, Kampen 1955, p. 221.

[108]   M. A. C. Warren, *The Christian Imperative, op. cit.*, p. 71.

[109]   Cf. some remarks of P. T. Forsyth: "You cannot separate the Mission and
the Passion in a universal Christianity. There is no World crown without the Cross.
The Church that missions really dies with Christ, and its missionaries but show
forth its death": D. W. Lambert, *The Missionary Message of P. T. Forsyth*, E.Q.
XXI (1949), p. 205. A similar thought we find in the Report of Commission II
of the North American study commission in preparation of the conference at
Willingen under the title: *Missionary Vocation* (1952), as quoted by R. Pierce
Beaver, *art. cit.*, pp. 362—363: "The cross is normative for the missionary vocation, "martyrdom" is the character of the missionary vocation ... the „martyr"
fixes his eyes on Christ, not on "martyrdom"."

[110]   Forsyth saw missions as "a debt on the Church by way of amends, not
only because of what Christ has done for it, but because of what it has done
against Christ": D. W. Lambert, *The Theology of Missions. The Contribution of
P. T. Forsyth*, The London Quarterly and Holborn Review CLXXVI (1951), p. 116.

the "already now" in the tension of the "not yet", it leads to an attitude of flight that falls short of the victorious character of Christian life. [111] But, if integrated with these motives, a certain form of asceticism can make it less difficult to follow Christ upon the road of the *hiddenness* of the Cross, which, as it has been remarked at the Willingen Conference, "is one of those facets of the Cross which we of this generation are all being called upon to accept". [112]

e. *Ekklesia and basileia*

Views with regard to the relation between Church and missions have undergone a remarkable change since the beginning of this century. Though Warneck had already devoted an important chapter of his *Evangelische Missionslehre* to the ecclesiastical foundation of missions, [113] it was still to be a long time before the integral relation between Church and missions was fully and generally recognized. Not until the Congress of Tambaran (1938) can we say that "mission and Church have found one another". [114] This change was not only due to historical circumstances (the growth and the coming to independence of the "younger Churches"), of it was above all a result of a trend in theological thinking which led to a deepening of insight into the true nature of the Church. [115] While fifty years ago missions could still be considered as a (more or less important) appendix to the life of the Church, it is now generally recognized that the missionary aspect belongs to the Church's essence. The *consensus* on this point is fully in accordance with the biblical view of the Church: while in the Old Testament the people of God is already seen as "the light of the nations", in the New Testament it becomes fully evident that the Church is not a closed, walled, self-sufficient community, but that she has been placed in the world in order to

---

[111] O. Cullmann, *op. cit.*, SS. 188—189: "Wo vom nicht neutestamentlichen Gegensatz "Zeit" und "Ewigkeit" ausgegangen wird, kommt es, wenn dieser Gegensatz bis zu den extremsten Konsequenzen geführt ist, zu asketischer Weltverneinung".

[112] By A. M. C. Warren in his lecture *Christian Mission and the Cross*, in N. Gooddall (ed.), *Missions under the Cross*, London 1953, p. 40.

[113] *Op. cit.*, I, SS. 240—260. See, however, also J. Dürr, who, gratefully recognizing the fact that Warneck laid such a close relation between Church and missions, yet remarks in his *Sendende und werdende Kirch in der Missionstheologie Gustav Warneck's*, Basel 1947, S. 84: „Die Grenze der Warneckschen Ausführungen liegt darin, dass es nicht zur klaren Erkenntnis der Tatsache kommt, dass *die* Begründung der Mission gerade die *kirchliche* ist".

[114] W. Andersen, *op. cit.*, p. 20.

[115] See: *The Church, Report of a Theological Commission on Faith and Order* (in preparation of the Lund Conference), London[2] 1952, p. 54: "There is a strong connection between the collapse of individualism in our own day and the recovery of the Church as a fellowship of men, governed by Christ in the Holy Spirit. This human longing for fellowship coincides providentially with a new approach to the New Testament conception of the Church".

give witness to Christ's redeeming work: "But ye are a chosen generation ... that ye should shew forth the praises of him who hath called you ..." (I Pet.2.9). We can also say that "the Church's very being is the continuation of Christ's redeeming mission in the world": [116] as the Church is the Body of Christ, her expansion is nothing less than the incorporation of the "lost sheep" into the communion with Christ. Professor Torrance remarks that there takes place in the Church a movement from particularity to universality, "for filled with the Spirit of Christ who has ascended to fill all things, the Church is caught up in the movement of *pleroma* ... This [*i. e.* the outpouring of the Spirit] is the point in the movement of *soma* to *pleroma* where we have to see the significance of the Apostolate". [117] In the same spirit the Lutheran theologian T. A. Kantonen writes: "The Word of God and the people of God can not be separated from each other. Christianity is not an impersonal body of abstract truth but the living body of Christ. Since Christ and His church form this unbreakable unity, there is truth in the ancient dictum: *extra ecclesia nulla salus* ... This is just another way of saying: apart from Christ there is no salvation ... In principle, all those for whom Christ died belong to the church. Evangelism consists in translating this principle into fact". [118]

Since Tambaram, however, the "Church-centred" view of missions has not remained unchallenged. Professor Hoekendijk especially tries to break through the dominance of the ecclesiocentric element in missionary thinking by pointing out that it revolves around an illegitimate centre: the Church is no end in itself, she has no other existence than *in actu Christi,* that is, *in actu apostoli.* [119] But however valuable Professor Hoekendijk's view may be as a correction to a one-sided Church-centric attitude, we yet miss in his exposition the recognition of the biblical datum that the Church is not only "Ereignis" but also "Anstalt", and that she does not only exist *in actu apostoli* but also before and behind the apostolic deed as the house of God in this world, as the "bridgehead" of the Kingdom. [120] In our opinion, Hoekendijk's dynamic view of the Church falls short of the full testimony of the New Testament with regard to the nature of the "Body of Christ". Grateful as we are for his strong protest against any conception which puts the "mission" of the Church behind the "establishment", we yet agree with Bishop Newbigin, when he remarks in his thankful and appreciative criticism of Hoekendijk's view that an un-

---

[116]   L. Newbigin, *The Household of God, op. cit.,* p. 94.
[117]   T. F. Torrance, *Royal Priesthood, op. cit.,* p. 26.
[118]   T. A. Kantonen, *The Theology of Evangelism,* Philadelphia 1954, pp. 93—94.
[119]   J. C. Hoekendijk, *The Church in Missionary Thinking,* I.R.M. XLI (1952), pp. 324—336.
[120]   So W. Andersen in his criticism of Hoekendijk: *op. cit.,* p. 49.

churchly mission is as much a monstrosity as an unmissionary Church. [121] In the movement from *soma* to *pleroma*, the Church as an institution is an indispensable link.

It is in the context of this view of the relation between Church and missions that we want to make some remarks on the ambivalent character of the ecclesiological motive. This motive finds its ground in the idea of the Church, and the stimulus to missionary action proceeds from the thought that there is a virtual identity between ecclesiastical expansion and missionary activity. Consequently the work of missions finds a sufficient motivation in the fact that it belongs to the essence of the Church to expand to the ends of the earth. This motive has an obviously negative aspect in that it is always in danger of making the mission a means to augment the this-worldly glory of the Church. This danger becomes reality when the mission is considered as *plantatio ecclesiae* and nothing more, when by means of its missionary activity the Church is trying to expand its influence and to strengthen its position in this world. It is especially the more Catholic Church-type, with its often rather massive ecclesiology and its strong emphasis upon the Church as "Anstalt", which stands open to this danger. We are not thinking here only of the Medieval Church and the Roman Catholic Church in later periods, but also of certain tendencies in the *ecclesia Anglicana*. In the first years after its foundation, as well as in a later period of its existence, the S.P.G. was in danger of falling into the error of what M. Kähler has called "Propaganda", *i. e.* the copying of its own ecclesiastical form of life on the mission-field. But other ecclesiastical groups, too, were not free from this form of missionary thinking: we need only recall the recurrent argument that missionary work was necessary because it strengthened the position of Protestantism over against Rome, while we could also point to the evil fruits of Protestant denominationalism upon the territory of the "younger Churches". We can even say, with Hoekendijk, that it is "one of our most painful and most frequent experiences that evangelism is almost always concealed in a form of propaganda". [122] But the main fault of this distortion of the ecclesiological ideal is not that it gives too heavy an accent to the idea of the Church. On the contrary, it does not take seriously enough the full meaning of the idea of the Church, it humanizes the idea of the Church by loosening it from its immediate relation to Him whose glory did not lay in the extension of earthly power but in the victory of the Cross. The Church is not in the world to save itself, but "in her the exalted Saviour continues His work of saving the world". [123] Here we meet with one of

---

[121]   L. Newbigin, *The Household of God, op. cit.,* p. 148.
[122]   J. C. Hoekendijk, *The Call to Evangelism, art. cit.,* p. 169.
[123]   J. H. Bavinck, *The Impact of Christianity on the Non-Christian World,* Grand Rapids (Mich.) 1949, p. 15.

the most real limitations of the ecclesiological motive: the Church in itself is not important, her only meaning lies in the fact that she is the instrument of Jesus Christ.

But at the same time this very point confronts us with the positive value of the ecclesiological motive. It is true that the definition of missions as *plantatio ecclesiae* is in itself "too poor a conception". [124] But, on the other hand, it cannot be denied that the plantation of the Church is an integral element of missionary work, if only the idea has been purified from two opposite tendencies, each of which threatens to darken the right view of the Church: denominationalism on one hand, spiritualism and anti-institutionalism on the other. We must not try to call into life on the missionfield a duplicate of the Church on the home-base; we are going out to plant the Church of Jesus Christ, which stands in a direct relation to the Lord and which is constituted through the work of the Spirit. [125] But we also know that this Church has to take visible form in an institution which in its visibility testifies to the fact that the Kingdom of God has a concrete bridgehead in this world. In this way we can agree with Dürr's remark that the mission is the road from Church to Church; [126] Christ sends through his Body, the Church, and the *pleroma* which becomes visible through the missionary work of the Church is integrated with the *soma* in its institutional form: one Lord, one faith, one *baptism* (Eph. 4.5). As an additional fruit of her missionary labours the Church receives a new health and vigour—this is the element of truth in M. Schmidt's remark that in the fulfilment of her missionary task the Church learns to understand again the purity of original Christianity—, [127] while Tillich remarks that "only missions can prove that the Church is the agent through which the Kingdom of God continually actualizes itself in history". [128]

But the ecclesiological motive may never be isolated. The Church is no "terminal station": [129] on one side it is the face of the earth which has to be renewed (the theocratic ideal), on the other hand

---

[124] J. C. Hoekendijk *in loco citato.*

[125] See: J. Dürr, *Sendende und werdende Kirche* etc., *op. cit.,* SS. 241 ff.

[126] *Op. cit.,* S. 34: „Von der Kirche her arbeitet die Mission zur Kirche hin. Mission ist die Wegstrecke von Kirche zu Kirche".

[127] See above, p. 95; cf. also D. van Swigchem, who remarks that in the word κερδαινειν, which frequently occurs in the Epistles, something can be seen of the "advantage" which the congregation receives from the conversion of the Gentiles: *op. cit.,* pp. 142, 221.

[128] *Art. cit.,* p. 4.

[129] Cf. J. Dürr: „Wie steht es den nur eigentlich mit der Mission, wenn sie in der Entstehung „Junger Kirchen" ihr gestrecktes Ziel erreicht hat? Hört die Mission dann einfach auf? Die Mission wäre nun also — um es in einem Bild zu sagen — in den Bahnhof der Kirche eingefahren. Ist es ein „Sackbahnhof" in welchem die Mission, die brave Lokomotive, nun blockiert ist, weder vorwärts noch rückwärts mehr sich bewegen kann?": *Kirche, Mission und Reich Gottes.* E.M.M. IIIC (1953), S. 134.

man in his individual need has to be brought into the communion of Christ (the soteriological emphasis). But above all the concept of the Church has to be integrated with the eschatological motive: the *ekklesia* is determined by the *basileia*. It is this viewpoint which takes a central place in contemporary missionary reflection. In the circle of missionary science there is a growing *consensus* with regard to the eschatological aspect, a *consensus* which is not unrelated to the development of contemporary theology. The tendency to break away from an idealistic eschatology and to return to a more realistic understanding of the events which are promised in the New Testament [130] is reflected in the latest development of missionary thinking. Missions are seen as having a place in the period between Christ's Resurrection and his Second Advent. They are part of the drama of eschatology, not only because they are the sign of the coming of the end, but even more because they are the solution of the secret of the postponement of the end. The world still exists because of the apostolate, because of the preaching of the Gospel to all nations. "The final consummation of God's purpose awaits the fulfilment of the world mission, and this not because of any defect in God's power or grace, but because this belongs to the character of the salvation He has purposed for us". [131] Consequently, it is generally felt that in the eschatological tension and expectation lies one of the most important motives of missionary action. [132] The relation between eschatology and missions is not new—but the new element is the way in which the historical and the apocalyptical factors are seen in their mutual relationship: God is bringing about the realization of his plans in the process of history, while history yet finds its consummation in the Second Advent, which is prepared by the mission of the Church.

If, however, the unity of the historical and the apocalyptic element is broken, the eschatological attitude can become a danger to the purity of the missionary motive and consequently of the missionary work. Either the apocalyptic element is eliminated, which means that eschatology becomes "this-wordly" and reaches no farther than the penultimate phase, or the apocalyptical element is loosened from the historical time-process, which means that the value of historical

---

[130]   See: T. F. Torrance, *The Modern Eschatological Debate*, E.Q. XXV (1953), pp. 45—54, 94—106, 167—178, 224—232.

[131]   L. Newbigin, *The Household of God*, op. cit., p. 142.

[132]   See among others: O. Cullmann, *Christus und die Zeit*, op cit., SS. 138 ff.; F. W. Dillistone, *The Hope Set Before Us*, in: M. A. C. Warren (ed.), *The Triumph of God*, London-New York-Toronto 1948; J. Dürr, *Kirche, Mission und Reich Gottes*, art. cit.; J. C. Hoekendijk, in several articles and in his *Kerk en Volk*, op. cit., pp. 223 ff.; E. Jansen Schoonhoven, *Apostolaat en Eschatologie*, De Heerbaan VIII (1955); W. Manson, *Mission and Eschatology*, I.R.M. XLII (1953), pp. 390—997, H. N. Ridderbos, *Het Nieuwe Testament en de Zending*, art. cit.; G. Rosenkranz, *Weltmission und Weltende*, Gütersloh 1951; M. A. C. Warren, *The Truth of Vision*, London and Edinburgh, 1948.

development is denied and that missionary work receives an unrealistic character. It is remarkable that the development of British missionary life around 1800 affords a point of contact for both deviations. The idea of the *gradual* approach of the Millennium could lead to a form of missionary work which was so much determined by the thought of a continuous process in history that the eschatological haste and tension was lost, while on the other hand the apocalyptic element could be so overemphasized that it ultimately led to the rise of an Adventist type of missions. The first type of missions so stresses the "already now" that it forgets the "not yet". The other type does not take seriously enough the fact that God is working out his purpose in the continuing process of history from the day of Pentecost onwards, and that the whole time between the outpouring of the Spirit and the Second Advent of Christ is "the last of the days". The first type tends to take a more or less agnostic attitude with regard to the end of history. The other is prone to fall into speculations with regard to the exact time of Christ's coming in glory. [133] The first type is in danger of neglecting the note of urgency in the missionary proclamation, while the second has not always the patience to build up a more lasting form of missionary work. The first type is too optimistic with regard to the possibilities of realizing the Kingdom of God in this dispensation, while the second type concentrates upon the saving of individual souls from the imminent judgment of God. It is not difficult to recignize the presence of these two types even in our own days.

But if it is seen in its scriptural unity, the ecclesiological motive appears to be of the greatest importance for the development of the missionary ideal. In the first place, it dynamizes the Church. The New Testament shows us that a living eschatological expectation is closely related to a fervent activity of the congregation: [134] the Church has to be active in preparing the coming of Christ, and "the activity of the Holy Spirit which is supremely significant for the End is the activity of building up and securing the unity of the Body of Christ". [135] The amazing missionary activity of British Christianity cannot be explained without taking into account the dynamizing influence of a reawakening of the eschatological ideal. In the second place, the eschatological motive teaches us to take history seriously. Though, in its speculations with regard to the temporal and sometimes

---

[133] Cf. O. Cullmann, *op. cit.*, S. 138: „Das Widerchristliche an der apokalyptischen Bewertung von Zeitereignissen, wie wir sie in den spätern apokalyptischen Sekten bis auf den heutigen Tag finden, ist nicht etwa die Tatsache, dasz solche Ereignisse irgendwie als „Vorzeichen" interpretiert werden, sondern dasz daraus das *Ende berechnet wird*".

[134] See: D. van Swigchem, *op. cit.*, pp. 233 ff.

[135] M. A. C. Warren, *Eschatology and History*, I.R.M. XLI (1952), p. 347.

even geographical localization of the Millennium, eighteenth century chiliasm was no doubt a backward step compared with the sober reserve of reformatory theology on this point, yet it is perhaps the lasting service which this form of millennianism has rendered to the Church that it has once more opened Christian eyes to the real problems around the doctrine of the last things it relates to the cause of missions. [136] Missionary work is taken up in the time-process, which is guided by God towards its fulfilment in the *basileia*, and the Church has to give heed to the "signs of the times", which ever and again point to the urgent character of the missionary task in this dispensation. [137] That the Evangelicals around 1800 were not deterred from missionary action by the events of the times, but that these events proved rather to have a stimulating influence, results from the fact that they saw these events in the light of God's promises with regard to his way of fulfilling his plan with this world. This brings us to a third point: the relation which exists between the conversion of Israel and that of the Gentiles. There are still many unsolved problems on this point, but at any rate it is clear that Paul in Romans 9—11 speaks of an interaction between the coming in of the fulness of the Gentiles and the salvation of Israel. [138] When missions are seen in eschatological perspective, our attention is directed to this special aspect of the work of missions among Israel (Simeon!). In the fourth place, the eschatological factor teaches us to see in one perspective the ends of the earth and the end of the times: Bishop Newbigin remarks that in speaking of the judgment of the *world*, the redemption of the *world*, the end of the *world*, we have to accept the hard geographical meaning of the word. [139] Only in this way can we break through the misconception which believes it is sufficient when the Church fulfils its missionary task in its own surroundings. The whole *oikoumenè* has to become *theatrum gloriae Dei*. It was eschatology which cooperated in making even simple Evangelicals think in the category of "the ends

---

[136] Cf. Karl Barth in his *Die Protestantische Theologie im 19. Jahrhundert, op. cit.*, S. 113: „Der chiliastische Pietismus des 18. Jahrhunderts ... hat in seinem Schranken und doch auch über sich selbst hinausweisend jedenfalls die eschatologische Frage, die Frage nach Christus als dem Wiederkommenden wieder gestellt ...".

[137] It is a result of Holsten's Bultmannian view of eschatology that he leaves no room for this aspect; though he must recognize: „Historisch steht es — in der Neuzeit — so, dasz es nur dort zur Missionstat kam, wo die endgeschichtliche Eschatologie maszgebend war", he remarks nevertheless: „Die Mission lebt nicht vom Blick auf die letzte Generation der Menschheit, sie kann die Parusie nicht auf diese letzte Generation beschränken, da sie ein die ganze Menschheit angehendes Ereignis ist und damit nur in dem Sinne das Ende der Geschichte bedeuten kann, als sie die Aufhebung der Geschichte ist", *Das Kerygma und der Mensch, op. cit.*, SS. 118—119.

[138] See for this point: G. Ch. Aalders and H. N. Ridderbos, *Israel* (Exegetica II, 2), 's Gravenhage 1955.

[139] *Op. cit.*, p. 135.

of the earth". And lastly, the expectation of the coming Kingdom gives to the missionary Church the certitude of victory. When we pray "Thy Kingdom come" we may know that through our work God is fulfilling our prayer, and that we shall see the day when the knowledge of the Lord shall cover the earth. This is the concrete background of Carey's saying: "expect great things from God".

Without this eschatological motive, the other motives are powerless and void. It is the idea of the *shalom* which gives a foundation to the theocratic ideal. It is the knowledge that the Kingdom is imminent which gives to the motive of love its deep urgency: "if any man love not the Lord Jesus Christ, let him be anathema, Maranatha" (I Cor. 16.22). The eschatological expectation makes it possible to accept the hard road of the Cross: "after that ye have suffered *a while*" (I Pet. 5.10). And the eschatological motive reminds us of the fact that the Church can never rest in her own existence, because she is on the way to the coming Kingdom, in which she shall be saved, "yet as by fire"! [140]

f.   Conclusion

It is under the influence of a renewed theocentric thinking that from more than one side protests have been launched against a foundation of missionary work upon anything other than the command, the will, the love of *God as revealed in Jesus Christ*. We think here of Barth, who subjected all "secondary motives" to the fire of his theological criticism. [141] We think also of Schärer, who protested passionately against any form of a "double" foundation and motivation of missions, [142] while of late Holsten has given us a doctrine of missions which is primarily a criticism of the anthropocentric attitude in missionary work on the ground of his view of the Pauline kerygma. [143] No doubt this criticism is valuable as a correction to a missionary attitude in which man threatened to receive a central place: we may think here among others of H. Vernon White, who saw as the essence of missions a "service to man in all his needs". [144] Ultimately, the mission of the Church finds its source only in the heart of God. This does not

---

[140]   Profesor Kraemer remarks that if the Church is true to its nature "it can never feel 'at home' in the world because of its eschatological character, for it looks forward to a consummation which transcends our human strivings and achievements, the realization of the Kingdom of God by himself": H. Kraemer, *The Christian Message in a Non-Christian World, op. cit.*, p. 418.

[141]   K. Barth, *Die Theologie und die Mission in der Gegenwart, op. cit.*, SS. 203—205.

[142]   See: H. Schärer, *Die Begründung der Mission in der katholischen und evangelischen Missionswissenschaft* (Theologische Studien Heft 16), Zürich 1944.

[143]   *Das Kerygma und der Mensch, op. cit.*, passim.

[144]   See H. Kraemer, *The Christian Message in a Non-Christian World, op. cit.*, pp. 431 ff., and R. Pierce Beaver, *art. cit.*, pp. 351 ff.

exclude, however, the so-called "secondary motives". On the contrary, these motives are taken up in the one great motive of God who loved the *world*, who loved mankind in all its need and misery, who came down in Christ to heal the brokenness of our existence and to create in the midst of this world a new form of life which finds its consummation in the Kingdom of heaven. Is is the special value—though not the exclusive one—of the British missionary awakening that it was moved primarily by the love of Jesus, but that within the frame of this love the Methodist and Evangelical missionaries had a regard for man's individual and communal needs. We heartily agree with Professor Korff when he remarks that faith feels constrained to missionary work not only by looking on Christ but also by looking on man. [145] The anthropocentric element has a legitimate plac in the motivation of Christian missions, if it is only seen in its correlation with and dependence on the theocentric motive. Not man in himself, but man seen through the eyes of God (which means to us, seen through the spectacles of God's revelation in the Bible), man standing in need of divine forgiveness and divine healing, can move us to that love which is the presupposition of all missionary work. When he saw the multitudes, Jesus was moved with compassion, because they fainted ...

In Jesus the motives are one, because the triune God, who is One in his works, his virtues, his being, reveals in Him his heart. His glory is the salvation of men; because He loves man He wants to create a new earth; He has a right to ask for obedience, because through his sacrifice He has saved the world; the Church is his Body, through which He continues his healing ministry in this world, until all the nations have been confronted with the message of this love; He is the coming God, who is himself the guarantee of his great promise: "behold, I make all things new". The more the Church is conscious of her deep unity with Christ, the more also the different motives become melted together into one great motive which transcends the possibilities of human formulation: " ... missionary obligation is not a deduction, but a reflex of faith. It is spontaneous, not studied; primary, not secondary; prior, not subsequent; reflexive, not derivative ... It is the normal relation of every disciple to his Lord". [146]

Human motives are always ambivalent. Even the purest motive has a strain of impurity in so far as it is but a faint reflection of the

---

[145] F. W. A. Korff, *Het Christelijk Geloof en de niet-Christelijke Godsdiensten*, Amsterdam 1946, p. 133. Professor Korff even appeals to Barth, who remarked in his *Der Römerbrief* (Neue Bearbeitung), Zürich 1940, S. 348 on Rom. 9. 30: „Wer sollte denn übersehen, wie sehr die Heiden anschaulicherweise wirklich arme Heiden sind?".

[146] From the Report of the North American Study Commision in preparation of „Willingen" under the title *Why Missions* (1952) as quoted by Pierce Beaver, *art. cit.*, pp. 361—362.

hidden motive which moved God to send his Son into the world. The Church has to struggle for the purity of her missionary work: it is for this reason that she cannot dispense with a continuous purification of her conscious or subconscious motives. Our historical survey has shown us how easily it can happen that, through a subtle process of secularization, the missionary motives are loosened from their integration with the motive of Christ and are drawn within the sphere of human interests and human motivations. From the evident correlation between aim and motive (*quod primum est in intentione ultimum est in executione*), it follows that when the aim lies in the greater glory of man—man in his political, his cultural and his ecclesiastical context [147]—the purity of the motive becomes sullied. The history of the sector of the missionary awakening which had our special attention affords ample proof of this proposition.

And when the motive is below the standard of the biblical motives the repercussions are to be seen in the mission-field. We gives some examples. When the missionary motive was connected in a one-sided way with the idea of the *corpus christanum,* a form of missionary work came into being which threatened to lose the indispensable element of loving attention to the problems of the peoples to whom the missionary call was directed. In a naive way, the pattern of Western culture was impressed upon a world with a totally different cultural pattern, and as a result of this attitude the Eastern peoples began to see the missionary activity of Western Christianity as an appendix to Western imperialism. When, on the other hand, the missionary motive was one-sidedly soteriological, the outlook of the missionary was generally limited to the spiritual sphere, and the economic and political problems remained outside the circle of his attention. Hence the complaint of the African student, which we quoted above. [148] And when the eschatological tension by itself fully determined the missionary motive, missionary work became restless and fragmentary— we need only mention the work of the China Inland Mission in its initial stage! The negative sides of more than one missionary method can be reduced to a defect in the missionary motive. [149]

But right through human considerations and motivations runs the thread of the divine motive, manifesting itself in various forms; in theocratic ideals, in compassion for the fate of the heathen, in love

---

[147]   Cf. P. Althaus, *Um die Reinheit der Mission,* E.M.Z. X (1953), p. 101: „Das Wesen der Mission wird aber auch verletzt durch die *Koppelung* des einzig legitimen Motivs mit illegitimen. Wir können deren drei unterscheiden: den nationalen (kolonialen), den kulturellen, den kirchlichen Imperialismus. Die Mission kann politisiert, kulturisiert, klerikalisiert werden".

[148]   See above, p. 192.

[149]   Cf. P. Althaus, *art. cit.,* S. 102: „Es ist klar dasz dem Motiv je eine bestimmte Methode zugeordnet ist, dasz also mit dem Motiv auch die Methode unrein wird".

for man in his struggle and his misery, in the wide vistas opened up by new eschatological expectations. The history of the missionary awakening points to the mystery of the presence of God in history, working through his Spirit in the hearts of men: "Constrained by Jesus' love to live the servants of mankind!" [150]

---

[150] From one of Charles Wesley's hymns: see above, p. 96 note 181.

EPILOGUE

During the course of our inquiry, we have been confronted with one of the most important periods in the history of Protestant missions, a period which still determines to a large degree our present missionary activity. But what can we do with this confrontation in the missionary situation of to-day? In the first place, we shall have to accompany our own work with the same critical questions with which in the present study we have accompanied the activities of former generations in the field of missions. This criticism has to go down to the roots of our work, to the motives which are determining our work in its phenomenal aspect. A living confrontation with the past, which still in its many forms is so near to us, can help to reveal to us the true nature of our own motives. It can bring us to a renewed reflection on the problems of theocracy and soteriology, of asceticism and eschatology. It can guard us against an uncritical continuity as well as against an ungrateful discontinuity. It makes us see the parallels between our own situation and that of the "fathers and founders": our life "has returned to its frontier simplicities" [1] and we are feeling the tension of standing on the verge of an apocalyptic period. It reveals to us also the great difference between our period and theirs: the sheltering influence of the *corpus christianum* has fallen away, and the life of the Church begins to take on once more the pattern of the Cross; missionary work is losing something of its human self-evidency and is receiving again the accent of toil and sacrifice which it has always possessed in the individual sphere, but which begins now to determine the totality of its existence.

"The frontier is aflame!". [2] Will our motives stand the test of these flames? Again and again we have to reconsider them in the critical light of the Bible, to submit them to the (purifying) fire of the Word of God, which casts down "every high thing that exalteth itself against the knowledge of God" (II Cor. 10.5). But it is not sufficient to accompany our work and its motives with critical questions: our critical questions must have their foundation in a missionary theology which forms the positive background of our missionary work. This theology has to be *ecumenical* in that it knows that only together with all saints

---

[1] So John A. Mackay in: *With Christ to the Frontier*, G. W. Randson (ed.), *Renewal and Advance*, London 1948, p. 199.
[2] J. A. Mackay *in loco citato*.

is it able to comprehend "what is the breadth and length and depth and height" (Eph. 3.18) of the dimensions of the Church's mission, and *reformatory* in that it sees in the Reformation a purification of the Church in her broadest scope and her widest activities. It has to be *confessional* in that in the problems around the *kerygma* which has to be transmitted it wants to listen together with the "fathers" to the voice of God, while at the same time it has to possess a sense of understanding *contemporaneity* with our own searching and struggling, despairing and expecting age. And above all it has to be *scriptural* in that it sees in the Word of God, in the Bible, the only rule for faith and order, for life and work, for missions and evangelism. But even the most perfect form of theology—and how defective, how far below the mark of God's revelation is all our theological thinking!—cannot render one real service to our missionary work, if that work is not rooted in a Christian community which is marked by a living faith in Christ and in which the flame of love and expectance is fed by the life-giving stream of the Spirit. It is because of this, that our confrontation with the missionary motives of a past generation has to end with this searching and urgent question: do we, —as Churches, as missionary agencies, as individual Christians—still feel ourselves "constrained by Jesus' love"?

SAMENVATTING

De hier gegeven studie handelt over de motieven der Angelsaksische Zending in de periode tussen 1698 en 1815. Het onderzoek naar het motief als zodanig vindt zijn legitimatie in het feit dat juist de crisis van deze tijd de Kerk terugwerpt op de oude fundamentele vraag: ,,waarom zending"? Deze vraag is gesteld in historisch perspectief, omdat wij haar niet zullen kunnen beantwoorden indien wij niet getracht hebben te luisteren naar het gesprek van vorige generaties met Hem, wiens oproep tot zending in alle perioden der Kerkgeschiedenis opnieuw tot zijn gemeente uitgaat. Tal van factoren hebben een rol gespeeld in het ontwaken der zendingsgedachte — factoren, die werden tot motieven zodra zij in het bewuste of onderbewuste leven der christelijke gemeenschap een plaats ontvingen van waaruit zij bewogen en drongen tot het ter hand nemen van de zendingstaak. In deze studie is de noodzakelijke begrenzing gezocht in de Angelsaksische wereld van — ruim genomen — de achttiende eeuw. De chronologische begrenzing vindt hierin haar oorzaak, dat juist in deze periode de moderne zending *in nuce* haar vorm ontving; de geografische limiet wordt gerechtvaardigd door het eigen karakter der Angelsaksische zending.

In een inleidend hoofdstuk wordt ingegaan op de periode vóór 1700. Deze valt in twee delen uiteen: de reformatorische en de na-reformatorische tijd. In de periode der Reformatoren is van de zendingsgedachte nog opvallend weinig te bespeuren. Wel is de zendingsgedachte, zoals bij nader onderzoek blijkt, onder de oppervlakte verborgen aanwezig, maar zij blijft latent tengevolge van een samentreffen van politieke en theologische factoren, onder welke laatste de reformatorische *epochè* ten aanzien van de ,,eigenmachtigheid" der Rooms-Katholieke zending — vrijwel de enige vorm van Zendingswerk die de Reformatoren in de practijk kenden —, een niet te onderschatten rol speelt. Bij de secten gelden deze overwegingen minder; daar zijn het veeleer het individualisme, het anti-institutionalisme en de overspannen eschatologie, die remmend gewerkt hebben op een evenwichtige realisering der zendingsgedachte. Aan de andere zijde der Reformatoren staat Erasmus, die ook in zijn zendingsoproep Rooms-Katholieke en humanistische tendenzen verbond. Vermelding verdient nog, dat in deze tijd de zending nog zeer sterk ligt binnen de sfeer van het *corpus christianum*.

216

In de zeventiende eeuw zien wij de zendingsgedachte ontwaken in de kringen van de voorlopers van het Duitse Piëtisme, in die van de Nadere Reformatie in Nederland en in die van het Puritanisme in de Angelsaksische landen. Verschillende motieven zijn reeds te constateren, waarvan wij — inzonderheid voor de laatste twee groepen — het theocratische en het soteriologische motief vermelden.

Wij gaan nu over tot het eigenlijke onderwerp van deze studie: de motieven der Angelsaksische zending in de periode tussen 1698 en 1815. In deze periode zijn drie — steeds hogere — golftoppen van zendingsbelangstelling waar te nemen. De eerste is die van de oprichting der *Society for the Propagation of Christian Knowledge* (1698) en de *Society for the Propagation of the Gospel in Foreign Parts* (1701), de tweede die van het Methodisme en de Opwekkingsbeweging in Amerika (omstreeks de helft der achttiende eeuw), de derde die van de oprichting der *Baptist Missionary Society* (1792), *London Missionary Society* (1795) en *Church Missionary Society* (1799), en van het nieuw ontwaken der Zendingsgedachte in de Schotse Kerken.

De eerste periode wordt gekenmerkt door een verbinding van de geest der "Aufklärung" met die van het Piëtisme. Enerzijds ontwaren wij de invloed van Leibniz, andererzijds die van Francke. Het is de combinatie van piëtistische elementen en rationalistische idealen die een van de meest karakteristieke kenmerken is van de in die tijd gevormde organisaties. Hun „vader" was de Anglicaanse predikant Thomas Bray: eerst richtte hij de *Society for the Propagation of Christian Knowledge* op, een nog slechts semi-officiële organisatie, echter niet gebonden aan de grenzen der Engelse koloniën. Haar vele doeleinden omvatten ook de zending. Drie jaar later werd, nu met officiële steun van de Kerk, de *Society for the Propagation of the Gospel in Foreign Parts* opgericht, die de geestelijke verzorging der Britse koloniën ten doel had. Zij heeft — zij het niet altijd met voldoende élan — de zending onder Indianen en Negers ter hand genomen. Haar zuster-organisatie, vrijer in haar beweging, droeg later een gedeelte van het zendingswerk in Zuid-India. Buiten Anglicaanse kring waren zendingsgedachten aanwezig bij de Quakers, bij sommige Dissenters (Watts, Doddridge) en in Schotland (Robert Millar). In deze periode speelden politieke en culturele motieven naast soteriologische motieven een rol.

Tijdens de periode van het Methodisme in Engeland en Schotland en van de „Grote Opwekking" in Amerika verschuift het beeld. Bij de volgelingen van Wesley, Whitefield en Jonathan Edwards is een intense missionaire drang aanwezig. Deze drang uit zich niet steeds onmiddellijk in activiteit op het gebied der heidenzending: inzonderheid Wesley zag zozeer het moederland als een „verheidenst" gebied, dat hij op de bekering daarvan alle krachten concentreerde. Edwards daarentegen had een open oog voor de noodzaak der heidenzending. De onder zijn invloed staande opwekkingsbeweging heeft verschillende grote zendelingen voortgebracht (David Brainerd!). In deze periode was de invloed van politieke en culturele motieven gering, groot daarentegen die van het soteriologisch motief, terwijl inzonderheid bij Edwards ook eschatologische motieven een belangrijke rol speelden: het zendingsideaal werd opgetild op de golven van grootse eschatologische verwachtingen!

In de periode die hierop volgt kunnen wij de lijnen der beide voorafgaande perioden doortrekken. Ook in deze periode spelen politieke motieven een slechts zeer geringe rol: enerzijds waren de „Evangelicals" zich zeer wel bewust van de distantie die er bestond en behoorde te bestaan tussen zending en koloniale politiek, terwijl aan de andere zijde de politici zich evenzeer van de afstand tussen beide grootheden bewust waren. Wel is er invloed aanwijsbaar van humanitair-culturele motieven, zij het ook dat deze motieven aan de zuiver religieuze motieven zijn gesubsumeerd. Tegelijkertijd komt er plaats voor het „schuldmotief": men begint zich de schuld der Westerse wereld bewust te worden. Romantische motieven zijn niet geheel afwezig — de invloed van Rosseau reikt ver — maar het zou volkomen onjuist zijn daaruit de zendingsbeweging in haar geheel te willen verklaren. Het soteriologisch motief oefent een niet minder sterke invloed uit dan in de voorafgaande periode, al hoedt men zich in het algemeen voor een speculatieve beantwoording van de vraag naar het eeuwig lot der heidenen. Een bijzondere plaats neemt het eschatologisch motief in. Algemeen was in de kring der „Evangelicals" het geloof in een komend duizendjarig vrederijk dat aan de wederkomst van Christus vooraf zou gaan. Sommigen meenden zelfs in de grote gebeurtenissen op internationaal terrein de eerste tekenen van het millennium te ontwaren. Dit was dan tevens een signaal om de zending onder de volkeren met meer enthousiasme ter hand te nemen. Maar ook daar, waar geen rechtstreeks verband werd gelegd tussen de grote politieke gebeurtenissen en de komst van het millennium, putte men niettemin kracht voor de vervulling van de zendingsgedachte uit het visioen van het naderend vrederijk. Tenslotte: het zendingsbevel functionneerde alleen als stimulans in verbinding met andere motieven.

Thans zijn wij toegekomen aan de confrontatie van de empirische motieven met het Bijbels motief. In deze confrontatie wordt het ons duidelijk dat alle motieven een ambivalent karakter bezitten: enerzijds zijn zij een antwoord op de roepstem Gods, maar tegelijkertijd wordt dit antwoord op het menselijk vlak gegeven. Aan vier groepen van motieven zouden wij dit duidelijk willen maken. De eerste groep is die van de motieven die liggen in de sfeer van het *corpus christianum*. Dit begrip heeft een negatief aspect in zoverre het een poging is om het leven der Kerk aan te passen aan de gestalte dezer wereld, maar tevens een positief aspect inzoverre het ernst tracht te maken met de gedachte van de heerschappij van Christus over het totale leven. Het *corpus christianum* is gebroken. Voor de zending is de periode van theocratische dromen en culturele visioenen voorbij. Maar waar in „comprehensive approach" het leven wordt gebracht tot een nieuwe integratie en een diepere eenheid, wordt een teken zichtbaar van de realisering der oudtestamentische profetie: „Hij zal heersen van zee tot zee" (Ps. 72 : 8).

De tweede groep is die van de motieven die liggen in de sfeer van de *liefde*. Het gevaar van een anthropocentische fundering der zending is hier niet denkbeeldig. De gedachte der liefde kan zo zeer worden gehumaniseerd dat zending wordt tot missionaire philanthropie. Toch is er in Bijbels verband plaats voor een positieve waardering van het liefdesmotief. Door de ogen van Christus leren wij de echte noden van de mensheid zien. Wij horen dan in de sociale ellende en de religieuze nood van de mens de roepstem Gods. Zonder het motief der liefde wordt het zendingswerk koud en steriel.

Het gehoorzaamheidsmotief kan komen te liggen in een legalistische sfeer. Niettemin kan het juist in tijden van geestelijke neergang noodzakelijk zijn om de Kerk te confronteren met het bevel van de verrezen Heer. Wij doen er dan wèl aan, te spreken over „vreugdevolle gehoorzaamheid" — al dienen wij terzelfder tijd te beseffen dat de Kerk op haar missionaire tocht ook deelt in de verdrukkingen van Christus.

Tenslotte spelen de begrippen „Kerk" en „Koninkrijk" in de zendingsmotivering een grote rol. Reeds uit het wezen van de Kerk vloeit de zendingsroeping voort: de zending is een essentiële functie van de Kerk (niet omgekeerd!). Deze stelling leidt echter niet tot zendingsdynamiek, indien de Kerk niet leeft uit de spanning van het verwachten van het Koninkrijk. De zending is immers een onderdeel van het eschatologisch drama, teken èn wegbereidster van het grote Einde.

In Christus zijn alle motieven één. Daarom dienen wij onze ambivalente motieven altijd weer te stellen onder zijn oordeel, en ons de vraag te stellen of wíj ons nog gedragen weten door de liefde van Jezus.

ABBREVIATIONS

A.M.Z.	=	Allgemeine Missions Zeitschrift
B.M.S.	=	Baptist Missionary Society
C.M.S.	=	Church Missionary Society
C.R.(O.C.)	=	Corpus Reformatorum (Opera Calvini)
E.M.M.	=	Evangelisches Missions Magazin
E.M.Z.	=	Evangelische Missions Zeitschrift
E.Q.	=	Evangelical Quarterly
I.M.C.	=	International Missionary Council
I.R.M.	=	International Review of Missions
L.M.S.	=	London Missionary Society
N.Th.T.	=	Nederlands Theologisch Tijdschrift
S.P.C.K.	=	Society for the Propagation of Christian Knowledge
S.P.G.	=	Society for the Propagation of the Gospel in Foreign Parts
S.S.P.C.K.	=	Society in Scotland for the Propagation of Christian Knowledge
Th.W.N.T.	=	Theologisches Wörterbuch zum Neuen Testament
W.A.	=	Martin Luthers Werke, Weimarer Ausgabe
Z.M.R.	=	Zeitschrift für Missionskunde und Religionswissenschaft

BIBLIOGRAPHY

G. Ch. Aalders en H. N. Ridderbos, *Israel* (Exegetica II, 2), 's-Graven-hage 1955.

Acta van het Zendingscongres, gehouden te Amsterdam, Amsterdam 1890.

R. Allen, *The Spontaneous Expansion of the Church*, London 1927.

W. B. Allen and E. Mc Clure, *Two Hundred Years: The History of the S.P.C.K.*, London 1898.

P. Althaus, *Um die Reinheit der Mission*, E.M.Z.X. (1953).

[An.], *Publick Spirit illustrated in the Life and Designs of the Rev. Thomas Bray D.D.*, London² 1808.

[An.], *The Spiritual Expansion of the Empire*, London 1900.

H. A. van Andel, *De Zendingsleer van Gisbertus Voetius*, Kampen 1912.

W. Andersen, *Towards a Theology of Mission*, London 1955.

G. Baez - Camargo, *The Earliest Protestant Missionary Venture in Latin America*, Church History XXI (1952).

E. W. Baker, *A Herald of the Evangelical Revival*, London 1948.

F. Baker, *Charles Wesley as Revealed by his Letters*, London 1948.

J. T. Bakker, *Coram Deo, Bijdrage tot het Onderzoek naar de Structuur van Luther's Theologie*, Kampen 1956.

G. R. Balleine, *A History of the Evangelical Party in the Church of England*, London etc. 1908.

R. Barclay, *The Inner Life of the Religious Societies of the Commonwealth*, London³ 1879.

W. C. Barclay, *Early American Methodism*, I, New York 1949.

K. Barth, *Die Theologie und die Mission in der Gegenwart*, Zwischen den Zeiten X (1932).

K. Barth, *Der Römerbrief* (Neue Bearbeitung), Zürich 1940.

K. Barth, *Kirchliche Dogmatik* I 2, II 2, Zürich 1945, 1946.

K. Barth, *Die Protestantische Theologie im 19. Jahrhundert*, Zürich 1947.

H. Bavinck, *Gereformeerde Dogmatiek*, IV, Kampen⁴ 1930.

J. H. Bavick, *The Impact of Christianity on the Non - Christian World*, Grand-Rapids 1949.

J. H. Bavinck, *Inleiding in de Zendingswetenschap*, Kampen 1954.

J. H. Bavinck, *Bonifatius de Missionaris*, De Heerbaan VII 1954.

Th. Beck, *The Mission, a Poem*, London 1796.

D. Beaton, *The "Marrow of Modern Divinity" and the Marrow Controversy*, Records of the Scottish Church History Society I (1926).

E. Benz, *Pietist and Puritan Sources of Early Protestant World Missions*, Church History XX (1951).

J. van den Berg, *Calvins Missionary Message*, E.Q. XXII (1950).

H. Berkhof, *De Kerk en de Keizer*, Amsterdam 1946.

G. C. Berkouwer, *Geloof en Rechtvaardiging*, Kampen 1949.

G. C. Berkouwer, *De Verkiezing Gods*, Kampen 1956.

H. Bett, *The Spirit of Methodism*, London 1937.

E. Beyreuther, *Die Bedeutung des 17. Jahrhunderts für das deutsche Missionsleben*, E.M.Z. VIII (1951).

Th. Beza, *Ad Tractationem de Ministrorum Evangelii Gradidus ... Theodori Bezae Responsio*, 1593 s. 1.

H. Boer, *Pentecost and the Missionary Witness of the Church*, Franeker 1955.

C. W. Th. Baron van Boetzelaer van Asperen en Dubbeldam, *De Protestantsche Kerk in Nederlandsch Indië*, 's-Gravenhage 1947.

D. Bogue and J. Bennett, *The History of the Dissenters from the Revolution to the Year 1808*, II, London² 1833.

D. Bogue, *Discourses on the Millennium*, London 1818..

J. Bohatec, *Calvins Lehre von Staat und Kirche mit besonderer Berücksichtigung des Organismusgedankens*, Breslau 1937.

J. Bohatec, *Budé und Calvin, Studien zur gedankenwelt des französischen Frühhumanismus*, Graz 1950.

R. Boon, *Het Probleem der Christelijke Gemeenschap, Oorsprong en Ontwikkeling der Congregationalistische geordende Kerken in Massachusets*, Amsterdam 1951.

J. N. Bowman, *The Protestant Interest in Cromwell's Foreign Relations*, Heidelberg 1900.

D. Brainerd, *The Diary and Journal of* —, I, II, London 1902.

R. H. Bremmer, *Enkele karakteristieke trekken van Calvijn's eschatologie*, Gereformeerd Theologisch Tijdschrift XXXXIV (1943).

Y. Brilioth, *Three Lectures on Evangelicalism and the Oxford Movement*, London 1934.

G. Brillenburg Wurth, *Heroriëntering ten aanzien van de ontmoeting tussen Kerk en Wereld*, Kampen 1955.

R. Bronkema, *The Essence of Puritanism*, Goes 1929.

A. W. Brown, *Recollections of the Conversation Parties of the Rev. Charles Simeon*, London 1863.

W. Brown, *History of the Propagation of Christianity among the Heathen*, I, London³ 1854.

J. R. Brutsch, *La pensée missionnaire dans le Protestantisme de Luther à Zinzendorf* (thèse en manuscrit de l'université de Genève), Genève 1946.

J. de Bruijn, *Thomas Chalmers en zijn Kerkelijk Streven*, Nijkerk 1954.

Claudius Buchanan, *The Works of the Rev.* —, New York 1812.

R. Buchanan, *The Ten Years' Conflict*, I, Glasgow 1852.

W. Burggraaff, *The Rise and Development of Liberal Theology in America*, Goes and New York 1928.

G. Burnet, *History of his own Times*, I, Edinburgh 1753.

J. Calvin, *Institutio; C.R.* 57, 73, 78.

A. J. Campbell, *Two Centuries of the Church of Scotland*, Paisley 1930.

W. Carey, *An Enquiry into the Obligation of Christians to use Means for the Conversion of the Heathen*, reprinted in fascimile from the edition of 1792, London 1891.

E. Carpenter, *Thomas Tenison, Archbishop of Canterbury*, London 1948.
S. C. Carpenter, *Church and People 1789—1889*, London 1933.
H. Carter, *The Methodist Heritage*, London 1951.
B. Citron, *New Birth, A Study of the Evangelical Doctrine of Conversion in the Protestant Fathers*, Edinburgh 1951.
E. Clowes Chorley, *The Seal of the S.P.G.* Historical Magazine of the Protestant Episcopal Church XII (1943).
H. Cnattingius, *Bishops and Societies*, London 1952.
Th. Coke, *To the Benevolent Subscribers for the Support of the Mission . . . for the Benefit of the Negroes and Carribs*, London 1789.
G. R. Cragg, *From Puritanism to the Age of Reason*, Cambridge 1950.
C. D. Cremean, *The Reception of Calvinistic Thought in England*, Urbana (Ill.), 1949.
O. Cullmann, *Christus und die Zeit*, Zürich 1946.

W. F. Dankbaar, *Het Apostolaat bij Calvijn*, N.Th.T. IV (1949-1950).
C. J. Davey, *The March of Methodism*, London 1951.
A. P. Davis, *Isaac Watts*, London 1948.
F. Deaville Walker, *The Call of the West Indies*, London s.a.
O. Dibelius, *Das Kirchliche Leben Schottlands*, Gieszen 1911.
O. Dibelius, *Die Epochen der Kirchengeschichte und die Mission*, E.M.Z. IV (1943).
K. Dijk, *Het Rijk der Duizend Jaren*, Kampen 1933.
P. Drews, *Die Anschauungen Reformatorischen Theologen über die Heidenmission*, Zeitschrift für praktische Theologie XIX (1897).
P. Drews, *Mission und Askese*, Die Christliche Welt XI (1897).
J. Dürr, *Sendende und Werdende Kirche in der Missionstheologie Gustav Warneck's*, Basel 1947.
J. Dürr, *Die Reinigung der Missions-Motive*, E.M.M. XCV (1951).
J. Dürr, *Kirche, Mission und Reich Gottes*, E.M.M. IIIC (1953).

J .Edwards, *Works*, II, VI, London 1817.
W. Elert, *Morphologie des Luthertums*, I, München 1931.
L. E. Elliott-Binns, *The Early Evangelicals*, London 1953.
O. W. Elsbree, *The Rise of the Missionary Spirit in America*, Williamsport 1928.
P. Eppler, *Die Gedanken der Reformatoren über die Frommigkeit und Seligkeit der Heiden*, E.M.M. LXII (1918).
J. Erskine, *Discourses preached on Several Occasions*, Edinburgh 1798.
R. B. Evenhuis, *De Biblicistisch-Eschatologische Theologie van J. A. Bengel*, Wageningen 1931.
J. A. Fabricius, *Salutaris Lux Evangelii*, Hamburg 1731.
N. F. S. Ferré, *Fear, Duty and Love as Ultimate Motives for Christian Missions*, I.R.M. XXXVII (1948).
J. Foster, *World Church*, London 1945.
J. Foster, *The Bicentenary of Jonathan Edwards, "Humble Attempt"*, I.R.M. XXXVII (1948).
J. Foster, *A Scottish Contributor to the Missionary Awakening, Robert Millar of Paisley*, I.R.M. XXXVII (1948).
Four Sermons preached in London, London 1798.

George Fox, *The Journal of* — (ed. by W. Nickalls), Cambridge 1952.

W. Freytag, *Vom Sinn der Weltmission*, E.M.M. XCIV (1950).

H. Frick, *Die Evangelische Mission, Ursprung, Geschichte, Ziel*, Bonn-Leipzig 1922.

H. Frick, *Vom Pietismus zum "Volkskirchentum"*, Gütersloh 1924.

K. Fröhlich, *Gottesreich, Welt und Kirche bei Calvin*, München 1930.

L. J. Frohnmeyer, *Freiherr von Leibniz und die Mission*, E.M.M. LXI (1917).

A. Fuller, *The Complete Works*, II, III, V, London 1831.

M. Galm, *Das Erwachen des Missionsgedankens im Protestantismus der Niederlände*, St. Ottilien 1915.

F. Gärtner, *Barth und Zinzendorf*, München 1953.

J. van Genderen, *Herman Witsius*, 's-Gravenhage 1953.

W. F. Gidney, *The History of the London Society for Promoting Christianity among the Jews*, I, London 1918.

F. C. Gill, *The Romantic Movement and Methodism*, London 1937.

L. H. Gipson, *The British Empire in the Eighteenth Century*, Oxford 1952.

J. P. Gledstone, *George Whitefield, Field-Preacher*, New York s. a.

M. Godwyn, *The Negro's and Indian's Advocate*, London 1680.

K.Goldammer, *Aus den Anfängen evangelischen Missionsdenkens, Kirche, Amt und Mission bei Paracelsus*, E.M.Z. IV (1943).

N. Goodall, *Missions under the Cross*, London 1953.

A. Goslinga, *Die Anfänge des Missionslebens in Holland*, A.M.Z. II (1922).

G. Goyau, *L'idée missionnaire dans le Protestantisme et dans le Catholicisme aux seizième et dix-septième siecles* (l'Eglise en marche, 1re série), Paris 1933.

J. de Graaf, *Het Apostolaat in een gereduceerde Kerk*, N.Th.T. VII (1953).

S. W. Green, *The Story of the Religious Tract Society*, London 1899.

F. W. Grosheide, *De Tweede Brief van de Apostel Paulus aan de Gemeente te Korinthe*, Amsterdam 1939.

[J. A. Grothe], *Archief van de Geschiedenis der oude Hollandsche Zending*, I, Utrecht 1884.

S. P. Grover, *The Planting of Christianity in Africa*, I, London and Redhill 1948.

A. Haldane, *The Lives of Robert Haldane of Airthrey and of his brother James Alexander Haldane*, London 1853.

E. Halévy, *Histoire du Peuple Anglais au XIX ième Siecle*, I, Paris[3] 1924.

Th. Hardy, *The Progress of the Christian Religion. A Sermon preached before the S.S.P.C.K. . . . 30 May 1793, on Hebr. 2.8*, Edinburgh 1794.

V. T. Harlow, *The Founding of the Second British Empire 1763—1793*, I, London—New York—Toronto 1952.

A. von Harnack, *Die Mission und Ausbreitung des Christentums*, I, Leipzig[4] 1924.

G. M. den Hartogh, *De Secession in Schotland van 1843 en het Schotse Seminarie in Nederland*, Vox Theologica XIV (1942—1943).

Th. Haweis, *An Impartial and Succinct History of the Rise, Declension and Revival of the Church of Christ*, III, London 1800.

J. Hawkesworth, *An Account of the Voyages, undertaken... by Comm. Byrom, Captain Wallis, Capt. Carteret and J. Cook*, II, London 1773.

G. D. Henderson, *The Church of Scotland*, Edinburgh 1939.

M. M. Hennett, *Henrij Venn of Huddersfield*, The Churchman LXVIII (1954).

[R. Heron], *Account of the Proceedings and Debate in the General Assembly of the Church of Scotland*, 27th May 1796, Edinburgh 1796.

J. Heurnius, *De Legatione Evangelica ad Indos capessenda Admonitio*, Leiden 1618.

G. H. G. Hewitt, *Reflections on the Early History of the R.T.S.*, I.R.M. XXXIX (1950).

E. Hirsch, *Geschichte der neueren evangelischen Theologie*, II, III, Gütersloh 1949, 1951.

C. W. H. Hochhuth, *Jane Leade und die Philadelphische Gemeinde in England*, Zeitschrift fur die historische Theologie XXXV (1865).

W. E. Hocking and others, *Re-Thinking Missions, A Layman's Inquiry after One Hundred Years*, New York and London 1932.

Ch. Hodge, *Systematic Theology, III*, London and Edinburgh 1884.

H. T. Hodgkin, *Friends Beyond Seas*, London 1916.

J. C. Hoekendijk, *Kerk en Volk in de Duitsche Zendingswetenschap*, s.l. [1948].

J. C. Hoekendijk, *The Call to Evangelism*, I.R.M. XXXIX (1950).

J. C. Hoekendijk, *The Church in Missionary Thinking*, I.R.M. XLI (1952).

J. C. Hoekendijk, *Rondom het Apostolaat*, Wending VII (1952).

Ch. Hole, *The Early History of the C.M.S.*, London 1896.

W. Holsten, *Das Evangelium und die Völker*, Berlin 1939.

W. Holsten, *Das Kerygma und der Mensch*, München 1953.

W. Holsten, *Reformation und Mission*, Archiv für Reformationsgeschichte XIVL (1953).

A. G. Honig, *Bijdrage tot het onderzoek naar de zendingsmethode der comprehensive approach in het Nieuwe Testament, Kampen* 1951.

S. Hopkins, *A Treatise on the Millennium*, Edinburgh 1794.

M. Horne, *Letters on Missions addressed to the Protestant Ministers of the British Churches*, Bristol 1794.

E. Marshall Howse, *Saints in Politics, The Clapham Sect and the Growth of Freedom*, Toronto 1952.

W. I. Hull, *Eight First Biographies of William Penn*, Swarthmore (Pennsylvania) 1936.

D. Humphreys, *An Historical Account of the Incorporated Society for the Propagation of the Gospel in Foreign Parts*, London 1730.

H. Hunter, *A Brief History of the Society in Scotland for Propagating Christian Knowledge in the Highlands and Islands*, London 1795.

J. Inglis, *Sermon preached before the S.S.P.C.K. in the High Church of Edinburgh on Is 49.6*, Edinburgh 1818.

E. Jansen Schoonhoven, *Critische Bespreking van enige Zendingsmotieven*, N.Th.T.V (1950—1951).

E. Jansen Schoonhoven, *Apostolaat en Eschatologie*, De Heerbaan VIII (1955).

M. G. Jones, *The Charity School Movement, A Study of Eighteenth Century Puritanism in Action*, Cambridge 1950.

T. K. Jones, *The Missionary Vocation*, I.R.M. XL (1951).

T. A. Kantonen, *The Theology of Evangelism*, Philadelphia 1954.

E. Kellerhals, *Der Islam*, Basel 1945.

J. T. van der Kemp, *Adres van het Zendelingsgenootschap te Londen aan de godsdienstige ingezetenen der Verenigde Nederlanden*, Dordrecht 1797.

W. M. Kirkland, *The Impact of the French Revolution on Scottish Religious Life and Thought with special Reference to Thomas Chalmers, Robert Haldane and Neil Douglas* (M.S. thesis of the University of Edinburgh), Edinburgh (New College) 1951.

F. J. Klingberg, *Contributions of the S.P.G. to the American Way of Life*, The Church Historical Publication No. 14 Philadelphia [1943].

I. Klug, *Het Katholieke Geloof*, Heemstede 1939.

K. E. Knorr, *British Colonial Theories*, Toronto 1944.

F. W. A. Korff, *Het Christelijk Geloof en de niet-Christelijke Godsdiensten*, Amsterdam 1946.

A. A. Koskinen, *Missionary Influence as a Political Factor in the Pacific Islands* (Annales Academiae Scientiarum Fennicae B 78 I), Helsinki 1953.

H. Kraemer, *The Christian Message in a Non-Christian World*, London[2] 1947.

D. H. Kromminga, *The Millennium in the Church*, Grand-Rapids 1945.

D. W. Lambert, *The Missionary Message of P. T. Forsyth*, E.Q. XXI 1949).

D. W. Lambert, *The Theology of Missions, The Contribution of P. T. Forsyth*, The London Quarterly and Holborn Review CLXXVI (1951).

A. Lang, *Puritanismus und Pietismus*, Neukirchen 1941.

G. Laws, *Andrew Fuller, Pastor, Theologian, Ropeholder*, London 1942.

R. Liechtenhan, *Die urchristliche Mission, Voraussetzungen, Motive und Methoden*, Zürich 1946.

A. Lincoln, *Some Political and Social Ideas of English Dissent*, Cambridge 1938.

J. M. van der Linde, *Het Visioen van Herrnhut en het Apostolaat der Moravische Broeders in Suriname, 1735—1863*, Paramaribo 1956.

J. Lindeboom, *Het Bijbelsch Humanisme in Nederland*, Leiden 1913.

J. M. Lloyd Thomas, *The Autobiography of Richard Baxter, being the Reliquiae Baxterianae, abridged from the Folio (1696)*, London 1925.

M. L. Loane, *Cambridge and the Evangelical Succession*, London 1912.

J. van Lodensteyn, *Beschouwinge van Zion*, Amsterdam 1729.

R. Lovett, *The History of the London Missionary Society*, I, London 1899.

Ch. W. Lowry, *The Spiritual Antecedents of Anglican Evangelicalism*, Historical Magazine of the Protestant Episcopal Church, XII (1943).

W. K. Lowther Clarke, *Eighteenth Century Piety*, London 1944.

H. de Lubac, *Le Fondement Théologique des Missions*, Paris 1946.

M. Luther, *W.A.* 8, 10 I a, 10 III, 30 II, 31 I.

J. Macinnes, *The Evangelical Movement in the Highlands of Scotland*, Aberdeen 1953.

D. Mackichan, *The Missionary Ideal in the Scottish Churches*, London 1927.

D. Maclean, *Aspects of Scottish Church History*, Edinburgh 1927.

D. Maclean, *Scottish Calvinism and Foreign Missions*, Records of the Scottish Church History Society, VI (1938).

J. Macleod, *Scottish Theology*, Edinburgh 1943.

H. Macpherson, *Alexander Shields*, in: Records of the Scottish Church History Society, VI (1938).

F. Mahling, C. Mirbt, A. Nebe, *Zum Gedächtnis A. H. Franckes*, Halle 1927.

B. Manning, *The Protestant Dissenting Deputies*, Cambridge 1952.

W. Manson, *Mission and Eschatology*, I.R.M. XLII (1953).

W. Manson and others, *Eschatology* (Scottish Journal of Theology Occasional Papers No 2), London and Edinburgh s.a.

J. C. Marshman, *The Life and Times of Carey, Marshman and Ward*, I, London 1859.

H. Martin, *Puritanism and Richard Baxter*, London 1954.

W. L. P. Martin, *Missionaries and Annexation in the Pacific*, London 1924.

H. Martyn, *Sermons*, Calcutta 1822.

H. Martyn, *Journals and Letters*, ed. by S. Wilberforce, I, II, London 1837,

J. Mayhew, *Observations on the Charter and Conduct of the Society for the Propagation of the Gospel in Foreign Parts*, Boston and London 1763.

J. Mc Kerrow, *History of the Secession Church*, II, Edinburg 1839.

J. Mc Leod Campbell, *Christian History in the Making*, London 1946.

S. Meckie, *The Marrow Controversy Reviewed*, E.Q. XXII (1950).

F. R. Merkel, *G. W. von Leibniz und die China-Mission*, Leipzig 1920.

F. R. Merkel, *The Missionary Attitude of the Philosopher G. W. von Leibniz*, I.R.M. IX (1920).

F. R. Merkel, *Des Philosophen G. W. Leibniz erste Bemühungen mit der Mission*, Mededelingen LXIV[2] (1929).

O. Michaelis, *Zur Frage des Missionsverständnisses der Reformatoren*, Z.M.R. XLI (1926).

John Mill, *The Diary of the Rev. —*, ed. by G. Goudie, Edinburgh 1889.

R. Millar, *The History of the Propagation of Christianity and the Overthrow of Paganism*, I, II, London 1731.

P. Miller, *Jonathan Edwards*, s. l. 1949.

Sir H. Moncreiff Wellwood, *Account of the Life and Writings of John Erskine D. D.*, Edinburgh 1818.

E. C. Moore, *The Spread of Christianity in the Modern World*, Chicago 1919.

J. Morison, *The Fathers and Founders of the L.M.S.*, I,s.l. 1839.

H. C. G. Moule, *Charles Simeon*, London[2] 1948.

L. Newbigin, *The Household of God*, London 1953.

G. F. Nuttall, *Richard Baxter and Philip Doddridge*, London 1951.

G. F. Nuttall (ed.), *Philip Doddridge 1702-1751*, London 1951.

W. Oehler, *Geschichte der Deutschen Evangelischen Mission*, I, Baden-Baden 1949.

J. N. Ogilvie, *Our Empire's Debt to Missions*, London 1924.

D. D. Oliver, *The Gospel in the Province of North Carolina*, The James Sprunt Historical Publications IX (1909).

A. H. Oussoren, *William Carey, especially his Missionary Principles*, Leiden 1945.

J. H. Overton and F. Relton, *The English Church from the Accession of George I to the End of the Eighteenth Century*, London 1906.

J. Owen, *The History of the Origin and First Ten Years of the British and Foreign Bible Society, I*, London 1816.

C. F. Pascoe, *Two Hundred Years of the S.P.G.* I, London 1901.

W. Pauck, *The Idea of the Church in Christian History*, Church History XXI (1952).

E. A. Payne, *The First Generation*, London [1936].

E. A. Payne, *The Prayer Call of 1784*, London 1941.

E. A. Payne, *The Church Awakes*, London 1942.

E. A. Payne, *The Evangelical Revival and the Beginnings of the Modern Missionary Movement*, The Congregational Quarterly XXI (1943).

E. A. Payne, *The Growth of the World Church*, London 1955.

S. Pearce Carey, *William Carey*, London[8] 1934.

F. Penny, *The Church in Madras*, London 1904.

C. H. Philips, *The East India Company 1784-1834*, Manchester 1940.

R. Pearce Beaver, *North American Thoughts on the Fundamental Principle of Missions during the Twentieth Century*, Church History XXI (1952).

M. Piette, *La Réaction Wesleyenne dans 'l Evolution Protestante*, Bruxelles 1925.

A. Plummer, *The Church of England in the Eighteenth Century*, London 1910.

F. J. Powicke, *Some unpublished Correpondence of Rev. R. Baxter and Rev. John Eliot*, Bulletin of the John Rylands Library XV (1931).

J. Pratt, *Propaganda, being an Abstract of the Designs and Proceedings of the Incorporated S.P.G., by a member of the Society*, London 1819.

Proceedings of the Society for Missions to Africa and the East, I, London 1805.

G. W. Ranson, (ed.), *Revival and Advance*, London 1948.

A. J. Rasker, *Christelijke Politiek. Gesprek over de Theocratie*, Nijkerk s.a.

M. Richter, *Der Missionsgedanke im evangelischen Deutschland des 18. Jahrhunderts*. Leipzig 1928.

H. N. Ridderbos, *De Komst van het Koninkrijk*, Kampen 1950.

H. N. Ridderbos, *Zending in het Nieuwe Testament*, De Heerbaan VII. (1954).

J. Ridderbos, *De Theologie van Jonathan Edwards*, 's Gravenhage 1907.

O. Riecker, *Das Evangelistische Wort*, Gütersloh 1935.

W. Robertson, *The Situation of the World at the Time of Christ's Appearance - A Sermon preached before the S.S.P.C.K. Jan. 6, 1775*, Edinburgh 1818.

H. Roddier, *J. J. Rousseau en Angleterre au XVIII ième Siècle*, Paris 1950.

G. Rosenkranz, *Weltmission und Weltende*, Gutersloh 1951.

R. Rouse, *The Missionary Motive*, I.R.M. XXV (1936)

R. Rouse, *William Carey's „Pleasing Dream"*, I.R.M. XXXVIII (1949).

R. Rouse and S. C. Neill, *A History of the Ecumenical Movement*, London 1954.

H. H. Rowley, *The Missionary Message of the Old Testament*, London [1944].

A. A. van Ruler, *Visie en Vaart*, Amsterdam 1947.

A. A. van Ruler, *De Bevinding*, Kerk en Theologie I (1950).

A. A. van Ruler, *Theologie van het Apostolaat*, Nijkerk s.a.

A. A. van Ruler, *Réveil en Revival*, Wending (1955).

H. Saravia, *De Diversis Ministrorum Evangelii Gradibus, sicut a Domino fuerunt Insituti, etc.*, Frankfort 1591.

H. Schärer, *Die begründung der Mission in der katholischen und evangelischen Missionswissenschaft* (Theologische Studien Heft 16), Zürich 1944.

A. A. van Schelven, *Het Calvinisme gedurende zijn Bloeitijd*, II, Amsterdam 1951.

E. Schick, *Vorboten und Bahnbrecher*, Basel 1943.

J. Schmidlin, *Erasmus von Rotterdam über die Heidenmission*, Z.M. IV (1914).

J. Schmidlin, *Katholische Missionsgeschichte*, Steyl 1924.

K. D. Schmidt, *Neue Zuge im Bild des Bonifatius*, E.M.Z. XI (1954).

M. Schmidt, *Der Missionsgedanke des jungen Wesley auf dem Hintergrunde seines Zeitalters* in Theologia Viatorum (Jahrbuch der kirchlischen Hochschule Berlin-Zehlendorf) I (1948-1949).

M. Schmidt, *Das Hallische Waisenhaus und England im 18 Jahrhundert*, Theologische Zeitschrift VII (1951).

M. Schmidt, *Der junge Wesley als Heidenmissionar und Missionstheologe*, Gütersloh 1955.

M. A. Schmidt, *Thomas von Aquino und Raymundus Lullus, zwei Grundtypen missionarischen Denkens im Mittelalter*, E.M.M. IIIC (1953).

H. W. Schomerus, *Missionswissenschaft*, Leipzig 1935.

G. Schrenk, *Gottesreich und Bund im älteren Protestantismus, vornehmlich bei Joh. Coccejus*, Gütersloh 1923.

Schrift en Kerk, Een Bundel Opstellen ... aangeboden aan Prof. Dr. Th. L. Haitjema, Nijkerk 1953.

Scientia Missionum Ancilla, Nijmegen-Utrecht 1953.

D. Scott, *Annals and Statistics of the Original Secession Church*, Edinburgh [1886].

K. Scott Latourette, *A. History of the Expansion of Christianity*, III, V, New York and London, 1939, 1943.

Sermons, preached in London at the Formation of the Missionary Society, 22, 23, 24 Sept. 1795, London 1795.

[Ch. Simeon], *Memorial Sketches of the Rev. David Brown, With a Selection of his Sermons, preached at Calcutta*, London 1816.

Ch. Simeon, *Horae Homileticae*, VI, XI, London 1820.

Ch. Simeon, *The Conversion of the Jews, Two Discourses preached before the University of Cambridge*, London 1821.

J. S. Simon, *The Revival of Religion in England in the Eighteenth Century*, London s.a.

J. S. Simon, *John Wesley and the Religious Societies*, London 1921.

Sydney Smith, *The Works of the Rev. —*, London 1850.

C. Smyth, *Simeon and Church Order*, Cambridge 1940.

R. P. Stacy Waddy, *250 Years of S.P.G.*, I R.M. XL (1951).

H. Stahl, *August Hermann Francke*, Stuttgart 1939.

L. Stephen, *History of English Thought in the Eigtheenth Century*, II, London 1876.

E. Stock, *The History of the Church Missionary Society*, I, London 1899.

V. F. Storr, *The Development of English Theology in the Nineteenth Century*, 1800-1860, London etc. 1913.

J. Stoughton, *History of Religion in England*, IV, V, London etc. 1913.

A. Streckeisen, *Die Kirchliche Missionsgesellschaft von England (C.M.S.) und die Basler Mission*, I-II, E.M.M. VIC (1950).

R. N.Stromberg, *Religious Liberalism in Eighteenth Century England*, London 1954.

G. Struthers, *The History of the Rise, Progress and Principles of the Relief Church*, Glasgow 1843.

G. Struthers, *The History of the Rise of the Relief Church*, Edinburgh and London 1848.

Lucy S. Sutherland, *The East India Company in Eighteenth Century Politics*, Oxford 1952.

W. W. Sweet, *The Story of Religions in America*, New York-London 1930.

W. W. Sweet, *Revivalism in America*, New York 1945.

D. van Swigchem, *Het Missionair Karakter van de Christelijke Gemeente volgens de brieven van Paulus en Petrus*, Kampen 1955.

N. Sykes, *E. Gibson, Bishop of London*, London 1926.

N. Sykes, *Church and State in England in the Eighteenth Century*, Cambridge 1934.

N. Sykes, *D. E. Jablonski and the Church of England*, London 1950.

N. Sykes, *The English Religious Tradition*, London 1953.

E. R. Taylor, *Methodism and Politics, 1791-1851*, Cambridge 1935.

W. Teellinck, *Ecce Homo ofte Oogen-Salve voor die noch sitten in Blintheyt des Ghemoets*, Dordrecht 1646.

Thanksgiving Sermons, preached before the Missionary Society, London 1798.

J. Thayer Addison, *The Medieval Missionary*, London en New York 1936.

The Authority of the Faith (The Madras Series I), London and New York 1939.

The Church, Report of a Theological Commission on Church and Order, London² 1952.

The Church's Witness to God's Design (The Amsterdam Assembly Series II), London 1948.

The Evangelical Magazine, 1794.

N. Thune, *The Behmenist and the Philadelphians*, Uppsala 1948.

H. P. Thompson, *Into All Lands, The History of the S.P.G.*, London 1951.

H. P. Thompson, *Thomas Bray*, London 1954.

P. Tillich, *The Theology of Missions*, Occasional Bulletin of the Missionary Research Library V, (1954).

A. Tindal Hart, *The Life and Times of John Sharp, Archbishop of York*, London 1949.

J. D. du Toit, *Het Methodisme*, Amsterdam-Pretoria 1903.

T. F. Torrance, *Calvin's Doctrine of Man*, London 1949.

T. F. Torrance, *The Modern Eschatological Debate*, E.Q. XXV (1953).

T. F. Torrance, *Royal Priesthood* (Scottish Journal of Theology Occasional Papers No 3), Edinburgh- London [1955].

W. J. Townsend, H. B. Workman, G. Eayrs, A. *New History of Methodism,*
    I, II, London 1909.
G. M. Trevelyan, *English Social History,* London² 1946.
G. M. Trevelyan, *History of England,* London-New-York-Toronto 1947.
L. J. Trinterud, *The Forming of an American Tradition,* Philadelphia
    1949.
E. Troeltsch, *Missionsmotiv, Missionsausgabe und neuzeitliches Humanitäts-
    christentum,* Z.M.R. XXII (1907).
E. Troeltsch, *Gesammelte Schriften,* I, II, Tübingen 1913.
P. A. Varg, *Motives in Protestant Missions 1890-1917,* Church History
    XXIII (1954).
G. Voetius, *Politica Ecclesiastica,* III, Amsterdam 1676.
K. Völker, *Die Religiöse Wurzel des Englischen Imperialismus,* Tübingen
    1924.
E. A. Walker, *The British Empire, its Structure and Spirit,* Londen-New
    York-Toronto 1943.
M. A. C. Warren, (ed), *The Triumph of God,* London-New York-To-
    ronto 1948.
M. A. C. Warren, *The Truth of Vision,* London and Edinburgh 1948
M. A. C. Warren, *The Christian Mission,* London 1951.
M. A. C. Warren, *Eschatology and History,* I R. M. XLI (1952).
M. A. C. Warren, *Caesar, The Beloved Enemy,* London 1955.
M. A. C. Warren, *The Christian Imperative,* London 1955.
H. Watt, *The Influence of Martin Luther on Scottish Religion in the
    Eighteenth Century,* Records in the Scottish Church History Society
    VI (1938).
H. Watt, *Thomas Chalmers and the Disruption,* Edinburgh etc. 1943.
H. Watt, *"Moderator, Rax me that Bible",* in: Records of the Scottish
    Church History Society X (1950).
G. A. Wauer, *Die Anfänge der Brüderkirche in England,* Leipzig 1900.
R. F. Wearmouth, *Methodism and the Common People of the Eighteenth
    Century,* London 1945.
R. W. Weir, *A. History of the Foreign Missions of the Church of Scot-
    land,* Edinburgh 1900.
J. Von Welz, *Der Missionsweckruf des Baron Justinian von Welz in
    neuer Wiedergabe des Originaldruckes vom Jahre 1664* (ed. by W.
    Faber), Leipzig 1890.
J. Wesley, *Works,* (ed. by Th. Jackson) London 1829. VI, VII, VIII,
    X, XIII.
J. Wesley, *The Letters of the Rev.* —, (ed. by J. Telford), I. VII, VIII,
    London 1938.
J. Wesley, *The Journal of the Rev.* —, (ed. by N. Curnoch), I, II, III, IV,
    V, VIII, London 1938.
G. Whitefield, *Works,* I, II, VI, London 1771.
G. Whitefield, *Sermons on Important Subjects,* London 1841.
H. C. Whitley, *Edward Irving* (M. S. Thesis of the University of Edin-
    burgh), Edinburgh (New College), 1953.
W. T. Whitley (ed), *Minutes of the General Assembly of the General
    Baptist Churches in England,* I, London 1908.
W. T. Whitley, *A History of British Baptists,* London² 1932.

W. Wilberforce, *A Practical View of the Prevailing Religious System of Professed Christians in the Higher and Middle Classes of this Country, Contrasted with Real Christianity,* London 1797.

B. Willey, *The Eighteenth Century Background,* London 1946.

E. Williams, *A Sermon and Charge delivered on Occasion of the Designation of the First Missionaries,* London 1796.

J. A. Williamson, *The Ocean in English History,* Oxford 1941.

J. A. Williamson, *Cook and the Opening of the Pacific,* London 1946.

O. E. Winslow, *Jonathan Edwards 1703—1758.* New York 1941.

Jhr. P. J. van Winter, *De Aanloop tot het Britse Imperialisme,* Groningen-Djakarta 1954.

J. Woodward, *An Account of the Rise and Progress of the Religious Societies,* London[3] 1711.

L. B. Wright and M. A. Fry, *Puritanism in the South Seas,* New York 1936.

L. B. Wright, *Religion and Empire,* Chapel Hill 1943.

A. C. Zabriskie, *The Rise and Main Characteristics of the Anglican Evangelical Movement in England and America,* Historical Magazine of the Protestant Episcopal Church XII (1943).

APPENDIX:

Works of General Reference:

Dictionary of American Biography.

Dictionary of National Biography.

Theologisches Wörterbuch zum Neuen Testament.

INDEX

A

Aalders, G. Ch., 209
Allen, R., 27
Allen, W. O. B., 46, 51
Althaus, P., 212
Andel, H. A. van, 20, 177
Andersen, W., 185, 188, 203, 204
Anne, Queen, 42, 44, 57
Aquino, Thomas of, 20, 173
Asbury, F., 88, 103, 105
Augustine (Bishop of Canterbury), 167

B

Bacon, Th., 51
Baez-Camargo, G., 8, 57
Baker, E. W., 74, 80, 95
Baker, F., 94, 95
Bakker, J. T., 174
Balleine, G. R., 67, 77, 113, 135
Bamberg, Otto of, 173
Barclay, R., 53
Barclay, W. C., 78, 80, 86, 87, 91, 103, 105
Barth, K., 2, 75, 79, 132, 186, 209, 210, 211
Bavinck, H., 26, 81, 195
Bavinck, J. H., 2, 5, 95, 103, 181, 196, 205
Baxter, J., 102
Baxter, R., 25, 26, 27, 28, 35
Beaton, D., 36
Beck, Th., 151
Benett, J., 55, 71, 114
Bengel, J. A., 82, 119, 125, 160, 182, 186
Benson, Archbishop, 47
Benz, E., 3, 17, 44, 104, 105
Berkhof, H., 167
Berkouwer, G. C., 11, 197
Berridge, J., 77
Bett, H., 116
Beyreuther, E., 13
Beza, Th., 20, 24, 164
Boehm, A. W., 51
Boer, H. R., 165, 177, 198, 199
Boetzelaer, C. W. Th. Baron van, 21

Bogue, D., 55, 71, 112, 114, 115, 117, 120, 121, 128, 130, 137, 139, 144, 154, 155, 156, 161, 162, 165
Bohatec, J., 168, 179, 182
Boniface, 168, 181
Boon, R., 72, 102
Bowman, J., 26
Boyle, D., 111, 142
Boyle, R., 28, 54
Bradford, W., 23
Brainerd, D., 56, 57, 88, 90, 92, 93, 96, 97, 98, 99, 100, 104, 117, 123, 127, 138, 148, 149, 180, 201, 202
Brainerd, J., 92
Brakel, W. à, 82
Bray, Th., 12, 40, 41, 44, 45, 46, 48, 50, 54, 60, 65, 132
Bremmer, R. H., 182
Brewer, J., 161
Brigden, Th. E., 88
Brilioth, Y., 113
Brillenburg Wurth, G., 87
Bronkema, R., 25, 61
Brown, A. W., 119, 122
Brown, D., 113, 135, 147, 157, 162, 164
Brown, W., 29, 61
Bruijn, J. de, 115
Brutsch, J. R., 6, 11, 14, 24
Bryce, J., 143
Bryne, G., 118
Bucer, M., 4, 7, 10, 169, 174, 182
Buchanan, C., 132, 133, 145, 147, 148, 154, 159, 162
Buchanan, R., 142
Burgess, Th., 147
Burggraaff, W., 69, 73, 78
Burke, E., 107, 119
Burnet, G., 26, 28, 34, 42
Burton, J., 88, 100
Butler, J., 37, 70
Butler, S., 145
Byington, E. Hoyt, 23, 25, 29

C

Calvin, 4, 7, 8, 10, 12, 14, 18, 22, 26, 57, 119, 164, 168, 169, 174, 179, 182, 183

(7)